Reasoning About Plans

THE MORGAN KAUFMANN SERIES
IN REPRESENTATION AND REASONING

Series editor, Ronald J. Brachman (AT&T Bell Laboratories)

BOOKS

James Allen, James Hendler, and Austin Tate, editors
Readings in Planning (1990)

James F. Allen, Henry A. Kautz, Richard N. Pelavin, and Josh D. Tenenberg
Reasoning About Plans (1991)

Ronald J. Brachman and Hector Levesque, editors
Readings in Knowledge Representation (1985)

Ernest Davis
Representations of Commonsense Knowledge (1990)

Matthew L. Ginsberg, editor
Readings in Nonmonotonic Reasoning (1987)

Judea Pearl
Probabilistic Reasoning in Intelligent Systems: Networks of Plausible Inference (1988)

Glenn Shafer and Judea Pearl, editors
Readings in Uncertain Reasoning (1990)

John Sowa, editor
Principles of Semantic Networks: Explorations in the Representation of Knowledge (1991)

Daniel S. Weld and John de Kleer, editors
Readings in Qualitative Reasoning about Physical Systems (1990)

David E. Wilkins
Practical Planning: Extending the Classical AI Planning Paradigm (1988)

PROCEEDINGS

Principles of Knowledge Representation and Reasoning:
Proceedings of the First International Conference (KR 89)
edited by Ronald J. Brachman, Hector J. Levesque, and Raymond Reiter

Proceedings of the Second International Conference (KR 91)
edited by James Allen, Richard Fikes, and Eric Sandewall

The Frame Problem in Artificial Intelligence: Proceedings of the 1987 Conference
edited by Frank M. Brown (1987)

Reasoning about Actions and Plans: Proceedings of the 1986 Workshop
edited by Michael P. Georgeff and Amy L. Lansky (1987)

Theoretical Aspects of Reasoning about Knowledge:
Proceedings of the First Conference (TARK 1986)
edited by Joseph P. Halpern

Proceedings of the Second Conference (TARK 1988)
edited by Moshe Y. Vardi

Proceedings of the Third Conference (TARK 1990)
edited by Rohit Parikh

Reasoning
About
Plans

James F. Allen
Henry A. Kautz
Richard N. Pelavin
Josh D. Tenenberg

Morgan Kaufmann Publishers, Inc.
San Mateo, California

Sponsoring Editor Michael B. Morgan
Production Editor Yonie Overton
Cover Designer Wells Larson & Associates
Copyeditor/Proofreader Susan Festa

Morgan Kaufmann Publishers, Inc.
Editorial Office:
2929 Campus Drive, Suite 260
San Mateo, CA 94403

94 93 92 91   5 4 3 2 1

Library of Congress Cataloging-in-Publication Data
Reasoning about plans/ James F. Allen ... [et al.].
          p. cm. -- (The Morgan Kaufmann series in representation and reasoning, ISSN 1046-9567)
     Includes bibliographical references and index.
     ISBN 1-55860-137-6 : $39.95
     1. Artificial intelligence.   2. Reasoning.   3. Problem solving.
4. Planning.   I. Allen, James, 1950– .   II. Title: Reasoning about plans. III. Series.
Q335.R45 1991
006.3--dc20
                                                    91-17369
                                                    CIP

Contents

Abstraction in Planning.................................213
Josh D. Tenenberg

Preface

This book addresses a fundamental problem in modeling intelligent behavior, namely, the ability to formulate, evaluate, and recognize plans. Any intelligent agent must be capable of reasoning about the environment it is in and modifying its behavior in order to achieve certain goals or conditions. This problem-solving behavior has been a central concern in artificial intelligence (AI) research since the beginning of the field. As a result, it is one of the few areas of AI where there is a fairly coherent history of ideas and where one can see evidence of incremental improvement. This book continues this process. It presents work that formalizes ideas that have been used only informally in plan reasoning systems in the past, and it then extends the range of situations that can be reasoned about. The fundamental assumption underlying all the work reported here is that it is necessary to build precise, formal models of plan reasoning systems. This is essential in order first, to identify the inherent expressive limitations of existing approaches, and second, to then extend the formalisms beyond those limits. In particular, we will present work that formalizes and develops extended models of reasoning about simultaneous actions, external events in the world, abstraction, and plan recognition.

One of the perennial problems in this area is defining what the notion of a plan is—and there have been many definitions put forth in the literature. One common definition is that a plan is a set (or sequence) of actions to be performed by a single agent, drawing on parallels between plans and programming languages. This definition is fine in situations where the only change in the world is a result of the agent executing its actions (just as the internal state of a computer changes only as a result of the program it is running), but it does not generalize well to real-world situations. In general, the effects of plan action depend on what certain other events are occurring at the same time. For instance, the action of walking down Main Street at 10 A.M. might have the effect that you meet a good friend of yours, if he or she is also walking at the same time. Otherwise, this effect does not hold. Thus a plan to meet your friend in this situation would have to account for your friend's actions as well. So the plan is not fully defined unless these other conditions are also included. Taking this argument to its limit, it may be difficult to distinguish a plan from any collection of facts about the world.

Another essential part of a theory of planning is the intentions that motivate plans. The intentions underlying a plan play a crucial role in defining the plan. For instance, except in the most trivial worlds, our knowledge of the world is quite incomplete. As a result, it is impossible to fully specify our behavior in advance. Even if our knowledge were complete, it would not be desirable to fully specify our behavior as it would take too much time. If we are executing an incomplete (or abstract) plan, then something is needed to evaluate what actual detailed responses are appropriate to the actual situation the agent finds itself in. Such a plan can only be defined in terms of the states that the agent wishes to achieve. It is the presence of intentions (or, more informally, goals) that distinguish plan reasoning from other forms of reasoning about causality and time. Thus, planning could be defined as reasoning about cause and effect in order to decide what behavior best fits the agent's intentions.

Precisely defining the notion of intention is very difficult (but see Cohen, Morgan, and Pollack [1990] for interesting work on this issue). We will not be attempting to define it here, but will rather depend on an intuitive notion of the term. The focus here will be on specifying an adequate representation of the world to allow reasoning about the causal aspects of plans. The discussion of plan recognition in chapter 2 will address some of the issues in attributing intention to agents, but it is mainly concerned with outlining a set of possible intentions based on causal coherence and assumptions about the behavior of goal-seeking agents.

Most existing planning systems use a much more limited notion of plans. In particular, most formulations assume a completely static world where change can result only from actions by the planning agent. They also assume that the agent has complete knowledge about the world and therefore can construct a plan in full detail. With these assumptions, defining a plan as the set of actions by the agent is reasonable, and, in fact, planning can be viewed as a specialized case of automatic programming. Goals in these systems are externally specified states that drive the reasoning process: the planner must find a set of actions that will transform the current state of the world into a state where the assertions described by the goals are true.

One reason for the popularity of these assumptions is the simplifying effects they have on the formalism needed to represent the world. Under these assumptions, a planning system may use a state-based representation of the world along the lines originally developed in the STRIPS system [Fikes and Nilsson 1971]. For over a decade after the STRIPS work, research in planning concerned itself entirely with the issue of search: given a goal and an initial state, how can we efficiently find a plan that will achieve the goal? Important progress was made on the search issues, with the major results being the use of abstraction to limit search [Sacerdoti 1973], the use of nonlinear plans [Sacerdoti 1975; Tate 1977], and the development of planners using the principles of least-commitment (e.g., Stefik [1981]). The limitations of the world representation, however, remained largely unexamined.

When we consider the representation of plans in detail, it is important to remember that there are many different forms of plan reasoning. The typical planning problem, which consists of taking an initial world specification and a goal state and finding a set of actions that will produce the goal state, is just one of many reasoning tasks involving plans. It is one example of a **plan construction** task. Other cases of plan construction might involve not so much a final state, but the actual processes of acting itself. For example, an agent might want to perform four actions, such as going to four different movies in different parts of town. However, time constraints limit the agent from performing them all in a single day. The plan reasoning task here is to find the best course of action that maximizes the number of these actions the agent actually gets to perform. Another class of plan reasoning tasks might simply involve evaluating courses of action in some way, rather than constructing plans. For example, an agent might be given four tasks to do and have to reason about how long it will actually take to accomplish them all (an essential task for preparing cost estimates). Another major class of plan reasoning tasks involves **plan recognition**. In these cases, one agent observes another agent performing certain actions and needs to infer what that agent is doing, that is, identify the intentions that motivated the observed behavior. Such an ability is crucial to allow cooperative actions between agents. Many actual tasks may involve a mix of construction, analysis, and recognition. Because of this, it is essential that the representation be adequate to support a wide range of different algorithms for plan reasoning. A representation that is specific to one task (i.e., plan construction) and not generalizable to other tasks is not going to be useful in general applications.

This book is motivated by the belief that progress in developing plan reasoning systems in realistic worlds depends not so much on issues of search (although search is obviously important) but on progress in representing more complex world situations. There are fundamental representational problems that need to be solved, and we hope this book makes a significant start in addressing these problems. Two classes of contributions are made here. The first is formalizing what already exists. Before we can identify the fundamental limits of existing approaches, we need to have a precise understanding of what they are. In this book, we present precise formulations of the representations used in STRIPS-like systems, we give a precise formulation of the notion of action abstraction, we clarify the notion of what is meant by nonlinear plans, and we identify the fundamental assumptions underlying work in plan recognition. The other class of contributions involves the development of new representations that are significantly more powerful than those used in previous work and the specification of new plan reasoning algorithms that use these representations. In most cases, prototype systems based on these algorithms have been developed and will be described.

Chapter 1 examines the representation of time in plan reasoning systems and develops a temporally explicit representation that is used as a starting point for the remainder of the book. A planning system is defined as a specialized form of a general temporal reasoning system. Chapter 2 examines the problem of plan recognition and presents a formalization that subsumes most previous work on the problem. Chapter 3 examines the representation of the world underlying planning systems and develops a new formal model that allows both simultaneous actions and reasoning about interacting with external events. Finally, chapter 4 gives a formal account of the STRIPS representation and uses this model to identify two very different forms of action abstraction. These two forms have quite different properties that generally have not been recognized.

Acknowledgements

This book reports on work done over almost a decade at the University of Rochester. During this time, the ideas have evolved from discussions with countless people and it would not be possible to list them all here. We all wish to thank the Department of Computer Science at Rochester for providing a friendly and supportive environment for this research and for support during the preparation of this book. In addition, also for their support during the preparation of the book, we would like to thank AT&T Bell Labs, Dick Wexelblat and Philips Research, and Chuck Hall, Bill Mark and the Lockheed AI Center.

This work would not have been possible without the long-term support from several granting agencies. We especially want to thank Nort Fowler at RADC (now Rome Labs) for continued support of our planning research from early on, when we're sure the ideas looked quite speculative and tentative. Similarly, Alan Meyrowitz at the Office of Naval Research has provided our research group at Rochester with long-term support over the last decade. Finally, the National Science Foundation also supported the work with a series of grants throughout the time of the research.

Many people have made direct contributions to the book, either in helping formulate the original ideas, or in the form of reviewing and criticizing earlier drafts. We would like to thank Tom Dean, Mark Drummond, and Len Schubert for substantive reviews of quite rough earlier drafts. In addition, John Anderson, Dana Ballard, Paul Benjamin, Ronald Brachman, Robin Cohen, Raymond De Lacaze, George Ferguson, Peter Haddawy, Leo Hartman, Pat Hayes, Lou Hoebel, Craig Knoblock, Hans Koomen, Diane Litman, Damian Lyons, Nat Martin, Ray Perrault, Martha Pollack, David Traum, Jay Weber, and Qiang Yang all provided advice and feedback through various versions of the documents.

Notation

We will be using standard first-order predicate logic throughout the book, using the following symbols:

- ~ (negation),
- ∧ (and),
- ∨ (or),
- ⊃ (implies),
- ≡ (equivalence),
- ∀ (universal quantifier), and
- ∃ (existential quantifier).

In addition, we use an n-ary "exactly one" operator ($\otimes$). For example, the formula ($\otimes$ A B C) is true if and only if one of the propositions A, B, or C is true and the other two are false.

We also use the following set-theoretic and metatheoretic symbols:

- ⊢ the provability relation,
- ⊨ the semantic entailment relation,
- ∈ set membership relation,
- ⊂ subset relation,
- ∪ set union, and
- ∩ set intersection.

Chapter 1
Temporal Reasoning and Planning

James F. Allen

1.1   Introduction

Currently, there is strong interest in designing planning systems that can reason about realistic worlds. In moving from the toy-world domains that characterized early work, researchers are looking at a wide range of issues, including reasoning in uncertain worlds, interacting with processes and events beyond the agent's direct control, and controlling mechanisms in real-time (i.e., robotics). Chapter 1 focuses on the temporal aspects of the knowledge representation formalism used to support plan construction. Starting with an examination of the assumptions built into representations based on the notion of state change, the chapter develops an alternative, temporally explicit representation that opens the door to investigating a range of plan reasoning problems.

The key intuitions motivating this development are the following:

1)   Actions take time—very few actions are instantaneous: a moment's reflection reveals that the effects of many actions result from applying some force over a period of time. Sometimes the effect of an action only holds while the action is being performed (e.g., a briefcase remains in your hand only as long as you are gripping it).

2)   More than one action may occur at the same time: in particular, one action might interfere or change the effects of another action while it is occurring. There may be additional effects, or some of the usual effects of one of the actions may not be realized. In fact, the effect of two actions together could be virtually independent of the effects of each action done alone. Many activities (e.g., carrying a piano) cannot be accomplished without close coordination and simultaneous action by multiple agents.

3)   Complex plans of activity may involve complex ordering constraints: two actions in a plan might need to overlap, or they might need to be temporally disjoint, although which occurs first might not matter. For example, to make cappuccino on my machine, I must hold down a button to heat the water to make steam. After a short wait, I then push another button to release the steam while still holding down the button to heat the water. Any other temporal ordering of these events will not produce the desired results.

4)   Actions may interact with external events beyond the agent's direct control: for example, to sail across a lake, the agent may put up the sail and so on, but the action will not succeed unless the wind is blowing. Thus, the plan must depend on the existence of external events.

Of these problems, the most central one is that of dealing with simultaneous events and actions. Without simultaneous action, the range of problems that can be addressed is very limited and is mainly restricted to specialized situations such as computer programming and game playing. It makes little sense to study planning in a dynamic, changing world if the planner cannot act while some other natural event is occurring. The problems that arise when an action and a natural event occur simultaneously parallel the problems of performing two or more simultaneous actions. To understand why this problem is so difficult, it is important to look at the assumptions underlying the world representation in many current planning systems. This is examined in detail in the next section.

1.1.1 Background: Actions as State Change

The predominant approach to modeling action in artificial intelligence and computer science has been to view action as state change. This view underlies all the state-based planning systems (e.g., STRIPS and its successors), formal models of planning (e.g., the situation calculus [McCarthy and Hayes 1969]), and work in dynamic logic for the semantics of programs (e.g., Harel [1979] and Rosenschein [1981]). In this view, the world is modeled by a succession of **states**, each **state** representing an instantaneous "snapshot" of the world. Actions are defined as functions from one state to another. Propositions in such models are relative to states. The notion of a proposition independent of a state is modeled as a function from states to truth-values. In the situation calculus [McCarthy and Hayes 1969], such functions are called **fluents**. For example, *On(A,B)* is a fluent that when applied to a state S is a proposition that is true if A is on B in state S.

In planning systems, knowledge about actions typically falls into several different categories. The **preconditions** of an action are those properties that must be true for the action to be executable. The **effects** of an action specify the resulting state when an action is applied in a state in which the preconditions hold. Finally, some systems also include a **body** or decomposition of an action that specifies additional details about the action's actual execution.

The STRIPS system [Fikes and Nilsson 1971] provides the representation of the world used by most implemented planning systems built to date. In STRIPS, a state is represented as a finite set of formulas, and the effects of an action are specified by two sets of formulas: the **delete list** specifies what propositions to remove from the initial state, and the **add list** specifies the new propositions to add. Together, they completely define the transition between the initial state and the resulting state. Figure 1 shows a simple blocks-world action that involves placing one block on top of another (the *stack* action). The preconditions on this action state that each block must be clear (i.e., it has no other block on top of it). The effects state that one block is now on top of the other (the add list) and that the bottom block is not clear (the delete list). The operation for constructing a resulting state applies the deletes first and then asserts the add list. This ordering is important if variables are allowed in the delete list, which is typically the case. Deleting a formula containing variables is

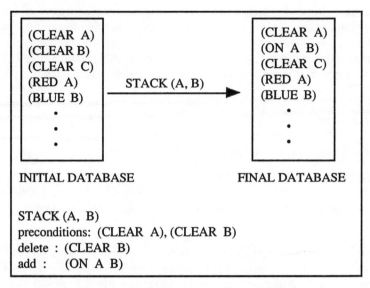

Figure 1: Actions as state change in STRIPS

defined as deleting all formulas in the state description that unify with that formula.

In state-change models such as STRIPS, actions are instantaneous and there is no provision for asserting what is true while an action is in execution. Also, since the state descriptions do not include information about action occurrences, such systems cannot represent the situation where one action occurs while some other event or action is occurring. Finally, there is no reasoning about the future in these models except by searching through different sequences of actions. Without some additional extensions, for example, one cannot assert that an event will occur at some time in the future when the event is not a result of the agent's actions.

While discussing the world representation in such models, it is important to include explicitly the **nonlinear planners** (e.g., Sacerdoti [1977], Tate [1977], Vere [1981], and Wilkins [1988]). The representational power of these systems is often misunderstood. In particular, the underlying world model used by such systems is essentially the same state-based model as used in STRIPS. Nonlinearity is a property of the search *process* in constructing plans, and not a property of the representation of the world. For example, figure 2 shows a very simple nonlinear plan in the notation of Sacerdoti [1977]. It represents a partial ordering of actions, where action ActA must precede ActB and ActC, and ActB and ActC must precede action ActD, but actions ActB and ActC are unordered with respect to each other. This is actually a compact representation of two distinct linear plans, namely, ActA, ActB, ActC, ActD in order, or ActA, ActC, ActB, ActD in order. It does not include the possibility that actions ActB and

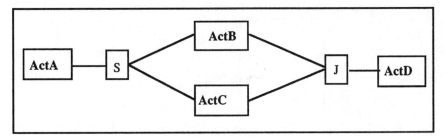

Figure 2:   A nonlinear plan

ActC are simultaneous. Extensions to include such a possibility are discussed below, but first consider the representation as Sacerdoti defined it. The representation was designed so that decisions about action ordering could be delayed as long as possible, avoiding the need for backtracking in cases where it was not necessary. The technique is very effective in some applications and has been adopted by many systems since. But information about a particular state can only be obtained by inferring what remains true throughout all the possible linear orderings. Thus, if we look at the example in figure 2, the only assertions the system could make about the state after ActD would be those assertions that were true both in the state obtained by applying ActA, ActB, ActC, and ActD in sequence and the state obtained by applying ActA, ActC, ActB, and ActD in sequence. For example, if ActB were "paint the room blue", and ActC were "paint the room crimson", then the color of the room after ActD would be undetermined, since the final color of the room given order ActA, ActB, ActC, ActD would be crimson, whereas the color of the room given the order ActA, ActC, ActB, ActD would be blue. If, instead, ActB were "paint the chair blue", then the result of the nonlinear plan would be that the room is crimson (from ActC) and the chair is blue (from ActB), since this is the resulting state given either the ordering ActA, ActB, ActC, ActD or the ordering ActA, ActC, ActB, ActD.

This final example suggests an extension to handle some cases of simultaneous action. In particular, in the last example above, the effect of performing the two actions ActB and ActC simultaneously could be the same as the result computed for any of the action orderings allowed by the nonlinear plan. Tate, Vere, and Wilkins have all used this extension in their systems and allow simultaneous action when the two actions are completely independent of each other. In such cases, the effect of the two acts performed together is the simple union of the individual effects of the acts done in isolation. Wilkins [1988] develops an interesting approach using the notion of resources to reason about the independence of actions.

The problem with this solution is that it excludes common situations of interest in realistic domains. In particular, interesting cases of interaction occur when the effect of two actions performed together is *different* from the sum of

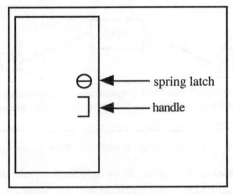

Figure 3: A door with a spring latch

Action	Precondition	Add-effects
TURN-LOCK	lock closed	lock open
HOLD-LOCK	lock open	lock open
PULL-DOOR	lock open door closed	door open

Figure 4: Encoding the spring-latch door in STRIPS

their individual effects. In particular, two actions may have additional effects when performed together, or they may partially interfere with each other's effects.

Here are several examples. The first concerns the door to the Computer Science Building at Rochester. A simplified version of this door is shown in figure 3. The door is designed so that it requires both hands to open it—very annoying since you have to put down whatever you are carrying! There is a spring lock that must be held open with one hand, while the door is pulled open with the other hand. If we try to formalize this in a STRIPS-like system, we might suggest the definitions summarized in figure 4. Each action is listed with its preconditions and the effects added. In each case, the delete-effects are the preconditions of the action and so are not listed.

This seems to come close to an adequate representation, but it is missing an essential fact, namely, that unless the lock is held open, it will snap shut. STRIPS, given the above definitions, would construct a plan to TURN-LOCK and then PULL-DOOR. The effect of TURN-LOCK would appear to satisfy the precondition for PULL-DOOR, and the plan in figure 5 appears well formed. Because STRIPS cannot represent change except as a result of the agent's actions, it cannot express the fact that the lock springs shut unless it is held open. Even if we could encode that, STRIPS still could not express the fact that

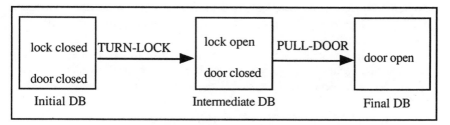

Figure 5: A faulty STRIPS "solution" to the door problem

Action	Precondition	Add-effects
TURN-LOCK	lock closed hand free	lock open holding lock open
RELEASE-LOCK	lock open holding lock open	lock closed hand free
PULL-DOOR	holding lock open door closed	door open

Figure 6: A state-encoding solution to the spring-latch door problem

doing PULL-DOOR and HOLD-LOCK simultaneously will have the effect that the door is open, even though neither PULL-DOOR nor HOLD-LOCK has this effect individually.

An approach to this problem that encodes the interaction of two actions in a special state has been used in several systems. We will call this technique **state encoding**. In particular, in the above example, we introduce a fluent that is true only if the agent is holding the lock open. The actions are now defined as in figure 6.

The action of holding the lock has been transformed into two actions, one to start holding the lock and another to release it. Pulling the door simply has a precondition that the agent is holding the lock open. The fluent "holding lock open", once asserted by the TURN-LOCK action, remains true until a RELEASE-LOCK action deletes it. While this might solve this particular problem, there are many potential disadvantages with this approach. The first objection is that it is ad hoc. While it may be the case that one can invent predicates to cover every specific example someone proposes, each must be done after the fact on an individual case-by-case basis. It is also not clear how the technique could be generalized to additional complexities involving simultaneous actions. The final objection is that holding the lock open is intuitively an action —it may take effort and will on the part of the agent to maintain and will constrain what other actions can be done simultaneously. Thus, it should explicitly be part of the plan. This is not reflected in the representation where holding the lock open is simply a fluent that will remain true until the agent does something to stop it.

In certain applications where a detailed causal theory is known, state-encoding approaches can be very powerful. If we cannot specify such a complete causal theory, however, or if we simply do not know enough about a situation to be able to use a causal theory, then other reasoning techniques must be explored. Both these problems arise in everyday planning situations: first, we have no detailed causal theory of the world, and second, we would not know the values for the parameters to the theory if such a theory was known.

Examples also exist where neither of the actions involved can be characterized as maintaining a state. In particular, consider the following problem in controlling a model train set. One of the tasks that the planner might have to do is to decouple cars from trains. In order to do this, the train must be moving and the particular car in question must be located at the decoupler when the decoupler is activated. The situation is shown in figure 7. If the train is not moving, then the cars will not pull apart. If the decoupler is left on and the train runs across it, it will simply decouple the engine from the rest of the train. The direct solution to this problem is to plan to perform the decouple action at the appropriate time while the move-train action is also occurring. In other words, the decouple action must be during a move-train action in order to succeed. A more realistic solution would need to model the train's momentum as well.

It might seem possible to introduce a fluent representing the fact that the train is being accelerated, but this fluent would have to cause dynamic changes to the world model as other actions were performed. In particular, the expected location of the train would be changing even when the agent is performing some completely unrelated action. Allowing this would violate the basic assumption that makes the state-based models feasible and so popular—that the only changes in the world are the result of planned actions.

While most likely there will be further extensions and improvements to the state-based models, progress on the problems discussed above cannot be made without moving to a representation where time plays a more central role.

1.1.2   Temporally Explicit Representations

There are several ways in which time can be introduced into planning models. The minimal change, which I shall call **temporal annotation**, is to simply associate times (or ranges of times) with each state. This extends traditional planners to handle some scheduling problems, but the primary assumptions built into the state-based models still hold. The more adventurous route is to start with a clean slate and consider what planning might be like given a temporally explicit representation of the world. In this section, I first briefly examine the models based on temporal annotation and then quickly move on to our proposal.

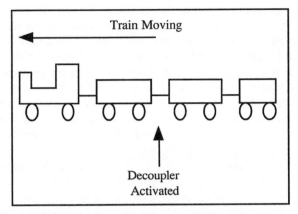

Figure 7: Decoupling a car in model train set

Temporal annotation was first used in **DEVISER** [Vere 1983], a planning application for controlling parts of the Voyager spacecraft. It used a hierarchical planner and added temporal information with each action. Each action had an earliest start time, latest start time, and constraints on its duration. Thus, this system is a cross between a planner and a PERT network. The system could use the ordering constraints introduced by the planner to refine the scheduling constraints on the actions and use the scheduling constraints to constrain the planner. While these techniques add expressive power to the plan representation and produce a system of great utility in certain domains, the system remains a state-based one. In particular, all the assumptions discussed above reappear in Vere's system, although sometimes in subtler forms. For example, this system can represent the fact that actions take time and can use this information in scheduling activities. However, it does not allow simultaneous events to interact, and so very little can be said about an action's execution except for its duration. In fact, to represent any forms of interaction for simultaneous actions, Vere must resort to state encoding, introducing new states for each interaction.

DEVISER can also represent the fact that some event will happen at some specific time in the future. The planner can then anticipate this future event in order to schedule the actions in the plan to avoid or take advantage of the event. This facility is limited, however, in that the planner cannot reason about changing the future event (e.g., preventing it). In addition, only interactions that can be captured by state encoding can be represented. This is all a result of the fact that it remains a state-based system in the way the world model is updated —using add lists and delete lists to transform the state before the action occurred into the state resulting from the action.

We will now eliminate the notion of state and build a new representation based on time. The simplest version of a system like this involves temporally explicit representation based on a linear time model (i.e., not a branching time model). This representation can be thought of as encoding the planning agent's knowledge of the world—past, present, and future. Since at the start, the agent has little knowledge of what it will be doing in the future, its predictions about the future will be quite incomplete. However, as the agent decides to perform certain actions in the future as a result of some planning process, the predictions of the future become more specific. The act of planning then looks like reasoning about what the future will be. The more an agent defines its plans, the more specific its knowledge of the future becomes. This approach allows significantly more complex worlds to be represented much more naturally than possible in the state-based formalisms, and a simple planner based on this model will be presented in some detail. While this model has known limitations, developing it will allow us to introduce the principal components needed for the more complex representations introduced in later parts of this book. In particular, many of the limitations of the simple approach can be removed by moving to a branching time logic that includes the notions of possibility and choice. This is explored in detail in chapter 3 of this book.

1.2   Representing Time

The literature on the nature and representation of time is full of different theories —continuous point-based models based on the real number line, discrete time, interval logics, branching time, and the like. We hope to avoid as many of these disputes as possible and introduce what seems to be the minimal requirements of a common-sense theory of time. This includes the intuition that time is fully ordered, that time can be naturally hierarchically organized, and that times are intimately connected with the events that occur in the world. The particular theory presented here is very simple, constructed out of one primitive object, the **time period,** and one primitive relation called **Meets**. It is the model developed by Allen and Hayes [1989], and those familiar with this logic and the computational model in Allen [1983a] may skip the rest of this section.

A time period is the intuitive time associated with some event or property of the world. Intuitively, two periods m and n meet if and only if m precedes n, yet there is no time between m and n, and m and n do not overlap. The axiomatization of the meets relation is as follows, where i, j, k, l, and m are logical variables restricted to time periods. These axioms are presented graphically in figure 8.

First, there is no beginning or ending of time and there are no semi-infinite or infinite periods. In other words, every period has a period that meets it and another that it meets.

(1.1) $\forall\, i, \exists\, j,k\, .\, Meets(j,i) \wedge Meets(i,k).$

Second, periods can compose to produce a larger period. In particular, for any two periods that meet, there is another period that is the "concatenation" of them. This can be axiomatized as follows:

(1.2) $\forall i,j,k,l$. $Meets(i,j) \land Meets(j,k) \land Meets(k,l)$
$\supset \exists m$. $Meets(i,m) \land Meets(m,l)$.

As a convenient notation, we will often write $j+k$ to denote the interval that is the concatenation of intervals j and k. This functional notation is justified because we can prove that the result of $j+k$ is unique [Allen and Hayes 1989].

Next, periods uniquely define an equivalence class of periods that meet them. In particular, if i meets j and i meets k, then any period l that meets j must also meet k:

(1.3) $\forall i,j,k,l$. $(Meets(i,j) \land Meets(i,k) \land Meets(l,j)) \supset Meets(l,k)$.

These equivalence classes also uniquely define the periods. In particular, if two intervals both meet the same period, and another period meets both of them, then the periods are equal:

(1.4) $\forall i,j$ $(\exists k,l$. $Meets(k,i) \land Meets(k,j) \land Meets(i,l) \land Meets(j,l))$
$\supset i=j$.

Finally, we need an ordering axiom. Intuitively, this axiom asserts that for any two pairs of periods, such that i meets j and k meets l, then either they both meet at the same "place", or the place where i meets j precedes the place where k meets l, or vice versa. In terms of the meets relation, this can be axiomatized as follows, using an n-ary exclusive-or:

(1.5) $\forall i,j,k,l$. $(Meets(i,j) \land Meets(k,l)) \supset$
$(\otimes Meets(i,l)$
$(\exists m. Meets(k,m) \land Meets(m,j))$
$(\exists m$. $Meets(i,m) \land Meets(m,l)))$.

Figure 8 shows these three possible orderings graphically.

Many of the properties that are intuitively desired but have not yet been mentioned are actually theorems of this axiomatization. In particular, it can be proven that no period can meet itself, and if one period i meets another j then j cannot also meet i (i.e., finite circular models of time are not possible).

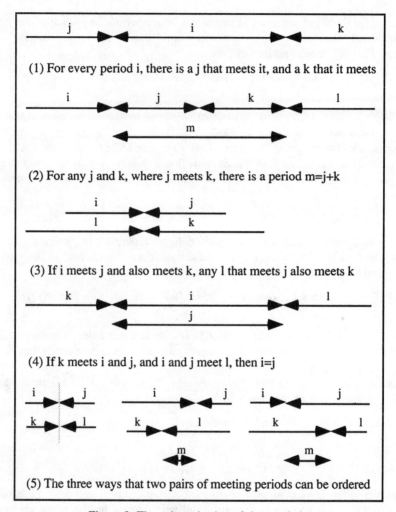

Figure 8: The axiomatization of time periods

With this system, one can define the complete range of the intuitive interval relationships that could hold between time periods. For example, one period is before another if there exists another period that spans the time between them, for instance:

Before(i,j) $\equiv \exists\ m\ .\ Meets(i,m) \wedge Meets(m,j).$

Figure 9 shows each of the interval relationships using the graphic notation and defines abbreviated character codes for each relation and its inverse (i.e., the relation obtained by reversing the order of the arguments).

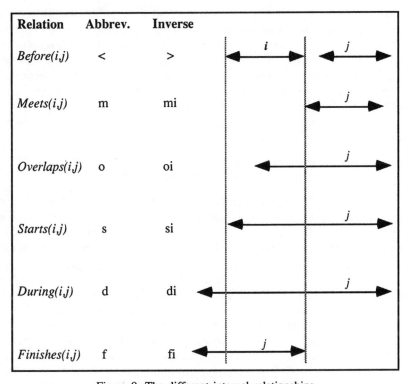

Relation	Abbrev.	Inverse
Before(i,j)	<	>
Meets(i,j)	m	mi
Overlaps(i,j)	o	oi
Starts(i,j)	s	si
During(i,j)	d	di
Finishes(i,j)	f	fi

Figure 9: The different interval relationships

A period can be classified by the relationships that it can have with other periods. For example, we call a period that has no subperiods (i.e., no period is contained in it or overlaps it) a **moment** and a period that has subperiods, an **interval**. In addition, we can define a notion of **time point** by a construction that defines the beginning and ending of periods. It is important to note that moments and points are distinct and cannot be collapsed. In particular, moments are true periods and may meet other periods, and if *Meets(i,m)* ∧ *Meets(m,j)* for any moment m, then i is before j. Points, on the other hand, are not periods and cannot meet periods. We will not need time points in this book. Full details can be found in Allen and Hayes [1989].

Any semantic model that allows these distinctions would be a possible model of time. In particular, a discrete time model can be given for this logic, where periods map to pairs of integers (I,J) where I<J. Moments correspond to pairs of the form (I,I+1), and points correspond to the integers themselves. A similar model built out of pairs of real numbers does not allow moments. A more complex model that is sometimes discrete and sometimes continuous would also be possible. Ladkin [1986] has characterized the possible models as precisely the arbitrary unbounded linear orders.

A computational system for reasoning about time periods has been built based on this logic. It can be shown that building a complete reasoner for this logic is NP-hard [Vilain, Kautz, and van Beek 1990]. However, a partial reasoner that captures a wide range of everyday reasoning situations and handles a useful range of disjunctive information can be built. In particular, the system can represent disjunctive information between a pair of periods. For example, it might be that period i meets, is before, or overlaps period j. Using the abbreviations for the relations, this disjunction can be expressed in the following form:

$i\ (m < o)\ j\ abbreviates$
$$Meets(i,j) \lor Before(i,j) \lor Overlaps(i,j).$$

The reasoning system represents such disjunctions directly. Each period is represented as a node in a directed graph. Arcs between nodes are labeled with a set of symbols to represent the disjunctive information between the two periods represented by the nodes. Thus, the disjunction above would be represented as the first graph shown in figure 10. If the system was also given the assertion $j\ (m)$ k, that is, j meets k, then it would automatically derive the consequence that k is strictly after i. It does this by maintaining consistency between any triple of periods using a transitivity table derivable from the axiomatization above and shown in figure 11. In particular, the system would check each possibility given the disjunction above: if i meets j and j meets k, then i must be before k, and if i is before j and j meets k, then i must be before k, and if i overlaps j and j meets k, then i must be before k. Since each possibility requires that i is before k, this relationship can be added to the network, possibily intitiating further inference.

The system uses the technique of constraint satisfaction to propagate effects through the network of interval relationships and is described in Allen [1983a]. An improved system that automatically restructures the network to eliminate redundant information is described in Koomen [1989]. For the purposes of this book, it is only important that such a reasoner can be constructed, so that the plan reasoning described below can be implemented.

There are several common combinations that we will use and hence define the following predicates:

$In(i,j) \equiv Starts(i,j) \lor During(i,j) \lor Finishes(i,j) \lor i=j$
$SameEnd(i,j) \equiv Finishes(i,j) \lor Finishes(j,i) \lor i=j$
$Disjoint(i,j) \equiv Before(i,j) \lor Meets(i,j) \lor Before(j,i) \lor Meets(j,i).$

Other disjunctions will be abbreviated by concatenating the predicate names involved. For example:

$BeforeMeetsOverlaps(i,j) \equiv Before(i,j) \lor Meets(i,j) \lor Overlaps(i,j).$

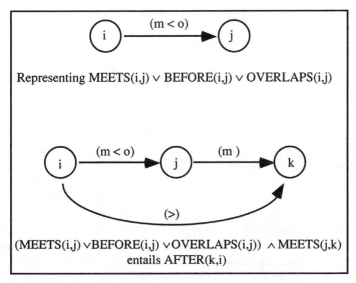

Figure 10: The network representation of interval relations

Note that the system cannot represent some disjunctions that are expressible in the general logic. For example, if *i* is either before *j* or before *k*, this situation cannot be represented as it involves a disjunction between more than two periods (i.e., *Before(i,j)* ∨ *Before(i,k)*). This limitation is a consequence of the notation based on labeling arcs—there is no way to express any disjunction except on an arc label, which connects exactly two periods.

A constraint propagation system based on intervals yields a more expressive system than a system that maintains a partial ordering on points. To see this, consider implementing intervals by a pair of time points *(begin,end)* and using constraints on the ordering between the points. Some relationships appear simpler with the point-based approach. For instance, consider representing the situation in which interval *A* begins before interval *B*, but nothing else is known. If *beg(A)* stands for the beginning point of *A*, and *end(A)* stands for the ending point of *A*, then this relationship is captured by

$beg(A) < beg(B)$

in the point-based representation, and by

A (< m o fi di) B

in the interval representation. The former appears simpler. However, the other side of the coin is that relationships that are very simple in the interval representation are much more complex in the point-based representation. For example, the situation where interval A overlaps B or interval B overlaps A is represented as

$A (o\ oi\ ) B$

in the interval logic, whereas it requires a complex disjunctive statement in the point-based logic:

$$((begin(A) < begin(B)) \wedge (end(A) > begin(B)) \wedge (end(A) < end(B)) \vee$$
$$((begin(B) < begin(A)) \wedge (end(B) > begin(A)) \wedge (end(B) < end(A))).$$

There is a significant difference between these examples. In particular, the disjunction in the point-based version cannot be expressed as a partial ordering on endpoints. On the other hand, the interval-based reasoner is designed to operate on disjunctions in the form of the examples. Ladkin and Madux [personal communication] demonstrate that out of the 2^{13} different ordering constraints that can be represented between two intervals in the interval logic, only 181 of these can be expressed as a partial ordering on the endpoints. Thus, the interval reasoner gives greater expressive power needed for plan reasoning. For example, a very common temporal constraint in a plan is that two actions must be disjoint, that is, $A (< m\ mi >) B$. This is not representable as a partial ordering on endpoints.

Given that this system is incomplete, how accurately can we characterize the effectiveness of the algorithm? Vilain, Kautz and van Beek [1990] show that the constraint propagation algorithm is complete on any set of relations that satisfies what they call the *continuous endpoint uncertainty* restriction. This subpart can express all the restrictions expressible in a point-based constraint algebra. Thus, we know that the interval algorithm is strictly more powerful than the point-based algorithm, since it can handle some cases of disjunctions not expressible as point-based constraints. We know, on the other hand, that the algorithm is incomplete. Allen [1983a] gives a specific network that does not make all the inferences that follow from the assertions. More precisely, Vilain, Kautz, and van Beek [1990] show that, while the problem is NP-hard, the interval propagation algorithm runs in $O(n^3)$. In practice, however, we have not yet found the incompleteness a problem in any particular application.

1.2.1 Temporal Logic

The preceding discussion developed a structure for time. We now will develop a temporal logic using this structure. The most obvious way to add times into a logic would be simply to add an extra argument to each predicate. For example, in a nontemporal logic, the predicate *Green* might denote the set of green objects. Thus, a formula such as $Green(FROG13)$ would be true only if the object named by the term $FROG13$ is in the set of green objects. To make this a temporal predicate, a time argument is added and *Green* now denotes a set of tuples consisting of all green objects with the times at which they were green.

A r1 B \ B r2 C	<	>	d	di	o	oi	m	mi	s	si	f	fi
"before" <	<	no info	< o m d s	<	<	< o m d s	<	< o m d s	<	<	< o m d s	<
"after" >	no info	>	> oi mi d f	>	> oi mi d f	>	> oi mi d f	>	> oi mi d f	>	>	>
"during" d	<	>	d	no info	< o m d s	> oi mi d f	<	>	d	> oi mi d f	d	< o m d s
"contains" di	< o m di fi	> oi di mi si	o oi dur con =	di	o di fi	oi di si	o di fi	oi di si	di fi o	di	di si oi	di
"overlaps" o	<	> oi di mi si	o d s	< o m di fi	< o m	o oi dur con =	<	oi di si	o	di fi o	d s o	< o m
"overlapped-by" oi	< o m di fi	>	oi d f	> oi mi di si	o oi dur con =	> oi mi	o di fi	>	oi d f	oi > mi	oi	oi di si
"meets" m	<	> oi mi di si	o d s	<	<	o d s	<	f fi =	m	m	d s o	<
"met-by" mi	< o m di fi	>	oi d f	>	oi d f	>	s si =	>	d f oi	>	mi	mi
"starts" s	<	>	d	< o m di fi	< o m	oi d f	<	mi	s	s si =	d	< o m
"started-by" si	< o m di fi	>	oi d f	di	o di fi	oi	o di fi	mi	s si =	si	oi	di
"finishes" f	<	>	d	> oi mi di si	o d s	> oi mi	m	>	d	> oi mi	f	f fi =
"finished-by" fi	<	> oi mi di si	o d s	di	o	oi di si	m	si oi di	o	di	f fi =	fi

Figure 11: The transitivity table for the twelve temporal relations (omitting "=")

Thus, the proposition *Green(FROG13,T1)* is true only if the object named by *FROG13* was green over the time named by *T1*.

This simple approach has been criticized as not providing any special status for time, and various other approaches have been suggested. These include introducing a modal operator that relates propositions to times, and logics such as Allen's [1984] and McDermott's [1982] in which events and propositions are reified and predicates such as *Holds* (or *Occurs*) are introduced that take a reified proposition (or event) and a time. Shoham [1987] has criticized these particular reified logics as unnecessarily complex and ill defined, and introduced an alternate with a variant of a first-order semantics without reified properties. Bacchus, Tenenberg, and Koomen [1989] then showed that the original approach of adding an extra parameter to every predicate is as powerful as Shoham's logic and is cleaner to define.

Notwithstanding all this, there are still good reasons for wanting reified events and possibly reified properties. However, for the moment, let us briefly introduce the logic of Bacchus, Tenenberg, and Koomen. They propose a sorted first-order logic using two sorts: times and everything else. Predicates are classified by the number of nontemporal and temporal arguments they take. For example, the predicate *Green* as defined above would now have arity $\langle 1,1 \rangle$: it takes one nontemporal argument and one temporal argument. On the other hand, a predicate of arity $\langle 2,1 \rangle$ takes two nontemporal arguments and one temporal argument. Semantically, this predicate denotes a triple consisting of two elements from the nontemporal domain and one from the domain of times. While their logic makes no commitment to the structure of time, we will use the structure introduced in the previous section.

By allowing time intervals as arguments, we open the possibility that a proposition involving some predicate P might be neither true nor false over some interval t. In particular, consider a predicate P such that P is true during some subinterval of t and also false in some other subinterval of t. In this case, there are two ways we might interpret the proposition $\sim P(t)$. In the **weak** interpretation, $\sim P(t)$ is true if and only if it is not the case that P is true throughout interval t, and thus $\sim P(t)$ is true if P changes truth-values during t. In the **strong** interpretation of negation, $\sim P(t)$ is true if and only if $\sim P$ is true throughout t, and thus neither $P(t)$ nor $\sim P(t)$ would be true in the above situation. Thus, a logic with only strong negation has truth gaps.

We use the weak interpretation of negation, as do Shoham [1987] and Bacchus, Tenenberg, and Koomen [1989], to preserve a simple two-valued logic. Weak negation also seems to be the appropriate interpretation for the standard definition of implication. In particular, the formula

$$P(t) \supset Q(t')$$

is typically defined as

$$\sim P(t) \vee Q(t').$$

Since we want the implication to mean—whenever P is true over t, then Q is true over t', this is best captured by the weak negation of the equivalent formula. With weak negation, $\sim P(t) \lor Q(t')$ says that either P is not true throughout t (but might be true in some subintervals of t), or Q is true over t'. This seems the right interpretation.

Of course, we can still make assertions equivalent to the strong negation. The fact that P is false throughout t can be expressed as

$$\forall\, t' \,.\, In(t',t) \supset \sim P(t').$$

There are several characteristics of propositions that allow them to be classified into broad classes based on their inferential properties. These distinctions were originally proposed by Vendler [1967], and variants have been proposed under various names throughout linguistics, philosophy, and artificial intelligence ever since (e.g., Dowty [1979], Allen [1984], Mourelatsos [1978], and Shoham [1987]). The first property is homogeneity. A proposition is *homogeneous* if and only if when it holds over a time period T, it also holds over any period within T.[1]

In the current formulation, this property is defined by a family of axiom schemata, one for each arity of predicate, for instance:

Homogeneity
For all homogeneous predicates P *of arity* $<n,1>$:
$\forall\, i,j \,.\, P(i_1,...,i_n,t) \land In(t,t') \supset P(i_1,...,i_n,t').$

The next property involves concatenation. A proposition is called *concatenable* if and only if whenever it holds over time i and j, where i meets j, then it holds over the time i+j:

Concatenability
For all concatenable predicates P *of arity* $<n,1>$:
$\forall\, i,j \,.\, P(i_1,...,i_n,t) \land P(i_1,...,i_n,t') \land Meets(t,t') \supset P(i_1,...,i_n,t+t')$
(*remember that* t+t' *is the concatenation of* t *and* t').

The final property we will need is countability. A proposition is *countable* if none of the times over which it holds overlap, that is, they are disjoint or equal.

Countability
For all countable predicates P *of arity* $<n,1>$:
$\forall\, i,j \,.\, P(i_1,...,i_n,t) \land P(i_1,...,i_n,t') \supset t\ (<m = mi>)\ t'.$

This is called *countability* because one can intuitively count the number of times such properties hold as there is no ambiguity introduced by overlapping

---

1. In a reified logic such as Allen's [1984], this would be expressed as follows, where p is a property and i and j are time periods: $\forall i,j,p\,.\, Holds(p,i) \land In(j,i) \supset Holds(p,j).$

intervals. For instance, a noncountable predicate is *Green*. If *Green(FROG13,T1)* is true and T1 contains other times T2 and T3, how many times was *FROG13* green? The answer certainly is not three (or more), which is the result one might get by counting the times over which the proposition holds. A predicate denoting an action such as dropping the ball, however, is countable. If John dropped the ball at time T3, then he did not drop the ball at any subtime of T3. It is simple to see that no countable predicate is either homogeneous or concatenable.

However, this logic is still insufficient to conveniently capture many of the situations that we need to reason about. In particular, we need to introduce events as objects into the logic. There are many reasons for this, and the most important of these are discussed in the remainder of this section. Davidson [1967] argued that there are potentially unbounded qualifications that could be included in an event description. For example, the event of Jack lifting a particular ball might be asserted to occur at some time by a <2,1>-arity predicate *Lift*, as follows:

   Lift(JACK34,BALL26,T1).

The problem now arises in representing the event "Jack lifted the ball onto the table". Either we need to add another argument to the *Lift* predicate, or we need to introduce a new predicate that represents a variant of lifting that includes an extra argument. Either is unsatisfactory. In the former case, all predicates describing event occurrences will contain a large number of argument positions, typically unspecified in any particular event description and thus requiring a large number of existential variables. In the latter case, we have a large class of predicates all asserting essentially the same thing. If we could put a bound on the number of argument positions needed, then one of these solutions might be viable. But in fact, it seems we could always add additional information about the event that has not yet been captured by a parameter, forcing us to add another. In natural language, this creates particular difficulty in representing adverbial modifiers. Davidson suggested the solution of reifying events, whereby additional modifiers would simply become additional predications on the event. Thus, the event of Jack lifting the ball onto the table with the tongs might be represented as

$$\exists e \,.\, Lift(JACK34,BALL26,e,T1) \wedge Dest(e) = TABLE555 \wedge$$
$$Instrument(e) = TONGS1.$$

In many subsequent works, this representation style has been extended so that all arguments of the predicate except the event variable itself have been moved to outside positions. This has been used extensively in representation based on case grammar developed in linguistics and used in AI in representations such as semantic networks. The assertion of the lifting event then becomes

$\exists\, e\, .\, Lift(e) \wedge Agent(e)=JACK34 \wedge Time\ (e)=T1 \wedge Theme(e)=BALL26$
$\wedge Dest(e)=TABLE555 \wedge Instrument(e)=TONGS1.$

These two styles of reifying events are essentially equivalent and are not mutually exclusive, so we will freely move between the two as is most convenient for each example.

The issue of reifying events is not only an issue for representing natural language meaning, however. A sophisticated plan reasoning system also needs to represent and reason about events of similar complexity. In addition, in many forms of plan reasoning, the system must be able to distinguish events even though it does not have any information to distinguish them. For instance, in a plan recognition task, an agent might know that two lifting events occurred, but it knows little else. In a reified logic this is easy to state, namely, as

$\exists\, e1,\, e2\, .\, Lift(e1) \wedge Lift(e2) \wedge e1 \neq e2.$

However, in a nonreified logic such a situation would have to be represented by a complex formula growing in size with the number of arguments. Thus, if the *Lift* predicate took five arguments, we would need a formula such as

$\exists\, a1,a2,a3,a4,t1,a6,a7,a8,a9,t2\, .\, Lift(a1,a2,a3,a4,t1) \wedge Lift(a6,a7,a8,a9,t2)$
$\wedge\ (a1 \neq a6 \vee a2 \neq a7 \vee a3 \neq a8 \vee a4 \neq a9 \vee t1 \neq t2).$

Besides being cumbersome, this formulation is committed to always being able to distinguish lifting events on the basis of the five arguments given. If Davidson's argument is accepted and the number of qualifications could be unlimited, we might not be able to express this situation at all. This technique might work in simple domains, but even then it rapidly becomes problematic if one needs to reason about action at an abstract level. For instance, both lifting and pushing could be viewed at an abstract level as classes of apply-force events. Specifically, it might be that we have the following relationships that capture this abstraction relationship:

$\forall\, a1,a2,a3,a4,t1\, .\, Lift(a1,a2,a3,a4,t1) \supset ApplyForce(a1,t1)$
$\forall\, a1,a2,a3,a4,t1\, .\, Push(a1,a2,a3,a4,t1) \supset ApplyForce(a1,t1).$

Consider now the situation where the plan reasoner learns that two distinct apply-force events occur, and its task is to identify the specific nature of these events given other evidence to come later. In the nonreified logic, this situation cannot be described. We could assert

$\exists\, a1,t1,a2,t2\, .\, ApplyForce(a1,t1) \wedge ApplyForce(a2,t2) \wedge (a1 \neq a2 \vee t1 \neq t2),$

but this does not allow the situation where a single agent did two apply-force actions simultaneously (e.g., possibly she lifted a balloon while pushing a ball). Since the arguments to the abstract predicate do not uniquely identify an event, there is no way to force the two events to be disjoint. In a reified logic, of course, this information can be expressed directly, namely, by

$\exists\ e1,e2\ .\ ApplyForce(e1) \wedge ApplyForce(e2) \wedge e1 \neq e2.$

The logic containing reified events also allows one to discuss events that do not occur. In particular, asserting that an event instance exists does not necessarily entail that it occurred. If this distinction is not necessary, then this assumption can be made. In fact, Kautz (chapter 2) only reasons about events that actually occur, and so his formulation does not make the distinction. Pelavin (chapter 3) considers certain events (plan instances) separately from their occurrence and thus uses an explicit predicate indicating occurrence. A new predicate *Occ* is introduced and the assertion that Jack lifted the ball (at time T1) would be represented as

$\exists\ e\ .\ Lift(JACK34,BALL26,e,T1) \wedge Occ(e).$

Using an explicit *Occ* predicate allows events to exist even if they do not actually occur, or could never occur. We will not need this expressive power in the temporal planner described next and so will proceed under the interpretation that only events that occur exist.

1.3   The Logic of Action

We will represent knowledge about action in several ways. The first is by defining the necessary conditions for the event consisting of the action occurring (or being performed). For example, consider the predication *Stack(a,b,e,t)*, taken to represent the fact that *e* is an event consisting of block *a* being placed on block *b* over time period *t*. The event variable plays a central role to this predicate—in fact, given the discussion in the previous section, the other parameters can be defined in terms of the event variable. In particular, every instance of a stacking event uniquely defines the blocks that it involves and the time over which it occurs. In fact, this is a general property of events captured by the following axiom schema:

Event Axiom Schema

For any $(n+2)$-ary Event predicate E,
$\forall\ e, i_1,...,i_n, t, i'_1, ..., i'_n, t'\ .\ E(i_1,...,i_n, e\ , t) \wedge E(i'_1,...,i'_n, e\ , t')$
$\supset (i_1 = i'_1 \wedge ... \wedge i_n = i'_n \wedge t = t').$

For the *Stack* predicate, this schema simply asserts that every stacking event uniquely defines two blocks and a time, namely,

$\forall\ e, a, b, t, a', b', t'\ .\ Stack(a, b, e, t) \wedge Stack(a', b', e, t')$
$\supset (a = a' \wedge b = b' \wedge t = t').$

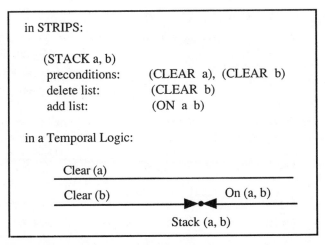

in STRIPS:

    (STACK a, b)
        preconditions: (CLEAR a), (CLEAR b)
        delete list: (CLEAR b)
        add list: (ON a b)

in a Temporal Logic:

    Clear (a)

    Clear (b)   On (a, b)

           Stack (a, b)

Figure 12: The temporal properties of stacking

The stacking event in a typical STRIPS-style system is defined by its preconditions: (both blocks must be clear) and by its transition function: (delete the formula $Clear(y)$ and add the formula $On(x,y)$). We can use the STRIPS definition to identify the conditions of the world that necessarily must be true whenever such a stacking event occurs. We see the following time course of properties whenever the stack(x,y) action occurs:

- the properties $Clear(x)$ and $Clear(y)$ must be true just before the action occurs.

- the property $On(x,y)$ must be true immediately after the action occurs.

These conditions could be be expressed directly in the temporal logic as shown graphically in figure 12, together with the STRIPS-style definition. A line signifies an interval and a dot signifies a moment. Ends of lines without arrowheads indicate an unconstrained endpoint for the interval.

STRIPS is required to make the assumption that the action is instantaneous. In the temporal representation, this assumption is neither necessary nor desirable, so we will develop a richer definition. Because an action takes time, we can define what is true while the action is occurring. This can be arbitrarily complex, but for this initial example, we shall make it simple. Let us define the action so that all we know is that the top block is held sometime during the execution of the action, and the effect is realized right at the end of the action. With these assumptions, we might have the following axiom representing our knowledge of the necessary conditions for a stacking action to have occurred:

$(*) \forall i,a,b,e$. $Stack(a,b,e,i) \supset$
$\exists j,k,l,m,n$. $Clear(a,j) \wedge Overlaps(j,i) \wedge Holding(a,k) \wedge Finishes(k,i)$
$\wedge Meets(j,k) \wedge Clear(a,l) \wedge Meets(i,l) \wedge Clear(b,m) \wedge SameEnd(i,m) \wedge$
$On(a,b,n) \wedge Meets(i,n)$.

A more useful form of this axiom for planning uses a more complex structure for events. In particular, we will introduce temporal functions on each event that define the structure of the temporal intervals needed for its definition. For example, for the class of stacking events, we need functions to produce times corresponding to the existential variables in $(*)$ above. Using new function names, we might define the temporal structure of the stacking event as follows:

Stacking Axiom 0: Temporal Structure

$\forall e , \exists a, b, i,$. $Stack(a, b, e, i) \supset$
$Overlaps(pre1(e), i) \wedge Finishes(con1(e), i) \wedge$
$Meets(pre1(e), con1(e)) \wedge Meets(i, eff1(e)) \wedge$
$SameEnd(i, pre2(e)) \wedge Meets(i, eff2(e))$.

The temporal functions are named to informally suggest the three classes of conditions that arise in an event definition. The "preconditions"—conditions that must hold prior to the event's occurrence—have the prefix "pre", the "effects"—conditions that must hold following the event—have the prefix "eff", and the other conditions that must occur during the event have the prefix "con". With this temporal structure defined for every stacking event, the axiom defining the necessary conditions for the event's occurrence now can be expressed as follows:

Stacking Axiom 1

$\forall i, a, b, e$. $Stack(a, b, e, i) \supset$
$Clear (a, pre1(e)) \wedge Holding(a, con1(e)) \wedge Clear(a, eff1(e)) \wedge Clear(b, pre2(e)) \wedge On(a, b, eff2(e))$.

The temporal functions can be viewed as Skolem functions justified by the original axiom $(*)$. The only aspect that might seem puzzling is why we can use the same Skolem functions in several axioms. This should be viewed as a notational convenience that allows a large conjunctive axiom (with a single universally quantified event variable) to be presented as several smaller axioms.

The above axiom asserts what is true whenever a stacking event occurs, independent of the situation. Other knowledge about action is relevant only in certain situations. For instance, if the block being moved in a stacking action was initially on another block, then this other block becomes clear. This is easily expressed in the logic by the following axiom, which states that if block a was initially on another block c, then c becomes clear when a is moved:

Stacking Axiom 2

$\forall i,a,b,c,t,e$. $Stack(a,b,e,i) \wedge On(a,c,t) \wedge Overlaps(t,i) \supset$
$Clear(c,eff3(e)) \wedge Meets(t,eff3(e)) \wedge Meets(t,con1(e))$.

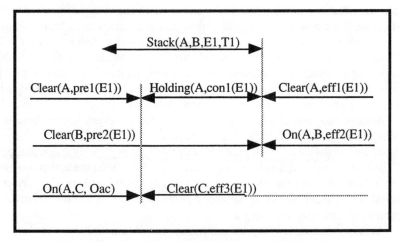

Figure 13: The necessary conditions for *Stack(A,B,E1,T1)* in a situation where A
is originally on C (using stacking axioms 1 and 2)

This axiom applies in a situation with three blocks, such as *A, B,* and *C,*
where *A* is originally on block *C*. The consequences of the assertion
Stack(A,B,E1,T1), based on the axioms above, are shown graphically in figure
13. Note that this definition does not assert that block C will be clear at the end
of the stacking event. In particular, if two stacking events overlap in time (say,
Stack(A,B,E1,T1) and *Stack(D,C,E2,T2)*), then this may not be the case, for *D*
may be placed on *C* before *A* is placed on *B*. This shows another weakness of
the STRIPS representation, which cannot easily represent such subtleties.

This development generalizes some of the information present in the
STRIPS formulation, but does not capture any sense of causality. In particular,
the formula above does *not* state what properties are caused by the stacking
action or what properties simply must be true whenever the action succeeds.
This is the distinction that STRIPS makes between preconditions and effects.
Intuitively, it is evident that the stacking action causes block *A* to be on block *B*
in situations where both blocks are clear at the start of the action. Furthermore,
the stacking action causes block *B* to become not clear while it does not affect
the condition that block *A* is clear.

To encode such knowledge, we need to be able to reason about attempting to
perform an action. The logic developed so far can express the fact that a certain
event occurred, but not that an agent attempted to perform some action. Until we
make such a distinction, we will not be able to explicitly describe the conditions
under which an action can be successfully executed, or describe what happens
when an action is tried in inappropriate circumstances. To do this, we need to
better define the distinction between events and actions. So far, we have only
talked about events occurring. The assertion that Jack lifted the ball onto the

table describes an event in which Jack performed some action that resulted in the ball being lifted onto the table. The action Jack performed, namely, the lifting, corresponds to some set of motions that Jack performed in order to lift the ball. If Jack were a robot, the action would be the execution of a program that involved the correct control sequences given perceptual input. Thus, in a robot world the action corresponds to the program, whereas the event corresponds to a situation in which the program was executed successfully.

Actions and events are easily confused since for every action there is a corresponding event consisting of an agent performing that action. Thus, for any action, we can define an event predicate that takes the arguments that it has, plus an agent and a time, and is true only if the agent performed the action over the time. Of course, there are other events that do not involve actions. For example, natural forces (such as the wind blowing) result in events but do not involve action in the sense we are using it.

Actions, of course, may be arbitrarily complex activities, but they are decomposable into other less complex actions, which themselves may be decomposable, until a certain basic level of action is attained. The primitive actions are called the *Basic* actions following Goldman [1970].

For every event predicate E that asserts that an action A occured over time t, we have an action that takes all the parameters of E except the event and time variables (and the agent variable if we used one). Thus, the action related to the event proposition $Stack(a,b,e,t)$ is $stack(a,b)$. If we wished, we could dispense with event predicates altogether and rewrite $Stack(a,b,e,t)$ in a style reminiscent of the situation calculus using a *Do* predicate: $Do(stack(a,b),e,t)$ would be true if and only if e is the event of action $stack(a,b)$ being successfully performed over time t.[2] We will however stick to the notation already introduced earlier.

The predicate *Try* is defined on actions, such that $Try(act,e,t)$ is true only if the *act* is attempted over time t causing event e to occur. In other words, $Try(stack(a,b),e,t)$ is true whenever the action $stack(a,b)$ is attempted by the agent over time t causing event e.

We can now assert an axiom defining the conditions sufficient to guarantee successful action attempts, namely, wherever the agent tries to stack a on b starting in a situation where a and b are clear, then the event that occurs is a stack event temporally constrained by the initial conditions:

Stacking Axiom 3

$\forall i,a,b,e \;.\; \exists j,k \;.\; Try(stack(a,b),e,i) \land Clear(a,j) \land Overlaps(j,i) \land$
$Clear(b,k) \land SameEnd(i,k)$
$\supset Stack(a,b,e,i)$

Of course, a realistic axiom would also include duration constraints on i so that the action is attempted sufficiently long enough to allow it to succeed.

---

2. or, for that matter, $Occurs(stack(a,b),t)$, as in Allen [1984].

It is interesting to consider why the information about the stacking action is captured by two different sets of related axioms: one capturing the necessary conditions whenever an event occurs, and the other relating action attempts to event occurrences. This is because the two sets of axioms represent two very different sources of knowledge. The first defines knowledge about what the world is necessarily like whenever the action occurs successfully, while the second defines the ability of the planning agent. In many situations, an agent may know the former but not the latter. For example, we all can recognize that the mechanic fixed our car, even if we have no idea what enabled the mechanic to do the job. In this case, we have knowledge of what it means to fix a car as expressed by the following axiom, which states that fixing something means that the thing was once broken and is now working:

$$\forall\ i,c,e\ .\ Fix(c, e, i) \supset$$
$$Broken(c, pre1(e)) \wedge Finishes(i, pre1(e)) \wedge Working(c, eff1(e)) \wedge$$
$$Meets(i, eff1(e)).$$

With this information, the agent knows what it means for the car to be fixed (although the agent does not know how it was done). Furthermore, once we incorporate the techniques used by Kautz (chapter 2), we could specify a system that could recognize situations in which the car has been fixed (again, without any knowledge of how it was done). Knowledge of this sort is also essential for much of natural language semantics, where many verbs are defined and used without the agent's knowing the necessary causal knowledge. Allen [1984] discusses this at length.

Do other planning formalisms use information about sufficient conditions for successfully attempting action or about necessary conditions given the event occurrence? It seems that the closer analogy is to attempting action, although it is hard to say since little attention is ever given to unsuccessful attempts. A STRIPS-like system, for instance, gives information about the effect of an action only in the class of situations where the precondition holds (i.e., where the attempt is guaranteed to succeed). There is no distinction made between action attempts and event occurrences, since they are equivalent under these conditions—the only action attempts considered are the successful ones. On the other hand, the situation calculus allows multiple axioms defining the result of performing an action in different situations and thus could include information about unsuccessful attempts. For instance, we could assert axioms

If a and b are clear in situation s,
    then On(a,b) is true in situation Stack(a,b,s).

If a is clear, and On(c,b) is true in situation s,
    then On(a,c) is true in situation Stack(a,b,s).

The second rule is actually providing information about attempting the action *stack(a,b)* when its preconditions do not hold (i.e., *b* is not clear). In other words, these axioms can be viewed as defining the effects of performing an action under different circumstances. So while the situation calculus can be viewed as capturing knowledge about action attempts, it does not then have a notion of successful action execution. Unless, of course, we view every action attempt as successful in that it has some effect on the world!

McDermott [1985] is one of the few other researchers to explicitly use a notion of attempting an action, and his approach is similar to that presented here. He defines an action to be feasible (i.e., can be executed successfully) if the task of trying the action ends in success.

1.4   The Logic for Planning

A planning system can now be specified using the temporal logic developed above. This system can reason about certain classes of interacting simultaneous events, and it has a limited capability for reasoning about the future. In particular, while it cannot plan to change any external events predicted to occur in the future, it can construct plans that take future events into account and reason about interactions with such events.

In order to construct plans, an agent needs to predict future states of the world. STRIPS-like problem solvers do this by using the add and delete lists to transform the current state into the next state. With a representation based on an explicit temporal logic, however, it is more complicated. In particular, if a proposition P is asserted to hold at a time $T1$ and then some action A occurs after $T1$ that makes P false, it is still true that P held at time $T1$. So, the representation of the world should still contain this assertion. What has changed once the new action is introduced is some prediction about whether P holds in the future. For example, before A is known about, the agent might have predicted that P still holds in the future. However, once the action A is expected, this prediction changes.

Thus, it is the predictions (or expectations) about the future that change as an agent plans. Since an agent may change its mind about what future actions it might do, most conclusions about the future must be retractable. This suggests that some form of nonmonotonic reasoning is necessary in order to maintain the world model, and some models such as deKleer's ATMS [deKleer 1986] might be useful. In this section, we take a simpler route: a model is outlined that views all predictions about the future as conditional statements based on what the agent assumes about the future, including its own actions. So, given an initial world description W and a goal statement G, a plan is a set of assumptions $A_1,...,A_n$ such that

$$W \vdash A_1 \wedge A_2 \wedge ... \wedge A_n \supset G.$$

Of course, if the Ai's are inconsistent then this statement is vacuously true, so we must also add the condition that

$A_1 \wedge A_2 \wedge ... \wedge A_n$ *is consistent.*

Finally, we want to avoid assuming the problem away. For instance, if A_1 is simply equivalent to the goal statement G, the above conditions are true, but we cannot say we have solved the problem! This is handled by restricting the form of assumptions that the planner can make, as described below. At any time, the world representation will consist of the agent's beliefs about the world—past, present, and future—based on a set of assumptions that the agent makes about the world and its future behavior.

With this analysis, we can view the planning problem as consisting of two types of reasoning:

- prediction—what is the world like, based on a given set of assumptions?

- planning—what assumptions should the agent make about its future behavior and the future world?

These two types of reasoning are explored in detail in the remainder of this section.

1.4.1   Predicting the Future

If an agent had full knowledge about a world, then predicting the future would be a relatively well-defined task. The agent would simply simulate the future course of events starting from the present state. In practice, however, the agent never has such detailed knowledge about the world—the agent's knowledge of the present state is partial, and the world is not well understood enough to make precise predictions. Even qualitative models, such as those discussed in Bobrow [1985], assume a level of knowledge about the state of the world and the processes that change it that are not realizable in most situations. Of course, in circumstances where such knowledge is present, the theory should allow such reasoning to be used. Thus, a continuum of methods is necessary, from the most simple forms of reasoning based on very partial knowledge, to the abstract simulations that are present in the qualitative-physics models, to detailed quantitative simulations of the world.

Here, we develop a model of prediction based on maintaining limited consistency of the agent's beliefs about the world. Essentially, given some set of beliefs about the future, the predictions are simply what is inferable from those beliefs using the agent's knowledge of the structure of the world and the definitions of actions and relationships between predicates. The particular system we will specify uses a forward chaining strategy on Horn clauses coupled with constraint propagation techniques (another form of forward inference) for temporal reasoning.

To drive the predictor, we need knowledge about the actions, such as defined in section 1.3, as well as general knowledge of the domain. All the axioms about actions in section 1.3 can be encoded as forward chaining rules. In a temporal logic, with a homogeneous predicate P, the propositions $P(t1)$ and $\sim P(t2)$ are inconsistent if interval $t2$ is contained in or equal to $t1$. If we consider a case of strong negation, where P is false throughout $t2$ (i.e., $\forall t$. $In(t,t2) \supset \sim P(t)$), then $t1$ and $t2$ must be disjoint. As a result, we can define an axiom where if we are given P is true throughout $t1$, and P is false throughout $t2$, then the proposition $Disjoint(t1,t2)$ is a consequence. This is captured by the axiom schema which we call the proposition constraint (in fact, this is a theorem of the temporal logic introduced previously):

Theorem: The Proposition Constraint

For any $<n,1>$ arity homogeneous predicate P,
$P(i_1,...,i_n,t1) \wedge (\forall\ t2\ .\ In(t2,\ t1) \supset \sim P(i_1,...,i_n,t2)\ ) \supset$
    $Disjoint(t1,t2).$

In general, we will not use this constraint directly, but use domain-specific axioms for predicates that are mutually exclusive. For instance, in the blocks world, every block is always either clear, being held, or has another block on top of it. For prediction purposes, we are interested in eliminating the inconsistencies that would arise if more than one of these properties held on a block at a particular time. This motivates a set of forward chaining rules that guarantees that this cannot occur. For instance, if a block b is clear at time t1, and another block a is on it at time t2, then t1 and t2 must be disjoint:

Domain Constraint 1

$\forall\ a,b,t1,t2$. $Clear(b,t1) \wedge On(a,b,t2) \supset Disjoint(t1,t2).$

Similarly, a block that is being held is not clear and cannot be on top of another block:

Domain Constraint 2

$\forall\ a,i,j$. $Clear(a,i) \wedge Holding(a,j) \supset Disjoint(i,j).$

Domain Constraint 3

$\forall\ a,b,i,j$. $On(a,b,i) \wedge Holding(a,j) \supset Disjoint(i,j).$

There are other facts about the blocks domain that can also be expressed by domain constraints. For example, in a domain with only one arm, only one block can be held at any particular time:

Domain Constraint 4

$\forall\ a,b,i,j$. $Holding(a,i) \wedge Holding(b,j) \wedge a \neq b \supset Disjoint(i,j).$

In addition, let us assume that a block can be on at most one other block, and have at most one block on top of it:

Domain Constraint 5

$\forall\ a,b,c,t1,t2$. $On(a,b,t1) \wedge On(c,b,t2) \wedge a \neq c \supset Disjoint(t1,t2).$

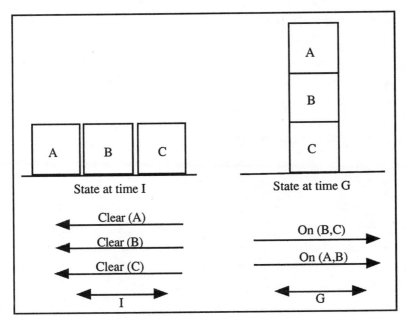

Figure 14: A simple blocks-world problem

Domain Constraint 6

$\forall\ a,b,c,t1,t2\ .\ On(a,b,t1) \wedge On(a,c,t2) \wedge b \neq c \supset Disjoint(t1,t2)$.

We can show that a forward chaining prediction algorithm using the axioms in the forms above can capture some important aspects of nonlinear planning systems quite well. In particular, nonlinear planners have used a set of heuristics to determine the ordering of actions in a plan. In our formulation, such heuristics are not needed and the ordering falls out from maintaining temporal consistency. For example, consider the simple example shown in figure 14. We have a simple blocks-world situation where blocks A, B, and C are clear at some initial time I. The goal is to build a tower with A on B and B on C such that the tower is standing over some time period G. The axiomatization of the initial state and the desired final state, where Ca, Cb, Cc, Oab, and Obc are all temporal constants, is as follows:

$Clear(A,Ca)$	$On(A,B,Oab)$
$Clear(B,Cb)$	$On(B,C,Obc)$
$Clear(C,Cc)$	$In(G,Oab)$.
$In(I,Ca)$	$In(G,Obc)$
$In(I,Cb)$	
$In(I,Cc)$	

Let us assume the planner has decided to solve this problem by planning two stacking actions, one to put A on B, and the other to put B on C. In both cases, the effect of the action should extend to include the time G in order to accomplish the goal. Techniques to derive these assumptions automatically will be described in the next section. The planner's assumptions about these two actions are as follows:

> $Stack(A,B,E1,I1)$ such that $In(G, \textit{eff2}(E1))$
> $Stack(B,C,E2,I2)$ such that $In(G, \textit{eff2}(E2))$.

When these assumptions are added, the predictor can use an encoding of stacking axiom 1 to infer the consequences of these actions on the world state, and new temporal constraints are derived by the temporal reasoner in order to maintain consistency. In particular, from $Stack(A,B,E1,I1)$ and stacking axiom 1 the system would infer

> $Clear(A, \textit{pre1}(E1)) \land Holding(A, \textit{con1}(E1)) \land Clear(A, \textit{eff}(E1)) \land$
> $\quad Clear(B, \textit{pre2}(E1)) \land On(A,B, \textit{eff2}(E1))$

plus the temporal constraints from stacking axiom 0:

> $Overlaps(\textit{pre1}(E1), I1) \land Finishes(\textit{con1}(E1), I1) \land$
> $\quad Meets(\textit{pre1}(E1), \textit{con1}(e1)) \land Meets(I1, \textit{eff1}(E1)) \land SameEnd(I1,$
> $\quad \textit{pre2}(E1)) \land Meets(I1, \textit{eff2}(E1))$.

When these are added, further inference may occur based on the domain constraints. The most interesting examples of this occur when the corresponding set of conclusions are made as a result of adding $Stack(B,C,E2,I2)$. A considerable number of constraints are derived that characterize the interactions between the two actions. In particular, the system would derive that $Clear(B)$ and $On(A,B)$ cannot overlap (domain constraint 1),

> $Disjoint(\textit{eff2}(E1), \textit{pre1}(E2)) \land Disjoint(\textit{eff2}(E1), \textit{pre1}(E2))$

that $On(A,B)$ and $Holding(B)$ cannot overlap (domain constraint 3),

> $Disjoint(\textit{eff2}(E1), \textit{con1}(E2))$

that $Clear(B)$ and $Holding(B)$ cannot overlap (domain constraint 2), and

> $Disjoint(\textit{pre2}(E1), \textit{con1}(E2))$

that $Holding(A)$ and $Holding(B)$ cannot overlap (domain constraint 4)

> $Disjoint(\textit{con1}(E1), \textit{con1}(E2))$.

The result of adding these additional constraints to the system creates a situation where $E1$ (stacking A on B) must be after $E2$ (stacking B on C). In particular, the time the system is holding block B must precede the time that the system is holding block A. This situation is shown in figure 15.

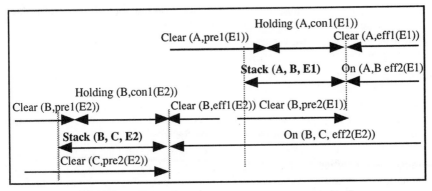

Figure 15: After introducing Stack (A,B) and Stack (B,C)

Note that the appropriate ordering of the two stacking actions is simply a logical consequence of the definition of the actions in the temporal representation, together with the domain constraints. There is no need to resort to special ordering heuristics to pick an order as in NOAH [Sacerdoti 1977]. In addition, had there been no constraint on what order two actions must occur, we could have represented this directly and not committed to an order. NOAH was often forced to pick an ordering at random to resolve conflicts and could not backtrack if it later turned out to be the wrong choice. NONLIN added backtracking to solve this problem, but still had to choose a specific ordering. Thus, we see that even in simple blocks worlds, the explicit temporal representation can be a conceptual advantage. Of course, the complexity of reasoning about action ordering is still present, but is now in the relatively well-defined temporal reasoner.

Before examining more complex problems, we must address a key issue that has been avoided so far: how were the particular actions selected that would solve this problem? From our viewpoint, this is the problem of what assumptions the agent should make about the future, and this is discussed in detail in section 1.4.2.

1.4.2   Planning With a Temporal World Model

There are roughly two classes of planning algorithms in the literature. The deductive planners, typified by STRIPS [Fikes and Nilsson 1971], Waldinger [1977], and Kowalski [1979], build plans from first principles using information about the preconditions and effects of actions. On the other hand, the hierarchical planners such as NOAH [Sacerdoti 1977], NONLIN [Tate 1977], SIPE [Wilkins 1988], and FORBIN [Dean, Firby, and Miller 1989], use preexisting knowledge about how to achieve single goals and reason about how to combine these simple tasks into more complex ones that achieve multiple goals simultaneously. Typically, this involves detecting interactions between the simple tasks and imposing ordering constraints on the substeps of each task so that they do not interfere with each other. These are very different forms of plan construction, and both are needed in a fully capable planning system. We will look at how each of these methods can be realized as specialized inference processes within our temporally-based representation. This section introduces the basic concepts essential to either approach and then develops a deductive planner. Section 1.7 shows how a hierarchical planner can also be specified. Along the way, we will show that the extended representation allows us to formulate plans in situations that cannot easily be handled in the state-based representations.

There are two main classes of assumptions that the planner must make. It must decide what actions it will attempt to perform, and it must make assumptions about how the external world will behave. The planner is built on the assumption that the agent may attempt any action at any time. Of course, the action will succeed only if the appropriate conditions hold, but an attempt can be made at any time. As we will see below, this is implemented by allowing the planner to add any assertion of the form $Try(a,e,t)$ without proof. The assumptions about the external world are limited at present to *persistence* assumptions (cf., Dean and McDermott [1987]), that is, once a property is established, it tends to remain true until explicitly changed. We can use persistence assumptions to complete the plan derived in section 1.4.1 (figure 15). In particular, we can assume that the preconditions of both the actions, which do hold in the initial time I, continue to hold until the actions occur. In particular, we can assume $Ca = pre1(E1)$, which guarantees that block A remains clear until the stacking action E1 begins. The other assumptions needed are $Cb = pre1(E2)$, $Cc = pre2(E2)$, and $eff1(E2) = pre2(E1)$. These assumptions produce a complete plan as shown in figure 16, where the persistence assumptions are indicated by grey lines.

Clearly, the problem facing the planner is what assumptions should be made. To find appropriate assumptions, the planner tries to prove the goals from the world description. Typically, this proof will fail, for otherwise the goal is predicted to follow without any further planned action. But by attempting to do the proof, the planner can discover what assumptions are needed to allow the proof to succeed.

Consider an example working on one of the simplest of tasks—given blocks A and B, where both are clear over a time I, achieve $On(A,B,G)$, where G follows sometime after I. Proofs of more complex goals in more complex situations follow along the same lines. The initial world description then consists of the following assertions:

> $Clear(A,Ca)$
> $Clear(B,Cb)$
> $In(I,Ca)$
> $In(I, Cb)$
> $Before(I,G)$.

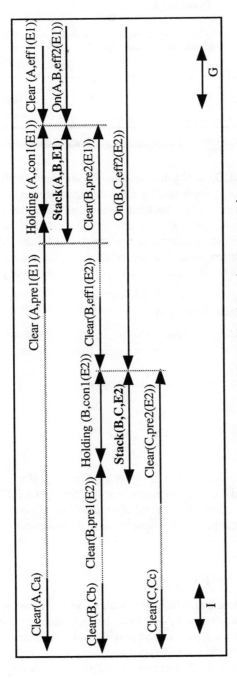

Figure 16: After making the persistence assumptions

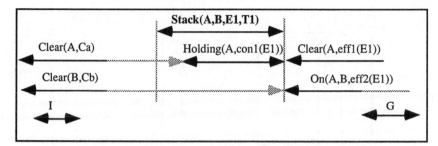

Figure 17: The situation after assuming a Stack action

We try to prove $On(A,B,G)$ using the axioms in section 1.3. Using the homogeneity axiom, we could prove $On(A,B,G)$ if we could prove $On(A,B,i)$ for some i containing G, such as $In(G,i)$. Stacking axiom 1 suggests that a stacking action could be applicable, where $i=eff2(E1)$, and $E1$ is the event of the stacking action occuring. Thus, we have a subgoal of proving $Stack(A,B,E1,T1)$, where T1 is a time satisfying the temporal structure of E1 (*stacking axiom 0*). Now using stacking axiom 3, we could prove $Stack(A,B,E1,T1)$ if we could prove

> $Try(stack(A,B),E1,T1) \land \exists j,k . Clear(A,j) \land Clear(B,k) \land$
> $Overlaps(j,T1) \land SameEnd(T1,k).$

This suggests the assumptions to make. The planner assumes that it will try *stack(A,B)* and that blocks A and B will remain clear from the initial state to the time the action is attempted.

In summary, if we make the following assumptions:

> $Try(stack(A,B),E1,Ts)$
> $Overlaps(Ca,Ts)$
> $SameEnd(Cb,Ts)$
> $In(G,eff2(E1)),$

then the goal $On(A,B,G)$ logically follows. More significantly, if we add these assumptions to the forward chaining predictor, it will derive $On(A,B,G)$. Figure 17 shows the final representation of the world after these assumptions are made. As before, the results of the persistence assumptions are indicated using grey lines.

1.5   The Planning System

Let us consider this example again from the point of view of the actual plan reasoning system. To distinguish the system from the logic developed so far, we will use a different notation closer to the actual implementation. A literal consists of a predicate name and a list of arguments enclosed in square brackets. Thus, the literal corresponding to the formula $On(A,B,G)$ is [On A B G].

Knowledge about actions is captured by a set of planning rules, which are a modified notation of Horn clauses using "?" as a prefix to indicate variables. For example, a planning rule for the stacking action is

(Stack.1)
   [On ?a ?b ?t'] <<< [Stack ?a ?b ?e ?t]   such that [EQ ?t' eff2(?e)].

In general, a planning rule is of the form

   C <<< A_1 A_2 ... A_n such that K_1, ..., K_k

and can be interpreted formally as a Horn clause: the consequent literal C is true (or provable) if the antecedent literals A_1, ..., A_n are true and the constraints K_1, ..., K_k are true.

Antecedants and constraints are distinguished to produce an efficient inference strategy with the temporal reasoning. Planning rules are used by the system in both a forward (from antecedent to consequent) and a backward (from consequent to antecedent) chaining manner. To apply a rule in a backward chaining manner, the rule's consequent C is unified with the goal. Then, the constraints K_1,..., K_n are added to the database, and the antecedent literals A_1,..., A_n are introduced as subgoals. To apply the rule in a forward manner, if a literal is added to the database that unifies with some antecedent literal A_i, and all the other A_j, $j \neq i$, and the constraints K_1,..., K_n are in the database, then we also assert the consequent C. For instance, rule (Stack.1) could be used to suggest that a goal [On A B Oab] could be accomplished by an event E1 if we can prove [Stack A B E1 T1] under the constraint eff2(E1)=Oab. The same rule is also used to predict the consequence of the same event E1 occurring at time T1. For instance, if [Stack A B E1 T1] is added then add [On A B eff2(E1)].

This simple example illustrates the basic technique for generating plans— planning rules are used to backward chain to suggested actions, and then in a forward manner to compute the consequences of those actions. In addition, all the domain prediction rules are also used in a forward chaining manner to compute additional consequences of the action. For example, domain constraint 1 above would be asserted as the following forward chaining rule:

   [Disjoint ?t1 ?t2] <forward< [clear ?b ?t1] [On ?a ?b ?t2].

All the other domain constraints can be expressed similarly.

There are several additional issues to consider before the algorithm can be fully specified. First, the planner must be able to create event structures as needed, since the appropriate events generally will not be known to occur in advance of the planning. This is accomplished during the backward chaining phase: whenever a literal containing an unbound event variable is to be introduced as a goal, a new event constant is generated, and the temporal structure associated with that event is added to the database together with any other constraints specified in the planning rule. As an example, given the goal

[On A B Oab], rule (Stack.1) suggests a subgoal of proving [Stack A B ?e ?t]. Before this is considered further, a new event, such as E1, and a new time, such as T1, are created, and the following constraints are added to the database from the definition of the temporal structure of stack events (stacking axiom 0):

> [Overlaps pre1(E1) T1], [Meets pre1(E1) con1(E1)], [Finishes con1(E1) T1], [Meets T1 eff1(E1)], [SameEnd pre2(E1) T1], [Meets T1 eff2(E1)],[Meets pre1(E1) eff3(E1)].

What we have done is create the temporal structure for an event that could accomplish the goal clause. We have not asserted that this event yet occurs. This will require further chaining to prove [Stack A B E1 T1]. This process of creating event and temporal constants to replace the unbound variables will be called *instantiating* the planning rule.

And finally, we need to elaborate on assumption making. There are two special ways in which a literal may be "proven" entirely by assumption. The first is an **ability assumption** in which an agent may assume that it can try any action that it chooses. Thus, any literal of the form $Try(a,e,t)$ is trivially proven by assumption. The second is the **persistence assumption**: a literal $P(i_1,...,i_n,t)$ can be proven by persistence if there is a literal in the database of form $P(i_1,...,i_n,t')$ where it is possible that t=t'. This definition will be considered in detail after the algorithm is presented and compared with the persistence technique of Dean and McDermott [1987]. Note that we have a constant time method of heuristically checking whether t=t' is possible given the network representation of temporal information: the system simply checks if "=" is one of the disjuncts still present on the arc connecting the node for t and the node for t'.

We can consider an example once we add one additional planning rule about stacking, namely, that if two blocks are clear, then attempting to stack them on top of one another will succeed. This is labeled *(Stack.3)* to correspond with the later fully elaborated example.

(Stack.3)
> [Stack ?a ?b ?e ?t] <<<
> > [Clear ?a pre1(?e)] [Clear ?b pre2(?e)] [Try [stack ?a ?b] ?e ?t].

Here is an informal trace of this simple system solving the simple goal of stacking A on B given the initial situation where A and B are clear, as described above. Following the example, we will specify the algorithm in further detail and discuss additional complications.

Given the goal [On A B Oab], the system uses rule (Stack.1) to create the subgoal [Stack A B E1 T1], where E1 and T1 are created when the rule is instantiated and the following constraints are added to the knowledge base from stacking axiom 0:

[Overlaps pre1(E1) T1], [Meets pre1(E1) con1(E1)],
    [Finishes con1(E1) T1], [Meets T1 eff1(E1)],
    [SameEnd pre2(E1) T1], [Meets T1 eff2(E1)],
    [Meets pre1(E1) eff3(E1)].

In addition, the assertion [EQ eff2(E1) Oab] is also added (the constraint for rule (Stack.1)). The system now has the goal [Stack A B E1 T1]. Using rule (Stack.3), it obtains the subgoals:

[Clear A pre1(E1)], [Clear B pre2(E1)], and [Try[stack A B] E1 T1].

The first subgoal is proven using a persistence assumption from the fact [Clear A Ca] in the initial situation description. Persistence is allowed since it is consistent with the current knowledge that Ca=pre1(E1). The assertion [Clear A pre1(E1)] is added to the database, triggering any forward chaining domain rules that apply to such assertions. The second subgoal is proven similarly since it is consistent that Cb=pre2(E1), and the assertion [Clear B pre2(E1)] is added to the knowledge base. Finally, the subgoal [Try[stack A B] E1 T1] is assumed since the agent can attempt any action. The assertion [Try[stack A B] E1 T1] is added to the knowledge base, and triggers forward chaining from rule (Stack.3) since all three antecedent conditions are now asserted. Thus, the assertion [Stack A B E1 T1] is added, triggering forward chaining using the rules (Stack.1) and (Stack.2), which add the assertions [On A B eff1(e1)] and [Holding A con1(E1)], respectively.

Remember that we already added the constraint that eff1(e1) = Oab, so the original goal is predicted to hold under these assumptions. However, this prediction is only valid if the two persistence assumptions that were made, namely, Ca=pre1(E1) and Cb=pre2(E1), are actually true. Once the assumptions pass the consistency tests, the algorithm accepts the plan. In this case, we have built a plan that corresponds to the proof that the formula

$$Try(stack(A,B),E1,T1) \wedge Ca = pre1(E1) \wedge Cb = pre2(E2) \supset On(A,B,Oab)$$

follows from the initial database W. Of course, if the heuristic consistency checks are invalid and the assumptions are inconsistent, then the formula proven is vacuously true since its antecedent is false.

While consistency cannot be proven absolutely, the algorithm uses the heuristic of rechecking the consistency of each persistence assumption now that all the constraints for the plan have been introduced. If the assumptions are still consistent, they are added to the knowledge base.

If the assumptions are not consistent, a modified plan must be found. In the easiest case, it may be that there is a different persistence assumption that can be made that preserves the existing plan. In other cases, the planner must be re-invoked to establish the precondition (or preconditions) that cannot now be assumed true by persistence.

1.5.1   A Nonlinear Planning Algorithm

The following algorithm defines a planner that does not commit to the persistence assumptions until the entire plan is otherwise complete. It uses the simple backward chaining technique from the goals as described informally above, and it uses forward chaining to compute the consequences of its assumptions about persistence of properties and action attempts.

It consists of two main parts: the **plan generator**, which creates a particular plan, and the **assumption verifier**, which takes a suggested plan and evaluates whether the persistence assumptions that support it still appear to be consistent. Let **GS** be the goal stack, which is initialized to the initial set of goals when the algorithm is invoked. The output of this algorithm is a set of actions to be attempted by the agent (the **action list**), a set of assumptions about the world (the **assumption list**), and the world state generated by the prediction reasoner. Each persistence assumption is a pair consisting of a literal P true over some time period T and an equality relation involving T that captures the persistence assumption.

Plan Generation

This is a nondeterministic version of the planning algorithm. A PROLOG-style search strategy to iterate through all possible proof paths can be added in the obvious way.

Do until **GS** is empty:

(0)   Remove the top element of **GS** and call it **G**;

(1)   Choose:

      (1.1)   If a formula unifying with **G** is found in the database, then bind any variables in **G** as necessary (i.e., **G** follows from the database);

      (1.2)   If **G** can be proven by a persistence assumption, then pass **G** to the prediction reasoner, and add **G** together with the equality assertion that justifies the assumption to the assumption list;

      (1.3)   If **G** is of the form $Try(A,e,t)$ for some action A, then add **G** to the action list, and pass **G** to the prediction reasoner;

      (1.4)   Find a planning rule **R** whose consequent unifies with **G**, instantiate the rule as defined above (i.e., binding the event and temporal variables and adding the constraints), and push the antecedents onto **GS**.

Verifying Assumptions

This algorithm uses the temporal reasoner to check that all the persistence assumptions appear to be globally consistent. It does this by first rechecking the temporal constraints for each assumption individually to see if it is still possible. It then adds all the assumptions together to see if they appear to be globally consistent (according to the temporal reasoning algorithm). If some assumptions are no longer consistent, the planning stage is reactivated.

(2) Check each persistence assumption individually to see if each is still possible given the current temporal network generated by the prediction reasoner. If not, add the literal associated with each assumption that is now impossible to **GS** and restart at step (0).

(3) If step (2) succeeded, add the persistence assumptions to the prediction reasoner.

(4) If step (2) failed, then an inconsistency has been found. We need to retract one of the assumptions and replan. We have not yet explored stategies to do this in any reasonable way. At the moment, we simply select an assumption at random. Remember that assumptions consist of a literal P and an equality assertion t=t'. Given the selected assumption, add t≠t' to the prediction reasoner, add P to **GS,** and restart at step (0).

Although this algorithm is based on a simple backward chaining scheme, it does not have the usual limitations of traditional backward chaining planners. In particular, the order of chaining does not correspond to the order of the planned actions. In fact, this planner can solve problems that require regression techniques as described by Waldinger [1977], as will be shown in the following example of the system running on the Sussman anomaly.

The complete set of planning axioms for stacking follows. For efficiency reasons, it is important to classify effects as *useful* or not. A **useful effect** is a proposition that starts during or is met by the time the event occurs, and which is not also true before the event (i.e., as a precondition). Thus, for the event *Stack(A,B,E1,T1)*, the propositions *On(A,B,eff2(E1))* and *Holding(A,con1(E1))* are useful effects, whereas *Clear(A,eff1(E1))* is not useful, since *Clear(A, pre1(E1))* indicates that A must be clear as a precondition as well. All useful effects are captured by planning rules such as the following two:

(Stack.1)
    [On ?a ?b ?t'] <<< [Stack ?a ?b ?e ?t]   such that   [EQ ?t' eff2(?e)].

(Stack.2)
    [Holding ?a ?t'] <<< [Stack ?a ?b ?e ?t]   such that   [EQ ?t' con1(?e)].

The axiom about attempting the action also becomes a planning rule:

(Stack.3)
    [Stack ?a ?b ?e ?t] <<<
        [Clear ?a pre1(?e)] [Clear ?b pre2(?e)] [Try [stack ?a ?b] ?e ?t].

Conditional effects also generate planning rules. For stacking, we have the following:

(Stack.4)

 [Clear ?c ?t"] <<<
  [On ?a ?c ?t'][Stack ?a ?b ?e ?t]
  such that [EQ ?t" eff3(?e)] [Overlaps ?t' ?t].

Finally, we have axioms for the nonuseful effects. These are encoded as forward chaining rules only, since we do not want the planner to attempt to achieve an effect by considering an action that has that very same effect as a precondition. The rule for stacking is as follows:

(Stack.5)

 [Clear ?a eff1(?e)] <forward< [Stack ?a ?b ?e ?t].

In addition, we have forward chaining rules based on all the domain constraints defined in section 1.4.1 and the definition of the temporal structure of stacking events (i.e., stacking axiom 0). This could be declared to the planning system as a set of forward chaining rules with [Stack ?a ?b ?e ?t] as the antecedent. But we will abbreviate that here with the following special form of forward chaining rule that allows multiple consequences:

(Stack.0)

 [Overlaps pre1(?e) ?t] [Finishes con1(?e) ?t] [Meets pre1(?e) con1(?e)]
  [Meets ?t eff1(?e)] [SameEnd ?t pre2(?e)] [Meets ?t eff2(?e)] <forward<
  [Stack ?a ?b ?e ?t].

Consider the planning process given the Sussman anomaly problem shown in figure 18. The initial knowledge base consists of the assertions:

[On C A Oca]	[In I Oca]
[Clear C Cc]	[In I Cc]
[Clear B Cb]	[In I Cb]
[Clear Table Ct]	[In I Ct]
[Before I G].	

The input to the planner consists of the goals: [On A B ?o1], [On B C ?o2] such that [In G ?o1] and [In G ?o2]. Following the same strategy as for rule instantiation described above, the system instantiates the temporal variables ?o1 and ?o2 to Oab and Obc, respectively, and the constraints [In G Oab] and [In G Obc] are added to the temporal database. The initial goals to the backward chaining algorithm are then as follows, where **GS** indicates the goal stack:

 GS: [On A B Oab] [On B C Obc].

Starting on the first goal, rule (Stack.1) matches, with ?a bound to A, ?b bound to B, and ?t' bound to Oab. The system instantiates the variables ?e and ?t on the left-hand side of the rule to E1 and T1, and adds to the knowledge base the constraint [EQ Oab eff2(E1)] together with all the constraints for E1 based on

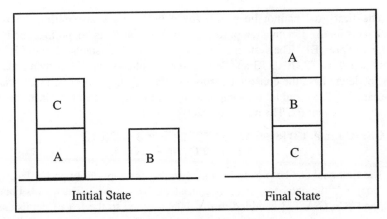

Figure 18: The Sussman anomaly

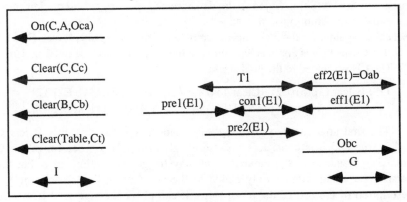

Figure 19: The temporal structure when E1 is defined

the temporal constraints defined by axiom (stack.0). The database is shown in figure 19. Note that while the temporal intervals are defined, no properties are yet true of most intervals except for those in the initial situation. This is because no assertions have been made except for the temporal structure.

The antecedent of (Stack.1) is added to the goal stack, which now is

GS: [Stack A B E1 T1] [On B C Obc].

Rule (Stack.3) matches the first goal, with ?a bound to A, ?b to B, ?e to E1 and ?t to T1. The antecedents of (Stack.3) are added to the goal stack, which now is

GS: [Clear A pre1(E1)] [Clear B pre2(E1)] [Try [stack A B] E1 T1]
       [On B C Obc].

The first goal cannot be proven by a persistence assumption, so rule (Stack.4) is invoked in an attempt to prove it. Variable ?c is bound to A, and ?t" is bound to pre1(E1). The system creates new temporal constants T2 and T3, and instantiates ?t to T2, ?t' to T3 and ?e to a new event constant E2. It then adds to the knowledge base the constraints from the rule—[EQ pre1(E1) eff3(E2)] and [Overlaps T3 T2]—and all the temporal constraints defined in (Stack.0) for the new stacking event E2. The new goal stack becomes

GS: [On ?a A T3] [Stack ?a ?b E2 T2] [Clear B pre2(E1)]
[Try [stack A B] E1 T1] [On B C Obc].

The first goal can be proven by a persistence assumption. In particular, [On C A Oca] is in the database, and it is consistent that Oca=T3. Thus, ?a is bound to C, and [On C A T3] is added to the database and to the list of persistence assumptions together with the justifying equality Oca=T3. Note that while the formula [On C A T3] is added to the database and may trigger prediction rules, the equality assumption is *not* added to the database at this time—it will be rechecked again once the plan appears complete. The next goal is [Stack C ?b E2 T2]. Rule (Stack.3) is applicable, with variable ?a bound to C, ?e to E2 and ?t to T2. The LHS is added to the goal stack:

GS: [Clear C pre1(E2)] [Clear ?b pre2(E2)] [Try [stack C ?b E2] T2]
[Clear B pre2(E1)] [Try [stack A B] E1 T1] [On B C Obc].

The first goal can be proven by a persistence assumption, since [Clear C Cc] is true and it is consistent that Cc equals pre1(E2). As before, [Clear C pre1(E2)] is added to the database and may trigger prediction rules, but the persistence assumption is only added to the assumption list. Shortening the description of the rest of the proof steps, it can prove the next goal [Clear ?b pre2(E2)] by a persistence assumption from [Clear Table Ct], and it can assume [Try [stack C Table] E2 T2] since it is an action attempt by the agent. When [Try [stack C Table] E2 T2] is added to the database, it triggers the prediction rules derived from rule (Stack.3), causing [Stack C Table E2 T2] to be added, which in turn triggers prediction rules derived from the rules (Stack.1), (Stack.2), and (Stack.5), causing the assertions [On C Table eff2(E2)], [Holding C con1(E2)], and [Clear C eff1(E2)] to be added. The goal stack now is

GS: [Clear B pre2(E1)] [Try [stack A B] E1 T1] [On B C Obc].

It can prove [Clear B pre2(E1)] from a persistence assumption from [Clear B Cb], and it can prove [Try [stack A B] E1 T1] since it is another action attempt. This initiates further forward chaining that results in [Stack A B E1 T1] and its effects being added to the database. The state of the temporal database at this stage is exactly as shown in figure 20 without the persistence assumptions shown in grey. Remember that the persistence assumptions are not in the database yet, they will be added in the second phase of the algorithm. The goal stack now contains one goal:

GS: [On B C Obc].

Rule (Stack.1) matches with variable ?a bound to B, ?b bound to C, and ?t' bound to Obc. The system instantiates variable ?t to a new constant T4 and ?e to a new event constant E3, and adds the assumption [EQ Obc eff2(E3)] and the temporal constraints for the new stacking event E3. The new goal stack is simply

GS: [Stack B C E3 T4].

Rule (Stack.3) matches the first goal, with ?a bound to B, ?b to C, ?e to E3 and ?t to T4. The left-hand side of (Stack 3) is added to the goal stack, which now is

GS: [Clear B pre1(E3)] [Clear C pre2(E3)] [Try [stack B C] E3 T4].

[Clear B pre1(E3)] can be proven by a persistence assumption from [Clear B Cb], [Clear C pre2(E3)] from a persistence assumption from [Clear C Cc], and [Try [stack B C] E3 T4] is proven since it is under the agent's control. Adding the final assertion triggers the prediction rules which add the assertion [Stack B C E3 T4] and all its effects. Since block B must be clear throughout *stack(A,B)* and have A on it after *stack(A,B)* until the goal time G, and B must be held during *stack(B,C)*, the domain constraints relating the *Holding, On,* and *Clear* predicates force *stack(B,C)* to precede *stack(A,B)*. The ordering between *stack(B,C)* and *stack(C,Table)*, however, has not yet been determined. This will be found when the persistence assumptions are found in the next phase of the algorithm.

A summary of the plan produced so far includes the actions the agent will attempt plus the propositions that were "proven" by persistence:

Actions: [Try [stack A B] E1 T1]
          [Try [stack C Table] E2 T3]
          [Try [stack B] C E3 T4].

Assumptions:
          [On C A T3], T3=Oca
          [Clear C pre1(E2)], pre1(E2)=Cc
          [Clear Table pre2(E2)], pre2(E2)=Ct
          [Clear B pre2(E1)], pre2(E1)=Cb
          [Clear B pre1(E3)], pre1(E3)=Cb
          [Clear C pre2(E3)] pre2(E3)=Cc.

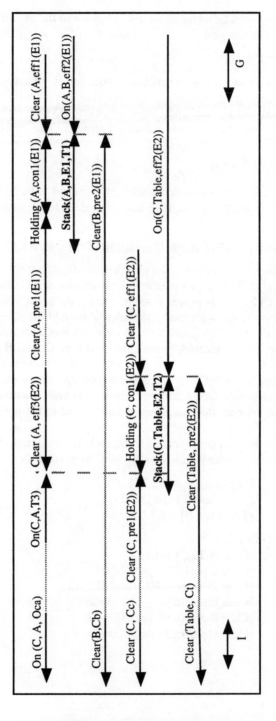

Figure 20: A plan to achieve On(A,B)

The assumption verifier now goes through each of the temporal persistence assumptions and checks if they are still possible. In this example, it finds that it is no longer consistent that pre2(E1) can equal Cb. This assumption was that block B would remain clear until stack(A,B) was performed. This assumption is not consistent with the fact that stack(B,C) will be performed before stack(A,B). The planner is reinvoked with the goal [Clear B pre2(E1)], and it finds another possible persistence assumption, namely, pre2(E1)=eff1(E3). Furthermore, the persistence assumptions that C is clear from the intial time I until stack(B,C) (i.e., pre2(E3)=Cc) and also clear until stack(C,Table) (i.e., pre1(E2)=Cc) are not consistent with the domain constraints. Another persistence assumption for pre2(E3), namely, pre2(E3)=eff1(E2), is consistent with pre1(E2)=Cc, however. Making this assumption forces stack(B,C) to follow stack(C,Table) as desired.

Finally, each of the equality assertions is added to the database in a final consistency check. In this case, everything is fine and the final plan is shown in figure 21. In particular, if you compare figures 20 and 21, you can see that the system has correctly ordered stack(B,C) between stack(C,Table) and stack(A,B).

1.5.2   Assumptions About Temporal Extension

One of the critical techniques used to construct plans was the use of assumptions about the equality of times. In essence, this technique allows a time period to extend as far as possible given its constraints to other periods. Thus, if a proposition P is known to be true over an interval that contains a time t, and nothing is known to prevent P remaining true after t, then an assumption may be made that P is true after t if needed in a plan. Similarly, if nothing prevents P from being true before t, an assumption might be made that P was true some time before t. This capability to extend forward or backward in time might seem strange at first, and we will take some time to justify it. Along the way, we will see two important differences between this approach and that of persistence as defined by Dean and McDermott [1987].

First, consider the technique used by Dean and McDermott. They use a temporal representation where temporal uncertainty is expressed by a range specifying how far apart two time points may be. This allows them to specify the time over which a property might hold by the earliest and latest time that it could start, and the earliest and latest time that it could finish. They allow special values for plus and minus infinity to allow for arbitrarily large ranges. As a concrete example, let us assume there is a reference time *REF*, which stands for 12 noon on a particular day. If block A was put on block B at 3 P.M., then the time over which $On(A,B)$ holds would be constrained to start no earlier than three hours after *REF* and no later than three hours after *REF*, that is, at exactly 3 P.M. Similarly, it must end sometime between three hours and plus infinity after *REF*. We will indicate these constraints using a simplified notation, $((3,3),(3,+inf))$, where each pair specifies the range from *REF* for the

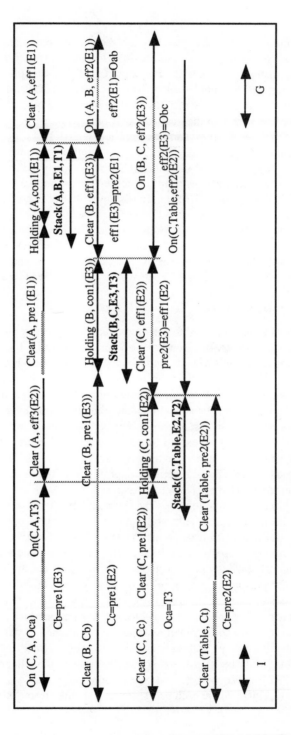

Figure 21: The Solution to the Sussman Anomaly

beginning and ending times, respectively. One can think of this constraint as selecting the set of intervals that begin three hours after *REF* and end three or more hours after *REF*. Any such interval will be said to satisfy the constraint. Given this is all that is known, they then can show that $On(A,B)$ is still true between times 7 and 8 by their persistence rule, which can be paraphrased as follows:

If P holds at time $((t1,t2),(t3,t4))$, then P may be shown by persistence at time $((t5,t6),(t7,t8))$ iff

a) $t2 \leq t5$;

b) $t7 \leq t4$.

In other words, there is an interval that satifies the constraint $((3,3),(3,+inf))$ that completely constrains any interval that satisfies $((7,7),(8,8))$.

Returning to the example, this rule can be used to show that $On(A,B)$ is still true at time $((7,7),(8,8))$, since

a) $On(A,B)$ starts at 3, which is before 7, and

b)   The end of the desired time interval 8 is before the end of when $On(A,B)$ could be true, namely, $+inf$.

On the other hand, if they try to prove $On(A,B)$ between times 2 and 7, the persistence rule fails since condition (a) is not satisfied (i.e., time 3 cannot be less than or equal to time 2).

Consider the same examples in interval logic: let M2, M3, and M7 be moments corresponding to their points 2, 3, and 7, respectively such that M2 < M3 < M7, then we can say that $On(A,B)$ holds over interval t such that M3 starts t. Now the question as to whether $On(A,B)$ still holds at time 7 corresponds to a query whether $On(A,B)$ holds over a time t' such that $In(M7,t')$. The situation is shown in figure 22, where lines without arrowheads indicate that the boundary of the time period is unconstrained. Querying the temporal reasoner, we see that it is possible that t=t' given the above facts, and thus, the persistence assumption can be made. The query whether $On(A,B)$ holds between 2 and 7 corresponds to asking whether $On(A,B)$ holds over t" where M2 starts t" and M7 finishes t". Given these facts, it is not consistent that t=t" (since they start at different times), so the query cannot be proven. Thus, the two representations give the same result.

The differences arise in two cases: first, when there is uncertainty as to the starting time of the property, and second, when a property is proven by extending a time period backward. In the first case, consider a slight modification to the above example: $On(A,B)$ is known to begin between 1 and 3, rather than exactly at 3, that is, at $((1,3),(3,+inf))$. Dean and McDermott's persistence rule cannot show that $On(A,B)$ holds between times 2 and 7, since $On(A,B)$ is not

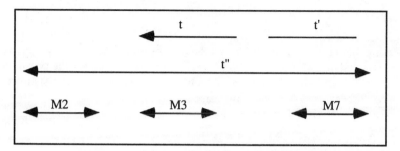

Figure 22: A persistence example (t=t') with intervals

guaranteed to have started by time 2. They require an additional mechanism using abductive premises to handle such cases [Dean 1985]. The interval logic technique allows this assumption directly as *On(A,B)* being true between 2 and 7 is consistent with the new constraints.

For an example of the second case, assume that the planner knows only that the night watchman turns off the lights at time 7 but does not know when they were turned on before that. The constraint on the property *LightOn* is that it ends at 7 and begins sometime before, ((-inf,7),(7,7)). Consider the planner reasoning about whether the light was on at time 3. Dean and McDermott's technique does not allow this by persistence (since time 7 is not before time 3). On the other hand, our technique allows it. In particular, given *T3* and *T7* as before, we know that *P* holds over time *t* such that *T7* finishes *t*. The query is whether *P* holds over *t'* where *T3* is during *t'*. Given these constraints, it is consistent that *t=t'* and so the assumption is allowed.

To summarize, the interval persistence rule is considerably more liberal than the rule used by Dean and McDermott. To handle these latter cases, Dean introduces another mechanism based on abduction. The different cases, however, all seem to reflect the same interactions, so a single uniform method for handling them seems preferable. In addition, the interval persistence rule is considerably simpler to describe and analyze. Situations requiring the more general interval persistence rule frequently appear in everyday situations. For instance, if one is trying to explain how a certain situation came about (e.g., *On(A,B)* at time 7), then we might reason that some action caused *On(A,B)* prior to time 7. If it were the case that if *On(A,B)* were true at time 6 some other facts would be explained, then it would be reasonable to assume *On(A,B)* at 6 on the basis of the evidence that it was known to be true at time 7.

In our model, the database represents an agent's beliefs and observations about the world. The database contains what is known about the world, and the temporal extension technique generates plausible hypotheses about the world given that knowledge. With this model, there may be considerable uncertainty about the present and past as well as the future. For example, if we are told that our airline tickets will be at the bursar's office at 3 P.M. on Tuesday, then that suggests that they might be there earlier—it depends on the unknown information about when they were delivered. Similarly, being there at 3 P.M. suggests that the tickets will be there after 3 P.M. as well, and how long depends on unknown information about when they were picked up. In a single-agent domain, we have a high degree of confidence that the tickets remain at the office until we pick them up, since no other agent exists to pick them up. Note, of course, in a single-agent domain, there would not be another agent to deliver the tickets to the office in the first place, so that the tickets would need to be at the office in the initial situation! Thus, with a single agent and a completely defined initial world, there is a strong bias to persistence only into the future (like Dean and McDermott's [1987] technique). With multi-agent worlds and partially defined situations, extension into the past becomes an equally important technique.

This is especially true as we move away from the traditional planning problem where the system reasons from an initial situation to a goal state, to the problem of an active reasoning agent that observes the present and must infer properties of the past in order to predict the future. For example, consider a situation in which you are looking for a colleague, Jack. You can either search the department for him, or call his home to see if he is there. You know that Jack always buys his coffee from the ACME grill on the other side of town near his house. You look in the seminar room and see an ACME coffee cup on the table with a little warm coffee in it. From this, you conclude that Jack must have been there recently and so you decide to look for him rather than call home. This simple everyday situation involves a current perception and causal reasoning about a past event that allows the planner to formulate the best plan for the future.

Finally, consider some examples where persistence is not allowed. We would not want to allow ridiculous conclusions: say, that if block A is on B now, it must have been there for the last year. But this is the same problem these techniques must face with persistence into the future: because A is on B now should not allow us to infer that it will be that way a year from now either. As another example, if you see a dollar bill lying on the sidewalk, you should neither be able to conclude that it will stay there long if you leave it, nor that it has been there long. As in Dean and McDermott, we depend on general world knowledge to constrain what extensions are allowable. One of the major sources of constraints would be based on information about the expected duration of events and the expected duration that properties may hold (without some active assistance). While we have done some work on duration reasoning, it will not be reported here. Rather, consider a few simple scenarios not involving durations to show that world knowledge can be effective in constraining persistence as well.

Consider a simple example in which the agent puts block A on B at time $T1$, which constitutes the event $E1$. This action has the effect $On(A,B,eff2(E1))$

over time *eff2(E1)* according to stacking axiom 1. This situation was shown graphically in figure 12 on page 23. Can we now prove that $On(A,B)$ was true before the action by extending the proposition backward, that is, that it holds over an interval t' such that $t' < T1$? Clearly, the answer is no, for it is not consistent that A be on B during the prior interval in which B is clear (i.e., t' cannot equal *eff2((E1))*.

Consider another case where block B is clear during time t. Can A be on B during any interval that overlaps t in any way? Again, the answer clearly is no. Domain constraint 1 forces any interval over which $On(A,B)$ holds to be disjoint from t. Thus, the property could not hold over any interval that overlaps t.

As a final note, it must be mentioned that reasoning based on persistence has its faults, and some difficult problems remain to be addressed. In particular, by basing the persistence rule on consistency, we produce a very optimistic planner. The planner will assume that the world will be as desired only on the basis that it is consistent that it is that way. Thus, if an office door is unlocked, and the planner does not know for certain whether the security guard has come by yet, then the planner may assume that the door remains unlocked (and infer that the security guard has not come by yet!). Thus, the planner will not perform well in worlds where there is considerable uncertainty. This issue is discussed at length in chapter 3.

1.5.3   Discussion of the Algorithm

It would be nice to be able to present some correctness and completeness criteria for the algorithm, say that it always finds a plan when one exists, or at least that every plan it finds is provably correct. This is difficult for several reasons. Discussing some of the problems that arise will reveal certain important properties of the approach.

Formally, we have defined the planner as a heuristic search given a set of goals G and an initial database D, which produces a set of assumptions A such that A and D together entail G. Thus the correlate of the *modal truth criterion* for nonlinear planners [Chapman 1987] is simple logical entailment—a property is true at time t if it logically follows from the database together with the assumptions. This analogy might seem strange at first because our approach treats persistence assumptions as part of the plan itself whereas the modal truth criterion builds persistence assumptions into its definition—a property p is true in a state if it is true in a previous state and nothing could have negated it since. Persistence can be built into the modal truth criterion in this way only because of the limited world representation used in which the STRIPS assumption holds. Of course, we must face the issue of whether the assumptions that the planner introduces are reasonable. This is the major factor that will determine whether the plan would actually accomplish its goals if executed.

The wrench in the works is that the temporal reasoner might allow an inconsistency to go undetected. We know from algorithmic complexity arguments that the temporal reasoner is not complete. In particular, certain temporal constraints may actually be inconsistent overall, yet not be detected as inconsistent by the reasoner. There are two ways we might try to eliminate this problem. We could limit the form of temporal expressions that are allowable (as in Vilain, Kautz, and van Beek [1990]) so that a complete temporal reasoner can be effectively built, but then we cannot express the assertions of disjointness needed for the planning algorithm. Alternately, we could generalize the constraint propagation algorithm so that it is complete, and accept a Np-hard execution time. Finally, we may prefer to stay with the incomplete temporal reasoner as it stands. It is expressive enough to handle most everyday situations, where the more limited reasoner is not, and all the known situations that generate undetectable inconsistencies are so complex that they require specialized problem-solving skills on the part of humans and so are probably not part of everyday common-sense reasoning. It is worth noting that because of our proof strategy, arbitrary propositions cannot be proven simply from the presence of an undetected temporal inconsistency, so the presence of an inconsistent set of assertions does not cripple the reasoning system.

The second point was that a plan is only as good as the assumptions that define it. If the assumptions are unrealistic, then the plan, in actual fact, will not be realistic. I have presented only the bare bones of a planning algorithm here, but the framework is laid for incorporating more sophisticated techniques. For instance, currently the planner assumes that it can try any action at any time (i.e., a proposition of form $Try(A,e,t)$ can always be assumed to be true). A more general planner would need to reason about the use of its limited resources (e.g., it only has two hands) and the limits on it performing actions simultaneously (e.g., some tasks may be too complex to perform simultaneously even though the resources are available). Pelavin [1988] presents formalisms that can express such constraints in a general way. This is described in chapter 3.

The other source of assumptions are the persistence assumptions about the world. Again, the current planner uses a very simple strategy—if it is consistent that the world behaves as required for the plan, then assume it will. Again, more complex strategies could be devised. One might introduce probability distributions for each property that can be used to predict how likely the assumption made is valid (e.g., see Dean and Kanazawa [1988b]), or one might use the statistical techniques in Weber [1989b].

1.6   The Door-Latch Problem

One of the major goals of this work was allowing plans that necessarily required simultaneous actions. The door-latch problem was posed as the simplest example of this type of situation. In this section, we show how the domain can be formalized and a plan constructed from first principles that will open the door.

First, we present the planning axioms that define the actions, and then give an overview of the solution.

Remember that the complication in this domain is that the agent must realize that it must continue to hold the latch open while it is pulling on the door. The actions involving the latch are turning the latch and holding the latch open. Unless it is held open, the latch snaps shut. Given that the planner uses persistence assumptions about the world, some technique must be introduced to prevent the planner from using this technique to infer that the latch stays open. This would best be handled by adding a more sophisticated causal reasoning to the predictor, but a simpler technique can be used in this class of situations. We will define the turn-latch action such that its effect holds exactly for a moment. Thus, any action that requires the latch to be open for an extended period of time cannot accomplish this by persistence, since by definition a moment cannot be equal to an interval. Remember that a moment is a nondecomposable period, whereas an interval is a decomposable period. The hold-latch action is then defined so that it requires the latch to be open at the time the action starts (which may be a moment) and has the effect that the latch stays open for the duration of the action. Specifically, we have the planning rules below which are used by the predictor to maintain the world representation. To simplify the axioms, we assume that the actions are specific to a single door and latch. They could easily be generalized by adding additional parameters.

The temporal structures for each event are axiomatized below and shown graphically in figure 23. *TurnLatch* events define a precondition interval (for the latch being closed) and an effect moment (for the latch being open):

(TurnLatch.0)

[Finishes ?t pre1(?e)] [Moment eff1(?e)] [Meets ?t eff1(?e)]
<forward< [TurnLatch ?e ?t].

HoldingLatch events define a single precondition period (for the latch being open) and an effect interval simultaneous with the event interval:

(HoldOpen.0)

[Meets pre1(?e) ?t] [EQ eff1(?e) ?t] <forward< [HoldOpen ?e ?t].

PullOpen events define two precondition intervals (for the latch being open, and the door being shut), and one effect interval (for the door being open):

(PullOpen.0)

[OverlapsDuring pre1(?e) ?t] [Meets ?t pre2(?e)] [Starts eff1(?e) ?t]
<forward< [PullOpen ?e ?t].

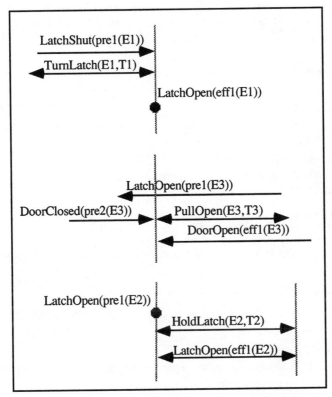

Figure 23: The temporal structures for three events in the
door-latch problem

The planning rules for these actions are as follows. Turning the latch has
the effect that the latch is momentarily open:

(TurnLatch.1)

[LatchOpen ?t'] <<< [TurnLatch ?e ?t]
        such that [Moment ?t'] [EQ ?t' eff1(?e)].

Turning the latch can be accomplished by trying to do it when the latch is shut:

(TurnLatch.2)

[TurnLatch ?e ?t] <<< [LatchShut pre1(?e)] [Try [turnlatch] ?e ?t].

The latch remains open if and only if it is held open. In particular, note that the
effect and the action in this rule must be simultaneous:

(HoldOpen.1)

[LatchOpen ?t'] <<< [Interval ?t'] [HoldOpen ?e ?t]
        such that [EQ eff1(?e) ?t'].

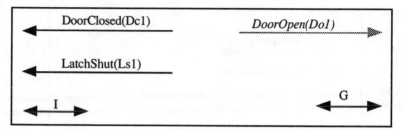

Figure 24: The initial situation in the door-latch problem

Holding the latch open succeeds whenever the latch is open at the start of the holding act:

(HoldOpen.2)

[HoldOpen ?e ?t] <<< [LatchOpen pre1(?e)] [Try [holdopen] ?e ?t].

Opening the door is an effect of pulling on the door when the latch is open:

(PullOpen.1)

[DoorOpen ?t'] <<< [PullOpen ?e ?t] such that [EQ eff1(?e) ?t'].

You may open the door any time you try to, if it is closed and the latch is unlocked:

(PullOpen.2)

[PullOpen ?e ?t] <<< [DoorClosed pre2(?e)] [LatchOpen pre1(?e)]
            [Try [pull] ?e ?t].

Assuming a situation in which the agent is near the door, the initial world description would be as follows, where I is the current time, and G is the time when the goal must hold:

[LatchShut Ls1]   [In I Ls1]
[DoorClosed Dc1]   [In I Dc1]
[Before I G].

The goal is simply to have the door open over time G, that is, [DoorOpen Do1] such that [In G Do1]. The initial planning situation is shown in figure 24.

Here is a brief sketch of the planner in operation. Given the goal [DoorOpen Do1], rule (PullOpen.1) applies and introduces the subgoals after instantiation:

GS: [PullOpen E1 T1],

where [EQ eff1(E1) Do1] and the temporal constraints for the new PullOpen event E1, i.e., [OverlapsDuring pre1(E1) T1], [Meets T1 pre2(E1)], and [Starts eff1(E1) T1] are added to the database. The subgoal [PullOpen E1 T1] can be proven by rule (PullOpen.2), producing the new set of subgoals:

GS: [DoorClosed pre2(E1)] [LatchOpen pre1(E1)] [Try [pull] E1 T1].

The first subgoal is proven by persistence from the initial state, using the assumption that pre2(E1)=Dc1. The second subgoal [LatchOpen pre1(E1)] requires further planning. Rule (TurnLatch.1) cannot apply here as it requires the interval pre1(E1) to be a moment. However, rule (HoldOpen.1) does apply and introduces the subgoal [HoldOpen E2 T2] and adds the constraints pre1(E1)=eff1(E2). When this rule was instantiated, the temporal constraints from (HoldOpen.0) asserted that T2=eff1(E2), thus T2=pre1(E1) as well by the transitivity of equality. The subgoals are now

GS: [HoldOpen E2 T2] [Try [pull] E1 T1].

Rule (HoldOpen.2) then applies to this subgoal and introduces the following subgoals after instantiation:

GS: [LatchOpen pre1(E2)] [Try [holdopen] E2 T2]
    [Try [pull] E1 T1].

This time, rule (TurnLatch.1) can apply (since it is consistent that pre1(E2) is a moment) and the action [TurnLatch E3 T3] is introduced. After using rule (TurnLatch.2) to reduce this goal, the following subgoals remain:

GS: [LatchShut pre1(E3)] [Try [turnlatch] E3 T3]
    [Try [holdopen] E2 pre1(E1)] [Try [pullOpen] E1 T1].

The first of these subgoals can be proven by persistence, since it is possible that pre1(E3)=Ls1, and the remaining three subgoals are trivially proven as they are under the control of the planner. As each of these is assumed, it is added to the database triggering the forward chaining prediction rules. As a result, the door is predicted to be open at time Do1.

Finally, the persistence assumptions must be verified and then added to the predictor producing the final plan as shown in figure 25. Note that the *pullOpen* action must start within the time when the *holdOpen* action occurs, as desired. If this were not the case, the final effect, namely, that the door is open, would not be predicted by the prediction mechanism. Thus, we have shown that the planner can find the correct plan, and that it would not accept the faulty plan arising from a STRIPS-style planner or from a naive persistence mechanism.

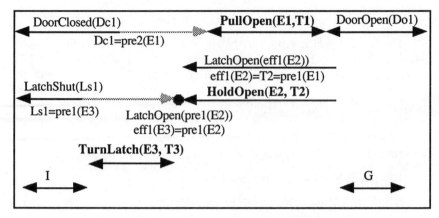

Figure 25: The solution to the door-latch problem

Another simple example of some interest shows that the planner can coordinate with external events that it knows will occur sometime in the future. For example, consider a different initial situation, which is the same as before except that the planner knows that the door is unlocked automatically between 8 A.M. and 9 A.M. every day, and the goal is to get the door open sometime between 7 A.M. and 9 A.M. This situation is shown in figure 26, where the times of day are represented by moments.

The initial database consists of the following assertions:

[In I Ls1]
[LatchShut Ls1]   [Meets Ls1 lo1]
[LatchOpen lo1]   [Meets Ls1 8AM]
[In I Dc1]   [DoorClosed Dc1]
[Before I 7AM]   [Before 7AM 8AM]
[Before 8AM 9AM]   [Before 7AM G]   [Before G 9AM]
[Moment 7AM]   [Moment 8AM]   [Moment 9AM].

The initial goal is as before—to accomplish [DoorOpen Do1] such that [In G Do1]. Using rule (PullOpen.1), we get the subgoal of [PullOpen E1 T1] where eff1(E1)=Do1. Rule (PullOpen.2) gives two preconditions for this action, namely,

[DoorClosed pre2(E1)] [LatchOpen pre1(E1)].

In this case, both can be proven by persistence. [DoorClosed pre2(E1)] would be true if pre2(E1)=Dc1, and [LatchOpen pre1(E1)] would be true if pre2(E1)=Lo1. Adding these assumptions creates a plan that involves pulling the door after 8 A.M. (since the latch must be open) and before 9 A.M. (to satisfy the goal conditions on G). Thus, we have constructed a plan that takes advantage of the automatic latch, a known event in the future, by scheduling its own actions

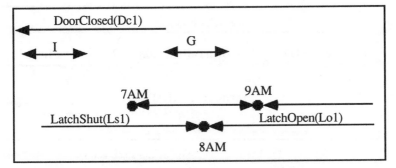

Figure 26: The door-latch problem with an automatic latch system

to take advantage of the latch being open. If, on the other hand, the goal had been to open the door before 8 A.M., that is, G is constrained to be before 8 A.M., then this plan will not be suggested since the persistence assumption pre1(E1)=Lo1 is not consistent with the database.

1.7 Hierarchical Planning

Hierarchical planning is a term used in many different ways in the planning literature. Here, we will examine those techniques used in planners that primarily employ decomposition or refinement to produce a plan. Such systems view planning as selecting and instantiating existing abstract plans in the database, rather than synthesizing new plans. However, new plans are created when multiple goals must be achieved simultaneously and plans for each individual goal must be combined. NOAH [Sacerdoti 1977] introduced this technique, and it has been used in many systems since (e.g., NONLIN, DEVISER, FORBIN). There are two issues to consider here: the *representation*, what information is being represented in a hierarchical planner, and *search strategy*, how plans are constructed. We will consider each in turn.

Hierarchical planners encode information about how an action is accomplished. For example, the action of constructing a house in Tate's NONLIN system is defined as a set of partially ordered actions: fastening the plaster to the walls and pouring the basement floor must precede laying the flooring, which precedes finishing the carpentry. Finishing the carpentry and painting must then precede sanding the floors. In addition, NONLIN maintained the necessary persistence facts for the successful plan, which were called the *supervised conditions*. For example, the effect of laying the flooring must still hold when the carpentry is being finished, and so on. In principle, there could be arbitrary constraints on the world state and action ordering for the action to be successfully performed.

We can extend our representation to include information like this by defining additional details on how actions are accomplished. We could do this by introducing axioms that allow us to prove formulas of the form *[Try a e t]* rather

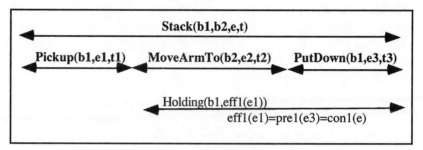

Figure 27: The decomposition of the stack action

than assuming them. But it turns out that the algorithm is easier to specify if we introduce a new predicate *Decomp* on actions. The relation between *Decomp* and *Try* is that you try an action by performing one of its decompositions, for instance:

$\forall\ e,t,a\ .\ Decomp(a,e,t) \supset Try(a,e,t).$

For example, a *stack* action could be accomplished by moving the arm to the block desired, opening the hand, lowering the hand over the block, grasping the block, raising the arm and moving it to the desired destination, and then lowering the arm and opening the hand again. Figure 27 shows the decomposition of the *stack* action together with the necessary persistence assumptions required to make the decomposition effective. In particular, the effect of picking up b1, namely, *Holding(b1,eff1(e1))*, must extend to satisfy the precondition on the *putDown* action. In addition, this effect is identical to the constraint originally defined for the *stack* action.

We capture this information by adding a planning rule that specifies this as one way to decompose the action:

(**Stack.6**)

    [Decomp [stack ?x ?y] ?e ?t] <<< [PickUp ?x ?e1 ?t1]
        [MoveArmTo ?y ?e2 ?t2] [PutDown ?x ?e3 ?t3]
        such that [Meets ?t1 ?t2] [Meets ?t2 ?t3] [Starts ?t1 ?t]
        [Finishes ?t3 ?t] [EQ eff1(?e1) pre1(?e3)]
        [EQ eff1(?e1) con1(?e)].

In words, one way of performing a stack action is to perform the three actions indicated in an order that satisfies the temporal constraints. This includes the fact that the effect of *pickUp*, namely, *Holding(?x,eff1(?e1))*, extends to satisfy the precondition on *putDown*, and is equal to the constraint originally defined in the definition of *Stack*.

To allow for multilevel decompositions, let us define the *pickUp* and *PutDown* actions as well. These actions have preconditions and effects as expected and are decomposable into yet finer-grained actions of grasping and releasing blocks and moving the arm. These decompositions are shown in figure

28. The *pickUp* action consists of moving the arm to the block, lowering the arm, grasping the block, and raising the arm. The effect of moving the arm, *ArmAt(bl)*, extends to satisfy the precondition of grasping, whose second precondition, *ArmPosition(LO)*, is satisfied by the effect of lowering the arm. The effect of grasping, namely, *Holding(bl)*, is identical to the effect of the *pickUp* action itself. The decomposition of the *PutDown* action is similar.

The following planning rules define the *pickUp* action. A *pickUp* action results in the block being held (PickUp.1), but it only succeeds if the arm is empty and is above the block when the action starts (PickUp.2). The decomposition of *pickUp* is defined in (PickUp.3) and reflects the information shown in figure 28.

(PickUp.0)
　　[Overlaps pre1(?e) ?t] [Overlaps pre2(?e) ?t] [Meets ?t eff1(?e)].
　　　　　　　<forward< [PickUp ?x ?e ?t]

(PickUp.1)
　　[Holding ?x ?t'] <<< [PickUp ?x ?e ?t] such that [EQ ?t' eff1(?e)].

(PickUp.2)
　　[PickUp ?x ?e ?t] <<<[HandEmpty pre1(?e)] [Clear ?x pre2(?e)]
　　　　　　　[Try [pickUp ?x] ?e ?t].

(PickUp.3)
　　[Decomp [pickUp ?x] ?e ?t] <<< [MoveArmTo ?x ?e1 ?t1]
　　　　　　　[LowerArm ?e2 ?t2] [Grasp ?x ?e3 ?t3] [RaiseArm ?e4 ?t4]
　　　　　　　such that [Meets ?t1 ?t2] [Meets ?t2 ?t3] [Meets ?t3 ?t4]
　　　　　　　[Starts ?t1 ?t] [Finishes ?t4 ?t] [EQ eff1(?e2) pre3(?e3)]
　　　　　　　[EQ eff1(?e1) pre1(?e3)] [EQ eff1(?e2) pre1(?e4)]
　　　　　　　[EQ eff1(?e3) eff1(?e)].

The *putDown* action causes any block that was held to be on the block at the location (PutDown.1) and the arm to become empty (PutDown.2). This action can be accomplished any time a block is being held (PutDown.3). Its decomposition is defined in (PutDown.4), reflecting the information in figure 28.

(PutDown.1)
　　[On ?x ?y ?t'] <<< [PutDown ?x ?t][ArmAt ?y ?t]
　　　　　　　such that [EQ ?t' eff1(?e)].

(PutDown.2)
　　[HandEmpty ?t'] <<< [PutDown ?x ?t]   such that [EQ ?t' eff2(?e)].

(PutDown.3)
　　[PutDown ?x ?e ?t] <<<
　　　　　　　[Holding ?x pre1(?e)] [Try [putDown ?x] ?e ?t].

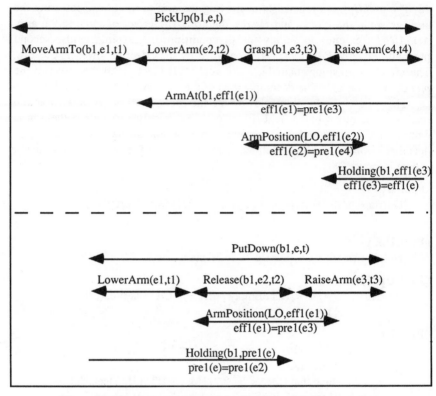

Figure 28: The decomposition of the PickUp and PutDown actions

(PutDown.4)

    [Decomp [putDown ?x] ?e ?t] <<<
        [LowerArm ?e1 ?t1] [Release ?x ?e2 ?t2] [RaiseArm ?e3 ?t3]
        such that [Meets ?t1 ?t2] [Meets ?t2 ?t3] [Starts ?t1 ?t]
        [Finishes ?t3 ?t] [EQ eff1(?e1) pre1(?e3)]
        [EQ pre1(?e2) pre1(?e)].

The planning rules for *moveArmTo*, *lowerArm*, *raiseArm*, *grasp*, and *release* are defined similarly and are shown in figure 29. An action a that does not have a decomposition defined for it is a primitive action, and [try a ?e ?t] is assumed as in the original algorithm.

Finally, we wish to restrict the domain to allow only one *moveArmTo*, *putDown* and *pickUp* action at a time. This is expressed as domain constraints:

    [Disjoint ?t1 ?t2] <forward< [PickUp ?x ?e1 ?t1][MoveArmTo ?y ?e2 ?t2]
    [Disjoint ?t1 ?t2] <forward< [PutDown ?x ?e1 ?t1][MoveArmTo ?y ?e2 ?t2]
    [Disjoint ?t1 ?t2] <forward< [PutDown ?x ?e1 ?t1][PickUp ?y ?e2 ?t2].

This completes the description of the action decompositions.

(MoveArmTo.1)

[ArmAt ?l ?t'] <<< [MoveArmTo ?l ?e ?t] such that [EQ ?t' eff1(?e)].

(MoveArmTo.2)

[MoveArmTo ?l ?e ?t] <<< [ArmPosition HI pre1(?e)]
                        [Try [moveArmTo ?l] ?e ?t].

(LowerArm.1)

[ArmPosition LO ?t'] <<< [LowerArm ?e ?t] such that [EQ ?t' eff1(?e)].

(LowerArm.2)

[LowerArm ?e ?t] <<< [ArmPosition HI pre1(?e)] [Try [lowerArm] ?e ?t].

(RaiseArm.1)

[ArmPosition HI ?t'] <<< [RaiseArm ?e ?t] such that [EQ ?t' eff1(?e)].

(RaiseArm.2)

[RaiseArm ?e ?t] <<< [ArmPosition LO pre1(?e)] [Try [raiseArm] ?e ?t].

(Grasp.1)

[Holding ?b ?t'] <<< [Grasp ?B ?e ?t] such that [EQ ?t' eff1(?e)].

(Grasp.2)

[Grasp ?b ?e ?t] <<< [ArmAt ?b pre1(?e)] [HandOpen pre2(?e)]
               [ArmPosition LO pre3(?e)][Try [grasp ?b] ?e ?t].

(Release.1)

[HandOpen ?t'] <<< [Release ?b ?e ?t] such that [EQ ?t' eff1(?e)].

(Release.2)

[Release ?b ?e ?t] <<< [ArmPosition LO pre1(?e)] [Holding ?b pre2(?e)]
               [Try [release ?b] ?e ?t].

Figure 29: The definitions of the nondecomposable actions

The second issue is the search strategy used by hierarchical planners. Essentially, such systems use a breadth-first search technique through action decompositions as the main control loop. A simple variant of the planning algorithm developed earlier will operate on these axioms in this way. Given a set of goals, the planning algorithm is run exactly as before, except that rather than simply assuming a formula *[Try a,e,t]* is true, we must prove the corresponding formula *[Decomp a,e,t]*. But this *Decomp* subgoal is placed at the *end* of the goal stack rather than the beginning. This simple change defines a planning algorithm that combines both the depth-first strategy used by precondition-effect chaining planners and the breadth-first strategy used by decomposition planners. Thus, the style of planner one builds will depend solely on the planning rules defined and may be purely decompositional, purely precondition-effect chaining, or any mix of these two techniques.

The only other complication is that the initial algorithm used a second stage to verify that all persistence assumptions made in the plan were still consistent.

We could leave this second stage until the entire plan is decomposed, but it is more in line with traditional hierarchical planners to verify these assumptions at each decomposition level before the next level is constructed. This can be accomplished simply in the new algorithm by adding a "dummy" goal on the bottom of the goal stack that invokes the consistency checking algorithm. When this goal rises to the top of the stack, one complete level of decomposition has been completed. The constraints are checked and the dummy goal is added again at the bottom of the goal stack to signal the end of the next level of decomposition. We will call this dummy goal [VerifyAssumptions]. A precise specification of the algorithm follows.

The Hierarchical Planning Algorithm

This algorithm is a slight variation on the nonlinear algorithm presented earlier. It differs in how action attempts are treated and in the time that assumptions are verified. As before, this is a nondeterministic version of the algorithm, and the goal stack **GS** is initialized to the goal statement and the goal [VerifyAssumptions].

Do until **GS** is empty:

(0)   Remove the top element of **GS** and call it **G**;

(1)   Choose:

    (1.1)   If a formula unifying with **G** is found in the database, then bind any variables in **G** as necessary (i.e., **G** is provable from the database);

    (1.2)   If **G** can be proven by a persistence assumption, then pass **G** to the prediction reasoner, and add **G** together with the equality assertion that justifies the assumption to the assumption list;

    (1.3)   If **G** is of the form [Try a e t] for some action A, add **G** to the action list, and pass **G** to the prediction reasoner. Also, if there are axioms with a consequence of form [Decomp a e t] in the database, add [Decomp a e t] to the end of **GS**;

    (1.4)   If **G** = [VerifyAssumptions], then invoke the assumption verifier. (Note, if verifying the assumptions fails, then **G** is not achieved and the algorithm backtracks.) Unless **GS** is now empty, add a new goal [VerifyAssumptions] to the end of **GS**;

    (1.5)   Otherwise, find a planning rule **R** whose antecedent unifies with **G** and instantiates the rule as defined above, and push the antecedents of **R** onto **GS**.

We can now demonstrate this planning algorithm using all the rules defined so far. For reasons of space, let us consider the hierarchical planning algorithm in detail with the simple problem of building a tower with A on B and B on C in a situation where A, B, and C are clear, as first shown in figure 14 (page 31) with the additional assertions that the hand is initially empty and in the HI position. The initial goal stack is

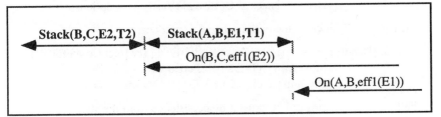

Figure 30: The initial plan before decomposition

GS: [On A B Oab] [On B C Obc] [VerifyAssumptions].

The new algorithm starts exactly as the old algorithm does. Rule (Stack.1) applies and produces the subgoal to execute the action [Stack A B E1 T1], and then rule (Stack.2) applies producing the goal stack:

GS: [Clear A pre1(E1)] [Clear B pre2(E1)] [Try [stack A B] E1 T1]
　　　[On B C Obc] [VerifyAssumptions].

Continuing on, both [Clear A pre1(E1)] and [Clear B pre1(E1)] can be proven by persistence assumptions as in previous examples, leaving the goal stack:

GS: [Try [stack A B] E1 T1] [On B C Obc] [VerifyAssumptions].

This is where the algorithms first differ. The goal [Try [stack A B] E1 T1] is proven by assumption, and a Decomp goal is added to the *end* of GS:

GS: [On B C Obc] [VerifyAssumptions] [Decomp [stack A B] E1 T1].

Rules (Stack.1) and (Stack.2) apply to the top goal, and then persistence assumptions are applied as before. The literal [Try [stack B C] E2 T2] is assumed as before and [Decomp [stack B C] E2 T2] is added to the end of **GS**. We are now at the stage where the first algorithm entered the verify assumptions phase. Exactly the same thing happens here, as [VerifyAssumptions] is now the top goal:

GS: [VerifyAssumptions] [Decomp [stack A B] E1 T1]
　　　[Decomp [stack B C] E2 T2].

In this case, all the assumptions are consistent and thus [VerifyAssumptions] succeeds. A new goal [VerifyAssumptions] is added at the end of **GS** producing the following:

GS: [Decomp [stack A B] E1 T1] [Decomp [stack B C] E2 T2]
　　　[VerifyAssumptions].

The actions planned so far, with their effects, are shown in figure 30. The planner now continues. The goal [Decomp [stack A B] E1 T1] is rewritten using rule (Stack.6) to produce the goal stack:

GS: [PickUp A E3 T3] [MoveArmTo B E4 T4] [PutDown A E5 T5]

[Decomp [stack B C] E2 T2] [VerifyAssumptions].

Rule (PickUp.2) rewrites the initial subgoal to produce:

GS: [HandEmpty pre1(E3)] [Clear A pre2(E3)] [Try [pickUp A] E3 T3]
[MoveArmTo B E4 T4] [PutDown A E5 T5]
[Decomp [stack B C] E2 T2] [VerifyAssumptions].

The first two subgoals can be proven by persistence from the state of the world at time I. The next goal is [Try [pickUp A] E3 T3], which is assumed as usual. Since there is a *Decomp* axiom defined for *pickUp*, it is added at the end of **GS:**

GS: [MoveArmTo B E4 T4] [PutDown A E5 T5]
[Decomp [stack B C] E2 T2] [VerifyAssumptions]
[Decomp [pickUp A] E3 T3].

As you can see, the planner is simply going through each of the subgoals in the decompositions, solving each one as usual and delaying further decomposition until later. It is also interesting to note that many of the conditions for other actions in decomposition are actually provably true given the constraints introduced by the decomposition axiom. For example, the precondition of [MoveArmTo B E4 T4], namely, [ArmPosition HI pre1(E4)], is provably true given the effect of the *pickUp* action and the equality assumption made on the decomposition of the *stack* action. The remainder of the trace should be straightforward to complete. Once we successively achieve the goals from the decomposition of *stack(A,B)* one level, we go and decompose *stack(B,C)*. Once this is done, the new assumptions are verified and the world shown in figure 31 is constructed and is ready for the final level of decomposition using

GS: [Decomp [pickUp A] E3 T3] [Decomp [putDown A] E5 T5]
[Decomp [pickUp B] E6 T6] [Decomp [putDown B] E8 T8]
[Verify Assumptions].

Note that there are no decomposition subgoals for the two actions [MoveArmTo C E7 T7] and [MoveArmTo B E4 T4], since these were defined as primitive (i.e., they have no *Decomp* axiom). In the final round of planning, all the remaining acts are primitive, and thus the algorithm terminates.

This algorithm thus expanded a plan level-by-level through a decomposition hierarchy, validating the consistency of the plan at each level before the next level was addressed. Constraints imposed by the higher levels makes the accomplishment of the actions at the lower levels considerably easier. Thus, we have defined the analog of a system such as NOAH or NONLIN within the temporal logic.

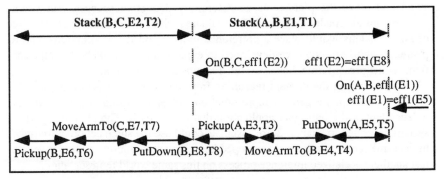

Figure 31: The plan after the first level of decomposition

1.8   Conclusions

We have introduced a temporally explicit representation for common-sense reasoning about causality and action and have shown how traditional planning systems could be recast within this framework fairly directly as a specialized inference process on a temporal logic. By recasting most of the procedural aspects of previous planning algorithms this way, we have produced a framework that is much easier to understand and extend. By separating the temporal aspects of a plan from the procedural aspects of plan construction, for example, we found that even the simplest backwards chaining planning algorithm can generate nonlinear plans. Similarly, a hierarchical planner can be generated by changing the set of assumptions about action attempts that the system is willing to make at any given time. As such, this work provides a uniform framework for examining many of the different planning frameworks developed to date.

While the actual system described duplicated the abilities of traditional planning algorithms, the situations that can be represented and reasoned about are more general than can be represented in a state-based model. In particular, it can reason about plans involving complex interactions between overlapping actions. It can reason about the effects of simultaneous actions that are not the effect of any one of the actions individually. However, the representation is limited in representing partial interference between actions. This limitation exists because the current representation cannot explicitly capture the notion of possibility (as found in branching time models). This topic is examined in depth in chapter 3, where this representation is extended and a new planning algorithm is specified.

The formalism is also limited in that it has the weakest possible criteria for deciding on the acceptability of assumptions: namely, that assumptions (of the allowed forms, of course) are reasonable if they are logically possible. Of course, in practice many things will be logically possible, but highly unlikely, and this representation has no means of accounting for this. It does lay the basis, however, for a formalism that can use probabilistic information to judge the worth of assumptions. For instance, we could leave the planning axioms as they stand and leave the planner as an essentially deductive process. But when assumptions are made, they would be evaluated with respect to their probability of holding. This would place a preference ordering on the assumptions, and a planning algorithm could be developed to explore the most likely assumptions first. At the present time, however, this remains as future work.

By separating the domain reasoning from the plan construction algorithm, we have developed a general representation for reasoning about action that is independent of the particular application that is driving it. The plan recognition system described in chapter 2, for instance, could use the same action definitions in the same representation we developed here. Plan recognition can be viewed as just another specialized inference process on this same world representation.

Chapter 2
A Formal Theory of Plan Recognition and its Implementation

Henry A. Kautz

2.1   Introduction

2.1.1   Background

While there have been many formal studies of plan synthesis in general [McCarthy and Hayes 1969; Moore 1977; Pednault 1988; Tenenberg 1990; Pelavin 1990], nearly all work on the inverse problem of plan recognition has focused on specific kinds of recognition in specific domains. This includes work on story understanding [Bruce 1981; Schank 1975; Wilensky 1983] psychological modeling [Schmidt 1978], natural language pragmatics [Allen 1983b; Carberry 1983; Litman 1987; Grosz and Sidner 1987], and intelligent computer system interfaces [Genesereth 1979; Huff and Lesser 1982; Goodman and Litman 1990]. In each case, the recognizer is given an impoverished and fragmented description of the actions performed by one or more agents and expected to infer a rich and highly interrelated description. The new description fills out details of the setting and predicts the goals and future actions of the agents. Plan recognition can be used to generate summaries, to provide help, and to build up a context for use in disambiguating natural language. Chapter 2 develops a formal theory of plan recognition. The analysis provides a formal foundation for part of what is loosely called "frame-based inference" [Minsky 1975], and accounts for problems of ambiguity, abstraction, and complex temporal interactions that were ignored by previous research.

Plan recognition problems can be classified as cases of either "intended" or "keyhole" recognition (the terminology developed by Cohen, Perrault, and Allen [1981]). In intended recognition, but not keyhole, the recognizer can assume that the agent is deliberately structuring its activities in order to make its intentions clear. Recognition problems can also be classified as to whether the observer has complete knowledge of the domain, and whether the agent may try to perform erroneous plans and plan recognition [Pollack 1986]. This chapter concentrates on keyhole recognition of correct plans where the observer has complete knowledge.

Plan synthesis can be viewed as a kind of hypothetical reasoning, where the planner tries to find some set of actions whose execution would entail some goal. Some previous work on plan recognition views it as a similar kind of hypothetical reasoning, where the recognizer tries to find some plan whose execution would entail the performance of the observed actions [Charniak 1985]. This kind of reasoning is sometimes called "abduction", and the conclusions "explanations". But it is not clear what the recognizer should conclude if many different plans entail the observations. Furthermore, even if the recognizer has complete knowledge and the agent makes no errors, cases naturally occur where no plan actually entails the observations. For example, suppose that the recognizer knows about a plan to get food by buying it at a supermarket. The recognizer is told that the agent walks to the A&P on Franklin Street. The plan to get food does not entail this observation; it entails going to some supermarket, but not specifically the A&P. One can try to fix this problem by giving it a more general plan schema that can be instantiated for any particular supermarket. But the entailment still fails, because the plan still fails to account for the fact that the agent chooses to walk instead of drive. Instead of finding a plan that entails the observations, one can only find a plan that entails some weaker statement entailed by the observations. Therefore, in order to make abduction work, the plan (or explanation) must be able to also include almost any kind of assumption (e.g., that the agent is walking); yet the assumptions should not be strong as to trivially imply the observations. The abductive system described in Hobbs and Stickel [1988] implements this approach by assigning costs to various kinds of assumptions and searching for an explanation of minimum cost. The problems of automatically generating cost assignments and of providing a theoretical basis for combining costs remain open.

Other approaches to plan recognition describe it as the result of applying unsound rules of inference that are created by reversing normally sound implications. From the fact that a particular plan entails a particular action, one derives the unsound rule that that action *may* imply that plan [Allen 1983b]. However, such unsound rules generate staggering numbers of possible plans. The key problems of deciding which rules to apply and when to stop applying the rules remain outside the formal theory.

By contrast, the framework presented in this chapter specifies what conclusions are absolutely justified on the basis of the observations, the recognizer's knowledge, and a number of explicit "closed world" assumptions. The conclusions follow by ordinary deduction from these statements. If many plans could explain the observations, then the recognizer is able to conclude whatever is common to all the simplest such plans. The technical achievement of this work is the ability to specify the assumptions the recognizer makes without recourse to a a control mechanism lying outside the theory.

Another natural way to view plan recognition is as a kind of probabilistic reasoning [Charniak and Goldman 1989]. The conclusions of the recognizer are simply those statements that are assigned a high probability in light of the evidence. A probabilistic approach is similar to the approach taken in this chapter in that reasoning proceeds directly from the observations to the conclusions and avoids the problems described above with the construction of explanations. The closed world assumptions employed by our system correspond to closure assumptions implicitly made in a Bayesian analysis, where the set of possible hypotheses is assumed to be disjoint and exhaustive. A major strength of the probabilistic approach over ours is that it allows one to capture the fact that certain plans are a priori more likely than others. While much progress is being made in mechanizing propositional probabilistic reasoning, first-order probabilistic reasoning is much more difficult. A propositional system can include a data element representing every possible plan and observation, and the effect of the change in probability of any element on every other element can be computed. This is not always possible in a first-order system, where the language can describe an infinite number of plans. The problem is not just one of selecting between hypotheses, but also selectively instantiating the first-order axioms that describe the parameterized plans. In our purely logical theory, one can simply deduce the parameters of the plans that are recognized.

2.1.2 Overview

In this chapter, plans and actions are uniformly referred to as **events**. The recognizer's knowledge is represented by a set of first-order statements called an **event hierarchy**, which defines the abstraction, specialization, and functional relationships between various types of events. The functional, or "role", relationships include the relation of an event to its **component** events. There is a distinguished type **End** which holds of events that are not components of any other events. Recognition is the problem of describing the End events that generate a set of observed events.[1]

In this work, we are limited to recognizing instances of plans whose types appear in the hierarchy; we do not try to recognize new plans created by chaining together the preconditions and effects of other plans (as is done in Allen [1983b]). Therefore, it is appropriate for domains where one can enumerate in advance all the ways of achieving a goal; in other words, where one wants to recognize stereotypical behavior, rather than understand truly unique and idiosyncratic behavior. This assumption of complete knowledge on the part of the system designer is fundamental to the approach. While abandoning this assumption might increase a system's flexibility, it would also lead to massive increase in the size of the search space, since an infinite number of plans could be constructed by chaining on preconditions and effects. We decided to maintain the assumption of complete knowledge and only construct plans by specialization and decomposition (as described below), until we have developed methods of controlling the combinatorial problem.

An event hierarchy by itself does not justify inferences from observations to End events. Consider the following set of plans. There are four kinds of End events (hiking, hunting, robbing banks, and cashing checks) and three other kinds of events (going to the woods, getting a gun, and going to a bank). The event hierarchy is illustrated in figure 1, where the thick grey arrows denote abstraction or "is a", and the thin black arrows denote component or "has part". The labels "s1" and "s2" serve to distinguish the component arcs; they denote the functions which map an event to the respective component. (The labels by themselves do not formally indicate the temporal ordering of the components.)

---

1. The idea of an End event may be problematic in general; see comments at the end of this chapter.

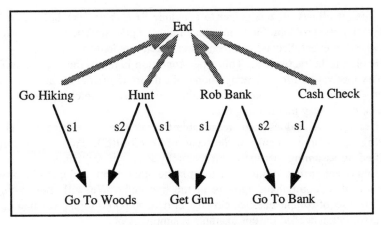

Figure 1: An event hierarchy

We encode this event hierarchy in first-order logic with the following axioms.

$\forall x \, . \, GoHiking(x) \supset End(x)$

$\forall x \, . \, Hunt(x) \supset End(x)$

$\forall x \, . \, RobBank(x) \supset End(x)$

$\forall x \, . \, CashCheck(x) \supset End(x)$

$\forall x \, . \, GoHiking(x) \supset GoToWoods(s1(x))$

$\forall x \, . \, Hunt(x) \supset GetGun(s1(x)) \wedge GoToWoods(s2(x))$

$\forall x \, . \, RobBank(x) \supset GetGun(s1(x)) \wedge GoToBank(s2(x))$

$\forall x \, . \, CashCheck(x) \supset GoToBank(s1(x)).$

The symbols $s1$ and $s2$ are functions which map a plan to its steps. Suppose $GetGun(C)$ is observed. This statement together with the axioms does not entail $\exists x.Hunt(x)$, or $\exists x.[Hunt(x) \vee RobBank(x)]$, or even $\exists x.End(x)$. The axioms let one infer that getting a gun is implied by hunting or going to the bank, but not vice versa.

It would not help to strengthen the implications to biconditionals in the last four axioms above in order to make them state sufficient as well as necessary conditions for the execution of the End events. Even if every single step of a plan were observed, one could not deduce that the plan occurred. For example, suppose that the recognizer learns $\{GetGun(C), GoToBank(D)\}$ and believes

$\forall x \, . \, RobBank(x) \equiv GetGun(s1(x)) \wedge GoToBank(s2(x)).$

The statement $\exists x.RobBank(x)$ still does not follow because of the missing premise that $\exists x.C=s1(x) \wedge D=s2(x)$. One could further strengthen the axiom to say that whenever someone gets a gun and goes to a bank he or she commits a robbery:

$[\exists x \, . \, RobBank(x)] \equiv [\exists y, z \, . \, GetGun(y) \wedge GoToBank(z)].$

This change allows the recognizer to conclude $\exists x.RobBank(x)$, but it does not really solve the problem. First, one cannot always give sufficient conditions for every kind of event. Second, the recognizer is still required to observe every step of the plan to be recognized. This latter condition is rarely the case; indeed, a primary motivation for plan recognition is the desire to *predict* the actions of the agent. Finally, such an axiom does not allow for a case in which a person cashes a check on his way to a hunting trip.

Nonetheless, it does seem reasonable to conclude that someone is either hunting or robbing a bank on the basis of $GetGun(C)$. This conclusion is justified by assuming that the event hierarchy is *complete:* that is, whenever a non-End event occurs, it must be part of some other event, and the relationship from event to component appears in the hierarchy. We will show how to generate a set of completeness or closed-world assumptions for a given hierarchy. The assumption needed for this example is simply

$\forall x . GetGun(x) \supset$
$\quad [\exists y . Hunt(y) \land x=s1(y)] \lor [\exists y . RobBank(y) \land x=s1(y)].$

We will also show that making these assumptions is equivalent to *circumscribing the event hierarchy* in a particular way [McCarthy 1980]. We borrow the model theory of circumscription to provide a model theory for plan recognition. Whatever deductively follows from the observations, event hierarchy, and assumptions holds in all "covering models" of the observations and event hierarchy. (The term "covering model" comes from the fact that every event in such a model is explained or "covered" by some End event which contains it.) In this example, the only covering models are isomorphic to (or contain a submodel isomorphic to) one of the two models:

$\{End(A), Hunt(A), GetGun(s1(A)), GoToWoods(s2(A)) \}$
$\{End(A), RobBank(A), GetGun(s1(A)), GoToBank(s2(A)) \}.$

Any model containing just an instance of $GetGun$ but no corresponding End event is not a covering model.

When several events are observed, additional assumptions are needed. Suppose that $\{GetGun(C), GoToBank(D)\}$ is observed. These formulas together with the assumptions

$\forall x . GetGun(x) \supset$
$\quad [\exists y . Hunt(y) \land x=s1(y)] \lor [\exists y . RobBank(y) \land x=s1(y)]$

$\forall x . GoToBank(x) \supset$
$\quad [\exists y . CashCheck(y) \land x=s1(y)] \lor [\exists y . RobBank(y) \land x=s2(y)]$

do not entail that an instance of bank robbery occurs. The first observation could be a step of a plan to hunt, and the second could be a step of a plan to cash a check. Yet in this example the *RobBank* plan is simpler than the conjunction of two other unrelated plans. It is reasonable to assume that unless there is reason to believe otherwise, all the observations are part of the same End event. Given the assumption

$$\forall\ x,y\ .\ End(x) \wedge End(y) \supset x=y,$$

the conclusion $\exists x.RobBank(x)$ deductively follows.[2] In model-theoretic terms, this assumption corresponds to selecting out the covering models that contain a minimum number of End events: these are the **minimum covering models** of the observations and hierarchy. Furthermore, this assumption can be blocked if necessary. If it is known that the agent is not robbing the bank, that is, if the input is $\{GetGun(C),\ GoToBank(D),\ \neg\exists\ y\ .\ RobBank(y)\}$, then the strongest simplicity assumption is that there are two distinct unrelated plans. It follows that these plans are hunting and cashing a check.

Why care about a formal theory of plan recognition? One advantage of this approach is that the proof and model theories apply to almost any situation. They handle disjunctive information, concurrent plans, steps shared between plans, and abstract event descriptions. We will illustrate the theory with examples of plan recognition from the domains of cooking and operating systems. The general nature of the theory suggests that it can be applied to problems other than plan recognition. We will show how a medical diagnosis problem can be represented in our system, by taking events to be diseases and symptoms rather than plans and actions. The similarity between the kind of reasoning that goes on in plan recognition and medical diagnosis has been noted by Charniak [1983]. Reggia, Nau, and Wang [1983] have proposed that medical diagnosis be viewed as a set covering problem. Each disease corresponds to the set of its symptoms, and the diagnostic task is to find a minimum cover of a set of observed symptoms. They work within a purely propositional logic and do not include an abstraction hierarchy. Extending their formal framework to first-order would make it quite close to the one presented here.

The formal theory is independent of any particular implementation or algorithm. It specifies the goal of the computation and provides an abstract mapping from the input information to the output. Section 2.5 provides specific algorithms for plan recognition. The algorithms implement the formal theory but are incomplete; however, they are much more efficient than a complete implementation, which simply used a general-purpose theorem prover. While the proof theory specifies a potentially infinite set of justified conclusions, the algorithms specify which conclusions are explicitly computed. The algorithms use a compact graph-based representation of logical formulas containing both conjunctions and disjunctions. Logical operations (such as substitution of equals) are performed by graph operations (such as graph matching). The algorithms use a temporal representation which is related to but different from that discussed in chapter 1. The times of specific instances of events are

---

2. The careful reader may note that the assumption $\forall x.\neg Hunt(x) \vee \neg RobBank(x)$ is also needed to make the proof go through; this kind of assumption will also be developed below.

represented by numeric bounds on the starting and ending instants. This metric information is constrained by symbolic constraints recorded in the interval algebra.

2.1.3   Plan Recognition and the Frame Problem

Although the work described in this chapter is the first to suggest that closed-world reasoning and circumscription in particular are relevant to plan recognition, the insight behind the connection is implicit in work on the "frame problem". Given an axiomatization of the changes actions make on the world, one wants to generate axioms that describe the properties that are *not* changed by each action. For example, in the situation calculus, the frame axiom that states that the color c of an object o is not changed by picking it up is often written as follows:

$$\forall\ s, c, o\ .\ Color(o,c,s) \supset Color(o,\ c,\ result(\ move(\ pickup(o)\ ),\ s)).$$

(In this particular representation, the last argument to a fluent such as *Color* is the state s in which the fluent holds. The function *result* maps the action *pickup(o)* and state s to the resulting state.) One of the primary motivations for the development of circumscription was to create a formal tool for specifying such frame axioms.

Several researchers have observed that there is another way of writing frame axioms [Haas 1987; Schubert 1989]. This is to state that if a particular property did change when any action was performed, then that action must be one of the actions known to change that property. In this example, suppose painting and burning are the only actions known to change the color of an object. The frame axiom for Color then becomes

$$\forall\ s, c, o, a\ .\ [Color(o,c,s) \wedge \neg Color(o,c,result(a,s)) \supset$$
$$[a{=}paint(o) \vee a{=}burn(o)].$$

This frame axiom looks very much like the assumptions needed for plan recognition. The frame axioms lead from the premise that a change occurred to the disjunction of all the actions that could make that change. The recognition assumptions lead from the premise that an action occurred to the disjunction of all plans that could contain that action as a substep.

Many difficult technical problems have arisen in applying circumscription to the frame problem. Apparently obvious ways of using circumscription can lead to conclusions that are much weaker than desirable [Hanks and McDermott 1986], and the formalism is generally unwieldy. This chapter shows how circumscription can be successfully and efficiently applied to a knowledge base of a particular kind in order to generate conclusions of a particular form. Like all formalisms, circumscription is of interest only if it is useful; and we hope that the use it has found in the present work is encouraging to those who continue to work on understanding and extending circumscription.

2.2 Representing Event Hierarchies

2.2.1 The Language

As described in chapter 1, the representation language we will use is first-order predicate calculus with equality. We make the following extension to the notation: a prefix $\wedge$ (similarly $\vee$) applied to a set of formulas stands for the conjunction (similarly disjunction) of all the formulas in that set. We will first introduce a standard semantics for this language and then extend it to deal with the plan recognition problem. A model interprets the language and maps terms to individuals, functions to mappings from tuples of individuals to individuals, and predicates to sets of tuples of individuals. If M is a model, then this mapping is made explicit by applying M to a term, function, or predicate. For example, for any model M:

Loves(Sister(Joe),Bill) is true in M if and only if
$\langle M[Sister](M[Joe]), M[Bill]\rangle \in M[Loves]$.

The domain of discourse of the model M is written **Domain(M)**. The fact that M interprets the constant *Joe* as an individual in its domain is written

$M[Joe] \in$ Domain(M).

Meta-variables (not part of the language) that stand for domain individuals begin with a colon. Models map free variables in sentences to individuals. The expression $M\{x|:C\}$ means the model that is just like M, except that variable x is mapped to individual :C. Quantification is defined as follows:

$\exists x . p$ is true in M if and only if
there exists :C $\in$ Domain(M) such that p is true in $M\{x|:C\}$
$\forall x . p$ is true in M if and only if $\sim\exists x .\sim p$ is true in M.

The propositional connectives are semantically interpreted in the usual way. Proofs in this chapter use natural deduction, freely appealing to obvious lemmas and transformations. It is convenient to distinguish a set of constant symbols called **Skolem constants** for use in the deductive rule of existential elimination. The rule allows one to replace an existentially-quantified variable by a Skolem constant that appears at no earlier point in the proof. Skolem constants are distinguished by the prefix "*". No Skolem constants may appear in the final step of the proof; they must be replaced again by existentially-quantified variables (or eliminated by other means). This final step is omitted when it is obvious how it should be done.

2.2.2 Representation of Time, Properties, and Events

Most formal work on representing action has relied on versions of the situation calculus [McCarthy and Hayes 1969]. This formalism is awkward for plan recognition: convolutions are needed to state that some particular action *actually occurred* at a particular time (but see Cohen [1984]). We therefore adopt the "reified" representation of time and events described in detail in chapter 1.

Recall from chapter 1 that time is linear, and time intervals are individuals, each pair related by one of Allen's interval algebra relations: *Before, Meets, Overlaps*, etc. The names of several relations may be written in place of a predicate, in order to stand for the disjunction of those relations. For example, *BeforeMeets(T1,T2)* abbreviates *Before(T1,T2)* ∨ *Meets(T1,T2)*. Intervals can be identified with pairs of rational numbers on some universal clock; two intervals meet when the first point of one is the same as the last point of the other [Ladkin and Maddux 1988].

Event **tokens** are also individuals, and event **types** are represented by unary predicates. All event tokens are real; there are no imaginary or "possible" event tokens. Various functions on event tokens, called **roles**, yield parameters of the event. Role functions include the event's agent and time. For example, the formula

$$ReadBook(C) \land object(C)=WarAndPeace \land time(C)=T2$$

may be used to represent the fact that an instance of book reading occurs, the book read is *War and Peace*, and the time of the reading is (the interval) *T2*. Role functions are also used to represent the steps of plans (or any other kind of structured event). For example, suppose that reading a book is a kind of plan which includes a step to pick up the book. The following formula could be used to represent the fact that two events have occurred, where one is reading a book and the other is the substep of picking up the book:

$$ReadBook(C) \land pickupStep(C)=D \land Pickup(D).$$

All other facts are represented by ordinary predicates. For example, the fact that John is a human may be represented by the formula *Human(John)*. Circumstances that change over time are also represented by predicates whose last argument is a time interval. For example, the fact that John is unhappy over the interval *T1* will be represented by the formula *Unhappy(John, T1)*.

2.2.3   The Event Hierarchy

An event hierarchy is a collection of restricted-form axioms, and may be viewed as a logical encoding of a semantic network [Hayes 1985]. These axioms represent the abstraction and decomposition relations between event types. This section defines the formal parts of an event hierarchy; Section 2.2.4 provides a detailed example. An event hierarchy H contains the following parts, H_E, H_A, H_{EB}, H_D, and H_G:

- H_E is the set of unary event type predicates. H_E contains the distinguished predicates *AnyEvent* and *End*. Any member of the extension of an event predicate is called an **event token**. *AnyEvent* is the most general event type, and *End* is the type of all events which are not part of some larger event.

- H_A is the set of abstraction axioms, each of the form
  $$\forall x . E_1(x) \supset E_2(x)$$
  for some E_1, $E_2 \in H_E$. In this case, we say that E_2 **directly abstracts** E_1. The transitive closure of direct abstraction is abstraction, and the fact that E_2 is the same as or abstracts E_1 is written E_2 **abstracts=** E_1. AnyEvent abstracts= all event types. The inverse of abstraction is specialization.

- H_{EB} is the set of basic event type predicates, that is, those members of H_E that do not abstract any other event type.

- H_D is the set of decomposition axioms, each of the form
  $$\forall x . E_0(x) \supset E_1(f_1(x)) \wedge E_2(f_2(x)) \wedge \ldots \wedge E_n(f_n(x)) \wedge \kappa$$
  where $E_0, \ldots, E_n \in H_E$; $f_1, \ldots, f_n$ are role functions, and κ is a subformula containing no member of H_E. The formula κ describes the **constraints** on E_0. E_1 through E_n are called **direct components** of E_0. Neither *End* nor any of its specializations may appear as a direct component.

- H_G is the set of general axioms, that is, those that do not contain any member of H_E. H_G includes the axioms for the temporal interval relations as well as any other facts not specifically relating to events.

Two event types are **compatible** if there is an event type they both abstract or are equal to. The **parameters** of an event token are the values of those role functions mentioned in a decomposition axiom for any type of that token applied to the token.

The direct component relation may be applied to event tokens in a model M as follows: Suppose $:C_i$ and $:C_0$ are event tokens. Then $:C_i$ is a **direct component** of $:C_0$ in M if and only if

1) there are event types E_i and E_0 such that $:C_i \in M[E_i]$ and $:C_0 \in M[E_0]$,

2) H_D contains an axiom of the form
   $$\forall x . E_0(x) \supset E_1(f_1(x)) \wedge \ldots \wedge E_i(f_i(x)) \wedge \ldots \wedge E_n(f_n(x)) \wedge \kappa,$$

3) $:C_i = M[f_i](:C_0)$.

In other words, one token is a direct component of another just in case it is the value of one of the role functions applicable to the former token. The **component** relation is the transitive closure of the direct component relation, and the fact that $:C_n$ is either the same as or a component of $:C_0$ is written $:C_n$ is a **component=** of $:C_0$. The component relation over event tokens does not correspond to the transitive closure of the direct-component meta-relation over event types because a token may be of more than one type.

A hierarchy is **acyclic** if and only if it contains no series of event predicates $E_1, E_2, \ldots, E_n$ of odd length (greater than 1) such that

1) E_i is compatible with E_{i+1} for odd i, $1 \le j \le n\text{-}2$,

2) E_{i-1} is a direct component of E_i for odd i, $3 \le i \le n$,

3) $E_n = E_1$.

Roughly speaking, an event hierarchy is acyclic if no event token may have a component of its own type. The definition above allows for the fact that all events are of type *AnyEvent*, and therefore any event token will share at least the type *AnyEvent* with its components. This chapter only considers acyclic event hierarchies.

2.2.4   Example: The Cooking World

The actions involved in cooking form a simple but interesting domain for planning and plan recognition. The specialization relations between various kinds of foods are mirrored by specialization relations between the actions that create those foods. Decompositions are associated with the act of preparing a type of food in the manner a recipe spells out the steps in the food's preparation. A good cook stores information at various levels in his abstraction hierarchy. For example, the cook knows the certain actions needed to create any cream-based sauce, as well as the certain conditions (constraints) that must hold during preparation. The sauce must be stirred constantly, the heat must be moderate, and so on. A specialization of the type cream sauce, such an Alfredo sauce, adds steps and constraints; for example, one should slowly stir in grated cheese at a certain point in the recipe.

We are assuming that the cook and the observer have the same knowledge of cooking—a hierarchically-arranged cookbook. Actions of the cook are reported to the observer, who tries to infer what the cook is making. We do not assume that the reports are exhaustive—there may be unobserved actions. A cook may prepare several different dishes at the same time, so it is not always possible to assume that all observations are part of the same recipe. Different End events may share steps. For example, the cook may prepare a large batch of tomato sauce and then use the sauce in two different dishes.

Figure 2 illustrates a very tiny cooking hierarchy. Thick grey arrows denote the abstraction meta-relation, while thin black arrows denote the direct component meta-relation. All event types are abstracted by *AnyEvent*. Here, there are two main categories of End events: preparing meals and washing dishes. It is important to understand that the abstraction hierarchy, encoded by the axioms in H_A, and the decomposition hierarchy, encoded by the axioms in H_D, are interrelated but separate. Work on hierarchical planning often confuses these two distinct notions in an action or event hierarchy. Figure 2 illustrates some, but not all, of the information in the axioms for the cooking domain. The formal description of the hierarchy is as follows:

- The set of event types H_E includes *PrepareMeal, MakeNoodles, MakeFettucini*, and so on.

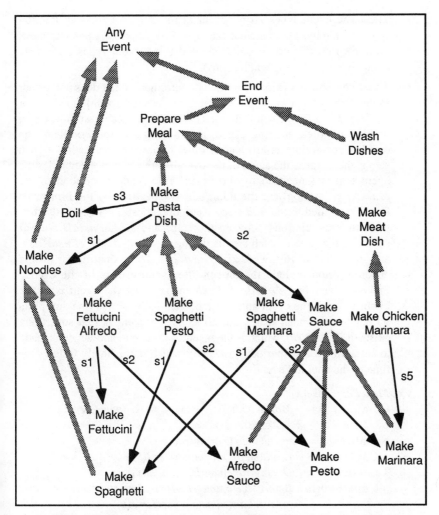

Figure 2: Cooking event hierarchy (The abstraction arc from MakeSauce to
AnyEvent is omitted for clarity.)

- The abstraction axioms H$_A$ relate event types to their abstractions. For
  instance, *MakeNoodles* is an abstraction of both *MakeSpaghetti* and
  MakeFettucini. A traditional planning system might call *Make–*
  Spaghetti and *MakeFettucini* different **bodies** of the *MakeNoodles*
  plan. This relationship is represented by asserting that every instance of
  the more specialized type is also an instance of the more abstract type.
  For example:

  $\forall x \, . \, MakeSpaghetti(x) \supset MakeNoodles(x).$
  $\forall x \, . \, MakeFettucini(x) \supset MakeNoodles(x).$

- The basic event types H_{EB} appear at the bottom of the abstraction (grey) hierarchy. These include the types *Boil, MakeSpaghettiMarinara, MakeFettucini,* and so on. Note that basic event types may have components (but no specializations).

- The decomposition axioms H_D include information that does not appear in the diagram. An incomplete version of the decomposition axiom for the *MakePastaDish* event follows. This act includes at least three steps: making noodles, making sauce, and boiling the the noodles. The equality constraints assert, among other things, that the agent of each step is the same as the agent of the overall act[3] and that the noodles the agent makes (specified by the **result** role function applied to the *MakeNoodles* step) are the thing boiled (specified by the *input* role function applied to the *Boil* step). Temporal constraints explicitly state the temporal relations between the steps and *MakePastaDish*. For example, the time of each step is during the time of *MakePastaDish*, and *Boil* must follow *MakeNoodles*. The constraints in the decomposition include the preconditions and effects of the events. Preconditions for *MakePastaDish* include that the agent is in the kitchen during the event and that the agent is dexterous (making pasta by hand is no mean feat!). An effect of the event is that something exists (a *PastaDish*), which is the result of the event, and which is ready to eat during a time period (*postTime*), which immediately follows the time of the cooking event.

$\forall x . MakePastaDish(x) \supset$

Components	$MakeNoodles(step1(x)) \land MakeSauce(step2(x))$
	$\land Boil(step3(x)) \land$
Equality	$agent(step1(x)) = agent(x) \land$
Constraints	$result(step1(x)) = input(step3(x)) \land$
Temporal	$During(time(step1(x)), time(x)) \land$
Constraints	$BeforeMeets(time(step1(x)), time(step3(x)))$
	$\land Overlaps(time(x), postTime(x)) \land$
Preconditions	$InKitchen(agent(x), time(x)) \land Dexterous(agent(x)) \land$
Effects	$ReadyToEat(result(x), postTime(x))$
	$\land PastaDish(result(x)).$

Note that the names of the component roles *step1, step2*, etcetera, are arbitrary; they do *not* indicate temporal ordering. The event types that specialize *MakePastaDish* add additional constraints and steps to its decomposition. For example, the event type *MakeSpaghettiMarinara* further constrains its

---

3. It is not necessarily the case that the agent of an event be the same as the agent of each of its components. One could as easily write constraints that they be different. For example, a plan for a cook could include steps to be carried out by the cook's helper.

decomposition to include *MakeSpaghetti* (rather than the more generic *MakeNoodles*) and *MakeMarinaraSauce* (rather than simply *MakeSauce*). One could also add completely new steps as well.

$\forall x$. *MakeSpaghettiMarinara(x)* $\supset$
    MakeSpaghetti(step1(x)) $\wedge$ *MakeMarinaraSauce(step2(x))* $\wedge$ ...

Assertions about particular event instances take the form of the predication of an event type of a constant, conjoined with equality assertions about the roles of the event token, and perhaps a proposition relating the time of the event to that of other events. The English statement, "Yesterday Joe made the noodles on the table." may be represented as follows:

MakeNoodle(Make33) $\wedge$ *agent(Make33)=Joe* $\wedge$
    result(Make33)=Noodles72 $\wedge$ *OnTable(Noodles72, Tnow)* $\wedge$
    During(time(Make33), Tyesterday).

2.3   The Formal Theory of Recognition

We have seen that the kind of inferences performed in plan recognition do not follow from an event hierarchy alone. The abstraction hierarchy is strengthened by assuming that there are no event types outside of H_E, and that all abstraction relations between event predicates are derivable from H_A. The decomposition hierarchy is strengthened by assuming that non-End events occur only as components of other events. These assumptions are reasonable because the hierarchy encodes all of our knowledge of events. If the hierarchy is enlarged, the assumptions must be revised. Finally, a simplicity assumption is used to combine information from several observations. We now consider the various kinds of assumptions in detail.

2.3.1   Exhaustiveness Assumptions (EXA)

Suppose you know that the agent is making some kind of sauce other than Alfredo sauce or pesto. Then you can reasonably conclude that the agent is making marinara sauce. Such a conclusion is justified by the assumption that the known ways of specializing an event type are the only ways of specializing it. In this case, the assumption is

$\forall x$. *MakeSauce(x)* $\supset$
    MakeMarinara(x) $\vee$ *MakeAlfredoSauce(x)* $\vee$ *MakePesto(x)*.

Another way to write this same statement is

$\forall x$. *MakeSauce(x)* $\wedge$ *~MakeAlfredoSauce(x)* $\wedge$ *~MakePesto(x)* $\supset$
    MakeMarinara(x).

This kind of assumption allows one to determine that a particular kind of event has occurred by eliminating all other possibilities. Fans of Sherlock Holmes will recognize it as an instance of his dictum, "When you have eliminated the impossible, whatever remains, however improbable, must be the truth." [Doyle 1890]

The set EXA of exhaustiveness assumptions are all statements of the following form, where E_0 is a predicate in H_A, and $\{E_1, E_2, \ldots, E_n\}$ are all the predicates directly abstracted by E_0:

$$\forall x . E_0(x) \supset (E_1(x) \vee E_2(x) \vee \ldots \vee E_n(x)).$$

2.3.2   Disjointness Assumptions (DJA)

Suppose the agent is making a pasta dish. It is clear from the example hierarchy that this particular event is not an instance of making a meat dish. That is, we make the assumption

$$\forall x . MakePastaDish(x) \supset {\sim}MakeMeatDish(x).$$

Why is this only an assumption? Suppose a new type were added to the hierarchy that specialized both *MakePastaDish* and *MakeMeatDish*:

$$\forall x . MakeMeatRavioli(x) \supset MakePastaDish(x).$$
$$\forall x . MakeMeatRavioli(x) \supset MakeMeatDish(x).$$

Then the assumption that meat dishes and pasta dishes are disjoint would no longer be reasonable. However, assuming that one's knowledge of events is complete, it is reasonable to assume that two types are disjoint, unless one abstracts the other, or they abstract a common type; that is, if they are compatible. The disjointness assumptions together with the exhaustiveness assumptions entail that every event has a unique basic type, where the basic types are the leaves of the abstraction hierarchy.

The set DJA of disjointness assumptions consists of all statements of the following form, where event predicates E_1 and E_2 are not compatible:

$$\forall x . {\sim}E_1(x) \vee {\sim}E_2(x).$$

2.3.3   Component/Use Assumptions (CUA)

The most important assumptions for recognition let one infer the disjunction of the possible "causes" for an event from its occurrence. They state that a plan or action implies the disjunction of the plans which use it as a component. The simplest case is when only a single type could have a particular event as a direct component. For instance, from the fact that the agent is boiling water one can conclude that the agent is making a pasta dish. Formally, the assumption is that

$$\forall x . Boil(x) \supset \exists y . MakePastaDish(y) \wedge x{=}step3(y).$$

More generally, the conclusion of this kind of assumption is the disjunction of all events having a component that is compatible with the premise. Consider the assumption for *MakeSauce*. This type is compatible with itself and all of its specializations: *MakeAlfredoSauce*, *MakePesto*, and *MakeMarinara*. The following formula describes all the events that could have a component of those types:

$\forall x . MakeSauce(x) \supset$
  $(\exists y . MakePastaDish(y) \land x=step2(y)) \lor$
  $(\exists y . MakeFettuciniAlfredo(y) \land x=step2(y)) \lor$
  $(\exists y . MakeSpaghettiPesto(y) \land x=step2(y)) \lor$
  $(\exists y . MakeSpaghettiMarinara(y) \land x=step2(y)) \lor$
  $(\exists y . MakeChickenMarinara(y) \land x=step5(y)).$

Note that *MakeChickenMarinara* has as a component *MakeMarinara*, which is compatible with *MakeSauce*. The formula can be simplified by using the abstraction axioms for *MakePastaDish*:

$\forall x . MakeSauce(x) \supset$
  $(\exists y . MakePastaDish(y) \land x=step2(y)) \lor$
  $(\exists y . MakeChickenMarinara(y) \land x=step5(y)).$

This example demonstrates that making such a component/use assumption is not the same as predicate completion in the style of Clark [1978]. Predicate completion yields

$\forall x . MakeSauce(x) \supset$
  $(\exists y . MakePastaDish(y) \land x=step2(y)).$

This assumption is too strong because it omits the use of *MakeSauce* as specialized by *MakeMarinara*, which is implicit in event hierarchy.

The definition of the set CUA of component/use assumptions follows. For any $E \in H_E$, define $Com(E)$ as the set of event predicates with which E is compatible. Consider all the decomposition axioms in which any member of $Com(E)$ appears on the right-hand side. The j-th such decomposition axiom has the following form, where E_{ji} is the member of $Com(E)$:

$\forall x . E_{j0}(x) \supset E_{j1}(f_{j1}(x)) \land ... \land E_{ji}(f_{ji}(x)) \land ... \land E_{jn}(f_{jn}(x)) \land \kappa.$

Suppose that the series of these axioms, where an axiom is repeated as many times as there are members of $Com(E)$ in its right-hand side, is of length $m > 0$. Then the following formula is the component/use assumption for E:

$\forall x . E(x) \supset End(x) \lor$
  $(\exists y . E_{1,0}(y) \land f_{1i}(y)=x) \lor$
  $(\exists y . E_{2,0}(y) \land f_{2i}(y)=x) \lor$
  $... \lor$
  $(\exists y . E_{m,0}(y) \land f_{mi}(y)=x).$

CUA is the set of all such formulas for a given hierarchy. It is usually possible to remove redundant subexpressions from the right-hand side of these formulas, as in the example above. Throughout the remainder of chapter 2 such simplifications will be made.

2.3.4   Minimum Cardinality Assumptions (MCA)

The assumptions described above do not combine information from several observations. Suppose that the agent is observed making spaghetti and making marinara sauce. The first observation is explained by applying the component/use assumption that the agent is making spaghetti marinara or spaghetti pesto. The second observation is similarly explained by the conclusion that the agent is making spaghetti marinara or chicken marinara. However, the conclusion cannot be drawn that the agent is making spaghetti marinara. The End event that explains the first observation could be distinct from the End event that explains the second. The theory as outlined so far sanctions only the statement

$$\exists x . [MakeSpaghettiMarinara(x) \vee MakeSpaghettiPesto(x)] \wedge$$
$$\exists y . [MakeSpaghettiMarinara(y) \vee MakeChickenMarinara(y)].$$

In many cases, it is reasonable to assume that the observations are related. A simple heuristic is to assume that there is a minimal number of distinct End events. In this example, all the types above are specializations of *End*. The statement above, the disjointness assumptions, and the assumption that there is no more than one End event entails the conclusion that the agent is making spaghetti marinara.

The three different kinds of assumptions discussed above are computed from the event hierarchy before any observations are made. The appropriate minimum cardinality assumption (MCA) is based on both the hierarchy and the specific observations that have been made. Consider the following sequences of statements:

MA_0. $\forall x . \sim\!End(x)$

MA_1. $\forall x,y . End(x) \wedge End(y) \supset x{=}y$

MA_2. $\forall x,y,z . End(x) \wedge End(y) \wedge End(z)$
$$\supset (x{=}y) \vee (x{=}z) \vee (y{=}z)$$

...

The first asserts that no End events exist; the second, no more than one End event exists; the third, no more than two; and so on. Let the observations be represented by a set of formulas Γ. The minimum cardinality assumption appropriate for H and Γ is the formula MA_i, where i is the smallest integer such that

$$\Gamma \cup H \cup EXA \cup DJA \cup CUA \cup MA_i$$

is consistent. (In general, this consistency test is undecidable; the algorithms described later in this chapter create separate data structures corresponding to the application of each assumption to the observations, and prune the data structures when an inconsistency is noticed. At any time the conclusions of the system are represented by the data structure corresponding to the strongest assumption.)

2.3.5   Example: The Cooking World

The following example shows how the different components of the event hierarchy and kinds of assumptions interact in plan recognition. As noted earlier, constants prefixed with a "*" stand in place of existentially-quantified variables. Suppose the observer initially knows that the agent will not be making Alfredo sauce. Such knowledge could come from information the observer has about the resources available to the agent, such as a lack of cream. Further, suppose that the initial observation is that the agent is making some kind of noodles.

Observation

   [1]   *MakeNoodles(Obs1)*

Component/Use Assumption [1] and Existential Instantiation

   [2] $MakePastaDish(*I1) \wedge step1(*I1)=Obs1$

Abstraction [2]

   [3]   *PrepareMeal(*I1)*

Abstraction [3]

   [4]   *End(*I1).*

Although the recognized plan is not fully specified, enough is known to allow the observer to make predictions about future actions of the agent. For example, the observer can predict that the agent will boil water:

Decomposition [2]

   [5] $Boil(\ step3(*I1)\ )\ \wedge After(time(Obs1),\ time(step3(*I1))\ ).$

The observer may choose to make further inferences to refine the hypothesis. The single formula *MakePastaDish(*I1)* above does not summarize all the information gained by plan recognition. The actual set of conclusions is always infinite, since it includes all formulas that are entailed by the hierarchy, the observations, and the assumptions. (The algorithms discussed later in this chapter perform a limited number of inferences and generate a finite set of conclusions.) Several inference steps are required to reach the conclusion that the agent must be making spaghetti rather than fettucini.

Given Knowledge

   [6] $\forall x\ .\ \sim MakeAlfredoSauce(x)$

Exhaustiveness Assumption [2]

   [7] $MakeSpaghettiMarinara(*I1) \vee MakeSpaghettiPesto(*I1)$
          $\vee MakeFettuciniAlfredo(*I1)$

Decomposition and Universal Instantiation

[8]   *MakeFettuciniAlfredo(*I1) ⊃ MakeAlfredoSauce(step2(*I1))*

Modus Tollens [6,8]

[9]   *~MakeFettuciniAlfredo(*I1)*

Disjunction Elimination [7,9]

[10]   *MakeSpaghettiMarinara(*I1) ∨ MakeSpaghettiPesto(*I1)*

Decomposition and Universal Instantiation

[11]   *MakeSpaghettiMarinara(*I1) ⊃ MakeSpaghetti(step1(*I1))*

[12]   *MakeSpaghettiPesto(*I1) ⊃ MakeSpaghetti(step1(*I1))*

Reasoning by Cases [10,11,12]

[13]   *MakeSpaghetti(step1(*I1))*.

Suppose that the second observation is that the agent is making marinara sauce. The minimal cardinality assumption allows the observer to intersect the possible explanations for the first observation with those for the second in order to reach the conclusion that the agent is making spaghetti marinara.

Second Observation

[14]   *MakeMarinara(Obs2)*

Component/Use Assumption [14] and Existential Instantiation

[15]   *MakeSpaghettiMarinara(*I2) ∨ MakeChickenMarinara(*I2)*

Abstraction [15]

[16]   *MakePastaDish(*I2) ∨ MakeMeatDish(*I2)*

Abstraction [16]

[17]   *PrepareMeal(*I2)*

Abstraction [17]

[18]   *End(*I2)*

Minimum Cardinality Assumption

[19]   ∀ *x,y . End(x) ∧ End(y) ⊃ x=y*

Universal Instantiation and Modus Ponens [4,17,19]

[20]   **I1=*I2*

Substitution of Equals [2,30]

[21]   *MakePastaDish(*I2)*

Disjointness   Assumption

[22] $\forall x . \sim\!MakePastaDish(x) \vee \sim\!MakeMeatDish(x)$

Disjunction   Elimination   [21,22]

[23] $\sim\!MakeMeatDish(*I2)$

Abstraction   and   Existential   Instantiation

[24] $MakeChickenMarinara(*I2) \supset MakeMeatDish(*I2)$

Modus   Tollens   [23,24]

[25] $\sim\!MakeChickenMarinara(*I2)$

Disjunction   Elimination   [15,25]

[26] $MakeSpaghettiMarinara(*I2)$.

2.3.6   Circumscription   and   Plan   Recognition

Earlier we discussed the relation of circumscription to plan recognition in informal terms. Now we will make that relation precise, and in so doing, develop a model theory for part of the plan recognition framework.

Circumscription is a syntactic transformation of a set of sentences representing an agent's knowledge. Let S[π] be a set of formulas containing a list of predicates π. The expression S[σ] is the set of formulas obtained by rewriting S with each member of π replaced by the corresponding member of σ. The expression $\sigma \leq \pi$ abbreviates the formula stating that the extension of each predicate in σ is a subset of the extension of the corresponding predicate in π, that is,

$$(\forall x . \sigma_1(x) \supset \pi_1(x)) \wedge \ldots \wedge (\forall x . \sigma_n(x) \supset \pi_n(x)),$$

where each x is a list of variables of the proper arity to serve as arguments to each σ_i. The circumscription of π relative to S, written Circum(S,π), is the second-order formula

$$(\wedge S) \wedge \forall \sigma . [(\wedge S[\sigma]) \wedge \sigma \leq \pi] \supset \pi \leq \sigma.$$

Circumscription has a simple and elegant model theory. Suppose M_1 and M_2 are models of S which are identical except that the extension in M_2 of one or more of the predicates in π is a proper subset of the extensions of those predicates in M_1. This is denoted by the expression $M_1 >> M_2$ (where the expression is relative to the appropriate S and π). We say that M_1 is minimal in π relative to S if there is no such M_2.

The circumscription Circum(S,π) is true in all models of S that are minimal in the π [Etherington 1986]. Therefore, to prove that some set of formulas S $\cup$ T entails Circum(S,π), it suffices to show that every model of S $\cup$ T is minimal in π relative to S.

The converse does not always hold because the notion of a minimal model is powerful enough to capture such structures as the standard model of arithmetic, which cannot be axiomatized [Davis 1980]. However, in the present work, we are only concerned with cases where the set of minimal models can be described by a finite set of first-order formulas. The following assertion about the completeness of circumscription appears to be true, although we have not uncovered a proof.

Supposition: If there is a finite set of first-order formulas T such that the set of models of $S \cup T$ is identical to the set of models minimal in π relative to S, then that set of models is also identical to the set of models of Circum(S,π). Another way of saying this is that circumscription is complete when the minimal-model semantics is finitely axiomatizable.

Given this supposition, to prove that Circum(S,π) entails some set of formulas $S \cup T$, it suffices to show that T holds in every model minimal in π relative to S.

Propositions

The major stumbling block to the use of circumscription is the lack of a general mechanical way to determine how to instantiate the predicate parameters in the second-order formula. The following propositions demonstrate that the first three classes of assumptions discussed above, exhaustiveness, disjointness, and component/use, are equivalent to particular circumscriptions of the event hierarchy. (Note: the bidirectional entailment sign $\Leftrightarrow$ is used instead of the equivalence sign $\equiv$ because the left hand-side of each statement is a set of formulas rather than a single formula.)

The first proposition states that the exhaustiveness assumptions (EXA) are obtained by circumscribing the nonbasic event types in the abstraction hierarchy. Recall that the abstraction axioms state that every instance of an event type is an instance of the abstractions of the event type. This circumscription minimizes all the event types, except those which cannot be further specialized. Therefore, something can be an instance of a nonbasic event type only if it is also an instance of a basic type, and the abstraction axioms entail that it is an instance of the nonbasic type. In other words, this circumscription generates the implications from event types to the disjunctions of their specializations.

$\quad$ 1) $H_A \cup EXA \Leftrightarrow$ Circum(H_A , H_E–H_{EB}).

The second proposition states that the disjointness assumptions (DJA) are obtained by circumscribing all event types other than *AnyEvent*, the most general event type, in the resulting set of formulas. The first circumscription entailed that each event token is of at least one basic type. This second circumscription ensures that each event token is of at most one basic type.

$\quad$ 2) $H_A \cup EXA \cup DJA \Leftrightarrow$ Circum($H_A \cup EXA$, H_E–{*AnyEvent*}).

The third proposition states that the component/use assumptions (CUA) result from circumscribing all event types other than *End* relative to the complete event hierarchy together with the exhaustiveness and disjointness assumptions. Note that in this case both the decomposition and abstraction axioms are used. Intuitively, events of type End "just happen" and are not explained by their occurrence as a substep of some other event. Minimizing all the non-*End* types means that events occur only when they are *End*, or a step of (a subtype of) *End*, or a step of a step of (a subtype of) *End*, and so on. This is equivalent to saying that an event entails the disjunction of all events that could have the first event as a component.

3) $H \cup EXA \cup DJA \cup CUA \Leftrightarrow$
   Circum($H \cup EXA \cup DJA$, $H_E-\{End\}$).

The minimum cardinality assumption (MCA) cannot be generated by this kind of circumscription. The minimum cardinality assumption minimizes the number of elements in the extension of *End*, while circumscription performs setwise minimization. A model where the extension of *End* is {:A, :B} would not be preferred to one where the extension is {:C}, because the latter extension is not a proper subset of the former.

Covering Models

The various completeness assumptions are intuitively reasonable and, as we have seen, can be defined independently of the circumscription schema. The propositions above might therefore be viewed as a technical exercise in the mathematics of circumscription rather than as part of an attempt to gain a deeper understanding of plan recognition. On the other hand, the propositions do allow us to use the model theory of circumscription to construct a model theory for the plan recognition. The original event hierarchy is missing information needed for recognition—or equivalently, the original hierarchy has too many models. Each circumscription throws out some group of models that contain extraneous events. The models of the final circumscription can be thought of as "covering models" because every event in each model is either of type End or is "covered" by an event of type End that has it as a component. (In fact, this is the lemma that appears below in the proof of proposition 3.)

The minimum cardinality assumption further narrows the set of models, selecting out those containing the smallest number of End events. Therefore, the conclusions of the plan recognition theory are the statements that hold in all "minimum covering models" of the hierarchy and observations. This model-theoretic interpretation of the theory suggests its similarity to work on diagnosis based on minimum set covering models, such as that of Reggia, Nau, and Wang [1983].

Proof of Proposition 1

$$H_A \cup EXA \Leftrightarrow Circum(H_A , H_E-H_{EB})$$

($\Leftarrow$) Suppose $\{E_1, E_2, \ldots , E_n\}$ are all the predicates directly abstracted by E_0 in H_A. We claim that the statement

$$\forall x . E_0(x) \supset (E_1(x) \vee E_2(x) \vee \ldots \vee E_n(x))$$

is true in all models of H_A that are minimal in H_E-H_{EB}. Let M_1 be a model of H_A in which the statement does not hold. Then there must be some :C such that

$$E_0(x) \wedge {\sim}E_1(x) \wedge \ldots \wedge {\sim}E_n(x)$$

is true in $M_1\{x/:C\}$. Define M_2 by

Domain(M_2)=Domain(M_1)
$M_2[Z]=M_1[Z]$ for $Z \neq E_0$
$M_2[E_0]=M_1[E_0] - \{:C\}$.

That is, M_2 is the same as M_1, except that :C $\notin M_2[E_0]$. We claim that M_2 is a model of H_A. Every axiom that does not contain E_0 on the right-hand side is plainly true in M_2. Axioms of the form

$$\forall x . E_i(x) \supset E_0(x) \quad 1 \leq i \leq n$$

are false in M_2 only if there is a :D such that

$$:D \in M_2[E_i] \wedge :D \notin M_2[E_0].$$

If :D $\neq$:C, then :D $\in M_2[E_i] \Rightarrow$:D $\in M_1[E_i] \Rightarrow$:D $\in M_1[E_0] \Rightarrow$:D $\in M_2[E_0]$, which is a contradiction. Otherwise, if :D=:C, then :D $\in M_2[E_i] \Rightarrow$:D $\in M_1[E_i] \Rightarrow$:C $\in M_1[E_i]$, which also is a contradiction. Therefore, there can be no such :D, so M_2 is a model of H_A and M_1 is not minimal.

($\Rightarrow$) First we prove the following **lemma:** Every event in a model of $H_A \cup EXA$ is of at least one basic type. That is, if M_1 is a model of $H_A \cup EXA$ such that :C $\in M_1[E_0]$, then there is a basic event type $E_b \in H_{EB}$ such that :C $\in M_1[E_b]$ and E_0 abstracts= E_b. The proof is by induction. Define a partial ordering over H_E by $E_j < E_k$ iff E_k abstracts E_j. Suppose $E_0 \in H_{EB}$. Then E_0 abstracts= E_0. Otherwise, suppose the lemma holds for all $E_i < E_0$. Since

$$\forall x . E_0(x) \supset (E_1(x) \vee E_2(x) \vee \ldots \vee E_n(x))$$

and :C $\in M_1[E_0]$, it must the case that

$$:C \in M_1[E_1] \vee \ldots \vee :C \in M_1[E_n].$$

Without loss of generality, suppose $:C \in M_1[E_1]$. Then there is an E_b such that E_1 abstracts= E_b and $:C \in M_1[E_b]$. Since E_0 abstracts E_1, it also abstracts= E_b. This completes the proof of the lemma.

We prove that if M_1 is a model of $H_A \cup EXA$, then M is a model of H_A minimal in H_E–H_{EB}. Suppose not. Then there is an M_2 such that $M_1 >> M_2$, and there is (at least one) $E_0 \in H_E$–H_{EB} and event $:C$ such that

$$:C \in M_1[E_0] \wedge :C \notin M_2[E_0].$$

By the lemma, there is an $E_b \in H_{EB}$ such that $:C \in M_1[E_b]$. Since M_1 and M_2 agree on H_{EB}, $:C \in M_2[E_b]$, and because E_0 abstracts E_b, $:C \in M_2[E_0]$, which is a contradiction. Therefore, there can be no such M_2, so M_1 is minimal. This completes the proof of the proposition.

Proof of Proposition 2

$$H_A \cup EXA \cup DJA \Leftrightarrow Circum(H_A \cup EXA, H_E-\{AnyEvent\})$$

($\Leftarrow$) We claim that if event predicates E_1 and E_2 are not compatible, then the statement

$$\forall x . \sim E_1(x) \vee \sim E_2(x)$$

is true in all models of $H_A \cup EXA$ that are minimal in $H_E-\{AnyEvent\}$. Let M_1 be a model of $H_A \cup EXA$ in which the statement is false and $:C$ be an event such that

$$E_1(x) \wedge E_2(x)$$

is true in $M_1\{/:C\}$. Using the lemma from the proof of proposition 1, let E_b be a basic event type abstracted by E_1 such that $:C \in M_1[E_b]$. Define M_2 as follows:

Domain(M_2)=Domain(M_1)
$M_2[Z]=M_1[Z]$ for $Z \notin H_E$
$M_2[E_i]=$ $\quad M_1[E_i]$ if E_i abstracts= E_b
$\qquad\qquad M_1[E_i]-\{:C\}$ otherwise.

In particular, note that $M_1[AnyEvent]=M_2[AnyEvent]$, since $AnyEvent$ certainly abstracts E_b. We claim that M_2 is a model of $H_A \cup EXA$.

(Proof that M_2 is a model of H_A) Suppose not; in particular, suppose the axiom

$$\forall x . E_j(x) \supset E_i(x)$$

is false in M_2. Since it is true in M_1, and M_2 differs from M_1 only in the absence of $:C$ from the extension of some event predicates, it must be the case that:$C \in M_2[E_j]$ and $:C \notin M_2[E_i]$ while $:C \in M_1[E_j]$ and $:C \in M_1[E_i]$. By the definition of M_2, it must be the case that E_j abstracts= E_b. Since E_i

abstracts E_j, then E_i abstracts= E_b as well. But then M_1 and M_2 would have to agree on E_i; that is, :C $\in$ $M_2[E_i]$, which is a contradiction.

(Proof that M_2 is a model of EXA) Suppose not; in particular, suppose

$$\forall x \, . \, Ej_0(x) \supset (Ej_1(x) \vee Ej_2(x) \vee \ldots \vee Ej_n(x))$$

is false. Then it must be the case that

$$:C \in M_2[Ej_0] \wedge :C \notin M_2[Ej_1] \wedge \ldots \wedge :C \notin M_2[Ej_n].$$

But :C $\in$ $M_2[Ej_0]$ means that Ej_0 abstracts= E_b. Since Ej_0 is not basic, at least one of $Ej_1, \ldots, Ej_n$ abstracts= E_b. Without loss of generality, suppose it is Ej_1. Then :C $\in$ $M_1[E_b]$ $\Rightarrow$:C $\in$ $M_2[E_b]$ $\Rightarrow$:C $\in$ $M_2[Ej_1]$, which is a contradiction.

Note that because E_1 and E_2 are not compatible, E_2 cannot abstract= E_b. Thus :C $\notin$ $M_2[E_2]$, so M_1 and M_2 differ at least on E_2. Therefore, $M_1 \gg M_2$ so M_1 is not minimal.

($\Rightarrow$) First we note the following **lemma**: Every event in a model of $H_A \cup$ EXA $\cup$ DJA is of exactly one basic type. By the lemma in the proof of proposition 1 there is at least one such basic type, and by DJA no event is of two basic types.

We prove that if M_1 is a model of $H_A \cup$ EXA $\cup$ DJA, then M_1 is minimal in H_E-{AnyEvent} relative to $H_A \cup$ EXA. Suppose there is an M_2 such that $M_1 \gg M_2$ and there exists (at least one) $E_0 \in H_E$-{*AnyEvent*} and event :C such that :C $\in$ $M_1[E_0]$ and :C $\notin$ $M_2[E_0]$. Then :C $\in$ $M_1[E_0]$ $\Rightarrow$:C $\in$ $M_1[AnyEvent]$ $\Rightarrow$:C $\in$ $M_2[AnyEvent]$. By the lemma in the proof of proposition 1 there is some $E_b \in H_{EB}$ such that :C $\in$ $M_2[E_b]$. Since $M_1 \gg M_2$, it must be the case that :C $\in$ $M_1[E_b]$. By the lemma above, E_b is the unique basic type of :C in M_1, and E_0 abstracts= E_b. But E_0 abstracts= E_b means that :C $\in$ $M_2[E_b]$ $\Rightarrow$:C $\in$ $M_2[E_0]$, which is a contradiction. Therefore, there can be no such M_2, and M_1 must be minimal. This completes the proof of proposition 2.

Proof of Proposition 3

H $\cup$ EXA $\cup$ DJA $\cup$ CUA $\Leftrightarrow$ Circum(H $\cup$ EXA $\cup$ DJA , H_E-{*End*})

($\Leftarrow$) First we prove the following **lemma**: Suppose M_1 is a model of H $\cup$ EXA $\cup$ DJA that is minimal in H_E-{*End*}. If :$C_1 \in M_1[E_1]$ for any event predicate E_1, then either :$C_1 \in M_1[End]$ or there exists some event token :C_2 such that :C_1 is a direct component of :C_2. Suppose the lemma were false. Define M_2 as follows:

$M_2[Z]=M_1[Z]$ for $Z \notin H_E$
$M_2[E]=M_1[E]$-{:C_1} for $E \in H_E$.

Note that M_1 and M_2 agree on *End*. We will show that $H \cup EXA \cup DJA$ holds in M_2, which means that $M_1 \gg M_2$ is a contradiction. We consider each of the types of axioms in turn.

(*Case 1*) Axioms in H_G must hold because they receive the same valuation in M_1 and M_2.

(*Case 2*) Axioms in H_A are of the form

$$\forall x \, . \, E_j(x) \supset E_i(x).$$

Suppose one is false; then for some :D,

$$:D \in M_2[E_j] \wedge :D \notin M_2[E_i].$$

But this is impossible because M_1 and M_2 must agree when $:D \neq :C_1$, as must be case because $:C_1$ does not appear in the extension of any event type in M_2.

(*Case 3*) Axioms in EXA must hold by the same argument.

(*Case 4*) Axioms in DJA must hold because they contain no positive uses of H_E.

(*Case 5*) The j-th axiom in H_D is of the form

$$\forall x \, . \, E_{j0}(x) \supset E_{j1}(f_{j1}(x)) \wedge E_{j2}(f_{j2}(x)) \wedge \, ... \, \wedge E_{jn}(f_{jn}(x)) \wedge \kappa.$$

Suppose it does not hold in M_2. Then there must be some $:C_2$ such that

$$E_{j0}(x) \wedge \{ \sim E_{j1}(f_{j1}(x)) \vee \sim E_{j2}(f_{j2}(x)) \vee \, ... \, \vee \sim\kappa \, \}$$

is true in $M_2\{x/:C_2\}$. M_1 and M_2 agree on κ, so it must the case that for some j and i, $M_2[f_{ji}](:C_2) \notin M_2[E_{ji}]$ while $M_1[f_{ji}](:C_2) \in M_1[E_{ji}]$. Because M_1 and M_2 differ on E_{ji} only at $:C_1$, it must be the case that $M_1[f_{ji}](:C_2)=:C_1$. But then $:C_1$ *is* a component of $:C_2$ in M_1, contrary to our original assumption. This completes the proof of the lemma.

Consider now an arbitrary member of CUA as defined above, which has predicate E on its left-hand side. Let M be a model of $H \cup EXA \cup DJA$ that is minimal in $H_E-\{End\}$ such that $:C \in M[E]$ and $:C \notin M[End]$. By the lemma above, there is an E_{j0}, E_{ji}, and $:D$ such that

$$:D \in M[E_{j0}]$$
$$:C \in M[E_{ji}]$$
$$:C=M[f_{ji}](:D),$$

where f_{ji} is a role function in a decomposition axiom for E_{j0}. Because M is a model of DJA, E and E_{ji} are compatible. By inspection, we see that the second half of the formula above is true in M when x is bound to :C because the disjunct containing E_{ji} is true when the variable y is bound to :D. Since the choice of :C was arbitrary, the entire formula is true in M. Finally, since the choice of M and the member of CUA was arbitrary, all of CUA is true in all models of $H \cup EXA \cup DJA$ that are minimal in $H_E-\{End\}$.

($\Rightarrow$) We prove that if M_1 is a model of $H \cup EXA \cup DJA \cup CUA$, then it is a model of $H \cup EXA \cup DJA$, which is minimal in $H_E-\{End\}$. Suppose not; then there is an M_2 such that $M_1 >> M_2$, and there exists (at least one) $E_l \in H_E-\{End\}$ and event $:C_1$ such that

$$:C_1 \in M_1[E_l]$$
$$:C_1 \notin M_2[E_l].$$

We claim that there is a $:C_n$ such that $:C_n \in M_1[End]$ and $:C_1$ is a component$=$ of $:C_n$. This is obviously the case if $:C_1 \in M_1[End]$; otherwise, for the axioms in CUA to hold there must be sequences of event tokens, types, and role functions of the following form

$$
\begin{array}{cccccc}
:C_1 & :C_1 & :C_3 & :C_3 & :C_5 & :C_5 & \dots \\
E_1 & E_2 & E_3 & E_4 & E_5 & E_6 & \dots \\
 & & f_{3i} & & f_{5i} & & \dots
\end{array}
$$

such that

For all j, $:C_j \in M_1[E_j]$
For odd j, E_j and E_{j+1} are compatible
For odd j, $j \geq 3$, E_{j-1} is a direct component of E_j, and $:C_{j-2}=M_1[f_{ji}](:C_j)$.

This sequence must terminate with a $:C_n$ such that $:C_n \in M_1[End]$ because H is acyclic. Therefore $:C_1$ is a component$=$ of C_n.

Because M_1 and M_2 agree on End, $:C_n \in M_2[End]$. Now for any odd j, $3 \leq j \leq n$, if $:C_j \in M_2[E_j]$, then since H_D holds in M_2, $:C_{j-2} \in M_2[E_{j-1}]$. If we prove that for all odd j, $1 \leq j \leq n$

$$:C_j \in M_2[E_{j+1}] \Rightarrow :C_j \in M_2[E_j]$$

we will be done; because we would then know that $:C_n \in M_2[End] \Rightarrow :C_n \in M_2[E_{n+1}] \Rightarrow :C_n \in M_2[E_n] \Rightarrow :C_{n-2} \in M_2[E_{n-1}] \Rightarrow \dots \Rightarrow :C_3 \in M_2[E_3] \Rightarrow :C_1 \in M_2[E_2] \Rightarrow :C_1 \in M_2[E_l]$, which yields the desired contradiction. So assume the antecedent $:C_j \in M_2[E_{j+1}]$. Because M_2 is a model of $H_A \cup EXA \cup DJA$, there is a unique $E_b \in H_{EB}$ such that $:C_j \in M_2[E_b]$. Because $M_1 >> M_2$, $:C_j \in M_1[E_b]$. Since M_1 is a model of $H_A \cup EXA \cup DJA$, by the lemma in the proof of proposition 2 it must be the case that E_j abstracts$=$ E_b. But then since H_A holds in M_2, $:C_j \in M_2[E_j]$, we are done. This completes the proof of proposition 3.

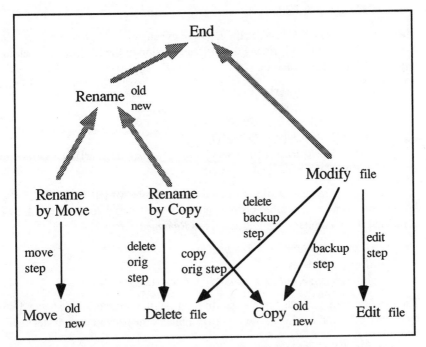

Figure 3: Operating system hierarchy

2.4 Examples

2.4.1 An Operating System

Several research groups have examined the use of plan recognition in "smart" computer operating systems that could answer user questions, watch what the user was doing, and make suggestions about potential pitfalls and more efficient ways of accomplishing the same tasks [Huff and Lesser 1982; Wilensky 1983]. A user often works on several different tasks during a single session at a terminal and frequently jumps back and forth between uncompleted tasks. Therefore a plan recognition system for this domain must be able to concurrently handle multiple unrelated plans. The very generality of the present approach is an advantage in this domain, where the focus-type heuristics used by other plan recognition systems are not so applicable.

Representation

Consider the hierarchy in figure 3. There are two *End* plans: to *Rename* a file, and to *Modify* a file.

$$\forall x \,.\, Rename(x) \supset End(x).$$

$\forall x$. $Modify(x) \supset End(x)$.

There are two ways to specialize the *Rename* event. A *RenameByCopy* involves *Copying* a file, and then *Deleting* the original version of the file without making any changes in the original file.

$\forall x$. $RenameByCopy(x) \supset Rename(x)$.
$\forall x$. $RenameByCopy(x) \supset$
    $Copy(s1(x)) \wedge Delete(s2(x)) \wedge old(s1(x))=old(x) \wedge$
    $new(s1(x))=new(x) \wedge file(s2(x))=old(x) \wedge$
    $BeforeMeet(time(s1(x)), time(s2(x))) \wedge Starts(time(s1(x)), time(x))$
    $\wedge Finishes(time(s2(x)), time(x))$.

A better way to rename a file is to *RenameByMove*, which simply uses the *Move* command.[4] A helpful system might suggest that a user try the *Move* command if it recognizes many instances of *RenameByCopy*.

$\forall x$. $RenameByMove(x) \supset Rename(x)$.
$\forall x$. $RenameByMove(x) \supset$
    $Move(s1(x)) \wedge old(s1(x))=old(x) \wedge new(s1(x))=new(x)$.

The *Modify* command has three steps. In the first, the original file is backed up by copying. Then the original file is edited. Finally, the backup copy is deleted.

$\forall x$. $Modify(x) \supset$
    $Copy(s1(x)) \wedge Edit(s2(x)) \wedge Delete(s3(x)) \wedge file(x)=old(s1(x))$
    $\wedge backup(x)=new(s1(x)) \wedge file(x)=file(s2(x)) \wedge$
    $backup(x)=file(s3(x)) \wedge BeforeMeet(time(s1(x)), time(s2(x)))$
    $\wedge BeforeMeet(time(s2(x)), time(s3(x)))$.

Assumptions

Some of the statements obtained by minimizing the hierarchy follow. The component/use assumptions include the statement that every *Copy* action is either part of a *RenameByCopy* or of a *Modify*.

$\forall x$. $Copy(x) \supset$
    $(\exists y$. $RenameByCopy(y) \wedge x=s1(y)) \vee (\exists y$. $Modify(y) \wedge x=s1(y))$.

Every *Delete* event is either the second step of a *RenameByCopy*, or the third step of a *Modify*, in any covering model.

$\forall x$. $Delete(x) \supset$
    $(\exists y$. $RenameByCopy(y) \wedge x=s2(y)) \vee (\exists y$. $Modify(y) \wedge x=s3(y))$.

---

4. Another way to represent this information would be to make *Move* a specialization of *Rename*. This would mean that *every Move* would be recognized as a *Rename* and therefore as an *End* event. This alternative representation would not be appropriate if there were End events other than *Rename* which included *Move* as a component.

The Problem

Suppose the plan recognition system observes each action the user performs. Whenever a new file name is typed, the system generates a constant with the same name and asserts that that constant is not equal to any other file name constant. We do not allow UNIX™-style "links". During a session, the user types the following commands:

```
1)          % copy foo bar
2)          % copy jack sprat
3)          % delete foo.
```

The system should recognize two concurrent plans. The first is to rename the file "foo" to "bar". The second is to either rename or modify the file "jack". Let us examine how these inferences could be made. Statement (1) is encoded

$$Copy(C1) \wedge old(C1)=foo \wedge new(C1)=bar.$$

The component/use assumption for *Copy* lets the system infer that *C1* is either part of a *RenameByCopy* or *Modify*. A new name *$*I1$* is generated (by existential instantiation) for the disjunctively-described event.

$$End(*I1) \wedge$$
$$(\qquad (RenameByCopy(*I1) \wedge C1=s1(*I1)\,)$$
$$\vee$$
$$(Modify(*I1) \wedge C1=s1(*I1)\,)$$
$$).$$

Statement (2) is encoded

$$Copy(C2) \wedge old(C2)=jack \wedge new(C2)=sprat \wedge Before(time(C1),\ time(C2)).$$

Again the system creates a disjunctive description for the event *$*I2$*, which has *C2* as a component.

$$End(*I2) \wedge$$
$$(\qquad (RenameByCopy(*I2) \wedge C2=s1(*I2)\,)$$
$$\vee$$
$$(Modify(*I2) \wedge C2=s1(*I2)\,)$$
$$).$$

The next step is to minimize the number of End events. The system might attempt to apply the strongest minimization default, that

$$\forall x,y\ .\ End(x) \wedge End(y) \supset x=y.$$

However, doing so would lead to a contradiction. Because the types *RenameByCopy* and *Modify* are disjoint, *$*I1=*I2$* would imply that *C1=C2*; however, the system knows that *C1* and *C2* are distinct—among other reasons, their times are known to be unequal. The next strongest minimality default—that there are two End events—cannot lead to any new conclusions.

Statement (3), the act of deleting "foo", is encoded

$$Delete(C3) \land file(C3)=foo \land Before(time(C2), time(C3)).$$

The system infers by the component/use assumption for *Delete* that the user is performing a *RenameByCopy* or a *Modify*. The name *I3* is assigned to the inferred event.

$$End(*I3) \land$$
$$(\qquad (RenameByCopy(*I3) \land C3=s2(*I3)\,)$$
$$\lor$$
$$\qquad (Modify(*I3) \land C3=s3(*I3)\,)$$
$$).$$

Again, the system tries to minimize the number of End events. The second strongest minimality default says that there are no more than two End events.

$$\forall x,y,z \,.\, End(x) \land End(y) \land End(z) \supset x=y \lor x=z \lor y=z.$$

In this case, the formula is instantiated as follows:

$$*I1=*I2 \lor *I1=*I3 \lor *I2=*I3.$$

We have already explained why the first alternative is impossible. Thus, the system knows

$$*I1=*I3 \lor *I2=*I3.$$

The system then reduces this disjunction by reasoning by cases. Suppose that *I2=*I3. This would mean that the sequence

```
2)          % copy jack sprat
3)          % delete foo
```

is either part of a *RenameByCopy* or of a *Modify*, described as follows:

$$End(*I2) \land$$
$$(\qquad (RenameByCopy(*I2) \land C2=s1(*I2) \land C3=s2(*I2) \land$$
$$\text{✗} \qquad old(*I2)=jack \land old(*I2)=foo\,)$$
$$\lor$$
$$\qquad (Modify(*I2) \land C2=s1(*I2) \land C3=s3(*I2) \land$$
$$\qquad new(s1(*I2))=jack \land file(*I2)=jack \land$$
$$\qquad backup(*I2)=sprat \land file(s3(*I2))=foo \land$$
$$\text{✗} \qquad backup(*I2)=file(s3(*I2))\,)$$
$$).$$

But both disjuncts are impossible, since the files that appear as roles of each event do not match up (as marked with ✗'s). Therefore, if the minimality default holds, it must be the case that

*I1=*I3.

This means that the observations

1)   % copy foo bar
3)   % delete foo

should be grouped together as part of a *Rename* or *Modify*. This assumption leads the system to conclude the disjunction as follows:

End(*I1*) ∧
((*RenameByCopy*(*I1*) ∧ *C1=s1*(*I1*) ∧ *C3=s2*(*I1*) ∧
           old(*I1*)=*foo* ∧ *new*(*I1*)=*bar*)

∨

           (*Modify*(*I1*) ∧ *C1=s1*(*I1*) ∧ *C3=s3*(*I1*) ∧
           new(*s1*(*I1*))=*bar* ∧ *backup*(*I1*)=*bar* ∧
           file(*s3*(*I1*))=*foo* ∧
✗   *backup*(*I1*)=*file*(*s3*(*I1*)))
).

The second alternative is ruled out, since the actions cannot be part of the same *Modify*. The system concludes that observations (1) and (3) make up a *RenameByCopy* act and that observation (2) is part of some unrelated *End* action.

End(*I1*) ∧
RenameByCopy(*I1*) ∧
old(*I1*)=*foo* ∧ *new*(*I1*)=*bar* ∧
End(*I2*) ∧
((*RenameByCopy*(*I2*) ∧ *C2=s1*(*I2*))

∨

           (*Modify*(*I2*) ∧ *C2=s1*(*I2*))
).

Further checking of constraints may be performed, but no inconsistency will arise. At this point, the plan recognizer may trigger the "advice giver" to tell the user the following:

```
*** You can rename a file by typing
*** % move oldname newname.
```

2.4.2   Medical Diagnosis

There are close links between the kinds of reasoning involved in plan recognition and that employed in medical diagnosis. The vocabulary of events can be mapped to one appropriate for diagnosis in a straightforward way. Events are replaced by pathological states of a patient. An abstraction hierarchy over pathological states is known as a **nosology**. The decomposition hierarchy corresponds to a **causation hierarchy**. If pathological state A always causes pathological state

B, then B acts as a component of A. If only certain cases of A cause B, then one can introduce a specialization of A that has component B. The most basic specializations of *End* (unexplainable) events correspond to **specific disease entities**, while states that can be directly observed are **symptoms**. (Note that a symptom may also cause other states: for example, high blood pressure can be directly measured, and it can cause a heart attack.)

The pattern of inference in plan recognition and diagnosis is similar as well. Each symptom invokes a number of different diseases to consider, just as each observed event in our framework entails the disjunction of its uses. Once several findings are obtained, the diagnostician attempts to find a small set of diseases that accounts for, or covers, all the findings. This step corresponds to the minimization of End events. A general medical diagnosis system must deal with patients suffering from multiple diseases; our plan recognition framework was designed to account for multiple concurrently executing plans. Finally, our work departs from previous work in plan recognition by explicitly dealing with disjunctive conclusions, which are winnowed down by obtaining more observations. These disjunctive sets correspond to the differential diagnosis sets that play a central role in medical reasoning. In some ways, medical diagnosis is easier than plan recognition. Often, medical knowledge can be represented in propositional logic. There is usually no need for diseases to include parameters as plans do, and most medical expert systems do not need to deal with the passage of time.

The following example is drawn from Pople [1982] and was handled by CADUCEUS, an expert system that deals with internal medicine. We have made a number of simplifications, but the key points of the example remain. These include the need to consider specializations of a pathological state (abstract event type) in order to explain a symptom, finding, or state, and the process of combining or unifying the differential diagnosis sets invoked by each finding.

Representation

Figure 4 illustrates a small part of CADUCEUS's knowledge base. The thin "component" arcs signify "can cause". We have added the type End as an abstraction of all pathological states not caused by other pathological states. The **basic** specializations of *End* are called **specific disease entities.** We have simplified the hierarchy by making the specializations of anemia and shock specific disease entities; in the actual knowledge base, anemia and shock are caused by other conditions.

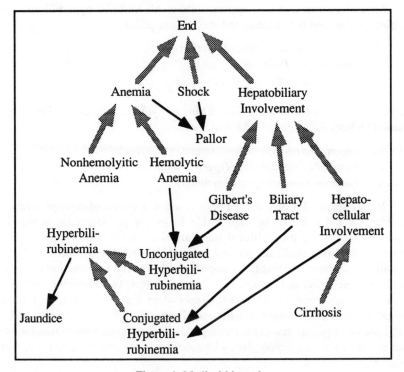

Figure 4: Medical hierarchy

The logical encoding of this network is as expected. The symptoms caused by a disease appear in the decomposition axiom for that disease. This is a considerable simplification over the original CADUCEUS model, in which the causal connections need only be *probable*. Symptoms of high probability, however, are taken by CADUCEUS as *necessary* manifestations, and CADUCEUS will *rule out* a disease on the basis of the *absence* of such symptoms. The *constraints* that appear at the end of a decomposition axiom would include conditions of the patient that are (very nearly) necessary for the occurrence of the disease, but which are not themselves pathological. These could include the age and weight of the patient, his immunization history, and so on. Thus, a constraint on Alzheimer's disease would be that the patient be over forty. Constraints are not used in this example.

For the sake of clarity, the names of the role functions have been omitted from component (symptom) arcs in the illustration, but such functions are needed in the logical encoding. We will use the letters j, h, p for role functions, where j is used for symptoms of type *Jaundice*, h for symptoms of type *Hyperbilirubinemia*, and p for symptoms of type *Pallor*. The names used are really not important; however, all the different symptoms caused by a particular disease must be related to it by different role functions.

Several axioms and assumptions follow. All kinds of hyperbilirubinemia cause jaundice, and both anemia and shock cause pallor.

$\forall y$. $Hyperbilirubinemia(y) \supset Jaundice(j(y))$
$\forall y$. $Anemia(y) \supset Pallor(p(y))$
$\forall y$. $Shock(y) \supset Pallor(p(y))$.

Unconjugated hyperbilirubinemia is a kind of hyperbilirubinemia which can be caused by hemolytic anemia, a kind of anemia.

$\forall x$. $Unconjugated\text{-}hyperbilirubinemia(x) \supset Hyperbilirubinemia(x)$
$\forall y$. $Hemolytic\text{-}anemia(y) \supset Hyperbilirubinemia(h(y))$
$\forall x$. $Hemolytic\text{-}anemia(x) \supset Anemia(x)$.

It may seem a bit odd that we need to use a first-order language, when the problem would seem to be expressible in purely propositional terms. The problem with using propositional logic arises from the abstract pathological states. A realistic medical knowledge base incorporates several methods of classifying diseases, leading to a complex and intertwined abstraction hierarchy. It is very likely that any patient will manifest at least two distinct pathological states (perhaps causally related) that specialize the same state. In a purely propositional system, such a pair would appear to be competitors as in a differential diagnosis set. (This corresponds to the disjointness assumptions in our system.) But this would plainly be incorrect if the two states were causally related.

Assumptions

Now we restrict our attention to the covering models of this hierarchy. The exhaustiveness assumptions include the fact that every case of *Hyperbilirubinemia* is either conjugated or unconjugated.

$\forall x$. $Unconjugated\text{-}hyperbilirubinemia(x) \supset$
$Conjugated\text{-}hyperbilirubinemia(x) \vee$
$Unconjugated\text{-}hyperbilirubinemia(x)$.

Disjointness assumptions include the fact that the pathological states of anemia, shock, and hepatobiliary involvement are distinct. It is important to note that this does *not* mean that the states cannot occur simultaneously; rather, it means that none of these states abstracts each other.

$\forall x$. $\sim Anemia(x) \vee \sim Shock(x)$
$\forall x$. $\sim Anemia(x) \vee \sim Hepatobiliary\text{-}involvement(x)$
$\forall x$. $\sim Shock(x) \vee \sim Hepatobiliary\text{-}involvement(x)$.

Finally, the component/use assumptions, better called the **manifestation/cause assumptions,** allow one to conclude the disjunction of causes of a pathological state, thus creating a differential diagnosis set. An important special case occurs when there is only one cause, usually at a fairly high level of abstraction, for a state. An example of this is the association of *Jaundice* with *Hyperbilirubinemia*. (Pople calls this case a *constrictor relationship* between the manifestation and cause, and argues that such cases play a critical role in reducing search in diagnostic problem solving.) A less conclusive assumption says that pallor indicates anemia or shock.

$\forall x$. *Jaundice*(*x*) $\supset \exists y$. *Hyperbilirubinemia*(*y*) $\wedge x=j(y)$
$\forall x$. *Pallor*(*x*) $\supset$
     ($\exists y$. *Anemia*(*y*) $\wedge x=p(y)$) $\vee$
     ($\exists y$. *Shock*(*y*) $\wedge x=p(y)$).

The Problem

We will sketch the kind of reasoning that goes on when the diagnostician is confronted with two symptoms, jaundice and pallor. From jaundice, the diagnostician concludes hyperbilirubinemia. This leads (by exhaustion) to either the conjugated or unconjugated varieties. At this point, CADUCEUS (and perhaps a human physician) may perform tests to decide between these alternatives. The framework we have developed, however, allows us to continue inference in each alternative. The first leads to either hemolytic anemia and then anemia, or to Gilbert's disease and then hepatobiliary involvement. The second leads to either biliary tract disease or hepatocellular involvement, both of which lead to hepatobiliary involvement. Figure 5 shows the final conclusion, which represents the logical sentence that follows. (Further steps in this example will be illustrated only in the graphical form.)

Jaundice(**J1*) $\wedge$ *Hyperbilirubinemia*(**H1*) $\wedge$
  ((*Unconjugated-hyperbilirubinemia*(**H1*) $\wedge$
     ((*Hemolytic-anemia*(**E1*) $\wedge$ *Anemia*(**E1*))
     $\vee$
     (*Gilbert's-disease*(**E1*) $\wedge$ *Hepatobiliary-involvement*(**E1*))
)
)
  $\vee$
  (*Conjugated-hyperbilirubinemia*(**H1*) $\wedge$
     (*Biliary-tract*(**E1*)
     $\vee$
     Biliary-tract(**E1*)
) $\wedge$
     Hepatocellular-involvement(**E1*)
)
) $\wedge$
End(**E1*).

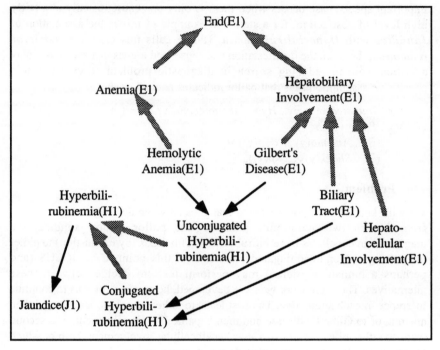

Figure 5: Conclusions from jaundice

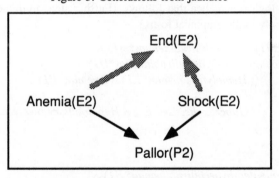

Figure 6: Conclusions from pallor

Next, the diagnostician considers pallor. This leads to a simple disjunction shown in figure 6.

Finally, the diagnostician applies Occam's razor, by making the assumption that the symptoms are caused by the same disease. This corresponds to equating the specific disease entities at the highest level of abstraction (*End*) in each of the previous conclusions. In other words, we apply the strongest minimum cardinality default. This allows the diagnostician to conclude that the patient is

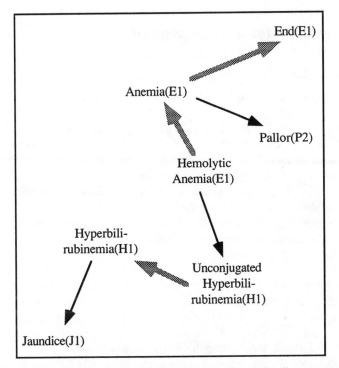

Figure 7: Conclusions from jaundice and pallor

suffering from hemolytic anemia, which has led to unconjugated hyperbilirubin-emia, as shown in figure 7.

A practical medical expert system must deal with a great many problems not illustrated by this simple example. We have not dealt with the whole problem of generating appropriate *tests* for information; we cannot assume that the expert system is passively taking in information, like a person reading a book. The entire CADUCEUS knowledge base is enormous, and it is not clear whether the complete algorithms discussed in section 2.5 could deal with it.

It seems clear, however, that our framework for plan recognition does formalize some key parts of diagnostic reasoning. In particular, we show how to "invert" a knowledge base which allows inferences from causes to effects (diseases to symptoms) to one which allows inferences from effects to causes. Like the minimum set covering model of Reggia, Nau, and Wang [1983], we combine information from several symptoms by finding the smallest set(s) of diseases which explains all the symptoms. One should note that our framework depends on having a model of disease but not a model of healthy processes. This is to be contrasted with work on "diagnosis from first principles", as in Reiter [1987], which models the correct or healthy functioning of a system and derives a diagnosis by trying to resolve inconsistencies between this model and the actual observations.

2.5   Algorithms for Plan Recognition

2.5.1   Directing Inference

An implementation of this theory of plan recognition must limit and organize the inferences drawn from the observations, hierarchy, and assumptions. As noted before, the formal theory sanctions an infinite set of conclusions. On the other hand, an implementation must compute some finite data structure in a bounded amount of time.

The framework developed in this chapter does not pose the plan recognition problem in such a way that a solution is simply the name of a specific plan. Instead, a solution is a partial description of the plans that are in progress. Different encodings of this description make aspects of the plan more or less explicit. For example, an encoding that leaves most aspects of the plans in progress implicit is simply the set of sentences in the observations, hierarchy, and assumptions. A more explicit encoding would be a disjunction of all the possible *End* plan types that explain the observations. A very explicit encoding may not only be expensive to compute, but may also involve a loss of detail. All information is contained in the observations, hierarchy, and assumptions, but the more explicit representation may include (for example) unnecessary disjunctions due to the incompleteness of the inference method employed. In fact, some degree of incompleteness is necessary in any implementation of our formal theory because the definition of the minimum cardinality assumption appeals to the consistency of a set of sentences—an undecidable property.

The less inference the plan recognition system performs, the more inference must be formed by the programs that call the plan recognizer as a subroutine. The implementation described in this section tries to strike a balance between efficiency and power. The choices we have made are to some degree arbitrary. We have not tried to develop a formal theory of limited inference to justify these choices, although that would be an interesting and useful project. Instead, we have been guided by the examples of plan recognition discussed in this chapter and elsewhere in the literature, and we have tried to design a system that makes most of the inferences performed in those examples and that outputs a data structure that makes explicit most of the conclusions drawn in those examples.

The implementation performs the following pattern of reasoning: from each observation, apply component/use assumptions and abstraction axioms until an instance of type End is reached. Reduce the number of alternatives by checking constraints locally. In order to combine information from two observations, equate the instances of *End* inferred from each and propagate the equality, further reducing disjunctions. If all alternatives are eliminated, then conclude that the observations belong to distinct End events. Multiple simultaneous End events are recognized by considering all ways of grouping the observations. As noted earlier, it is not possible to detect all inconsistencies. Therefore, the "best" explanation returned by the system (by the function **minimum-Hypoths** described below) may, in fact, be inconsistent because observations which logically could not be combined were grouped together.

The algorithms presented here only handle event hierarchies in which the abstraction hierarchy is a forest. That is, they do not deal with "multiple inheritance". (But note that the decomposition hierarchy is not necessarily a forest—one event type may be a component of many others. For example, *MakeMarinara* falls below both *MakeSpaghettiMarinara* and *MakeChicken–Marinara* in the decomposition hierarchy.) Furthermore, in order to limit inference, the implementation does not perform inferences that correspond to applications of the decomposition axioms. This restriction limits the predictive power of the system to some degree. The implementation could not reach one of the conclusions drawn in the example presented in section 2.3.5, where the observer concludes that the agent is making spaghetti because the agent is known to be making either spaghetti marinara or spaghetti pesto. However, the implementation described here does make explicit all the other conclusions presented in the examples in this chapter.

2.5.2   Explanation Graphs

Chaining through all the component/use assumptions raises the prospect of generating extremely long disjunctive conclusions. The first assumption generates a disjunction, applying the assumptions to each disjunct in this formula generates another disjunction, and so on. In general, this process multiplies out the event hierarchy from the bottom up, creating a number of literals exponential in the size of the original hierarchy. This problem has led other plan recognition systems to limit component/use type inferences to a single application.

Our implementation meets this problem by using a nonclausal representation of the plan description. The representation takes the form of a labeled acyclic graph, called an "explanation graph" or **e-graph**. These graphs can encode disjunctive assertions in a compact form through structure-sharing. In the worst case, the e-graph generated by an observation can be exponential in the size of the event hierarchy; however, in all the examples we have considered, structure-sharing allows the e-graph to be smaller than the hierarchy. Figure 8 shows the e-graph that is generated for an observation of *MakeMarinara*.

An e-graph contains the following three kinds of nodes. **Event nodes** consist of an event token and a single associated event type. An event token N appears at most once in an e-graph, so we can simply identify the token with the node and recover the associated type with the form $type(N)$. In figure 8, $N1$ through $N7$ are all event nodes. **Proper names** are unique names for objects other than events and times. **Fuzzy temporal bounds** are 4-tuples of real numbers. (No proper names or fuzzy temporal bounds appear in figure 8.)

There are two kinds of arcs, both of which can only lead out of event nodes. A **parameter** arc is labeled with a role function f_r and points to its value v.

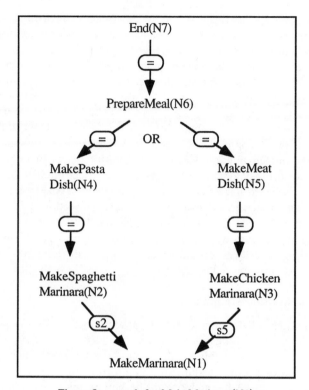

Figure 8: e-graph for MakeMarinara(N1)

When the value is an event node or a proper name, the arc means that $f_r(N)=v$. Figure 8 contains two parameter arcs, labeled *s2* and *s5*. When the value is a fuzzy temporal bound, the arc means that according to some universal clock, the beginning of the time interval $f_r(N)$ falls between the first two numbers, and the end falls between the last two numbers. Below we will discuss how fuzzy time bounds can be combined, so that temporal constraint propagation can be performed without recourse to a separate temporal database program.

The second kind of arcs are **alternative** arcs, which always point at event nodes. The meaning of these arcs is that the (event token identified with the) origin node is equal to one of the nodes pointed to by an alternative arc. Note that event nodes (tokens) are not unique names for events; in general, several nodes in an e-graph will represent the same real-world event. The alternative arcs point from a node of a particular type to a node of a more specialized type. The alternative arcs in figure 8 are labeled with an "=" sign.

Every e-graph G contains exactly one node N of type *End*. The translation of that graph into sentential logic is given by *TRANS(N)*, where *TRANS* is given by the following recursive definition:

$TRANS(n)=$

$type(n)$ (n) $\wedge$

$\bigwedge\{v=f_r(n) \wedge TRANS(v) \mid \langle n,f_r,v \rangle \in$ G and v is an event node$\}$ $\wedge$

$\bigwedge\{v=f_r(n) \mid \langle n,f_r,v \rangle \in$ G and v is a proper name$\}$ $\wedge$

$\bigwedge\{r1 \leq f_r(n)^- \leq r2 \wedge r3 \leq f_r(n)^+ \leq r4 \mid \langle n,f_r, \langle r1, r2, r3, r4 \rangle\rangle \in$ G$\}$ $\wedge$

$\bigvee\{n=m \wedge TRANS(m) \mid \langle n, =, m \rangle \in$ G$\}$.

In the first line of the translation, the expression $type(n)$ stands for the event type predicate associated with node n. The full expression $type(n)(n)$ means that this predicate is applied to the logical constant n. Arcs in the graph are represented by triples, consisting of a node, a label, and a node. In the definition above, $\langle n,f_r,v \rangle$ is an arc from event node n, labeled with role function f_r, to event node v. Similarly, $\langle n,f_r, \langle r1, r2, r3, r4 \rangle\rangle$ is an arc from event node n, labeled with temporal parameter f_r, to fuzzy temporal bound $\langle r1, r2, r3, r4 \rangle$. The triple $\langle n, =,$ $m \rangle$ indicates that node m is an alternative for node n in the graph. The postfix functions – and + apply to a time interval and return the metric time of the start and end of interval respectively. The event tokens in the translation are interpreted as Skolem constants (existentially quantified variables). The translation of figure 8 is the sentence

$End(N7) \wedge N7{=}N6 \wedge PrepareMeal(N6) \wedge$

$\quad (\; (\; N6{=}N4 \wedge MakePastaDish(N4) \wedge$

$\quad\quad\quad N4{=}N2 \wedge MakeSpaghettiMarinara(N2) \wedge$

$\quad\quad\quad step2(N2){=}N1 \wedge MakeMarinara(N1) \;)$

$\quad \vee (\; N6{=}N5 \wedge MakeMeatDish(N5) \wedge$

$\quad\quad\quad N5{=}N3 \wedge MakeChickenMarinara(N3) \wedge$

$\quad\quad\quad step5(N3){=}N1 \wedge MakeMarinara(N1) \;) \;).$

An e-graph describes a single End event. When the plan recognizer determines that more than one End event is in progress, it returns a set of End events whose interpretation is the conjunction of the interpretations of each e-graph. When the observations can be grouped in different ways, the recognizer returns a set of sets of End events whose interpretation is the disjunction of the interpretation of each set. For example, given three observations where no plan contains all three but some plans contain any two, the recognizer returns a set of the form $\{\{g1{\wedge}2, g3\}, \{g1, g2{\wedge}3\}, \{g1{\wedge}3, g2\}\}$.

2.5.3   Implementing Component/Use Assumptions

A component/use assumption leads from an event to the disjunction of all events that have a component that is compatible with the premise. It is desirable that this disjunction not be redundant; for example, it should not contain both an event type and a more specialized version of the event type. The algorithm below implements the component/use assumptions by: first, considering the cases that explicitly use the premise event type (plus a few others, as we shall explain in a moment); next, considering the cases that explicitly use a type that specializes

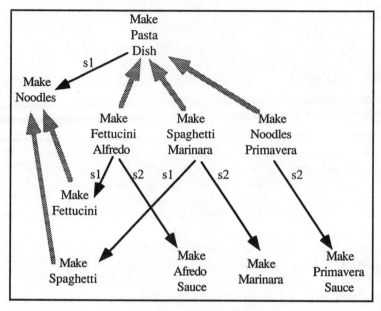

Figure 9: Example of implicit use

the premise type and that are not redundant with respect to the first group of cases; and finally, considering the cases that explicitly use a type that abstracts the premise type, and that are not redundant with respect to the previous cases.

A **use** is a triple $\langle E_c, f_r, E_u \rangle$ and stands for the possibility that (some instance of) E_c could fill the r role of some instance of E_u. The set **Uses** contains all such triples considered by the algorithm. We shall say that $\langle E_{ac}, r, E_{au} \rangle$ **abstracts** $\langle E_c, r, E_u \rangle$ exactly when E_{ac} abstracts E_c and E_{au} abstracts E_u. The inverse of abstraction is as before called **specialization**. This notion of abstraction is used to eliminate redundancy in the implementation of the component/use assumptions. For example, $\langle MakeNoodles, s_1, MakePastaDish \rangle$ abstracts $\langle MakeSpaghetti, s_1, MakeSpaghettiMarinara \rangle$. Therefore, once the algorithm has considered the possibility that an event of type *MakeSpaghetti* is a component of an event of *MakeSpaghettiMarinara*, it would be redundant to consider the possibility that the more abstract description of the premise *MakeNoodles* is a component of an event of type *MakePastaDish*.

Uses contains the inverse of the direct component relation, together with certain other "implicit" uses. Consider the modified cooking hierarchy in figure 9. This new hierarchy introduces the type *MakeNoodlesPrimavera*, which has no direct component filling the s_1 role, and which, therefore, inherits the component *MakeNoodles* from *MakePastaDish*. Suppose the observation is of type *MakeSpaghetti*. It would be wrong to conclude

$$\exists x \, . \, MakeSpaghettiMarinara(x),$$

because the observation could have been a step of *MakeNoodlesPrimavera*. The conclusion

$$\exists x \,.\, MakeSpaghettiMarinara(x) \lor MakePastaDish(x)$$

is sound but too weak; the check for redundancy would notice that the type of the second disjunct abstracts the first. The correct conclusion is

$$\exists x \,.\, MakeSpaghettiMarinara(x) \lor MakeNoodlesPrimavera(x).$$

Therefore, the set Uses should contain the implicit use $\langle MakeSpaghetti, s_1, MakeNoodlesPrimavera \rangle$ as well as $\langle MakeSpaghetti, s_1, MakeSpaghetti-Marinara \rangle$.

Define **Explicit** as the set of explicit uses corresponding to the direct-component relation. Then Uses is the union of Explicit together with the following set:

$\{ \langle E_c, r, E_i \rangle \mid$
    (1) There is an E_u such that $\langle E_c, r, E_u \rangle \in$ Explicit and
    (2) There is an $\langle E_{ac}, r, E_{au} \rangle \in$ Explicit that abstracts $\langle E_c, r, E_u \rangle$ and
    (3) E_{au} abstracts E_i and
    (4) There is no E_j that either specializes, abstracts, or is equal to E_i such that there is an $\langle E_d, r, E_j \rangle \in$ Explicit that specializes $\langle E_{ac}, r, E_{au} \rangle$ and
    (5) There is no E_{ai} that abstracts E_i for which conditions (3) and (4) hold (with E_{ai} in place of E_i). $\}$.

In this construction, E_i is a type such as *MakeNoodlesPrimavera* that inherits a role without further specializing it. Condition (5) prevents redundant uses (that simply specialize this new use) from being added (e.g., if there were a type *MakeSpicyNoodlesPrimavera*).

2.5.4   Constraint Checking

The algorithms check the various constraints that appear in the decomposition axioms by failing to prove that the constraint is false. As a side effect of constraint checking, the values of noncomponent parameters are propagated to a node from its components. (The algorithms presented here do not propagate values *from* a node *to* its components.) There are three different kinds of constraints.

An **equality constraint** equates two roles of a node or its components whose values are neither events nor times. An equality constraint fails if the values of the two items are distinct proper names. As a side effect, when a value for a parameter of a component is known, but it is not known for an equal parameter of the node, the value is assigned to the parameter of the node.

Temporal constraints take the form of binary predicates over the time parameters of a node or its components. As noted above, rather than passing around precise values for time parameters, the implementation passes fuzzy

relation	i	j	k	l
equals	$max(a,e)$	$min(b,f)$	$max(c,g)$	$min(d,f)$
before	a	$min(b,f)$	c	$min(d,f)$
after	$max(a,g)$	b	$max(c,g)$	d
meets	a	$min(b,f)$	$max(c,e)$	$min(d,f)$
met by	$max(a,g)$	$min(b,h)$	$max(c,g)$	d
overlaps	a	$min(b,f)$	$max(c,e)$	$min(d,h)$
overlapped by	$max(a,e)$	$min(b,h)$	$max(c,g)$	d
starts	$max(a,e)$	$min(b,f)$	$max(c,e)$	$min(d,h)$
started by	$max(a,e)$	$min(b,f)$	$max(c,g)$	d
during	$max(a,e)$	$min(b,h)$	$max(c,e)$	$min(d,h)$
contains	a	$min(b,f)$	$max(c,g)$	d
finishes	$max(a,e)$	$min(b,h)$	$max(c,g)$	$min(d,h)$
finished by	a	$min(b,f)$	$max(c,g)$	$min(d,h)$

Figure 10: The thirteen temporal relations

temporal bounds. It is straightforward to check if any particular temporal relation could hold between two times that have been assigned temporal bounds. For example, if $time(N)$ is bounded by $\langle 1\ 3\ 7\ 9 \rangle$, and $time(step1(N))$ is bounded by $\langle 4\ 5\ 6\ 7 \rangle$, it is clearly impossible for the relation $started\text{-}by(time(N),\ time(step1(N)))$ to hold. Furthermore, it is easy to generate a set of rules that can tighten the fuzzy bounds on an interval given its relation to another interval and the fuzzy bounds on that interval. One such rule is

If T_1 is bounded by $\langle a\ b\ c\ d \rangle$ and T_2 is bounded by $\langle e\ f\ g\ h \rangle$
and started-by(T_1, T_2) then
T_1 is bounded by $\langle max(a,e)\ min(b,f)\ max(c,g)\ d \rangle$.

The implementation uses such rules to update the fuzzy bounds assigned to the temporal parameters of a node during constraint checking. The table in figure 10 describes the rules for the thirteen basic temporal relations, where $\langle a\ b\ c\ d \rangle$ is the original bound on T_1, $\langle e\ f\ g\ h \rangle$ is the bound on T_2, and $\langle i\ j\ k\ l \rangle$ is the updated bound on T_1. All unknown times are implicitly bounded by $\langle -\infty\ +\infty\ -\infty\ +\infty \rangle$.

When the "matching" algorithm below equates two event tokens, the "intersection" of the fuzzy time bounds is taken. An advantage of this approach over a purely symbolic implementation of Allen's temporal algebra is that the system does not need to maintain a table relating every interval to every other interval (as in Allen [1983b]). A single data structure—the e-graph—maintains both temporal and nontemporal information. The use of fuzzy time bounds precludes the expression of certain kinds of relationships between specific event instances. For example, it is not possible to record an observation that the times of two event instances are disjoint, without saying that one is before or after the other. (It is possible, of course, to include a constraint that two times are disjoint in the decomposition axioms for an event *type*.) In many domains, however, it is reasonable to assume that specific observations can be "timestamped", and it seems important to provide some mechanism for metric information, even if symbolic information is not handled in full generality.

Fact constraints include the preconditions and effects of the event along with type information about the event's noncomponent parameters. Facts are checked only if values are known for all the arguments of the predicates in the constraint. The constraint is satisfied if a limited theorem prover fails to prove the negation of the constraint from a global database of known facts. A limitation of the implementation described here is that the global database is not augmented by the conclusions of the plan recognizer itself. A worthwhile extension of the system would make it assert in the global database the preconditions and effects of any unambiguously recognized plans. This would be useful for the kind of predictive reasoning discussed in chapter 1. A difficult problem we have avoided dealing with is recognizing that a fact constraint is violated because it is inconsistent with all the possible disjunctions encoded in the e-graph.

2.5.5   Algorithms

The algorithm **explain-observation** implements the component/use assumptions, and the algorithms **match-graphs** and **group-observations** implement the minimum cardinality assumptions. The code for each algorithm is followed by commentary on its operation.

Explain-observation

```
/* explain-observation
        Ec : type of observed event
        parameters : list of role/value pairs that describe the
        observation
returns
        G : explanation graph
*/
function explain-observation(Ec, parameters) is
        Let G be a new empty graph
        G := explain(Ec, parameters, ∅, {Up, Down})
        return G
end build-explanation-graph
```

/* explain
  Ec : type of event to be explained
  parameters : list of ⟨role value⟩ pairs that describe the event
  visited : set of event types visited so far in moving through
  abstraction hierarchy
  direction : direction to move in abstraction hierarchy; subset of
    {Up, Down}
returns
  N : node that represents the event of type Ec
  newVisited: updated value of visited
*/
function explain(Ec, parameters, visited, direction)**is**
    visited := visited ∪ {Ec}
    if G has a node N of type Ec with matching parameters **then**
        return ⟨N, visited⟩
    Add a new node N of type Ec to G
    Add the parameters of N to G
    if Ec=End **then return** ⟨N, visited⟩
    Propagate constraints for N
    if constraints violated **then return** ⟨N, visited⟩
    for all ⟨Ec, r, Eu⟩ ∈ Uses **do**
        if ⟨Ec, r, Eu⟩ does not abstract or specialize a use
            for any member of visited **then**
                explain(Eu, {⟨r,N⟩}, ∅, {Up, Down})
    if Down ∈ direction **then**
        for all Esc ∈ direct-specializations(Ec)
            ⟨M, visited⟩ := explain(Esc, parameters, visited,
            {Down})
    if Up ∈ direction **then {**
        Eac := direct-abstraction(Ec)
        p := the role/value pairs for N restricted to those roles
        defined
            for Eac or higher in the abstraction hierarchy
            ⟨M, visited⟩ := explain(Eac, p, visited, {Up})
        Add ⟨M, =, N⟩ to G **}**
    return ⟨N, visited⟩
end explain

The function **explain-observation** builds an e-graph on the basis of a single observation. For example, for the observation that Joe is making marinara sauce starting between times 4 and 5 and ending between times 6 and 7, the function call would be

explain-observation(MakeMarinara, {⟨agent Joe⟩, ⟨time ⟨4 5 6 7⟩ ⟩}).

Explain-observation calls the subroutine **explain** which operates as follows:

- Check whether the graph under construction already contains a node of the given type that exactly matches the given parameters. If this is the case, then the graph merges at this point, rather than getting wider and wider as one moves upward. Consider the e-graph shown in figure 8 (section 2.5.2). Suppose the left-hand side of the graph has been constructed (nodes *N1, N2, N4, N6,* and *N7*). Search is proceeding along the right-hand part of the graph, through *N3*. The invocation of **explain** that created *MakeMeatDish(N5)* is considering abstractions of *MakeMeatDish* (see below), and recursively calls **explain** with type *PrepareMeal*. The specific call would be

    explain(PrepareMeal, {...}, {MakeMeatDish}, {Up}).

    This description exactly matches previously created node *N6*, which is returned. Then *N5* is made an alternative for *N6* (in the third to last line of the procedure). Thus, the left path through *N2* and *N4* merges with the right path through *N3* and *N5*. This kind of merging can prevent combinatorial growth in the size of the graph.

- Create a new node of type **Ec**, and link all the **parameters** to it.

- Check whether the type of the newly created node is *End*, and if so, return.

- Propagate and check constraints. Suppose this is the invocation of **explain** that created *MakeSpaghettiMarinara(N2)*. **Parameters** is {⟨*step2 N1*⟩}, meaning that component *step2* of *N2* is *N1*. The equality constraints inherited from *MakePastaDish* state that the agent of any *MakeSpaghettiMarinara* must equal the agent of its *MakeMarinara* step. If initially ⟨*N1 agent Joe*⟩ appears in the graph, then ⟨*N2 agent Joe*⟩ also appears after this step. Fuzzy time bounds are also propagated. *N2* is constrained to occur over an interval that contains the time of *N1*. Suppose the graph initially contains ⟨*N1 time ⟨4 5 6 7⟩*⟩. After this step, it also contains ⟨*N2 time ⟨−∞ 5 6 +∞⟩*⟩. This step can also eliminate nodes. The agent of every specialization of MakePastaDish is constrained to be dexterous. If the general world knowledge base contains the assertion *~Dexterous(Joe)*, **explain** does not continue to build a path to *End* from this node.

- Consider Uses of **Ec**, as described above. If **Ec** is *MakeMarinara*, then **explain** is recursively invoked for *MakeSpaghettiMarinara* and *MakeChickenMarinara*.

- Explain **Ec** by considering its specializations. This step is not performed if **Ec** was reached by abstracting some other type. Suppose **explain** were initially invoked with **Ec** equal to *MakeSauce*. Then the specialization *MakeMarinara* is considered. In the recursive invocation of **explain**, the Uses of *MakeMarinara* are examined. The use ⟨*MakeMarinara, step2, MakeSpaghettiMarinara*⟩ is eliminated (by the test in the **if** statement within the first **for all** statement in the procedure) because it specializes ⟨*MakeSauce, step2, MakePastaDish*⟩. The use ⟨*MakeMarinara, step5, MakeChickenMarinara*⟩, however, *does* lead to a path to *End*.

- Explain **Ec** by considering its abstractions. This step is not performed if **Ec** was reached by specializing some other type. The node becomes an alternative for its abstractions. Suppose the current invocation has created *MakePastaDish(N4)*. This step calls

  explain(PrepareMeal, {⟨agent Joe⟩ ⟨time ⟨−∞ 5 6 +∞⟩⟩},
            {MakePastaDish}, {Up})

  which returns *N6*.

Not all abstractions lead to *End*; some are pruned and do not appear in the final graph. Consider the invocation that created *MakeMarinara(N1)*. It calls **explain** for *MakeSauce*. The only Use for *MakeSauce*, however, is ⟨*MakeSauce, step2, MakePastaDish*⟩, but that use is eliminated by the redundancy test. Therefore, no node of type *MakeSauce* appears in the final graph.

The worst-case complexity of **explain** is exponential in the size of the event hierarchy because an event can have several different components of the same type. In practice, the first step in **explain** frequently finds a similar node and cuts off search. For example, suppose that the event hierarchy contains no noncomponent roles, and if a type has components, only its abstractions (but not itself or its specializations) appear as components of another type. Under this restriction, the worst-case complexity of **explain** is $O(|H_E|)$. If the algorithm did not merge search paths at abstraction points, its worst-case complexity would still be exponential.

Match-graphs

```
/* match-graphs
       G1, G2 : graphs to be matched
returns
       G3 : result of equating End nodes of G1 and G2 or FAIL if no
       match possible    */
```

function match-graphs(G1, G2) **is**
   Create a new empty graph G3
   Initialize Cache, a hash-table that saves results of matching
   event nodes
   if match(End-node-of(G1), End-node-of(G2))=FAIL
     then return FAIL
     else return G3
end match-graphs
/* match
   n1 , n2 : nodes to be matched from G1 and G2 respectively
returns
   n3 : node in G3 representing match or FAIL if no match
*/
function match(n1, n2) **is**
   if n1 and n2 are proper names **then**
     if n1=n2 **then return** n1 **else return** FAIL
   else if n1 and n2 are fuzzy temporal bounds **then** {
     $\langle$a b c d$\rangle$:= n1
     $\langle$e f g h$\rangle$:= n2
     $\langle$i j k l$\rangle$:= $\langle$max(a,e) min(b,f) max(c,g) min(d,h)$\rangle$
     if i > j **or** k > l **or** i > l **then return** FAIL **else return** $\langle$i j k
     l$\rangle$ }
   else if n1 and n2 are event nodes **then** {
     if Cache(n1,n2) is defined **then return** Cache(n1,n2)
     if type(n1) abstracts= type(n2) **then** n3Type := type(n2)
     else if type(n2) abstracts type(n1) **then** n3Type :=
     type(n1)
     else {Cache(n1,n2) := FAIL
       return FAIL }
     Add a new node n3 of n3Type to G3
     Cache(n1,n2) := n3
     for all roles r defined for n3Type or higher **do** {
       Let V1 be the value such that $\langle$n1,r,V1$\rangle \in$ G1 (or
         undefined)
       Let V2 be the value such that $\langle$n2,r,V2$\rangle \in$ G2 (or
         undefined)
       if either V1 or V2 is defined **then** {
         if V1 is defined but not V2 **then**

```
                    V3 := match(V1,V1)
           elseif V2 is defined but not V1 then
                    V3 :=match(V2,V2)
           else V3 := match(V1,V2)
             if V3=FAIL then {         Cache(n1,n2) := FAIL
                                return FAIL }
             Add ⟨n3, r, V3⟩ to G3 } }
      Propagate constraints for n3
      if constraints violated then { Cache(n1,n2) := FAIL
                                       return FAIL }
      alts1 := { A1 | ⟨n1, =, A1⟩∈ G1 }
      alts2 := { A2 | ⟨n2, =, A2⟩∈ G2 }
      if alts1 ∪ alts2 ≠ ∅ then {
        if alts1=∅ then alts1 := {n1}
        if alts2=∅ then alts2 := {n2}
        noneMatched := TRUE
        for all a1 ∈ alts1 do
          for all a2 ∈ alts2 do {
            A3 := match(A1, A2)
            if A3 ≠ FAIL then {
              Add ⟨n3, =, A3⟩ to G3
              noneMatched := FALSE } }
          if noneMatched then { Cache(n1,n2):=FAIL
                                return FAIL } }
        return n3 }
      else return FAIL
end match
```

The function **match-graphs** creates a new e-graph that is the result of equating the *End* nodes of the two e-graphs it takes as inputs and propagating that equality. Figure 11 shows two e-graphs: the first is built from an observation of *MakeMarinara*, and the second from an observation of *MakeNoodles*. **Match** is initially invoked on the *End* nodes of the two graphs **match**(*N7*, *N11*) and returns *N12*, which is the *End* node of the combined graph. The following example steps through the operation of **Match**.

- If the objects to be matched are proper names, they must be identical.

- If the objects are fuzzy temporal bounds, then take their intersection. If **n1** is $⟨-\infty \ 5 \ 6 \ +\infty⟩$ and **n2** is $⟨-\infty \ 8 \ 7 \ +\infty⟩$, then **match** returns $⟨-\infty \ 5 \ 7 \ +\infty⟩$.

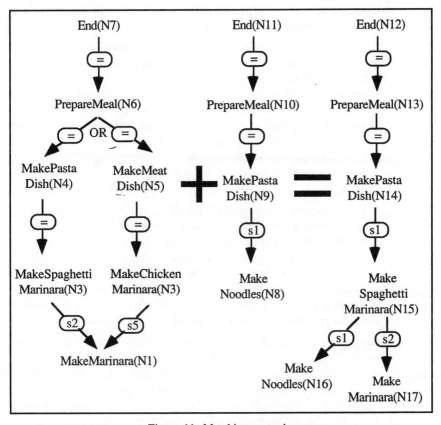

Figure 11: Matching e-graphs

- Check whether **n1** and **n2** have already been matched, and if so, reuse that value. Suppose that the first e-graph in figure 11 were matched against an e-graph of identical shape; for example, there were two observations of *MakeMarinara* that *may* have been identical. During the match down the left-hand side of the graphs through *N4* and *N2*, *MakeMarinara(N1)* would match against the *MakeMarinara* node in the second graph (say, *N1'*), resulting in some final node, for instance, *N1"*. Then the right-hand side of the graphs would match through *N5* and *N3*. *N1* would match against *N1'* a second time, and the value *N1"* would be used again. This would retain the shape of the digraph and prevent it from being multiplied out into a tree.

- Add a new node **n3** to the graph to represent the result of the match, which is of the most specific type of **n1** and **n2**. Matching *MakeSpaghettiMarinara(N2)* against *MakePastaDish(N9)* results in *MakeSpaghettiMarinara(N15)*. The match fails if the types are not compatible. Thus, *MakeMeatDish(N5)* fails to match against *MakePastaDish(N9)*.

- Match the roles of **n1** and **n2**. If a parameter is defined for one node but not the other, match the role against itself in order to simply copy the structure into the resulting graph. This is what happens when *N2* matches *N9*, yielding *N15*. The new node gets both the *step2* parameter from *N2* (a copy of *N1*, which is *N17*) and the *step1* parameter from *N9* (a copy of *N8*, which is *N16*). If *N2* had the role *step1* defined, that value would have had to match against *N8*.

- Check and propagate the constraints on **n3**. New constraint violations may be detected at this point because more of the roles of the nodes are filled in.

- Try matching every alternative for **n1** against every alternative for **n2**. The successful matches are alternatives for **n3**. If one of the nodes has some alternatives, but the other does not, then match the alternatives for the former against the latter directly. This occurs in figure 11. *MakePastaDish(N4)* matches against *MakePastaDish(N9)*. *N4* has the alternative *N2*, but *N9* has none. Therefore, *MakeSpaghetti-Marinara(N2)* matches against *MakePastaDish(N9)* as well. If there were some alternatives but all matches failed, then **n3** fails as well.

Calling **match-graphs(G_1,G_2)** frequently returns a graph that is smaller than either G_1 or G_2. Unfortunately, sometimes the resulting graph can be larger. This occurs when two nodes are matched that have several alternatives, all of which are mutually compatible. Therefore, the worst-case complexity of **match-graphs(G_1,G_2)** is $O(|G_1|*|G_2|)$. The key feature of **match-graphs** is the use of a cache to store matches between nodes. Without this feature, **match-graphs** would always multiply the input digraphs into a tree, and the algorithm would be no better than $O(2^{|G_1|*|G_2|})$.

Group-observations

global Hypoths
/* *A set (disjunction) of hypotheses, each a set (conjunction) of explanation graphs. Each hypothesis corresponds to one way of grouping the observations. Different hypotheses may have different cardinalities.* */
function minimum-Hypoths **is**
    smallest := min { |H| | H ∈ Hypoths}
    return { H | H ∈ Hypoths ∧ card(H)=smallest }
end minimum-Hypoths

```
procedure group-observations is
    Hypoths := {∅}
    while more observations do {
        Observe event of type Ec with specified parameters
        Gobs := explain-observation(Ec, parameters)
        for all H ∈ Hypoths do {
            remove H from Hypoths
            Add H ∪ {Gobs} to Hypoths
            for all G ∈ H do {
                Gnew := match-graphs(Gobs, G)
                if Gnew ≠ FAIL then
                    Add (H − {G}) ∪ Gnew to Hypoths } } }
end group-observations
```

The function **group-observations** continually inputs observations and groups them into sets to be accounted for by particular e-graphs. The function **minimum-Hypoths** is called to retrieve a disjunctive set of current hypotheses, each of which is a conjunctive set of e-graphs that accounts for all of the observations, using as few End events as possible. It works as follows:

- Input an observation and generate a new e-graph **Gobs**.

- *Conjoin* **Gobs** with each hypothesis. This handles the case where **Gobs** is *unrelated* to the previous observations. Note that this case is included in **Hypoths** even when **Gobs** matches one of the previous e-graphs. This is necessary because a later observation may be able to match **Gobs** alone, but *not* be able to match **Gobs** combined with that previous e-graph. In any case, the function **minimum-Hypoths** will select those members of **Hypoths** which are of minimum cardinality, so hypotheses containing an "extra" unmatched **Gobs** will be effectively invisible to user until needed.

- Try to match **Gobs** with each e-graph in each hypothesis. This handles the case where **obs-graph** is *related* to a previous observation.

- The current conclusion corresponds to the *disjunction* of all hypotheses of minimum size.

Sometimes a member of **Hypoths** may contain an undetected inconsistency. In this case, the answer returned by **minimum-Hypoths** may be incorrect: for example, it may return an inconsistent e-graph which groups all the observations as part of a single End event rather than as part of two or more distinct End events. However, if this inconsistency is detected when later observations are being incorporated, the system can usually recover. In the inner loop of the algorithm **group-observations**, the new e-graph **Gobs** will fail to match against every member of the inconsistent hypothesis **H**. Although **Hypoths** is updated to contain **H** ∪ {**Gobs**}, if any matches against other hypotheses containing the same or fewer number of e-graphs *do* succeed, **H** ∪ {**Gobs**} will not be returned by **minimum-Hypoths**. Furthermore, it would not be difficult to modify **group-observations** to explicitly eliminate **H** ∪ {**Gobs**} from **Hypoths** in this special case.

Some of the most intimidating complexity results arise from this algorithm. In the worst case, there could be $O(2^n)$ consistent ways of grouping n observations, and **Hypoths** could contain that number of hypotheses. In practice, it appears that stronger assumptions than simply minimizing the number of End events are needed. One such stronger assumption would be that the current observation is part of the End event whose previous steps were most recently observed—or if that is inconsistent, then the next more recent End event, and so on. This assumption limits **Hypoths** to size O(n). All previous plan recognition systems implement some version of this stronger assumption.

2.6 Conclusions and Caveats

Chapter 2 has developed a framework for plan recognition that includes a proof theory, a model theory, and a set of algorithms. It would not be an exaggeration to say that the most difficult task was to define the rather amorphous problem of "plan recognition" at the most abstract level. Similar algorithms for plan recognition problems have been hashed over for years, since the early work of Schmidt and Genesereth. The formal theory we have developed suggests what some of these algorithms are algorithms *for*.

The theory is extremely general. It does not assume that there is a single plan underway that can be uniquely identified from the first input, or that the sequence of observations is complete, or that all the steps in a plan are linearly ordered. We know of no other implemented plan recognition system that handles arbitrary temporal relations between steps. On the other hand, there are some limitations inherent in our representation of plans. In particular, the current framework does not explicitly represent propositional attitudes, such as goals or beliefs. The use of quantification and disjunction in the event hierarchy is restricted, although some of these limitations can be easily circumvented. For example, existential quantifiers cannot appear in the axioms which make up the event hierarchy, but in most cases, it should be possible to use function symbols instead. Disjunctions cannot appear in the body (the right-hand side) of a decomposition axiom. One way around this limitation is to create a new event event type to stand for the disjunctive formula, and then assert that each disjunct is a different specialization of the new type.

Another expressive limitation of the theory revolves around the whole idea of End events. We have used End events as a way to determine when "nothing more" needs to be explained. But, in general, it may prove difficult to define a set of End events (perhaps "stay alive" is the only one). Context must ultimately play a role in determine the scope of explanation.

It is important to note that the input to the algorithms presented here is still more expressively limited. For example, the algorithms do not handle theories in which an event type can have more than one direct abstraction (i.e., multiple inheritance), and they do not explicitly handle "general axioms" which lie outside the event hierarchy. (The actual LISP implementation included some special purpose inference procedures, such as those used to infer that certain pairs of predicates could not hold true of the same time period.)

The theory is limited in its ability to recognize erroneous plans. We have assumed that all plans are internally consistent and that all acts are purposeful. Yet real people frequently make planning errors and change their minds in midcourse. Some simple kinds of errors can be handled by introducing an End event called *Error*. For each observable action, there is a specialization of *Error* that contains that action as its only component. Therefore, every observation can be recognized as being part of some meaningful plan or simply an error.

Another serious limitation of the theory is the inability to recognize new plans whose types do not already appear in the recognizer's knowledge base. One might argue that plan recognition essentially deals with the recognition of stereotypical behavior, and the understanding of new plans is better treated as an advanced kind of learning.

In some domains, the theory described in this chapter is simply too weak. Rather than inferring the disjunction of all the plans that could explain the observations, the recognizer may need to know the most likely such plan. Nothing in this theory contradicts the laws of probability, probability, and plan recognitionand it should be possible to extend the theory with quantitative measures.

A more philosophical problem is the whole issue of what serves as primitive input to the recognition system. Throughout chapter 2, we have assumed that arbitrary high-level descriptions of events are simply presented to the recognizer. This assumption is reasonable in many domains, such as understanding written stories or observing the words typed by a computer operator at a terminal. But a real plan recognizer—a person—does not always get his or her input in this way. How are visual impressions of simple bodily motions—John is moving his hands in such and such a manner—translated into the impression that John is rolling out dough to make pasta? There is a great deal of work in low-level perception and a great deal in high-level recognition. The semantic gap between the output of the low-level processes and the high-level inference engines remains wide, and few have ventured to cross it.

Chapter 3
Planning With Simultaneous Actions and External Events

Richard N. Pelavin

3.1   Introduction

Planning refers to synthesis: from a description of individual actions, one reasons about the various compositions of these actions (i.e., plans). Thus, central to a formalization for planning is a notion of action and action composition. The original and still most prevalent treatment of action in the planning literature is the state-change model [McCarthy and Hayes 1969], where an action is modeled as a function that transforms one state into another, and actions are composed sequentially. This treatment of action provides a simple and natural basis for the state-based planning paradigm; in this framework, a planning problem is given by a description of an **initial state**, a set of actions, and goal conditions to achieve. The planner then searches for a sequence of actions that transforms the initial state into a state where the goal conditions hold.

The state-based framework, however, is limited because it does not treat plans with concurrent actions or plans that are executed in dynamic environments, environments where events not controlled by the planning agent(s) may be occurring. These **external events** may be caused by natural forces as well as agents other than the ones for which we are creating plans. These limitations of the state-based planning paradigm can be traced to the limitations of its underlying model of action; the state-change model does not directly support concurrent action composition or treat external events that may occur during plan execution. Consequently, the few extensions to the state-based framework, such as SIPE [Wilkins 1988], which treats concurrent actions, and DEVISER [Vere 1981], which treats external events, have no formal basis and are difficult to extend in any general way, as discussed in chapter 1.

This chapter develops a formal basis for planning with concurrent actions and external events by developing an appropriate model of action. This model provides a basis for planners handling concurrent actions and external events much in the same way that the state-change model of action provides a basis for state-based planners.

3.1.1   Key Considerations

Chapter 1 of this book motivated the need for an explicit temporal representation to address the limitations of the state-change model. The temporal model developed there serves as the starting point in this chapter. We extend this temporal model, focusing on considerations such as

1)   modeling concurrent interactions,

2)   modeling interactions between the agent and the external world, and

3)   planning with an incomplete world description.

Modeling Concurrent Interactions

Whether two or more actions can be executed concurrently, and what their joint effects would be, depends on how they interact. There are a variety of concurrent interactions that we wish to model. **Interference** refers to interactions where two or more actions can be executed separately, but not together. Interference may result from a resource conflict. For example, there may be a single burner on a stove, and two pans to be heated. Either pan can be heated at one time, but not both together under any circumstances. This is an example of **necessary interference**. We must also model **conditional interference**, the case where concurrent actions interfere only under certain conditions. A typical example of this interaction is where two or more actions share the same type of resource, such as a power supply or a pool of money, and consequently interfere if there is not enough of this resource available.

Another way that concurrent actions interact is by having joint effects. For independent actions, joint effects are simply the conjunction of the individual action's effects. We also wish to model cases where the joint effect differs from the conjunction. We refer to this interaction as **simultaneous effects**. Consider an example where an object is lifted by applying pressure to both its ends and then lifting upwards. If pressure were only applied to one of the ends, a pushing event would arise, rather than a lifting event. Thus, the effect of applying pressure at both ends is a lifting event, not two pushing events.

There are also more subtle forms of simultaneous effects. For example, consider a scenario where there are two cups of water which can be poured individually or simultaneously into an empty bucket. This situation might be described by stating that the effect of pouring a single cup of water into an empty bucket is that the bucket will have one cup of water upon completion. If the cups are poured simultaneously, then their joint effect is that two cups of water will be in the bucket upon completion. This joint effect is a simultaneous effect since it differs from the conjunction of the individual effects. This is because "one cup is in the bucket" conjoined with "one cup is in the bucket" is logically equivalent to "one cup is in the bucket", not "two cups are in the bucket".

Interactions Between the Agent and the External World

Capturing the interaction between the planning agent's actions and external events is another important consideration. There are a variety of interactions that we wish to model. For example, there are external events that the agent cannot influence, such as events relating to weather conditions. These type of external events must be distinguished from ones that the agent can affect—events that can be prevented or enabled by the agent's actions. For example, the agent may be able to prevent someone from walking in the room by locking the door. Conversely, the agent may be able to perform an action to enable some desirable occurrence, such as placing an assembly on a conveyor belt which causes the assembly to move to the next work cell. Enablement and prevention can also go the other way: external events can enable or prevent the agent's actions. For example, the wind must be blowing in order for the agent to sail across the lake.

Planning With a Partial World Description

When forming a plan to be executed in a dynamic environment, one typically has only a limited view of the external world in the which the plan will be executed. Such a partial description may not indicate the values of all conditions in the world or just constrain the possible values. If information is missing at planning time, there are a number of courses that may be taken. For example, one may construct a plan with conditional actions [Warren 1976; Schoppers 1989], that is, steps whose behaviors are functions of the environment, or one may suspend planning until the relevant information is gathered.

An objective of this work is to develop a notion of planner correctness that is appropriate when only a partial world description is given. We want to develop a conservative notion of correctness that holds when a planner reserves judgement, rather than one that jumps to conclusions when relevant information is missing. As we will see, complications arise from the pervasive use of non-monotonic inference in planning systems to handle such things as the frame problem and concurrent action interactions.

3.1.2   Overview

Our starting point is the temporal logic developed in chapter 1 of this book, namely, the Interval Logic temporal model. Section 3.2 examines why this temporal model must be extended to address the considerations described above. It also considers why other logics in the AI literature that treat time and/or simultaneous events (e.g., McDermott [1982], Lansky [1985], Haas [1985], Georgeff [1986], and Shoham [1989]) are not adequate for our purposes.

Section 3.3 presents a semantic model for a logic that supports planning with concurrent actions and external events. This model of action extends the Interval Logic model with a structure analogous to the *result function* found in the state-change model of action. This allows us to exploit the complementary strengths of these two types of models. While Interval Logic can represent concurrent actions and external events, it does not adequately capture how an action affects the world or how actions interact and can be composed together. The state-change model is the opposite: its strengths are that it captures the conditions that an action affects and does not affect, and it provides a simple basis for (sequential) action composition.

In our model, **action instances** and **world-histories** take the place of actions and states. An action instance refers to an action at a specified time and is used to construct **plan instances**, our analog to plans. A world-history refers to a complete world over time, rather than an instantaneous snapshot, and serves as the context in which the execution of an action instance is specified. This enables us to model the interaction between action instances and external events that occur simultaneously.

Section 3.4 presents the language and defines its interpretation in terms of the model developed in section 3.3.

Section 3.5 begins by defining what it means for a planner to produce correct plans. This definition is in terms of semantic entailment. Such a definition of correctness allows us to examine planning using partial world descriptions without conflating the issue with nonmonotonic inference. Section 3.5 also illustrates how a planning problem is expressed in this new formalism and how the properties of a plan instance are computed from descriptions of its constituent parts. It examines the frame problem and illustrates the problems caused when standard approaches are used, such as the *STRIPS assumption* [Waldinger 1977] and its analog, the *persistence assumption* [McDermott 1982]. We show that our model provides a different conception of the frame problem for formalisms with concurrent actions and external events. As an alternative to using a STRIPS or persistence assumption, we present a simple approach based on plan instances that maintain properties.

Section 3.6 presents a simple algorithm for planning with concurrent actions and external events, which has been shown to meet our criteria for correctness [Pelavin 1988]. This algorithm can be viewed as an adaptation of the algorithm presented in chapter 1, modified so that it can be applied with partial world descriptions and can treat a wide variety of concurrent interactions. Our algorithm is novel in its use of **noninterference conditions**, which are conditions under which a pair of concurrent plan instances do not interfere, and the use of maintenance plan instances. All harmful interactions, both sequential and concurrent, are detected through concurrent conflicts.

Section 3.7 presents a summary and discusses issues outside the scope of the deductive planning problem.

3.2   Representations That Treat Simultaneous Events

In response to the deficiencies of the state-change model, a number of logics in the artificial intelligence literature have been developed, such as Allen [1984; see also chapter 1], McDermott [1982], Lansky [1985], Haas [1985], Shoham [1989], and Georgeff [1986]. All these representations can model simultaneous events in some fashion. However, we will see in this section that each of these logics lacks features that we seek in a model of planning. We start by examining Interval Logic, which serves as a basis for our extensions.

3.2.1   Interval Logic

In chapter 1, Interval Logic is cast as a sorted first-order theory having one sort to denote temporal intervals and another to refer to all other objects. To describe what is happening over time, predicates are used that refer to both properties that hold over intervals and events that occur over intervals. Interval Logic can represent simultaneous events by stating that they occur over intervals that overlap in time. It can capture simple concurrent interactions, such as a law stating that two events of the same type cannot occur simultaneously, or that two simultaneous events may have effects that are in addition to the conjunction of their individual effects.

Chapter 1 also presented a planning algorithm based on Interval Logic, which we will refer to by **ILP**, for Interval Logic Planner. By examining its limitations, we show where Interval Logic is deficient as a model for planning. By analyzing these limitations, we provide a glimpse of our model, which is presented in detail in section 3.3.

The Interval Logic Planner (ILP)

A planning problem is given by a world description, action specifications, and a goal. The world description in ILP is given by a set of Interval Logic statements describing external events, properties, causal laws, and definitions that hold in the world. Using Interval Logic one can describe conditions that hold in the future as well as conditions that hold during or prior to planning time. Interval Logic is a linear time model, that is, a model that can describe what is actually true, what was true, or what will be true, but not what is possibly true. In ILP one assumes that any future condition mentioned in the world description holds regardless of what the agent does; that is, it inevitably holds. Consequently, this formalization does not allow us to represent future conditions that may possibly hold, such as ones that may be prevented or enabled by the planning agent's actions.

The goal conditions in ILP are given by Interval Logic statements. This allows one to treat goals that refer to conditions that may hold during plan execution as well as at the completion of plan execution. One can also describe goals that refer to avoiding some condition while performing some task and achieving a number of conditions in a specified order.

The action specifications are modeled after the STRIPS approach, where actions are described by preconditions and effects. To distinguish between preconditions and effects, ILP uses the concept of **action attempts**; one asserts that if an action is attempted and its preconditions hold, then its effects will hold. By describing preconditions and effects using Interval Logic, one can treat preconditions that hold during execution (as well as prior to execution) and effects that hold during execution (as well as after execution). For example, to capture that the precondition for sailing is that the wind is blowing while the sailing takes place, and the effect of sailing is that the boat is moving, one would assert

$$Try(sail(i)) \land In(i,i2) \land WindBlowing(i2) \supset BoatMoving(i).$$

A plan in ILP is taken to be a set of assumptions about the future. Each assumption is either

    1)   a statement about an attempt of an action over some interval,

2)   a statement about a property that persists over some interval, or

3)   a statement constraining the temporal relationship between action attempts and persistences.

To investigate the effects of a plan, ILP reasons about conditional statements having the form

$$assum_1 \wedge assum_2 \wedge ... \wedge assum_n \supset G,$$

where each $assum_i$ refers to an assumption about the future. However, with this scheme there is a complication: a conclusion reached using a material implication is meaningless if the antecedent is false. ILP addresses this problem by checking if the set of assumptions is consistent with the world description and action specifications. Thus, ILP concludes that the plan $\{assum_1, assum_2, ..., assum_n\}$ achieves goal G with respect to the world description W and the action specifications AS if and only if the following two conditions hold:

COND1) $W \cup AS \vdash assum_1 \wedge assum_2 ... assum_n \supset G$, and

COND2)   the set $W \cup AS \cup \{assum_1, assum_2, ..., assum_n\}$ is consistent in Interval Logic,

where $\vdash$ denotes provability in Interval Logic.

As mentioned earlier, one limitation of ILP is that it cannot express possible future events, and thus cannot plan to prevent or enable possible future events. This problem is addressed by extending the Interval Logic to explicitly allow possibility, as do the branching time models we will discuss later in this section. The other problems arise from the fact that ILP uses logical consistency (COND2) as a test for whether a set of actions can be done together. As a result, ILP is not applicable with a partial or imprecise world description and cannot encode certain types of concurrent interactions. We now examine this issue in some detail.

Limitations of ILP and Interval Logic

When reasoning about concurrent actions, it is important to consider action interference. Recall that we say that two concurrent actions interfere if they cannot be done together even if both their preconditions hold (i.e., when they can be executed individually). As an example, consider *MoveBackward(i)*, which refers to the action where the agent moves backward during interval i, and *MoveForward(i)*, which refers to the action where the agent moves forward during interval i. The precondition for *MoveBackward(i)* is that there are no obstructions in back of the agent and the effect is that the agent moves backward. Similarly, the precondition for *MoveForward(i)* is that there are no obstructions in front of the agent, and the effect is that the agent moves forward. Now, it might be the case that the preconditions for both actions hold, but clearly an agent cannot move forward and backward at the same time, as *MoveBackward(i)* and $MoveForward(i)$ interfere. To capture this relationship in ILP, one could include the following Interval Logic statement in the world description:

~ $(MoveBackward(i)) \wedge MoveForward(i))$.

If this statement is in the world description, any plan containing both actions would not be acceptable because condition COND2 would not hold. This is the desired behavior; if two concurrent actions interfere, we want to reject any plan that contains them.

If, on the other hand, the world description is incomplete, and in particular omits the above formula and all equivalents, then a plan containing $MoveBackward(i)$ and $MoveForward(i)$ could be accepted. However, this conclusion is not necessarily the desired result. The omission of information might just signify that the agent does not know how the two actions interact. We do not want a planner to jump to the conclusion that there is no interference just when it is consistent to do so. Rather, we seek a notion of planner correctness that is conservative in the sense that if relevant information is missing, the planner reserves judgement rather than jumping to a nonmonotonic conclusion. ILP, on the other hand, can accept a plan when relevant information is missing.

The above problem is quite pervasive. ILP can jump to conclusions not only when information is omitted from the world description, but also when information is given imprecisely, as the following example demonstrates. Suppose that the agent has fifteen minutes to catch a train and to do so requires getting to the train station and purchasing a ticket. Suppose also that the agent knows that taking a bus will take between nine and sixteen minutes and purchasing a train ticket takes five minutes. With this imprecise information about temporal durations, ILP can accept a plan consisting of the assumptions:

taking the bus is attempted during interval Ib,

purchasing the ticket is attempted during interval Itp,

Ip meets Ib,

Ib meets Itp, and

Itp meets or is before Ig,

where Ip refers to the time of planning, and Ig refers to the time that the goal of catching the train must be achieved. This plan can be accepted because it is consistent to assume that its temporal relations hold given only that the duration of Ib is between nine and sixteen minutes, the duration of Itp is five minutes, and the duration of an interval that is met by Ip and meets Ig is fifteen minutes. This, however, is not the conservative behavior we are seeking; instead, we would want to accept such a plan only if it can be determined that taking the bus takes ten minutes or less to insure the train will be caught.

Now let us consider conditional interference, where actions can be executed simultaneously only under certain conditions. We want to accept a plan containing two actions that conditionally interfere only if it is derivable that the conditions needed to execute them together hold in the world description, or if an additional action is introduced into the plan to provide for their joint execution. ILP has difficulty with conditional interference even with a complete world description.

Consider reasoning about a space heater and power saw, where it is known that each machine requires one unit of power. Thus, they can be run together if the circuit can provide two units of power. We could try to capture this in ILP with the following axiom:

$Try(runHeater,i) \wedge Try(runSaw, i) \wedge CircuitProvides(2,i) \supset$
$HeaterRunning(i) \wedge SawRunning(i).$

With this statement, we can deduce that $HeaterRunning(i)$ and $SawRunning(i)$ both occur if we can deduce that there are at least two units of power available. However, problems arise when we include the following statements, which are intended to capture that *runHeater* or *runSaw* can be executed *individually* if there is at least one resource available:

$Try(runHeater,i) \wedge CircuitProvides(1,i) \supset HeaterRunning(i)$

$Try(runSaw, i) \wedge CircuitProvides(1,i) \supset SawRunning(i).$

From these two statements and the fact that at least one resource is available, ILP can accept a plan with both actions occurring simultaneously—not what we want! The reason for this is that using these axioms we can derive $HeaterRunning(i)$ and $SawRunning(i)$ from the assumptions $Try(runHeater,i)$ and $Try(runSaw,i)$ and $CircuitProvides(1,i)$. Moreover, these assumptions are not inconsistent unless it can be derived that at least two units of power are not available. For cases where the planning agent is responsible for setting the appropriate amount of power, any fact about the amount of power available would not be derivable from the world description because it would not be an inevitable fact. To fix this problem, we would need to replace these axioms with

$Try(runHeater,i) \wedge \sim Try(runSaw, i) \wedge CircuitProvides(1,i) \supset$
$HeaterRunning(i)$

$Try(runSaw, i) \wedge \sim Try(runHeater,i) \wedge CircuitProvides(1,i) \supset$
$SawRunning(i),$

which captures that if one action is attempted and the other is not, then the attempted action occurs if there is at least one resource available. Although this solution fixes our problem, it comes at a great expense: we are no longer able to describe actions *in isolation*. These last axioms are not about the individual actions, but about both actions taken together. Moreover, if there were other actions sharing the power supply, they too would have to be mentioned in the formulas above.

We seek a formalism where one can describe each action in isolation and use these descriptions to compute the properties of their compositions. The state-change model has this feature: from the description of each action's preconditions and effects, one can compute the properties of any composition (i.e., sequence). However, our task is more difficult because we are handling concurrency, and thus to describe actions in isolation, we must distinguish the effects of an action from what is happening simultaneously, but not related. Now, by appealing to the concept of interference in our previous discussions, we have been implicitly solving this problem in part. When we introduced the concept of interference we referred to the *individual* execution of an action. Specifically, we said that it might be the case that two actions can be executed individually, but not together, that is, they interfere. We also have been assuming that if two actions can be executed individually and they do not interfere, then they can be executed together. Thus, interference is the concept that links individual executions to joint execution. In the previous discussion, we have been criticizing ILP, not because it makes use of interference, but because of the way that interference is encoded.

A Glimpse at Our Solution

The above problems arise because ILP uses consistency to determine a lack of interference and more generally what an action does not affect. That is, "$A1(i)$ and $A2(i)$ do not interfere" is implicitly equated with "$A1(i) \land A2(i)$ is consistent with the world description". As we have just seen, this treatment causes problems if the world description is incomplete or imprecise or if we wish to treat conditional interference. If two actions interfere, but there is no statement in the world description capturing this relationship, then it is consistent to assume they can be attempted together, and consequently a plan containing both of them may be accepted.

To develop a framework to avoid these problems, we will extend Interval Logic to explicitly state that two actions do not interfere, rather than treating noninterference by appealing to consistency, a meta-theoretic concept. In such a logic, an axiom can be included that states that two concurrent actions can be executed together only if they do not interfere. This approach enables us to work with partial world descriptions since we conclude that two concurrent actions can be done together only if we can *deduce* that they do not interfere. Thus, if there is no information indicating whether or not two actions interfere, we make no conclusion about whether they can be executed simultaneously. Conditional interference is handled by describing the sufficient conditions under which two concurrent actions do not interfere.

3.2.2   A Model Based on Events

The GEM system [Lansky 1985, 1988] is a linear time model that treats simultaneous events. In this system, events are the basic entities; time and properties are built on top of them. A world model is equated with an evolving sequence of events, some of which may be simultaneous. A first-order language, which has constructs to specify temporal and causal relations between events, is provided to describe these models. The causal statements describe a relationship between two sequential events where the first is needed to enable the second, and a relationship between two events that need to be executed simultaneously. These causal statements play the same role that action attempts play in ILP; they capture preconditions relationships

A world description is given by GEM statements capturing the causal and temporal relationships between events that are assumed to hold. Thus, like ILP, the world description can only describe or put constraints on the events that are expected to occur; it cannot describe possible events that the planning agent may wish to prevent.

A plan, like the world description, is taken to be a set of temporal and causal constraints on a set of events. Given a goal statement and a world description, the planner must find a plan having the property that all its completions meet the constraints given in the world description and achieve the goal. Thus, in formulating what it means for a plan to solve a goal, GEM appeals to constraint satisfaction, which in this case is the same as logical consistency. As a result, the GEM system suffers from the same problems that we mentioned in ILP; namely, it is not applicable with a partial or imprecise world description.

GEM, however, provides additional structure that can capture event independence (i.e., noninterference), which is used to facilitate the process of finding whether a plan meets the world constraints. This structure allows one to partition events into a hierarchically organized set of classes. One can then specify how events in different classes affect each other, such as specifying that two classes are independent, meaning that events in the two classes do not affect each other, or by identifying the "ports" through which two classes can influence each other. As explained in Lansky [1988], this structure allows one to do "localized constraint satisfaction" because, for example, one does not have to check the relationship between events belonging to two independent classes.

While the structure that Lansky introduces can explicitly capture that two actions do not interfere, the approach does not meet all our needs. First, even with the structure for partitioning events, GEM still must appeal to consistency checking to determine whether actions in the same group can be executed together. Second, we want more flexibility in how noninterference can be described. In GEM, to capture that two events do not interfere, one must introduce event classes, specify which classes the events belong to, and specify the relationship between the event classes; one cannot simply assert "events *ev1* and *ev2* do not interfere".

3.2.3 Branching Time Models

Branching time models have been considered as alternatives to linear time models. A branching time model typically refers to a structure in which a set of instantaneous states are arranged into a tree that branches into the future. Each branch in the tree represents a different way that the future might unfold. For instance, McDermott [1982], Haas [1985] and Shoham [1989][1] have developed such models for reasoning about actions and time and have suggested they can be used for planning.

Unlike a linear time model, a branching time model can distinguish future conditions that inevitably hold from ones that only possibly hold. Thus, one can describe possible conditions that the agent may be able to prevent or enable as well as inevitable conditions, which the agent can only work with or plan around. However, the branching time structure still is not adequate as a model for planning. In particular, it does not provide an adequate basis for computing whether actions in a plan can be done together from a description of the individual actions.

In the linear time models, consistency is needed to model whether the steps in a plan can be done together. This is not the case for branching time models. One approach to modeling the statement "plan P can be done" in a branching time model is to let possibility serve the role that consistency played in ILP. That is, "plan P can be executed in state s" can be equated with "there is a branch going through s where P occurs". However, as McDermott [1986] notes, with this definition one could conclude that I can win the lottery, but there is no useful sense in which this is true (or is *feasible* in his words) because it rests on conditions out of an agent's control. To solve the above problem, McDermott introduced the notion of plan (action) attempts, as is done in ILP. An attempt is something that can be done at will; that is, an action or plan can be attempted in any state. Armed with the concept of plan attempts, McDermott then equates "plan P can be executed in state s" with "in every branch through s where P is attempted, P (successfully) occurs." This enables one to assert that a plan or action can be executed, or to assert the conditions under which a plan or action can be executed (i.e., a precondition specification). However, a critical problem still remains: how does one relate the attempt of a plan to the attempt of its constituent actions? McDermott notes that this is a difficult problem and only provides a partial solution.

What is lacking from McDermott's treatment is a basis for developing simple axioms that relate the attempt of a plan to the attempt of its actions in isolation. In our approach, this problem is addressed by describing individual actions not just by what they affect but also by what they do not affect, such as statements that describe lack of interference.

---

1. Strictly speaking, Shoham's model is not a branching time model; rather than introducing a temporal structure having branches, a similar structure is obtained by integrating a linear time model with a semantic structure for capturing an agent's knowledge about the world. Possibility in this case stems from a lack of knowledge.

3.2.4   Adapting the State-Change Model to Handle Simultaneous Events

Georgeff [1986] adapts the state-change model to provide for simultaneous events by redefining an event as a function from a state to a *set of states*, rather than as a function from a state to a state. The state transition associated with an event *ev* captures the possible effects of applying *ev* in conjunction with any other events that can occur simultaneously with *ev*. The concurrent composition of two events applied in a state is defined as the intersection of the individual events applied in the state. If two events lead to disjoint sets in a state, then these events cannot simultaneously occur in that state.

Georgeff discusses why further structure is needed to reason about whether two actions can be performed simultaneously and for describing actions in isolation. The problem that he identifies is analogous to the problem we identified in a branching time model. To address this problem, Georgeff introduces the **direct effects formula**, which distinguishes, in each state, between the properties that an action can affect and the properties it cannot affect. For example, this formula can be used to capture that the action "move block A" can affect the location of block A, but not the location of any other blocks. If two actions do not affect any of the same properties in state s, then they are considered independent and consequently can be executed together in state s. On the other hand, if they affect the same property, then either they interfere or are *compatible*, a concept that Georgeff does not clearly define.

Georgeff's approach is one way to describe what actions affect and do not affect. It has some limitations, however, which we address in our solution:

1)   It is not clear how the interaction between three or more actions is treated, such as the case where any two, but not three, actions can be executed simultaneously.

2)   Whether a single action or set of actions can be executed is contingent only on the state in which it is executed, and thus not on simultaneous conditions. For example, Georgeff's formalism cannot capture that to sail across the lake the wind must be blowing *simultaneously*. Now, one can make the assertion

   $$OCC(sailing,s1,s2) \supset OCC(wind\text{-}blowing,s1,s2),$$

   where $OCC(a1,s1,s2)$ means that action $a1$ occurs between states $s1$ and $s2$. This formula, however, does not indicate whether the wind is blowing is an effect or a necessary condition for sailing. As we have seen, this distinction can be made by introducing action attempts, the approach taken by both Allen and McDermott. In our work, we also introduce action attempts, and develop a notion of interference that can be contingent on simultaneous conditions.

3) The direct effects formula is not tightly related to the rest of the structure. For example, there is no axiom capturing that the statements "action *al* brings about property *p*" and "*al* does not affect *p*" are inconsistent.

Summary

In summary, we can divide the logics we have examined into linear time models and branching time models, where Georgeff's logic can be considered a branching time model. Linear time models are inadequate as models for planning because they do not represent possibility; instead, the approaches to planning based on these models [Lansky 1985; Allen 1984; see also chapter 1] appeal to logical consistency to determine if a set of actions can be executed together. We saw, however, that equating possibility with consistency amounts to nonmonotonic inference and consequently is problematic when working with an incomplete or imprecise world description.

While branching time models explicitly treat possibility, they are still inadequate because they do not provide a basis for relating plans to their constituent actions. Ideally, we seek a model that provides a "compositional semantics", where a plan is defined in terms of its constituent actions.

As we mentioned, a key idea behind our approach, which we present in section 3.3, is that our models can explicitly represent what actions do not affect. This allows us to employ simple axioms for composition; for instance, one capturing that if two actions can be executed individually and they do not affect each other, then they can be executed jointly. Now, both GEM and Georgeff's system provide structures that can capture what actions do not affect, but they do not meet all our objectives. The structure in GEM that partitions events into groups can be cumbersome to specify. Moreover, it cannot encode independence relationships between events in the same group. Consequently, consistency checking is still needed to determine if events in the same group can be done together. The use of direct effects formulas in Georgeff's system cannot treat interactions between three or more actions, such as the case where two, but not three, actions can be executed, or interactions that are conditional on what is happening during execution.

In the next sections, we present a new logic of action by extending Interval Logic. Section 3.3 describes the semantic model, and Section 3.4 presents the logical language and its interpretation. Appendix A provides an encapsulated formal description of the semantic model and the interpreted logic, and appendix B presents a sound proof theory.

3.3   The Semantic Model

We seek a model of action that provides a basis for describing and reasoning about concurrent actions in a dynamic world. As described earlier, this model should support

1) external events that may take place while an action is being executed;

2) conditions needed for execution that may be a function of what is happening during execution as well as just prior to execution;

3) the explicit treatment of what an action does *not* affect;

4) simultaneous interactions between actions, such as interference (including noninterference and conditional interference), and simultaneous effects; and

5) the sequential and concurrent composition of actions.

Let us first consider an overview of the model. The starting point for our development is the introduction of semantic structures that serve as a model for Interval Logic. A set of Interval Logic statements describe a world over time, rather than an instantaneous state. Consequently, a model for Interval Logic includes a set of intervals arranged in a linear time line and a **world-history,** which is a complete world over time. So that we can talk about different possibilities, the new model includes a *set* of world-histories, rather than a single one, capturing the different possible ways that the world can evolve. We also introduce a relation that arranges a set of world-histories into a tree that branches into the future, giving us a branching time model.

Now, one cannot simply say that an action can be executed or what its effects would be without also identifying the time that the action is to be executed. Consequently, we will speak of **action instances**, which refer to actions at specified times (given by an interval). To provide a basis for describing action instances individually, capturing what they affect and do not affect and how they are composed, we introduce a function that is analogous to the result function in the situation calculus [McCarthy and Hayes 1969]. This function,which is referred to as the **closeness function**, takes a world-history h and an action instance ai as arguments and yields the world-histories that differ from h solely on the account of executing ai in the context given by h. World-history h and any closest world-history differing on the account of ai will agree on all conditions that are not affected by ai. Thus, like the result function, the closeness function captures the result of executing an action instance in different contexts, indicating the parts of the world that the action affects and the parts that it does not affect. World-histories and action instances are our analogs to states and actions.

The closeness function also captures the simultaneous interactions between actions and provides a basis for composition. Simultaneous interactions are captured because world-histories indicate the actions that the agent is performing, as well as the conditions in the external world. Thus, in specifying a world-history that differs by executing an action instance, the closeness function must take into account simultaneous actions. For example, consider two simultaneous action instances $ai1$ and $ai2$ that do not interfere with each other. If h is a world-history where $ai1$ occurs, then $ai1$ would also occur in any closest world-history to *h* differing on the account of *ai2*, and vice versa. This would not be the case if these two action instances interfered.

Because each action instance has a time associated it, only one type of composition operator is needed to form plans with concurrent actions, sequential actions, as well as plans with gaps between execution times. For example, by composing action instances with execution times that overlap, we are forming a plan with concurrent actions. On the other hand, by composing action instances with execution times where one meets the other, we are forming a plan with sequential actions. To capture the relationship between a composition and its constituents, a closeness function taking a set of action instances is defined in terms of the closeness function taking individual action instances. Algebraically, this relationship is similar to the relationship between actions and action sequences in the state-change model.

The following sections describe the model in detail. Section 3.3.1 describes the part of the model that relates to the Interval Logic fragment, section 3.3.2 describes the branching time structure, and section 3.3.3 discusses plan instances. Section 3.3.4 provides a detailed discussion of the closeness function, including an intuitive account of this function and the constraints that we impose in accordance with these intuitions. Finally, section 3.3.5 discusses action interactions and composition, showing how a composition is defined in terms of its parts.

3.3.1   The Interval Logic Structure

Each model identifies a set of world-histories, a set of propositions, and a set of temporal intervals. As mentioned above, a world-history is a complete world over time and is complete in the same sense that a state is complete; it captures everything about the world, although typically, we are only concerned with a set of sentences that just partially describe the world. More specifically, a world-history captures exactly what the planning agent does and what is happening in the external world at all times.

Each temporal interval picks out a common time across the set of world-histories. The intervals are arranged by the *Meets* relation to form a global date line. *Meets(i1,i2)* is true if and only if interval *i1* meets interval *i2* (to the left). In chapter 1, it is shown that all temporal interval relations, such as "overlaps to the right" and "starts", can be defined in terms of the *Meets* relation. The model includes the constraints on *Meets* described in [Allen and Hayes 1989] and in chapter 1. We will also use the following interval relations defined in terms of *Meets* presented in chapter 1:

In(i1,i2) for *i1* is contained in or equal to *i2*,

Starts(i1,i2) for *i1* starts at the same time but ends before *i2*,

Finishes(i1,i2) for *i1* ends at the same time but starts after *i2*,

Equal(i1,i2) for *i1* equals *i2*, and

EndsBeforeEqual(i1,i2) for *i1* ends before or at the same time as *i2*.

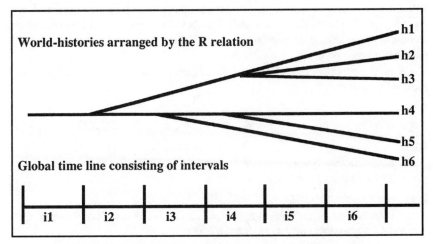

Figure 1: The branching time structure with a global time line

We also use the convention presented in chapter 1 where a relation such as *BeforeMeets(i1,i2)* refers to the disjunction *Before(i1,i2)* ∨ *Meets(i1,i2)*.

The model identifies a set of **propositions** to capture what happens in each world-history at each time. Formally, a proposition is given by a set of ordered pairs, each consisting of an interval and a world-history. If *<i,h>* belongs to proposition *p*, then we say that proposition *p* holds over interval *i* in world-history *h*. As before, propositions refer to both properties, namely, static aspects of the world, and events, which include actions.

3.3.2   The Branching Time Structure

To capture that at each time there may be many possible futures, the model includes an accessibility relation *R*. This relation arranges a set of world-histories into a tree that branches into the future. The set of temporal intervals pick out common times in the tree-like structure as shown in figure 1. The different possible futures arise because of the different behaviors that the planning agent can choose and because of nondeterminism in the external world.

The *R* relation takes an interval and two world-histories as arguments. Intuitively, *R(i,h1,h2)* means that world-histories *h1* and *h2* share a common past through the end of interval *i* and are possible alternatives with respect to their common past. Constraints are placed on *R* as follows:

R0)   For all world-histories *h1* and *h2* and intervals *i1* and *i2*, if *EndsBeforeEqual(i1,i2)* and *R(i2,h1,h2)* then *R(i1,h1,h2)*.

This constraint can be explained as follows. Because *R(i,h1,h2)* means that *h1* and *h2* share a common past through the end of interval *i*, its truth-value depends on the end of interval *i*, not its starting point. That is, if two intervals *i1* and *i2* end at the same time, then *R(i1,h1,h2)* and *R(i2,h1,h2)* will have the same truth-value irrespective of the intervals' starting points. Now, if $i1$ ends before $i2$, we want $R(i1,h1,h2)$ to hold if $R(i2,h1,h2)$ does because if two world-histories share a common past through the end of interval $i2$, then they clearly share a common past though the end of $i1$, an earlier time.

R is an equivalence relation for a fixed interval, and thus has the following standard constraints:

R1)

R is reflexive: For every world-history h and interval i, $R(i,h,h)$

R2)

R is symmetric: For all world-histories $h1$ and $h2$ and every interval i, if $R(i,h1,h2)$ then $R(i,h2,h1)$

R3)

R is transitive: For all world-histories $h1$, $h2$, and $h3$ and every interval i, if $R(i,h1,h2)$ and $R(i,h2,h3)$ then $R(i,h1,h3)$.

The last constraint that we impose relates to the events and properties constituting the propositions. Any world-histories that share a common past through the end of interval i must agree on all propositions that end at the same time or before i. Formally this is captured by

R4)

For all world-histories $h1$ and $h2$, every proposition p and all intervals $i1$ and $i2$, if $EndsBeforeEqual(i1,i2)$ and $R(i2,h1,h2)$ then $<i1,h1>\in p$ iff $<i1,h2>\in p$.

3.3.3   Plan Instances and Basic Actions

To capture the planning agent's possible behaviors, our model identifies a subset of the propositions that we refer to as **basic actions**, following Goldman [1970]. Intuitively, a basic action is an event brought about by the planning agent that is primitive in the sense that no other action brings it about: if $a1$ is a basic action, then there does not exist another action $a2$ where we could say that $a1$ is done by doing $a2$. Everything the agent does boils down to the performance of a set of temporally coordinated basic actions.[2] Goldman, in his theory of human action, equates basic actions with the performance of body movements, such as raising the left arm or taking a step with the right foot. We adopt a more general notion of basic actions: rather than restricting basic actions to be the performance of body movements, we take basic actions to be actions that are at the finest level of detail for the domain under consideration. For example, in modeling a game of chess, we might take our basic actions to be simple chess

---

2. Our theory does not distinguish the actions performed by agents other than the planning agent from the other propositions. They are modeled just like external events or processes. If one can influence another agent, then this can be treated like a process that the agent can partially control.

moves, such as moving the queen from Q1 to Q3. There is no need to look at chess moves at a finer level of detail, such as actions that refer to the arm movements that physically move the pieces. In the case of a robot agent, the basic actions could be the different signals that can be sent to the robot's effectors.

We also let basic actions refer to inactivity, such as keeping one's arm still, and the nonperformance of some behavior, such as not moving one's arm in a particular way, because what happens depends on not only what an agent does, but also on what an agent does not do. For example, if a ball is rolling down a hill, then it will reach the bottom unless the agent puts out its arm to stop it. Thus, a plan to have the ball reach the bottom would need to ensure that the agent does not put out an arm, thereby stopping the ball.

An alternative approach to having basic actions refer to inactivity and nonperformance is to have actions only refer to activity, and capture behavior as a set of basic actions such that the agent performs *only* these specified basic actions. In contrast, we explicitly treat inactivity and nonperformance as actions because this approach is more general. It allows us to specify a behavior that only mentions basic actions that are critical to some goal, and is noncommittal to all other basic actions. The alternative approach does not distinguish between nonperformances that are critical to achieving the goal and ones that are irrelevant to the goal.

Typically, when describing an agent's behavior, one does not directly describe the basic actions that are executed. Rather, one describes what happens in more abstract terms. As an example, one might say that the agent opened the door, rather than describing the set of body movements that the agent performed. As another example, one might say that the agent does not knock over the cup, rather than listing the nonperformances of all the precise body movements that would knock the cup over. For planning, we are interested in reasoning about what the agent *can* do. The standard approach—and one we wish to follow—is to describe what the agent can do by identifying a set of abstract actions at the agent's disposal and specifying conditions under which each one can be done. Thus, in our object language, we will introduce terms that make reference to abstract behavior. For our semantic theory, we must decide what type of objects these "action terms" denote.

One approach that may come to mind is to simply let these action terms refer to abstract actions in our model (i.e., propositions in our model that are actions, but not basic actions). There is a problem with this approach, however. It is not proper to describe the conditions under which an abstract action can be done without also having in mind how it is to be performed. For example, saying "the door can be opened if it is unlocked" implies that one is intending to open the door by twisting its knob and pulling the door open, rather than by using a key or dynamite. Thus, if we want to talk about the conditions under which an action term can be executed, the term must refer to both an abstract action and a particular way of executing it, which can be given by a set of temporally coordinated basic actions. We do this by introducing plan instances, which serve as our analog to actions and plans.

Plan Instances

A plan instance is given by two parts: a set of propositions at particular times, which we call **proposition instances**, and a set of basic actions at particular times, which we call **basic action instances**. The set of proposition instances indicates the abstract steps associated with the plan instance. The set of basic action instances indicates precisely how the plan instance is to be performed. Formally, a plan instance is an ordered pair of the form $<priS,baiS>$, where $priS$ is a nonempty set of proposition/interval pairs, and $baiS$ is a nonempty set of basic action/interval pairs.

It is important to note that plan instances differ from actions and plans because a plan instance identifies a time with each of its abstract steps and basic actions. There are a number of reasons why we take temporally annotated entities as our basic units. To begin with, we want to talk about plan entities that accomplish goals. In a dynamic world whether a plan accomplishes a goal depends on the time that it is executed. Thus, while it is proper to say that a plan instance achieves a goal, it is not proper to say that a plan achieves a goal without also specifying when the actions in the plan are executed. As we will see shortly, another advantage of using temporally annotated entities is that it allows us to introduce one composition operator for both sequential and concurrent composition.

We restrict the temporal relationship between the set of basic action instances and set of proposition instances so that

1) the time when the earliest basic action instance(s) begins coincides with the time when the earliest proposition instance(s) begins, and

2) the time when the latest basic action instance(s) ends is before or equal to the time when the latest proposition instance(s) ends.

Restriction 1 is imposed because it does not make sense to say that a basic action instance brings about a proposition instance that begins earlier than it. Restriction 2 is imposed because we assume that the only reason that a basic action instance belongs to a plan instance is to bring about a proposition instance in the plan instance. If all the proposition instances ended at time t, there would be no reason to specify what to perform after time t. We must also note that we allow plan instances in which the latest basic action instance ends before the latest proposition instance. This allows us to model a plan instance such as one corresponding to breaking the vase by pushing it off the table. In this case, the time when the vase actually breaks is after the time that the pushing takes place.

Formally, the two restrictions above are captured by stating that an interval that **covers** the set of basic action instances equals or starts (i.e., starts at the same time but ends before) an interval that covers the set of proposition instances

PI1)

For every plan instance $<priS,baiS>$, there exists intervals $ic1$ and $ic2$ such that $Covers(ic1,INTS(priS))$ and $Covers(ic2,INTS(baiS))$ and $EqualStarts(ic2,ic1)$

where $Ints(S) =_{def} \{ i \mid$ such that $<p,i> \in S \}$

and $Covers(i,S)$ is true iff for all intervals $ix \in S$, $In(ix,i)$ is true, and there exists intervals iy and $iz \in S$ such that $EqualStarts(iy,i)$ and $EqualFinishes(iz,i)$.

Plan Instance Attempts and Occurrences

As in chapter 1, we make a distinction between the attempt of a plan instance and its (successful) occurrence. This distinction allows us to define what it means to say that a plan instance can be done, and to talk about failed plan instances. A plan instance can be attempted under any conditions (i.e., in any world-history), but only under certain conditions will it occur rather than fail. If the attempt of a plan instance *would* lead to its occurrence, then we say that it is **executable**.

Formally, we say that a plan instance occurs in a world-history h, if all of its proposition instances hold in h and all its basic action instances occur in h. This definition can be given by

$$OccursIn(<priS,baiS>,h) =_{def}$$
$$\text{for every proposition instance } <p,i> \text{ in } priS \cup baiS, <i,h> \in p.$$

We say that a plan instance is attempted in a world-history if and only if all its basic action instances occur in the world-history. The functions described in sections 3.3.4 and 3.3.5 capture what *would happen* if a basic action or set of basic actions were executed in each world-history. In other words, these functions capture what would happen if a plan instance were attempted under different circumstances, providing the formal basis for concepts such as *executable* and what the plan instances does not affect.

Composing Plan Instances

When planning, one reasons about ways of composing actions to form plans that achieve goals. Thus, a model for planning must include operators for forming compositions and must capture how a composition relates to its constituent parts. In our framework, we must be able to compose plan instances to form more complex plan instances. To form compositions, we introduce one composition operator, captured by set union defined on pairs; that is, given two plan instances $<priS1,baiS1>$ and $<priS2,baiS2>$, their composition is given by $<priS \cup priS2, baiS1 \cup baiS2>$. Because plan instances have times associated with them, we are able to use this operator to form plan instances with sequential steps, concurrent steps, and steps with gaps between them. Thus, it is not necessary to introduce separate composition operators for each type of temporal relation.

To capture that any two plan instances can be composed to form a more complex one, we place the following restriction on the model:

> **PI2)** For all plan instances *<priS1,baiS1>* and *<priS2,baiS2>*, *<priS1∪priS2, baiS1∪baiS2>* is a plan instance.

Note that this constraint provides for the composition of three or more plan instances because, for example, the composition of three plan instances can be cast as first composing two of them together, forming a plan instance that is composed with the third. Because union is commutative and associative, the order of composition has no bearing. Also note that although any two plan instances can be composed, a plan instance can be produced that may not be executable under any circumstances. This would be the case if, for example, "move up during *i*" and "move down during *i*" were composed.

By modeling composition with union, we relate a composite plan instance to its parts. It is easily seen that a composite plan instance occurs in a world-history *h* if and only if both its parts occur in *h*. That is, the following relation holds in our model:

> For every world-history *h* and all plan instances *<priS1,baiS1>* and *<priS2,baiS2>*,
> *OccursIn(<priS1 ∪ priS2,baiS1 ∪ baiS2>,h)* if and only if
> *OccursIn(<priS1,baiS1>,h)* and *OccursIn(<priS2,baiS2>,h)*.

In section 3.3.5, we show how the result that would be produced by jointly executing a set of basic action instances is defined in terms of the results that would be produced by executing the individual members.

Plan Instances That Refer to Properties

Because propositions refer to both events and properties, plan instances can contain proposition instances that refer to properties. Such a proposition instance takes place if the property stays true over the designated interval. The need to keep properties true over time periods in a plan has been widely discussed in the planning literature under the name *protection*. If a property is true at some time and the planner needs to make this property true at a later time (say to achieve a precondition), the planner may try to keep this property true, that is, protect it, between these two times.

Our treatment is more general than the typical approach to protections in which a protection can be introduced only if no other action in the plan negates the property. In our framework, protections correspond to steps that are brought about by basic action instances that refer to nonperformance or nonactivity. We, however, can also have propositions that are kept true by executing basic actions corresponding to activity. For example, we can have a plan instance corresponding to the action of keeping the door open by preventing anyone from closing it. The need for plan instances of this type arises in a dynamic environment where there are other agents and forces that can negate a property unless prevented. We return back to these issues in section 3.5.5, showing the advantages of our more general approach.

3.3.4   The Closeness Function

To capture what each basic action affects and does not affect in different settings, the model includes a **closeness function**, based on a similarly named function found in semantic treatments of conditionals [Stalnaker 1968; Lewis 1973]. Our closeness function, which we designate by CL, takes a basic action, interval, and world-history as arguments and yields a nonempty set of world-histories. All world-histories in $CL(ba,i,h)$ that differ from h do so solely on the account of the occurrence of basic action ba during interval i. Equivalently, we say that the world-histories belonging to $CL(ba,i,h)$ are the **closest** world-histories to h where ba occurs during i. We will use the term $ba@i$ to refer to basic action ba with execution time i. Also, we will use the phrase "$ba@i$ occurs" synonymously with "$ba@i$ is executed."

As we mentioned in the overview, the closeness function can be seen as an analog to the result function in the situation calculus [McCarthy and Hayes 1969], namely, the function that indicates the result of executing each action in each state. Typically, if $h2$ is a closest world-history to h, then the two world-histories will agree on many conditions. If $h2$ belongs to $CL(ba,i,h)$, then h and $h2$ must coincide on all conditions that are not affected, directly or indirectly, by the occurrence of ba during i. This includes conditions out of the agent's control, such as whether or not it is raining during some interval, and conditions that hold and occur at times that end before interval i.

Because a world-history is a complete world over time, a basic action instance $ba@i$ either occurs or does not occur in a world-history h. If $ba@i$ occurs in h (i.e., $<i,h> \in ba$), then $CL(ba,i,h)$ is simply set to $\{h\}$:

BA1) For every basic action ba, interval i, and world-history h, if $<i,h> \in ba$, then $CL(ba,i,h) = \{h\}$.

This treatment makes sense since $CL(ba,i,h)$ captures what world-history h would be like if $ba@i$ were to be executed in it. But if $ba@i$ actually occurs in h, then the answer is h itself. This treatment is also compatible with the restrictions placed on semantic models for subjunctive conditionals [Stalnaker 1968; Lewis 1973].

Let us now examine the nontrivial cases of $CL(ba,i,h)$, where $ba@i$ does not occur in h and the world-histories in $CL(ba,i,h)$ differ from h. In these cases, a world-history $h2$ belonging to $CL(ba,i,h)$ will differ from h not only by the fact that $ba@i$ occurs in $h2$, but also by the consequences of $ba@i$ occurring.

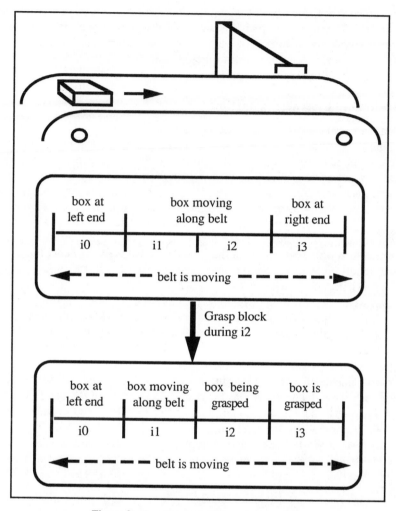

Figure 2: A robot arm with a conveyor belt

As an example, consider figure 2, which depicts a scenario where there is a robot arm that is used to grasp items on the conveyor belt next to it. We consider evaluating the action instance "grasp block during $i2$" with respect to a world-history h, where a block rests on the left end of the conveyor belt and moves toward the right end because the belt is moving and no actions or events occur to disturb the block's position. We assume that interval $i2$ is the appropriate time when the block can be grasped because of its position at that time on the belt. In this case, the closest world-history to h on the account of "grasp block during $i2$" is a world-history $h2$, where the block moves along the belt until the beginning of interval $i2$, then during $i2$ the block is being grasped resulting in the condition that the block is grasped during interval $i3$. Because the basic action instance is executed during *i2*, world-histories h and *h2* agree on all conditions prior to *i2*. The basic action instance "grasp block during *i2*" directly affects the position of the robot arm which causes the position of the block to be affected. Thus, *h* and *h2* differ on the positions of the arm and the block at times during and after *i2*. However, the basic action instance does not affect other aspects of the world, such as the motion of the conveyer belt. Thus, in world-history *h2*, we find that the belt is moving during intervals *i1* through *i4* because the belt is moving in *h* from *i1* through *i4*, and it is not affected by the grasping action instance.

As a second example, consider the scenario depicted in figure 3 where a ball can be placed at the top of a hill, behind a gate that prevents the ball from rolling down the hill if it is closed. We consider evaluating the basic action instance "lift the gate during *i1*" with respect to a world-history *h*, where a ball is at the top of the hill during interval *i1* and remains there during intervals *i2* through *i4* because the gate remains closed throughout this time period. The closest world-history to *h* on the account of "lift the gate during *i1*" is a world-history in which the gate is being lifted during *i1*, and as a result, the ball rolls down the hill until it reaches the bottom. If we considered "lift the gate during *i1*" with respect to a world-history where there are obstructions on the hill during *i2* through *i3*, then the ball would not reach the bottom of the hill in a resulting closest world-history.

Multiple World-Histories

The function $CL(ba,i,h)$ yields a set of world-histories, instead of a single one, because there may be many ways to minimally modify *h* to account for the occurrence of *ba@i*. For example, multiple world-histories can be used to model nondeterministic actions, such as the rolling of a fair die. In this case, there will be (at least) six different ways that a world-history can be revised to account for the six different outcomes that can be produced.

Multiple world-histories can also be produced by the conflict between alternative basic action instances. For example, suppose that only two of the three basic action instances *ba1@i*, *ba2@i*, and *ba3@i* can be executed together. Also assume that both *ba2@i* and *ba3@i* occur in *h*. In this case, $CL(ba1,i,h)$ must contain (at least) two world-histories: one where both *ba1@i* and *ba2@i* occur, but not *ba3@i*, and another where *ba1@i* and *ba3@i* occur, but not *ba2@i*.

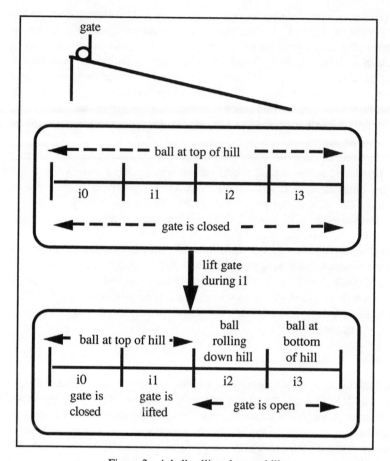

Figure 3: A ball rolling down a hill

Temporal Restrictions on the Closeness Function

There are two constraints that relate the closeness function and the temporal structure. Both derive from the asymmetric property of time: earlier conditions can affect later conditions, but later conditions cannot influence earlier ones. We capture these restrictions by relating the CL function to the R relation, which, recall, captures world-histories that are possible alternatives to a common past.

Our first constraint captures that if world-history $h2$ differs from h on the account of executing ba during i, then they are **R-related** at any interval that meets i:

BA-R1)

For all world-histories $h1$ and $h2$, every basic action ba, and all intervals $i1$ and $i2$, if $h2 \in CL(ba,i2,h1)$ and $Meets(i1,i2)$ then $R(i1,h2,h1)$.

This restricts CL so that if $h2$ belongs to $CL(ba,i2,h1)$, then, as a result of constraint R4, $h1$ must agree on all propositions holding during intervals that end at the same time or before interval $i2$ starts. This constraint also serves to more precisely capture what we mean by "two world-histories that are *possible* alternatives to their common past". In particular, BA-R1 captures that if $h2$ differs from h on the account of some basic action instance, then h and $h2$ are possible alternatives to each other.

Our second constraint stems from the intuition that in evaluating a closest world-history $h2$ to h, later conditions in h do not influence earlier conditions in $h2$: if world-history $h2$ differs from h on the account of basic action instance $ba@i$, then the conditions that hold in $h2$ up until some time ix are a function only of $ba@i$, and the conditions that hold in h up until ix, not conditions after ix. The ramification of this principle is that if two world-histories $h1$ and $h2$ are R-related at time ix (and thus share a common past up until at least time ix), the valuation of CL at $h1$ must be compatible with $h2$ in the following manner: for every member $hcl1$ of $CL(ba,i,h1)$, there exists a member of $CL(ba,i,h2)$ that is R-related to $hcl1$ at time ix. Formally, this is given by

BA-R2)

For all world-histories $h1$, $h2$, and $hcl1$, every basic action ba, and all intervals i and ix, if $R(ix,h1,h2)$ and $hcl1 \in CL(ba,i,h1)$, then there exists a $hcl2 \in CL(ba,i,h2)$ such that $R(ix,hcl1,hcl2)$.

We can help to explain this constraint by illustrating one of its ramifications. Plan instance $<\{<p,i>\},\{<ba,i>\}>$ is executable in world-history h if the result of executing basic action ba during i in the context given by h would lead to proposition p holding over interval i (i.e., for all $h2 \in CL(ba,i,h)$, $<i,h2> \in p$). Now, we do not want conditions in h after i to determine whether this plan instance is executable. In other words, if the plan instance is executable in a world-history hx but not executable in world-history hy, then hx and hy must differ on at least one condition holding over a time that starts before i ends. Thus, these world-histories cannot be R-related at interval i, a conclusion that would be enforced by BA-R2 (using also the constraints on R).

Standard Conditions

We have seen that $CL(ba,i,h)$ yields the trivial result $\{h\}$ when $ba@i$ occurs in h. $CL(ba,i,h)$ is also set to $\{h\}$ when $ba@i$'s **standard conditions** do not hold in h. The term *standard conditions* is taken from Goldman [1970] and refers to conditions that must hold in order for a basic action to occur. For example, the standard conditions for "the agent moves its right arm up during time i" include the condition that the arm is not broken during time i. As a second example, in a game setting, the standard conditions would refer to the conditions under which a move is legal. Also, we must note that $CL(ba,i,h)$ is defined for all interval arguments i. Consequently, $CL(ba,i,h)$ can refer to the situation where ba cannot be executed for the duration captured by i. In these cases, we treat $CL(ba,i,h)$ as if its standard conditions do not hold. For example, *ba* might refer to taking a step which takes a certain amount of time. If *i* refers to an interval with duration not equal to this amount of time, we treat *ba@i* as if its standard conditions do not hold in all world-histories.

The reason that we set $CL(ba,i,h)$ to $\{h\}$ when *ba@i* 's standard conditions do not hold in *h* requires some explanation. Now, one might ask: why not treat the lack of standard conditions like the other cases and let $CL(ba,i,h)$ return a set of world-histories where *ba@i* occurs? The problem with this treatment is that it would force us to either violate our assumption that all world-histories adhere to the causal laws or our assumption that the execution of a basic action cannot affect its standard conditions. For example, suppose that "the right arm is broken during *i*" holds in world-history *h*. Consider a world-history *h2* differing from *h* on the account of the basic action instance "the right arm moves up during *i*". If we allowed this basic action instance to occur in *h2*, then either i) we would have a world-history where the arm moves while broken, which is a violation of a causal law, or ii) we would have the situation where the arm is broken in *h*, but not in *h2*, which can be interpreted as capturing that moving the arm causes the arm to become fixed.

The above argument shows why if *ba@i* 's standard conditions do not hold in *h*, $CL(ba,i,h)$ must not contain any world-histories where *ba@i* occurs. By setting $CL(ba,i,h)$ equal to $\{h\}$, this is accomplished. In effect, we are treating a basic action instance when its standard conditions do not hold as a *no-op*, an action that produces no change. One can think of the situation where $CL(ba,i,h) = \{h\}$ and *ba@i* does not occur in *h* as the way that our semantic model encodes the lack of standard conditions. To capture that the lack of standard conditions is the only case when *ba@i* does not occur in every world-history in $CL(ba,i,h)$, we impose the following constraint:

BA2)

> For every world-history *h*, basic action *ba*, and interval *i*, if $CL(ba,i,h)\neq\{h\}$ then $CL(ba,i,h) \subseteq \{h2 \mid <i,h2>\in ba\}$.

3.3.5   Composition and Interaction of Basic Action Instances

The closeness function CL captures the *individual* execution of a basic action instance. In this section, we show how the joint execution of a set of basic action instances is defined in terms of CL applied to the members of the set. We will define the F_{cl} function, which takes a set of basic action instances *baiS* and a world-history *h* as arguments and yields the set of world-histories that "differ from *h* solely on the account of the occurrences of the basic action instances in *baiS*".

The function F_{cl} can take any set of basic action instances as an argument regardless of its members' temporal relationships. Moreover, the definition of F_{cl} applied to *baiS* does not need to be conditionalized on the temporal relationship between the members of *baiS*. So, for example, the composition of two concurrent basic action instances is defined in the same way as the composition of two basic action instances that do not overlap in time.

In this section, we will first provide an intuitive presentation of the F_{cl} function, showing how the composition of a set of basic action instances depends on how its members interact. We will then provide the formal definition of the F_{cl} function.

Intuitive View of Composition and Interactions

The basic principle that we wish to exploit is as follows:

> To find the world-histories that minimally differ from h on the account of a set of basic action instances, one can successively revise h to account for each member of the set. To determine how to make individual revisions, we use the CL function.

It is important to keep in mind that each basic action instance has a time associated with it. Thus, the order of revision does not have any bearing on the temporal ordering of the action instances. For example, revising a world-history first by basic action instance $ba1@ix$ then by basic action instance $ba2@iy$ does not necessarily indicate the result of doing $ba1$ followed by $ba2$. This would only be the case if interval ix meets or is before interval iy. On the other hand, if iy overlaps in time with ix, then the successive revision captures a concurrent relationship.

As an example, consider the basic action instances "move right arm up during time i" and "move left arm down during time i". Figure 4 depicts the result of successively modifying a world-history h in both orders. In this example, the order of revision makes no difference; whether we start with "move right arm up during time i" or "move left arm down during time i", we arrive at the same world-history, one where they both occur. In this case, we define a closest world-history to h that differs by both these action instances as being the result of either successive revision.

We will see that the simple rule above for computing joint execution only applies in certain cases. There are complications that must be taken into account to provide for the various ways that basic actions can interact. In particular, we must handle the cases where

1) the action instances interfere;

2) one action instance (or set of action instances) ruins another one's standard conditions;

3) one action instance (or set of action instances) is needed to enable another's standard conditions; and

4) the standard conditions for both do not hold.

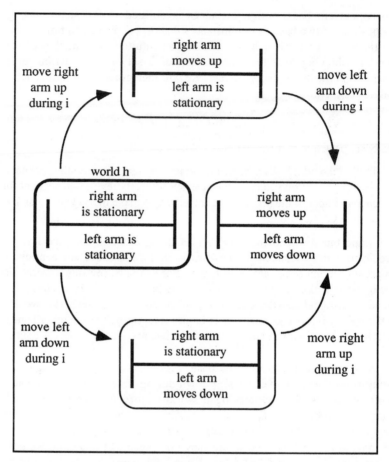

Figure 4: Action composition

Interference

In the case where *baiS* contains two or more basic action instances that interfere with respect to world-history h, we set $F_{cl}(baiS,h)$ to $\{h\}$, treating *baiS* just like a basic action instance with standard conditions that do not hold in h.

We detect whether two (or more) basic action instances interfere in a world-history by examining the *CL* function. Consider world-history h and two basic action instances *bai1* and *bai2*. If they interfere, then one or neither, but not both, can occur in h. If one of them occurs in h, say *bai1*, then the world-histories produced by revising h by *bai2* are those where *bai2* occurs, but not *bai1*. This is because we are assuming that there are conditions that hold in h that preclude *bai1* and *bai2* from both occurring.

Now, in the case where neither *bai1* nor *bai2* occur in h, we have the following. If we revise h by *bai1*, we get to world-histories where *bai1* occurs.

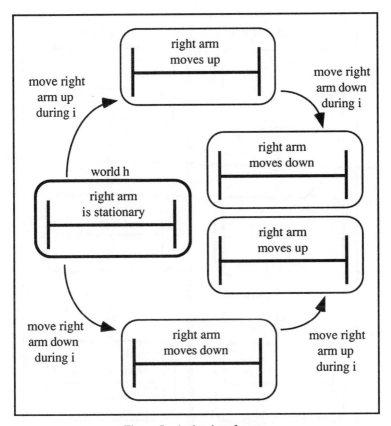

Figure 5: Action interference

Revising these world-histories by *bai2* yields world-histories where *bai2* occurs and where *bai1* does not occur. If we revised *h* in the opposite direction, we would get to world-histories where *bail* occurs, but not *bai2*. Thus, we see that if we have two basic action instances that interfere with respect to a world-history, successively modifying this world-history in the different orders yields different results; however, in both cases, both *bai1* and *bai2* do not jointly occur in the resulting world-histories.

An example of interference is shown in figure 5, where we are composing "move right arm up during *i*" and "move right arm down during *i*". These basic action instances interfere at world-history *h*, and also at all other world-histories. This is an example of necessary interference. Because interference is defined *with respect to a world-history*, we can also model conditional interference. As an example, consider figure 6. Basic action instances "machine1 is on during *i*" and "machine2 is on during *i*" can be performed separately if there are one or more units of power available during interval *i*. However, they interfere if they are

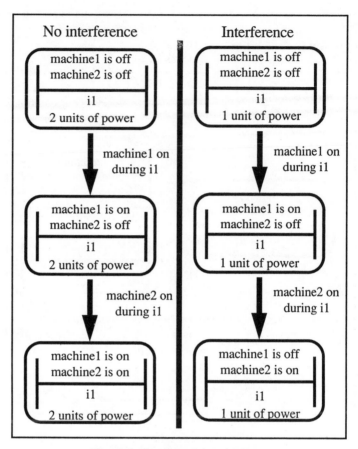

Figure 6: Conditional interference

evaluated with respect to a world-history in which there are not at least two units of power available during i.

Negating Standard Conditions

In the example in figure 5, the two basic action instances could not be executed together because they interfered. Another similar interaction is where the execution of one of the basic action instances ruins the other's standard conditions, and hence, they cannot be done together. In this case, we also treat the composition as if its standard conditions do not hold: if execution of $bai1$ would ruin $bai2$'s standard conditions in the context given by world-history h, then $F_{cl}(baiS,h)$ is set to $\{h\}$. This type of interaction typically arises when an earlier basic action instance negates a later one's standard conditions. For example, consider world-history h where "the arm is not broken" holds during interval i. With respect to this world-history, a basic action instance just prior to *i* that would cause the arm to break, would ruin the standard conditions for "move the arm during *i*". This type of interaction can also take place between concurrent action instances.

Enablement

Another relationship that must be considered is enablement—where one basic action instance (or set of basic action instances) brings about another's standard conditions (with respect to a world-history). In this case, the two basic action instances can be executed together. However, this case differs from the one where we have basic action instances that can be executed individually and together because in this case the order of revision makes a difference. Meaningful results are only produced by the revision where we start with the basic action instance doing the enabling. As an example, consider figure 7. In the initial world-history *h*, there is no power supplied during interval *i2* and consequently the standard conditions for "the saw is on during *i2*" do not hold in *h*. Now, if we revise *h* to account for "turn power on during *i1*", we get to a world-history where the standard conditions for "the saw is on during *i2*" hold. Consequently, by revising this world-history to account for "the saw is on during *i2*", we get a world-history where both basic action instances occur. We define the closest world-history to *h* that differs by both "turn power on during *i1*" and "the saw is on during *i2*" as this resulting world-history. As figure 7 illustrates, revision in the other direction produces meaningless results. In this example, the enablement relation was between an earlier and later basic action instance. Enablement can also relate simultaneous basic action instances, such as the case where "hold the block still during *i*" enables "drill a straight hole in the block during *i*".

Neither Standard Condition Holds

The last case to consider is where the standard conditions of both *bai1* and *bai2* do not hold in *h*. In this situation, $F_{cl}(\{bai1,bai2\}, h)$ is simply set to $\{h\}$, treating it as if the composition's standard conditions do not hold.

Formal Treatment

The following notation is introduced to succinctly present the formal definition of F_{cl} and two related constraints. The constructor function * combines two functions from H to 2^H to form a function from H to 2^H, where H denotes a set of world-histories:

$$fx*fy(h) =_{def} \bigcup_{hx \in fx(h)} fy(hx).$$

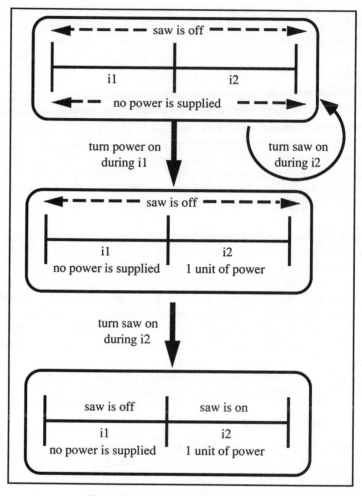

Figure 7:   An example of enablement

The set of composition functions of a basic action instance set, which we denote by the function **CompF**, is recursively defined by

1) A singleton basic action instance set $\{ba@i\}$ has one composition function: $CompF(\{ba@i\}) =_{def} \{\lambda h.CL(ba,i,h)\}$.

2) A basic action instance set $baiS$ with more than one element is defined as:

$$CompF(baiS) =_{def}$$
$$\{bai*cmp \mid bai \in baiS \text{ and } cmp \in CompF(baiS - \{bai\})\}.$$

If *cmp* is a composition function of *baiS*, then *cmp(h)* yields the set of world-histories that would be reached by successively modifying *h* by the basic action instances belonging to *baiS* in some order.

The predicate *AllOccur* relates world-histories, composition functions, and basic action instance sets. For every world-history *h*, composition function *cmp* and basic action instance set *baiS*:

$$AllOccur(h,cmp,baiS) =_{def}$$
$$cmp \in CompF(baiS) \land$$
$$cmp(h) \subseteq \{h2 \mid <i,h2> \in ba \text{ for all } <ba,i> \in baiS\}.$$

So *AllOccur(h,cmp,baiS)* is true if and only if *cmp* is a composition function of *baiS* and the result of modifying *h* successively by all the members in *baiS*, in the order implicit in *cmp*, yields a set of world-histories where all the members in *baiS* occur.

$F_{cl}(baiS,h)$ is defined such that if there is a composition function that produces a set of world-histories where all the members of *baiS* occur, then $F_{cl}(baiS,h)$ is defined as this set. If we cannot find such a set, then two or more members of *baiS* interfere or one member ruins another's standard conditions. In these cases, we set $F_{cl}(baiS,h)$ to $\{h\}$. More formally, F_{cl} is defined by

1) If there is a composition function *cmp* of *baiS* such that *AllOccur(h,cmp,baiS)*:

$$F_{cl}(baiS,h) =_{def} cmp(h)$$

2) Otherwise, $F_{cl}(baiS,h) =_{def} \{h\}$.

We also impose the following constraints:

BA-CMP1)

For every world-history *h*, every basic action instance set *baiS*, and all composition functions *cmp1* and *cmp2*, if *AllOccur(h,cmp1,baiS)* and *AllOccur(h,cmp2,baiS)* then *cmp1(h)=cmp2(h)*.

BA-CMP2)

For every world-history *h*, all basic action instance sets *baiS1* and *baiS2* and all composition functions *cmp1* and *cmp2*, if *AllOccur(h,cmp2,baiS2)* and *AllOccur(h,cmp1*cmp2,baiS1∪baiS2)* then
    AllOccur(h,cmp2*cmp1,baiS1∪baiS2) .

Constraint BA-CMP1 is necessary for F_{cl} to be well defined. It captures that if the result produced by different orders both produce world-histories where all the members of *baiS* occur, then these resulting sets are equal. Constraint BA-CMP2 entails that if we revise world-history *h* first by *bai1* then by *bai2* yielding a set of world-histories where they both occur, then the only way that the same result would not be produced using the other order is if *bai2*'s standard conditions do not hold in *h*, meaning that *bai1* was needed to enable *bai2*.

Now, to carefully show the applicability of the definition of the F_{cl} function and the two constraints, we would have to show how it applies in all cases. For example, we would have to consider the composition of more than two basic action instances, and the complication caused by the fact that revision by a basic action instance or set of basic action instances produces multiple world histories, not just a single one. The reader interested in a more comprehensive analysis can refer to Pelavin [1988].

How Time Comes Into Play

Although we define composition independently from the temporal relationships between the components, there are properties that fall out because of the relationship between the basic actions and the temporal structure. In particular we find that

1) If basic action instance *bai1* is prior to basic action instance *bai2*, then we only need to consider a successive revision that starts with *bai1* to see if they can be jointly executed. This is because a later action instance cannot enable or ruin an earlier one's standard conditions.

2) Only action instances that overlap in time can interfere; the only type of harmful interaction between nonoverlapping action instances is a case in which the earlier one ruins the later's standard conditions.

One can deduce these relationships from the constraints on the model we have presented.

3.4 The Language

In this section, we discuss the syntax and semantic interpretation for our logic, focusing on the highlights. (Appendix A provides a complete presentation of the syntax and its interpretation.) This provides a definition of semantic entailment, which we in turn use to define planner correctness in section 3.5. We also present a sound axiomatic theory in appendix B.

The language is a simple extension of the Interval Logic syntax presented in chapter 1, which is cast as a sorted first-order language. In Interval Logic, there are two sorts, one to denote temporal intervals and the other to denote all other objects. We define a third sort to denote plan instances, and we introduce the functions *TimeOf* and *Comp* and the predicate *Occ* to talk about them. Second, we extend the language with two modal operators *INEV* and *IFTRIED*. The modal operator *INEV* takes an interval term and a sentence as arguments and is used to describe the branching time structure. The modal operator *IFTRIED* takes a plan instance term and a sentence as arguments and is used to describe what a plan instance can and cannot affect.

We must also note that there are other languages that can be used to describe our models. For example, one might use a first-order language with terms that denote world-histories, this being similar to Moore [1977] and McDermott [1982] who use first-order languages to describe models with possible worlds.

3.4.1   The Syntax: Additions to Interval Logic

Technically, the logic is a sorted first-order language with modal operators. The primitive symbols for forming such a language are

1) variables,

2) function symbols, which include constants,

3) predicate symbols, which include propositional atoms,

4) modal operators, and

5) logical connectives.

Associated with each function and predicate symbol is a nonnegative integer denoting its arity, that is, how many arguments it takes. If a function symbol has arity zero we say that it is a constant, and if a predicate has arity zero we say that it is a propositional atom.

Terms

Variables and the function symbols are used to form terms, the syntactic entities that denote objects in the model. The set of terms are recursively defined by

1) Any function symbol that is a constant or a variable is a term.

2) If f is a function symbol with arity $n > 0$, and $t_1, t_2, ..., t_n$ are terms, then $f(t_1, t_2, ..., t_n)$ is a term.

Example of terms are v, *Machine1*, *PowerReq(Machine1)*, and *Add(v,Add(1,2))*. Associated with each term is its sort. Sorts are also associated with each argument in a function to indicate its domain.

Recall that a plan instance is a set of temporally annotated propositions to be performed in a particular way. Thus, a plan instance is a complex object, one composed of constituents. But this does not mean, of course, that a plan instance term must also be complex. For example, a constant term may be used to refer to plan instances. In section 3.5, where we present many examples of plan instance terms, we will use plan instance terms of the form $f(i)$, where i is a interval term. Moreover, we will use function terms such as *GraspWrench(i)* or *PushVaseOff(i)*, which intuitively refer only to abstract steps, leaving implicit the way that the step is to be attempted. If we want to talk about two different ways of performing the same abstract action, such as *PushVaseOff*, we could use unary function symbols, such as *PushVaseOff1* and *PushVaseOff2*, or introduce a second argument to *PushVaseOff* to denote how the abstract action is to be performed.

To describe plan instances, the language includes two interpreted function symbols: **TimeOf(pi)**, which denotes the interval corresponding to the total execution time of the plan instance denoted by *pi*, and **Comp(pi1,pi2)**, which denotes the plan instance formed by composing the plan instances denoted by *pi1* and *pi2*. Note that the order of the arguments in the term *Comp(pi1,pi2)* do not capture a temporal order because each plan instance has a time of occurrence associated with it. As we have seen, this allows us to form sequential and concurrent compositions, as well as compositions with gaps between the execution times. Moreover, the *Comp* function is associative and commutative. Because *Comp* is associative, we introduce the following defined term to succinctly describe the composition of three or more plan instances:

$$Comp(pi_1, pi_2,...., pi_n) =_{\text{def}} Comp(pi_1, Comp(pi_2, ..., pi_n)).$$

Sentences

The set of sentences is given as follows:

1) Every predicate symbol of arity 0 (i.e., a propositional atom) is a sentence.

2) If *p* is a predicate symbol with arity *n*, and t_1, t_2,..., t_n are terms, then $p(t_1, t_2,..., t_n)$ is a sentence.

3) If *i* is an interval term, and *s* is a sentence, then *INEV(i,s)* is a sentence.

4) If *pi* is a plan instance term, and *s* is a sentence, then *IFTRIED(pi,s)* is a sentence.

5) If *v* is a variable and *s1* and *s2* are sentences, then the following are sentences: ~*s1*, *s1* ∨ *s2*, *s1* ∧ *s2*, ∀*v* . *s1*, and ∃*v* . *s1*.

We divide the set of predicates into **temporal predicates**, which are associated with propositions in the model, and all other predicates, which we call **eternal predicates** because they refer to relations that either hold at all times or are false at all times. A temporal predicate is used to state that an event occurs or a property holds over some time interval. The general form is given by $p(t_1,t_2, ...,t_n,i)$, where *i* is an interval term. By asserting $p(t_1,t_2, ...,t_n,i)$, we mean that the proposition in the model, identified by *p* and the first *n* arguments, holds over the interval denoted by *i*. The set of eternal predicates includes the interpreted predicates *Meets* and *Occ*. *Meets(i1,i2)* is defined as before, this being the syntactic entity corresponding to the relation of the same name that we introduced in the model structure. *Occ(pi)* means that the plan instance denoted by *pi* occurs. This predicate does not need a temporal argument because plan instances have times associated with them.

The *INEV* modal operator is used to describe the branching time structure captured in the model. The statement *INEV (i,s)* means that at the end of interval *i*, statement *s* is inevitable, that is, it holds in all branches that are possible at the end of time *i*. To talk about what is possibly true, we make use of the following definition:

$$POS(i,s) =_{def} \sim INEV (i,\sim s).$$

$POS(i,P)$ means that it is not true that $\sim s$ is inevitable at time i; in other words, s is possible at time i.

The *IFTRIED* modal operator is used to capture how individual plan instances can and cannot affect the external world and other plan instances. This operator takes a plan instance and sentence as arguments. We give the statement *IFTRIED(pi,s)* the English reading: "if plan instance *pi* were to be attempted, then *s* would be true". As we discussed earlier, we distinguish between the attempt of a plan instance and its (successful) occurrence, which we describe using the predicate *Occ*. If the attempt of a plan instance would lead to its occurrence, we say that it is **executable**. We introduce the following definition to talk about this concept:

$$Executable(pi) =_{def} IFTRIED(pi,Occ(pi)).$$

Along with capturing what a plan instance affects and the concept of executability, we can use *IFTRIED* to describe what a plan instance does not affect. To state that plan instance *pi* cannot make statement P false we can write

$$P \supset IFTRIED(pi,P).$$

That is, if P is true then the attempt of *pi* would not have made it false. The statement P can refer to any statement, modal or nonmodal, in the language. Typically, we will write statements where P refers to a proposition (i.e., event or property) at a particular time, which *pi* cannot affect, or P has form $Occ(pi2)$ to capture that *pi1* does not affect plan instance *pi2*. Section 3.5 shows many statements of this form and illustrates how they are used to draw useful conclusions.

3.4.2   Interpretations

An interpretation relates the terms and sentences in the language to the model structure. Terms are mapped to objects in the model, and sentences are given truth-values with respect to each world-history in a model. In our treatment, the denotation of a term is given by a unary function. We use $V(t)$ to refer to the object in the model that term t denotes. This treatment is a simplification in that a term's denotation does not vary from world-history to world-history. This is in contrast to a treatment where there is a two place interpretation function that can assign a term a different denotation in different world-histories. This would allow us to use terms such as "the block on the top of the stack", which could refer to different blocks in different world-histories.

We distinguish between different types of objects, which correspond to the different sorts in the language. Interval terms are mapped to intervals, plan instance terms are mapped to plan instances, and object terms are mapped to a set distinct from the intervals and plan instances. In this section we will discuss the interpretation of plan instance terms and the functions *Comp* and *TimeOf* defined on them. The interpretation of the other terms are straightforward and are given in appendix A.

Recall that a plan instance is an ordered pair of the form $<priS,baiS>$, where *priS* refers to a set of proposition instances (i.e., proposition/interval pairs) and *baiS* refers to a set of basic action instances (i.e., basic action/interval pairs). The set *priS* indicates the temporally annotated propositions associated with the plan instance, and *baiS* indicates the particular way that the plan instance is to be attempted. We use the notation $V(pi)|_1$ (the first element of the ordered pair) to refer to the set of proposition instances that *pi* refers to, and $V(pi)|_2$ (the second element of the ordered pair) to refer to the set of basic action instances instances that *pi* refers to.

The interpretation of the term $Comp(pi1,pi2)$ is given by

$$V(Comp(pi1, pi2))=<V(pi1)/_1 \cup V(pi2)/_1, V(pi1)/_2 \cup V(pi2)/_2>.$$

Thus, the composition of two plan instances is obtained by combining their abstract steps together and by combing their basic action instances together. The denotation of $TimeOf(pi)$, which describes *pi*'s execution time, is given by

$V(TimeOf(pi)) =$
$cover(\{i \mid$ there is a proposition p such that $<p,i> \in V(pi1)|_1\}$,
where $cover(iS)$, which was defined earlier, refers to the smallest interval
that contains the set of intervals, iS, given as its argument.

This definition specifies that the time associated with a plan instance is the smallest interval that contains all the times associated with its set of proposition instances (which necessarily contains all the times associated with the plan instance's set of basic action instances).

Interpretation of Sentences

The interpretation of a sentence indicates whether it is true or false in each world-history, which is a standard treatment of a modal language [Hughes and Cresswell 1968]. We will also use the function V to specify the interpretation of sentences. For each sentence S and world-history h, $V(S,h)$ is equal to T (i.e. true) if and only if S is true in world-history h. We now examine the interpretation of sentences formed with the temporal predicates and the eternal predicates *Occ* and *Meets* as well as the interpretation of the modal operators *INEV* and *IFTRIED*.

As we have seen, a sentence of the form $p(t_1, t_2,..., t_n,i)$, where p is a temporal predicate, refers to a proposition at a particular time. V is also defined for each predicate. For each temporal predicate symbol p having $n+1$ arguments, we define $V(p)$ as a function from AO^n to the set of propositions, where AO refers to the set of all objects in the model. This function indicates the proposition associated with the predicate symbol p and its first n arguments. Using $V(p)$, we can specify the interpretation of $p(t_1, t_2,..., t_n,i)$ by

$$V(p(t_1, t_2,..., t_n,i),h)=T \quad \text{iff} \quad <V(i),h> \in V(p)(V(t_1),V(t_2),...,V(t_n)).$$

Recall that propositions in the model refer to sets of interval/world-history pairs. If $<i,h> \in pr$, then proposition pr holds during interval i in world-history h. Thus, the interpretation captures that $p(t_1, t_2,..., t_n,i)$ is true in world-history h if and only if the property denoted by $"p(t_1, t_2,..., t_n)"$ holds during the interval denoted by i in world-history h.

The interpretation of the statement $Occ(pi)$ is given by

$V(Occ(pi),h)=T$ iff for every proposition instance $<x,i>$ in $V(pi)|_1 \cup V(pi)|_2$, $<i,h> \in x$.

Thus, this interpretation captures that a plan instance occurs in a world-history h if and only if all of its proposition instances and basic action instances occur in h.

The interpretation of interval relations are given by specifying the interpretation of $Meets(i1,i2)$ because all other interval relations, such as $Starts$ and $Equals$, are defined in terms of $Meets$ and the logical connectives. In our model, we introduced a semantic counterpart to the function symbol $Meets$, which we designate as $Meets'$ here to distinguish the two:

$V(Meets(i1,i2),h) = T$ iff $Meets'(V(i1),V(i2))$.

Because the right-hand side of the interpretation does not mention the world-history h, the truth-value of $Meets(i1,i2)$ does not vary from world-history to world-history. This means that intervals refer to a global time line and do not have temporal orders that vary from world-history to world-history.

Interpretation of the Modal Operators

While the truth-value of a nonmodal statement only depends on the world-history at which it is being evaluated, the truth-value of a modal operator depends on other world-histories linked by the accessibility relations, which in our case refer to the R relation and the closeness function. The interpretation of $INEV(i,P)$ is given by

$V(INEV(i,P),h)=T$ iff for every world-history $h2$,
  if $R(V(i),h,h2)$ then $V(P,h2) = T$.

This says that $INEV(i,P)$ is true at world-history h if and only if sentence P is true in all world-histories that are possible with respect to h at time i. In Pelavin [1988] we show that $INEV$ with a fixed temporal argument can be viewed as a S5 necessity operator [Hughes and Cresswell 1968]. We also discuss properties relating to its temporal argument, such as the fact that if $INEV(i,P)$ holds then $INEV(i2,P)$ holds for any interval $i2$ that ends before or the same time as i. To see these properties, the reader should refer to the axioms in appendix B.

The interpretation of $IFTRIED$ is given in terms of the F_{cl} function, which as we saw in section 3.3.5 is defined in terms of CL, the closeness function for individual basic action instances. The interpretation of $IFTRIED(pi,P)$ is given by

$V(IFTRIED(pi,P),h)=T$ iff for every world-history $h2$, if $h2 \in F_{cl}(V(pi)/2,h)$ then $V(P,h2) = T$.

Recall that $V(pi)/2$ refers to the set of basic action instances which captures what it means to attempt pi, and $F_{cl}(baiS,h)$ yields the world-histories that differ from h solely on the account of the basic action instances in $baiS$. Thus, $IFTRIED(pi,P)$ is true at world-history h if the effect of executing the basic action instances associated with pi in a context given by h yields world-histories where P holds in each of them.

3.5   Planning

In general, a planning problem can be given by

1)   a description of the external world in which plan execution is to take place, the **world description**;

2)   a description of the actions at the agent's disposal and their interactions, the **action specifications**; and

3)   a description of desired conditions, **the goal.**

The output is a temporally ordered collection of actions, the **plan** (instance), that would achieve the goal if executed in any world meeting the world description.

For standard state-based planners, such as STRIPS [Fikes and Nilsson 1971] and NOAH [Sacerdoti 1977], the goal refers to a set of properties that must hold at the completion of plan execution. The world description refers to a description of the initial state, and the action specifications refer to descriptions of each action's preconditions and effects. A plan that solves the goal is either taken to be a linear sequence of actions or a partially ordered set of actions. In our framework, the world description can include conditions describing the world during plan execution as well as conditions that hold prior to plan execution, the goal condition is given by an Interval Logic statement describing desired future conditions, and the action specifications are descriptions of (simple) plan instances, which are combined using the *Comp* operator to form composite plan instances.

3.5.1   Planner Correctness

We appeal to semantic entailment to define correctness, capturing what it means to say that a plan instance solves a goal with respect to the world description and action specifications. Semantic entailment, which we designate by $\models$, relates a set of sentences to a sentence. The relation $S \models P$ means that P holds in all world-histories in all models where each member of S holds. Given a goal G and a set of sentences S capturing the world description and the action specifications, we seek a composition $Comp(pi_1,pi_2, ...,pi_n)$ having the following properties:

C1) $S \vDash INEV(Ip, Executable(Comp(pi_1, pi_2, ..., pi_n)))$

C2) $S \vDash INEV(Ip, Occ(Comp(pi_1, pi_2, ..., pi_n)) \supset G,$
where *Ip* refers to the time of planning.

Condition C1 guarantees that in any world model that meets S, $Comp(pi_1, pi_2, ..., pi_n)$ can be executed under all possible circumstances (at planning time *Ip*). Condition C2 guarantees that in any world model that meets S, if $Comp(pi_1, pi_2, ..., pi_n)$ occurs successfully then the goal will hold under all possible circumstances.

This definition provides a notion of correctness that is appropriate with partial world descriptions. A planner meeting this correctness criteria will not accept a plan when relevant information is missing. Not meeting this criteria does not necessarily mean that the plan does not achieve the goal, but rather it is not known whether the plan achieves the goal with the information currently available. Being able to make a three-way distinction between knowing that a plan works, knowing that it does not work, and not knowing whether it works is a necessary first step towards working with partial world descriptions. It allows us to model the situation where relevant information is missing, a situation that should lead to gathering additional information or using conditional actions. This is in contrast to a notion of correctness involving nonmonotonic inference, where, unless one is very careful, the three-way distinction is blurred.

We must also note that defining correctness with respect to semantic entailment does not mean that the planner must be implemented as a theorem prover operating on our object language. Any algorithm may be used. To show that it meets our notion of correctness requires that one maps the possible inputs and the possible results of the algorithm to their equivalents in our language. Once these mappings are established, one could then try to prove or disprove that the algorithm meets our notion of correctness. In Pelavin [1988], we use this approach to show that the algorithm presented in section 3.6 is correct.

The remainder of this section discusses the statements that can be included in S, which consist of the world description and action specifications. We also demonstrate how to compute the effects of a composite plan instance and the conditions needed for its execution from the description of its individual components. Finally, we discuss the use of the STRIPS assumption and its analog "the persistence assumption" [McDermott 1982]. We demonstrate that these assumptions are inappropriate when planning with a partial world description. As an alternative, we introduce plan instances that maintain properties over intervals.

3.5.2   The World Description

We can think of two different approaches that may be taken to describe the external world: i) describe the possible futures that can arise, taking into account all the possible courses of action that the agent may take, or ii) describe the external world under the assumption that the agent remains inactive. In this development, we take the former approach. Thus, the world description is given by statements that describe a branching time structure. This branching tree structure captures possibilities that can be produced by the planning agent as well as possibilities that can be caused by other agents and external forces. We also assume that for any course of action the agent can take, there is at least one branch where these actions are taken.

The statements making up the world description can be divided into two categories: ones that indicate conditions and relations that hold in all branches, namely, ones that are inevitably true, and ones that describe conditions and relations that may only hold in some branches, namely, ones that are possibly true.

We use the modal statement $INEV(Ip, ILS)$, as defined earlier, to capture that Interval Logic statement ILS is inevitably true at time Ip. There are basically two types of Interval Logic statements that are inevitably true: i) statements that capture causal laws and definitions, and ii) statements describing properties or external events that hold (occur) in the scenario under consideration that cannot be affected by the agent's actions or nondeterminism in the external world.

Causal laws and definitions refer to relations between properties and events that are general principles, and thus, we assume they hold in all world-histories. For example, one can capture that a vase will break if it drops off the table by:

$$INEV(Ip, \forall i . VaseDrops(i) \supset \exists i2 . Meets(i,i2) \wedge VaseBreaks(i2)).$$

As another example, one might capture the relationship between the predicates *On* and *Clear* by saying that an object is clear over interval i if and only if there is no object on top of it at any time during i:

$$INEV(Ip, \forall obj, i . Clear(obj,i) \equiv \forall i2 . In(i2,i) \supset \\ \sim\exists obj2 . On(obj2,obj,i2)).$$

We also use statements that are inevitably true for conditions that the agent cannot affect. For example, one can state that the bank will open sometime between 9:00 A.M. and 9:30 A.M.

$$INEV(Ip, \exists i . BankOpens(i) \wedge DURING(i, i\_9:00\_9:30)),$$
where $i\_9:00\_9:30$ refers to the interval between 9:00 A.M. and 9:30 A.M.

The planning agent can only plan around or work with conditions that are inevitably true. These conditions will hold regardless of what the agent does; thus, they cannot be prevented and do not need to be enabled by the agent's actions.

To describe conditions that may only possibly hold, one can use statements of the form $POS(Ip, ILS)$, where ILS is an Interval Logic statement. Conditions that are possibly true (but not inevitably true) are ones that the agent may be able to enable or prevent.

3.5.3   The Action Specifications

Actions in the state-change model are described by identifying preconditions and effects. It is also necessary to capture what each action does not affect, namely, what properties remain true as the action is applied, either by including *frame axioms* or by making a STRIPS assumption.

In our framework plan instances, our analog to actions can be described in a similar manner. Recall that the effect of executing a plan instance is given by a function from world-history to set of world-histories. A plan instance's executability conditions serve as our analog to preconditions: they capture the world-histories in which a plan instance can be executed. A plan instance's effects describe conditions that hold in all world-histories where the plan instance (successfully) occurs.

To describe what a plan instance does not affect, we introduce statements that can be viewed as analogs to frame axioms. These statements are more general, however, because they can describe simultaneous conditions and simultaneous behaviors not affected by a plan instance. The reason that we introduce an analog to frame axioms, rather than an analog to the STRIPS assumption, is because in this initial development we want to stay within a deductive framework to avoid the problems caused when nonmonotonic inference is used with partial world descriptions. Moreover, we feel that it is important to first understand "deductive planning" in a concurrent, dynamic environment before bringing in nonmonotonicity. After we understand the problem deductively, we can carefully bring in nonmonotonicity to capture the analog to the STRIPS assumption in order to afford a more succinct description of actions. In section 3.7 we discuss this issue in more detail.

Executability Conditions

If we say that the Interval Logic statement EC captures plan instance pi's executability conditions, then we assume that pi is executable in all possible branches where EC holds; that is, the following holds:

$INEV(Ip, EC \supset Executable(pi))$.

Recall that $Executable(pi)$ is defined as $IFTRIED(pi,Occ(pi))$, meaning that pi is executable if it would occur if it were to be attempted. For example, one can encode that block A can be stacked on block B during i if both blocks are clear just prior to execution:

$INEV(Ip,Clear(A,ia) \wedge Meets(ia,i) \wedge Clear(B,ib) \wedge Meets(ib,i) \supset$
$Executable(Stack(A,B,i)))$.

Executability conditions are more general than preconditions. While preconditions refer to properties that hold just prior to execution, executability conditions can refer to properties, events, and other plan instances that have times prior or during execution. For example, one can encode that to sail across the lake, the wind must be blowing while the sailing takes place:

$INEV(Ip, WindBlowing(i0) \wedge In(i,i0) \supset Executable(Sail(i)))$.

Executability conditions can also mention other plan instances as well. For example, one can write

$INEV(Ip,Occ(GraspWrench(i0)) \wedge Meets(i0,i) \supset Executable(TightenBolt(i)))$

to capture that the agent can tighten the bolt if just previously it has grasped the wrench.

Effects

The effects of plan instances are given by Interval Logic statements. If we say that the Interval Logic statement EFF specifies plan instance pi's effects, then we assume that under all possible conditions if pi occurs then EFF holds; that is, the following holds:

EFF-CND)
$INEV(Ip,Occ(pi) \supset EFF)$.

It should be noted that EFF-CND is just a necessary condition that must hold to conclude that EFF specifies pi's effects. EFF-CND does not contain sufficient conditions because, for example, any tautology substituted for EFF would make EFF-CND true.

As an example of a statement describing effects, one can encode that the effect of stacking block A on block B during i is that A is on B immediately following execution:

$INEV(Ip,Occ(Stack(A,B,i)) \supset \exists i2 . Meets(i,i2) \wedge On(A,B,i2))$.

This treatment of effects is more general than the treatment of effects in state-based systems. Effects in our system do not just refer to properties that hold immediately following execution. They can also mention events and refer to any time period during or after execution. For example, one can state that the effect of sailing across the lake is that the boat is moving as the sailing takes place:

$INEV(Ip, Occ(Sail(a,b,i)) \supset Moving(i))$.

Simultaneous Effects

Ideally, we want to describe the effects of each plan instance in isolation and use these descriptions to compute the properties of their compositions. However, achieving this objective can be difficult. For example, there are situations where actions produce **simultaneous effects**, which are effects that are a function of two or more actions working in conjunction. For example, consider an object that is lifted by applying pressure to two ends of the object, one hand at each end, and then lifting. If pressure is only applied to one end, the result is a pushing action, not part of a lifting action. This situation can be captured by the following statements:

$INEV(Ip,Occ(PushLeft(i)) \land \sim Occ(PushRight(i)) \supset BoxSlidesLeft(i))$

$INEV(Ip,\sim Occ(PushLeft(i)) \land Occ(PushRight(i)) \supset BoxSlidesRight(i))$

$INEV(Ip,Occ(PushLeft(i)) \land Occ(PushRight(i)) \supset BoxLifted(i)).$

The statements above do not describe the effects of either action $PushLeft(i)$ or $PushRight(i)$ in isolation; rather, they describe the effects of the two actions together. Our formalism provides the flexibility to come closer to the ideal of describing actions in isolation by allowing us to describe effects as a *difference* between the case where an action is performed and the case where it is not. This allows us to formulate $PushLeft(i)$ and $PushRight(i)$ as applying different forces to the box over time as is done in physics. We can then determine how the box would move by summing all the forces that are being applied. In particular, we can introduce a predicate *ForceApplied* to describe the forces on an object over some time period. *PushLeft* then adds a *LeftForce* to the object being pushed:

$INEV(Ip, \forall v,i \ . \sim Occ(PushLeft(i)) \land ForcesApplied(v,i) \supset$
$IFTRIED(PushLeft(i), ForcesApplied(sum(v,LeftForce), i))).$

The above statement captures if v is the force on the box over time i if $PushLeft(i)$ does not occur, then the force on the box if $PushLeft(i)$ is tried will be v plus the new *LeftForce*. Similarly, we can describe $PushRight(i)$.

Describing the effects of a plan instance as a difference also arises in cases with simultaneous actions that consume resources, such as money. For example, consider the plan instance $BuyCD(cd,i)$, which refers to buying CD cd during interval i. To capture that a CD costs fifteen dollars, one might try the following specification:

CD1)
$INEV(Ip,\forall cd,x,i \ . \ Occ(BuyCD(cd,i)) \land \exists i0 \ . \ STARTS(i0,i) \land$
$MoneyAvail(x,i0)) \supset$
$(\exists i2 \ . \ Meets(i,i2) \land MoneyAvail(minus(x,15),i2))).$

CD1 captures that the agent has fifteen dollars less than when the "buying event" started. However, this is incorrect because there might be other "buying events" occurring simultaneously, in which case more than fifteen dollars is spent during i. The problem with CD1 is that it uses the amount of money prior to execution as a reference point. Instead, the amount of money that would be available if $BuyCD(cd,i)$ did not take place should be used. That is, we want to capture that the effect of buying a CD is that one has fifteen dollars less than one would have if one did not buy the CD. This can be represented by

CD2)
$INEV(Ip, \forall cd,x,i \ .(\sim Occ(Buy(cd,i)) \land \exists i2 \ . \ MoneyAvail(x,i2) \land$
$Finishes(i2,i) \land x \geq 15) \supset$
$IFTRIED(BuyCD(cd,i),$

$$\exists \; i3 \; . \; MoneyAvail(minus(x,15),i3) \wedge Finishes(i3,i)).$$

CD2 captures that if x is that amount of money that the agent has if it does not buy the CD (and the agent has more than fifteen dollars), then the agent would have $x\text{-}15$ dollars, if it were to purchase the CD.

Describing What a Plan Instance Does Not Affect

In our framework, saying that a plan instance does not affect a condition in a world-history means that if the condition holds in the world-history and the plan instance were to be attempted, then the condition would hold in the resulting world-histories. The general form to describe that plan instance pi does not affect condition P is given by

$$P \supset IFTRIED(pi,P).$$

It is important to keep in mind that both plan instance pi and condition P have times associated with them. This allows us to make statements about simultaneous activity or static conditions not affected by a plan instance, as well as about future conditions that are not affected. For example, to capture that under all circumstances placing an object on the table does not move the table while the moving takes place we can assert

$$INEV(Ip,TableStationary(i) \supset$$
$$IFTRIED(Place(Obj,Table,i),TableStationary(i))).$$

To capture that there is nothing that the agent can do to move the table during time i (i.e., because the table is rigidly fastened to the floor), we could assert

$$INEV(Ip,\forall pi \; . \; TableStationary(i) \supset IFTRIED(pi,TableStationary(i))).$$

Now, the statements above describe situations where a plan instance or set of plan instances could not affect a condition *under all circumstances*. However, in many situations an action has conditional effects and thus what the agent does not affect is also conditional. For example, if the agent flips the switch on the lamp to the on position, it does not affect the condition "the lamp is off" if the lamp is not plugged in. This can be expressed as follows:

$$INEV(Ip,LampUnplugged(i) \supset$$
$$(LampOff(i) \supset IFTRIED(FlipSwitch(i),LampOff(i)))).$$

As a final observation, note that it is not necessary to explicitly assert that a plan instance does not affect any condition in the past, since this is a general property of the *IFTRIED* operator. (See section 3.3.4 for the related constraints in the model and appendix B for the related axioms.)

Interactions Between the Agent and the External World

By being able to represent what the agent can affect and what the agent cannot affect, the formalism can capture how the agent and the external world can influence each other. To illustrate the flexibility of the representation, we consider a scenario where the planning agent shares a computer terminal with another agent, which we will denote by *agt2*. We will let *UsingTerm(agt,i)* refer to the condition that holds if agent *agt* is using the terminal during interval *i*. We will let *UseTerm(i)* refer to the plan instance "the planning agent uses the terminal during interval *i*".

In the world description, one can capture that agent *agt2* and the planning agent cannot be using the terminal at the same time under any possible circumstances by asserting

TERM-USE)
$$\forall\ i1,i2\ .\ {\sim}Disjoint(i1,i2)\ \supset$$
$$INEV(Ip,\ {\sim}(UsingTerm(agt2,i1)\ \wedge\ Occ(UseTerm(i2))))).$$

While this captures that the two agents cannot use the terminal at the same time, it does not capture the way in which the two agents can affect each other. For example, it does not capture whether the planning agent can prevent *agt2* from using the terminal, or whether one of the agents has priority over the other and can gain access at any time. In order to capture these causal relations, we must appeal to the *IFTRIED* operator. We now describe three types of interactions, showing how they can be encoded in our formalism.

The first case to consider is where under all circumstances, agent *agt2* has priority over the planning agent. That is, if *agt2* is using the terminal, the planning agent must wait until *agt2* is done. Furthermore, *agt2* can interrupt the planning agent at any time and gain use of the terminal. This type of relationship can be captured by the following specification:

Priority Scheme 1)
$$\forall i,pi\ .\ INEV(Ip,UsingTerm(agt2,i))\ \supset\ IFTRIED(pi,UsingTerm(agt2,i))),$$

which captures that under all conditions if agent *agt2* is using the terminal, there is nothing the planning agent can do to prevent this from happening. Using priority scheme 1 and the TERM-USE constraint, one can deduce that the following holds:

$$\forall i,i2\ .\ {\sim}Disjoint(i,i2)\supset INEV(Ip,UsingTerm(agt2,i2))\supset$$
$${\sim}Executable(UseTerm(i))).$$

This captures that the planning agent cannot use the terminal during interval *i* if the other agent is going to be on the terminal during any time that overlaps with *i*. Thus, under priority scheme 1, the planning agent has no influence over the other agent; it cannot prevent this agent from using the terminal. Instead, if the planning agent wants to use the terminal during interval *i* it must refer to its world description to determine whether the other agent is expected to be using the terminal during any time that overlaps with *i*. If this information is not available, the agent may plan to gather it.

Let us now consider a case that is the reverse of the above priority relationship, where the planning agent has priority over *agt2*. Thus, we assume that it is inevitable that the planning agent can interrupt *agt2* at any time and gain use of the terminal. This relationship can be captured by asserting

Priority Scheme 2)

$\forall i . INEV(Ip, Executable(UseTerm(i)))$,

which captures that *UseTerm(i)* is executable under all possible conditions. For simplicity we are ignoring other conditions needed for execution, such as being near the terminal. From priority scheme 2 and the TERM-USE constraint, one can deduce

$\forall i, i2 . \sim Disjoint(i, i2) \supset$
$INEV(Ip, IFTRIED(UseTerm(i), \sim UsingTerm(agt2, i2)))$.

That is, the planning agent can prevent *agt2* from using the terminal during a time *i2* by using the terminal during a time that overlaps with *i2*. Under this priority scheme, the planning agent can choose to use the terminal at any time without needing to consider the other agent's plans for using the terminal.

Let us now examine a third priority relationship where the agent that first tries to use the terminal gets the terminal until it is done. If both agents try to use the terminal at the same time, we assume that the planning agent gets it. This priority relationship can be captured by the following specification:

Priority Scheme 3)

$\forall i . INEV(Ip, \sim (\exists i0 . OverlapsFinishedbyContains(i0, i) \wedge$
$UsingTerm(agt2, i0))$
$\equiv Executable(UseTerm(i)))$.

Priority scheme 3 captures that the planning agent can use the terminal during interval *i* if and only if the other agent is not going to be on the terminal during any time that begins before or at the same time as *i* and extends into *i*.

Interactions Between Plan Instances

By describing what an action does not affect, we capture interactions between plan instances as well as the interactions between plan instances and conditions in the external world. To determine whether two plan instances can be executed together, we must determine whether they harmfully interact. Statements using the form $P \supset IFTRIED(pi, P)$ can describe the lack of harmful interactions.

To state that *pi1* and *pi2* do not harmfully interact, we define a new predicate *NoConflict*:

$NoConflict(pi1, pi2) =_{def}$
$(Executable(pi1) \supset IFTRIED(pi2, Executable(pi1))) \wedge$
$(Occ(pi1) \supset IFTRIED(pi2, Occ(pi1))) \wedge$
$(Executable(pi2) \supset IFTRIED(pi1, Executable(pi2))) \wedge$
$(Occ(pi2) \supset IFTRIED(pi1, Occ(pi2)))$.

In other words, if *pi1* is executable then it would be executable if *pi2* were attempted, and if *pi1* occurs then it would still occur if *pi2* were to be attempted, and vice versa. We can now assert that two plan instances *Pi1* and *Pi2* do not harmfully interact under any conditions:

$$INEV(Ip, NoConflict(Pi1,Pi2)).$$

We can also describe plan instances that conditionally interact in a harmful way, using

$$INEV(Ip,C \supset NoConflict(Pi1,Pi2)).$$

In the case where concurrent plan instances *Pi1* and *Pi2* meet the relation above, we say that the two plan instances **conditionally interfere**. For example, we can capture that the plan instances "Run heater during time *i*" and "Run saw during time *i*" do not interfere if their common power supply puts out two or more units of power over interval *i*:

$$INEV(Ip,MinPowerSupplied(2,i) \supset NoConflict(RunHeater(i),RunSaw(i))).$$

3.5.4   Plan Instance Composition

The central operation in planning is composition: given a description of the individual actions (plan instances), a planner determines whether there is a composition that solves the goal. This section discusses how the executability conditions and the effects of a composite action can be computed from the definitions of its component parts. It only examines pairwise composition because the composition of three or more plan instances is defined in terms of pairwise composition.

Executability Conditions for Composite Plan Instances

As we have discussed, the composition *Comp(pi1,pi2)* can refer to a sequential composition, concurrent composition, or one where the steps are separated by a gap of time. In the case where the plan instances are arranged sequentially or are separated by a gap, our treatment of composition parallels the treatment in the state-based framework. In order to draw some parallels with the traditional state-based approach, we will first consider the composition of sequential plan instances.

The Composition of Sequential Plan Instances

The state-based model provides a simple basis for computing the preconditions of a sequence of actions from the description of the actions in the sequence. The sequence *a1;a2* can be executed in a state *s* if i) the preconditions of *a1* hold in *s*, ii) applying action *a1* in state *s* does not negate *a2*'s preconditions, and iii) the preconditions of *a2* not brought about by *a1* hold in *s*. In our system there is an analogous relation that allows us to compute the executability conditions for a composition of two plan instances that do not overlap in time. In particular, if *pi1* is before or meets *pi2*, then the executability conditions for *Comp(pi1,pi2)* can be taken to be the conjunction of i') *pi1*'s executability conditions, ii') conditions that guarantee that *pi1* does not negate *pi2*'s executability conditions, and iii') *pi2*'s executability conditions not brought about by *pi1*'s effects.

The fact that *Comp(pi1,pi2)* is executable in world-history *h* if i') – iii') hold can be seen by examining the semantic constraints and interpretations presented in sections 3.3 and 3.4. Recall that *Comp(pi1,pi2)* is executable if attempting it would result in both *pi1* and *pi2* occurring. The result of jointly attempting two nonoverlapping plan instances in a world-history *h* is obtained by first modifying *h* to account for the attempt of the earlier one, *pi1* in our case, and then modifying this resulting world-history (really a set of histories) to account for the attempt of the later plan instance. If *pi1* is executable in *h*, attempting *pi1* leads to a world-history *h1* where *pi1* occurs. Modifying *h1* by attempting *pi2* leads to a world-history *h2* where *pi1* still occurs since *pi2* cannot affect conditions in its past. So if *pi2*'s executability conditions are either brought about by *pi1*, or hold in *h* and are not negated by *pi1*, then *pi2* is executable in *h1*. Thus, both plan instances occur in *h2*, and thus, by definition *Comp(pi1,pi2)* is executable in world history *h*.

The Composition of Concurrent Plan Instances

Concurrent composition is the composition of two (or more) plan instances with overlapping times of execution. For concurrent composition, we must determine whether the plan instances conflict with each other, that is, whether they interfere or one ruins another's executability conditions.

If two plan instances conflict under all conditions, that is, they necessarily conflict, then there are no conditions under which their composition is executable. The interesting case occurs when two plan instances conditionally conflict. As we have seen, a conditional conflict can be captured using a statement of the form

A1) $INEV(Ip,C \supset NoConflict(pi1, pi2))$.

If the above statement holds and neither *pi2* nor *pi1* can negate *C*:

A2) $INEV(Ip,C \supset IFTRIED(pi1, C)) \land INEV(Ip, C \supset IFTRIED(pi2,C))$,

then the executability conditions for *Comp(pi1,pi2)* can be given by the conjunction: $EC(pi1) \land EC(pi2) \land C$, where $EC(pi)$ refers to plan instance *pi*'s executability conditions.[3] This is seen as follows. Consider a world history *h* in which $EC(pi1) \land EC(pi2) \land C$ holds. We then revise it by attempting *pi1* to produce world-history *h2*, which in turn is revised to produce world-history *h3* by attempting *pi2*. Plan instance *pi1* is executable in *h*, since its executability

---

3. This relation is stronger than it needs to be for cases where *pi1* or *pi2* partially brings about the other's executability conditions.

conditions $EC(pi1)$ hold in h, and so $Occ(pi1)$ is true in $h2$. Condition C also holds in $h2$ by A2 above and the assumption that C holds in h. Thus, $pi1$ and $pi2$ do not conflict in $h2$ by A1. Now, using the assumption that $pi2$ is executable in h and $NoConflict(pi1,pi2)$ holds in h (because C does and A1), we can use the definition of $NoConflict$ to derive that $pi2$ is also executable in $h2$. Consequently, $pi2$ occurs in $h3$. Finally, we derive that $pi1$ occurs in $h3$ because it holds in $h2$ and the attempt of $pi2$ does not ruin this occurrence since $NoConflict(pi1,pi2)$ holds in $h2$. Thus we have shown that both $pi1$ and $pi2$ occur in $h3$ and hence, by definition, $Comp(pi1,pi2)$ is executable in h.

This argument can also be used to show that if $pi1$ and $pi2$ do not conflict under any circumstances (i.e., $INEV(Ip, NoConflict(pi1,pi2))$) holds), then the executability condition for $Comp(pi1,pi2)$ is simply the conjunction of $pi1$'s and $pi2$'s executability conditions.

The Effects Produced by Composite Plan Instances

We have seen that there are two ways to specify effects: by specifying conditions that will inevitably hold if the plan instance occurs, or by specifying the difference between a world-history in which the action is executed and one where it is not. In this presentation, we will just explore joint effects when individual effects are given in the first way. In this case, we have a very simple relation between joint effects and individual effects: the effects of $Comp(pi1,pi2)$ are given by the conjunction of $pi1$'s and $pi2$'s effects. That is, the following is a valid statement:

> **CE1)** $(INEV(Ip,Occ(pi1) \supset EFF1) \land INEV(Ip,Occ(pi2) \supset EFF2))$
> $\supset INEV(Ip,Occ(Comp(pi1,pi2)) \supset EFF1 \land EFF2).$

The reason that this is valid is because the connection between $pi1$ and $EFF1$ (and similarly between $pi2$ and $EFF2$) holds under all circumstances; that is, this connection holds no matter which external events or other plan instances are executed. If, for example, $pi1$ and $pi2$ cannot be executed together, that is, they necessarily interfere, then the conclusion in CE1 will vacuously hold; that is, $INEV(Ip,Occ(Comp(pi1,pi2)) \supset EFF1 \land EFF2)$ would hold because $INEV(Ip,\sim Occ(Comp(pi1,pi2)))$ would hold.

3.5.5   Persistence and Maintenance Plan Instances

A common situation that arises during planning is that an action's precondition is true at an earlier time and there are intermediate actions or events that occur between that time and the action. If none of these intermediate actions affects the precondition, then one does not have to reachieve this condition. In a state-based model, the STRIPS assumption [Waldinger 1977] can be used to make such an inference. In our system, we also need to reason about properties remaining true. For instance, if an action brings about a property, typically, we can only say that it holds right after execution, not how long it holds. As an example, the effect of a "stacking" action was earlier given by

$INEV(Ip,Occ(Stack(A,B,i))) \supset \exists i2 . Meets(i,i2) \wedge On(A,B,i2))$,

which captures that block A will be on block B immediately after $Stack(A,B,i)$ is performed. It does not, however, indicate for how long this property remains true. A generalization of the STRIPS assumption for a formalism with an explicit time line and simultaneous events has been called the *persistence assumption* [McDermott 1982]. This assumption can be given by:

> If property *pr* holds immediately prior to interval *i* and one cannot deduce that *pr* is not true throughout *i* assume that pr holds throughout *i*.

The persistence assumption, however, is problematic with a partial world description because it is a nonmonotonic rule. In addition, it has been geared towards *prediction* rather than *plan generation*. As a consequence, uses of the persistence assumption have not distinguished between properties that the agent can plan to keep true versus ones it has no control over. As we will see, it is important to make this distinction. In the literature, much attention has been paid to problems with the persistence assumption, the most notable being the "Yale shooting problem" [Hanks and McDermott 1986]. This has prompted a number of solutions to correct these problems [Kautz 1986; Lifschitz 1986; Morgenstern and Stein 1988; Shoham 1986]. However, none of these solutions addresses the problems with partial world descriptions and the distinction between the use for plan generation versus the use for prediction.

First consider the problems caused when the persistence assumption is used with a partial world description. Assume that interval *i0* meets interval *i1*, property Pr is true during interval *i0*, and if event Ev occurs during *i1*, Pr will not persist through *i1*. These relations can be captured by the following Interval Logic statement:

$Meets(i0,i1) \wedge Pr(i0) \wedge (Ev(i1) \supset \sim Pr(i1))$.

If there are no other statements in the world description from which we can infer whether or not event Ev occurs during *i1*, we can use the persistence assumption to infer that Pr remains true throughout *i1*, that is, $Pr(i1)$ holds because it is consistent to do so. Additionally, from $Ev(i1) \supset \sim Pr(i1)$ and $Pr(i1)$ we can conclude $\sim Ev(i1)$, that is, event Ev does not occur during *i1*. Thus, we can infer that a property holds even when there is an event instance that could negate it but we do not know if the event occurred. This then entails that the event instance does not occur, an unwarranted conclusion since Ev could be quite likely to occur. Unless its occurrence is provable, however, using the persistence assumption will commit us to its nonoccurrence.

An alternative approach can be used that makes the assumptions underlying the persistence rule explicit. If there exists a set $\{ei_1,ei_2, ...,ei_n\}$ containing all the event instances that could negate a property, then we could justify the persistence assumption by assuming that none of the events in $\{ei_1,ei_2, ...,ei_n\}$ occurs. This type of analysis is suggested by Georgeff [1986], Pelavin [1988] and Schubert [1990]. In this approach, one deduces that a property continues to hold if and only if one can deduce that no member of $\{ei_1,ei_2, ...,ei_n\}$ occurs. Thus, if our world description is noncommittal as to whether the elements of $\{ei_1,ei_2, ...,ei_n\}$ occur, we do not conclude whether the property holds or not. This is in contrast to the persistence assumption approach, which jumps to the conclusion that a property persists when there is no information about any member of $\{ei_1,ei_2, ...,ei_n\}$.

The analysis above applies to prediction as well as to planning. When we consider planning, however, an important distinction must be made. It is necessary to divide the set of event instances that can negate a property into those that are initiated by the planning agent and those that are caused by external events. If only the agent's actions can negate a property, then the agent can plan to keep the property true by not performing any of these actions. On the other hand, if some of the event instances that can negate the property are external events that the planning agent cannot prevent, the agent cannot assume that the property persists. The agent can only consult its world description (or gather more information) to see if any of the "negating external events" are expected to occur. We now present a scheme that allows us to make this distinction and to plan to achieve persistences just like we plan to achieve other goals and subgoals.

We introduce a class of plan instances that we call **maintenance plan instances** to reason about persistence. A maintenance plan instance is entered into a plan to keep a property true over some time period. These plan instances are used in place of making a STRIPS or persistence assumption. We will use the function term $mtn(pr,i)$ to refer to the plan instance where the agent maintains the property denoted by pr over interval i.[4] The effect of $mtn(pr,i)$ is that pr holds during i, which is captured by $INEV(Ip,Occ(mtn(Pr,i)) \supset Pr(i))$.

Whether an executable maintenance plan instance exists for a property depends on how the property is affected by the external world and the agent's actions. If only the agent's actions can negate a property, the property can be maintained at any time for any duration. Consider the following example. Suppose if the agent's car is parked, the only way it will be moved is if the agent drives it away (i.e., we assume that the car cannot be stolen, towed, etc.). In this case, the agent can always maintain the property that the car is parked:

$$\forall i,i0 . INEV(Ip, Meets(i0,i) \land CarParked(i0) \supset$$
$$Executable(mtn(CarParked,i))).$$

In other words, it is inevitable that if the car is parked during any interval $i0$, then the agent can keep the car parked during i, an interval that can have any duration. Of course, this maintenance plan instance must be defined to conflict with any plan to drive the car away so that the composite plan to maintain the car in the parking lot at i and to drive the car away during a time that overlaps with i would not be executable.

---

4. For simplicity we will not distinguish between the first argument to mtn, which is a *term* denoting a property, and the property itself.

If external events as well as the agent's actions can negate some property, the situation is more complicated. If we modify the above example by introducing a towing event that can negate *CarParked*, this situation must be captured by the following:

$$\forall i,i0 \; . \; INEV(Ip,(Meets(i0,i) \wedge CarParked(i0) \wedge$$
$$\sim(\exists i2 \; . \; \sim Disjoint(i,i2) \wedge CarTowed(i2))) \supset$$
$$Executable(mtn(CarParked,i))).$$

This says that under all possibilities the agent can keep the car parked during a time period *i* if previously the car was parked and a towing event does not occur any time that overlaps with *i*. In this case, the agent can determine that it can maintain *CarParked* over *i* if it knows that it is inevitable that no towing event will take place, or if it knows that it can prevent a towing event if one could possibly arise.

In general it is necessary to circumscribe the set of events that can negate the property *CarParked*. For example, if it is also possible that the car may be stolen, the above axiom would not be correct; instead, we would want:

$$\forall i,i0 \; . \; INEV(Ip, (Meets(i0,i) \wedge CarParked(i0) \wedge$$
$$\sim(\exists i2 \; . \; \sim Disjoint(i,i2) \wedge CarStolen(i2)) \wedge$$
$$\sim(\exists i2 \; . \; \sim Disjoint(i,i2) \wedge CarTowed(i2))) \supset$$
$$Executable(mtn(CarParked,i))).$$

The last type of properties to consider are those that can be negated only by external events that cannot be affected by the agent. In this case, there does not exist a plan instance that can maintain them. That is, there is no action the agent can take (or avoid) to make one of these properties remain true. If one is constructing a plan where it is desired that a persistence of this type holds, one must consult the world description to see if the persistence can be inferred.

In nonlinear planning systems [Sacerdoti 1977], the STRIPS assumption is implemented in the guise of *phantom nodes*. The function that phantom nodes provide is to prevent one from linking (maintaining) a property true at some state to a later state if there is an intermediate action that negates the property. Analogously, in our system, if a property *pr* is maintained over some interval *i*, then one cannot introduce a plan instance that negates *pr* sometime during *i*. The conflict between a property being maintained and an action that can negate it is detected as (concurrent) interference. If plan instance *pi* negates property *pr* any time during interval *i*, then *pi* and *mtn(pr,i)* necessarily interfere and thus cannot be done together. In the algorithm we present in the next section, we exploit this relation and detect all harmful interactions by just considering the interference between overlapping plan instances.

3.6   A Planning Algorithm

In this section, we present a simple planning algorithm applicable in domains with concurrent actions and external events. In Pelavin [1988] a proof is given showing that this algorithm meets the criteria for correctness that we presented in section 3.5.1. This algorithm adapts the algorithm (ILP) presented in chapter 1 to be applicable with a partial or imprecise world description, and to handle a wide variety of concurrent interactions. Our algorithm is novel in its use of noninterference conditions, which are specified by a user and capture the conditions under which a pair of concurrent plan instances do not interfere. All harmful interactions, both sequential and concurrent, derive from the noninterference conditions. A second departure from the standard approach is the use of maintenance plan instances in place of a STRIPS assumption.

This algorithm is presented to illustrate the novel perspective gained by using our logic. Our primary concern in this development is the expressiveness of the formalism and as such many specific implementation issues related to the planner are not addressed at this stage. In section 3.6.4, we discuss some efficiency issues that must be considered and the limitations of this simple algorithm, the most pressing being that when an action is entered into the plan, one must commit to the time that it is executed; this is more restrictive than nonlinear planners [Sacerdoti 1977] and ILP, which allow one to partially describe these times and to incrementally add constraints to avoid conflicts.

3.6.1 The Input to the Planning Algorithm

The input to the planning problem is given by the world description, the action specifications, and the goal. These are given using statements from the set of Interval Logic statements, which we designate by **ILS**. Formally, the input to our algorithm is given by the tuple $<W,G,SPI,EFF,EC,NI>$, where

$\quad$ **W:** $\quad$ the **world description**, a subset of ILS describing conditions and relationships that are inevitably true; and

$\quad$ **G:** $\quad$ the **goal**, a nonempty subset of ILS describing the goal conditions.

The action specifications are

$\quad$ **SPI:** $\quad$ a set of terms denoting the simple plan instances that can be used to form composite plan instances;

$\quad$ **EFF:** $\quad$ a function from SPI to 2^{ILS} describing the effects produced by each simple plan instance;

$\quad$ **EC:** $\quad$ a function from SPI to 2^{ILS} describing the executability conditions for each simple plan instance; and

$\quad$ **NI:** $\quad$ a function from SPI$\times$SPI to 2^{ILS}; the relation $NI(pi1,pi2)$ describes the noninterference conditions relating $pi1$ and $pi2$, which are conditions that must hold in order to execute $pi1$ and $pi2$ together. For nonoverlapping plan instances, $NI(pi1,pi2)$ is the null set.

In the following section, we discuss these components in more detail, showing how a planning problem, given by these components, corresponds to assertions in our logic. We then discuss the algorithm in section 3.6.2, present examples in section 3.6.3, and finally discuss its limitations in section 3.6.4.

The World Description

The world description W is given by a set of Interval Logic statements describing conditions and relationships that are inevitably true at planning time Ip. Thus, saying IL belongs to W is equivalent to saying that $INEV(Ip,IL)$ holds.

Both relative temporal descriptions, such as "event ev occurs after planning time", and temporal relations that are given by referring to intervals forming a date-line structure may be used. The user has the flexibility to describe any date-line structure that can be expressed using intervals. Thus, for example, the user can choose between a discrete model of time where there are primitive intervals that cannot be decomposed and one where any interval can be more finely divided. If a date-line structure is used, the temporal relations between the intervals forming this structure must be specified in the world description.

Sentences belonging to W may describe the events that occur and the properties that hold at various times, along with causal laws and definitions that relate events and properties. We do not place any restrictions on the form of the sentences belonging to W and do not require that it is complete. If one does not know whether or not an external event occurs, one simply omits it from W. The only ramification of using an incomplete or imprecise world description is that we may not be able to find a plan to solve the goal that could be solved if we had a more complete or precise description.

Effects

A plan instance's effects are given by a set of Interval Logic statements. Setting $EFF(pi)$ to $\{e_1, e_2, ..., e_n\}$ means that $INEV(Ip,Occ(pi) \supset e_i)$ holds for each i; that is, under all possibilities, if pi (successfully) occurs then each e_i will be true. A plan instance's effects are used to determine which conditions it achieves with respect to the world description. Plan instance pi can be used to achieve condition C if $W \cup EFF(pi) \vdash C$. That is, plan instance pi can be used to achieve condition C if C is derivable (in Interval Logic) from the world description augmented with pi's effects. Note that this also includes *indirect effects*, which refer to conditions that are produced by the action's execution, but not explicitly listed in the effect specifications. This type of capability has been treated by other planning systems such as SIPE [Wilkins 1988] and DEVISER [Vere 1981].

The only restriction placed on $EFF(pi)$ is that it does not refer to any conditions that hold earlier than pi's execution time. We allow specifications that may only partially describe an action's effects, specifications described by a material implication (for a conditional effect), and ones given by a disjunction (which can be used to describe the effect of a nondeterministic action). This flexible treatment of effects is not problematic because we do not make a STRIPS assumption.

Executability Conditions

A plan instance's executability conditions are given by a set of Interval Logic statements. Setting $EC(pi)$ to $\{ec_1, ec_2, ..., ec_n\}$ means that

$$INEV(Ip,(ec_1 \wedge ec_2 \wedge ... \wedge ec_n) \supset Executable(pi))$$

is true. That is, under all possibilities, if pi's executability conditions hold then if pi were to be attempted then pi would (successfully) occur. The only restriction placed on $EC(pi)$ is that it does not refer to any conditions that hold later than pi's time of execution.

Executability conditions pertain to the individual execution of a plan instance. If a plan instance's executability conditions hold in W, then a plan consisting of just this plan instance could be successfully executed. If, however, the plan contains other plan instances in addition to pi, then pi may not successfully occur because of conflicts with other plan instances in the plan. To encode the conditions under which two (or more) plan instances conflict, we appeal to noninterference conditions.

Noninterference Conditions

Noninterference conditions are given for each pair of overlapping (simple) plan instances by a set of Interval Logic statements. Setting $NI(pi1,pi2)$ to $\{n_1, n_2, ..., n_n\}$ means that

$$INEV(Ip, (n_1 \wedge n_2 \wedge ... \wedge n_n) \supset NoConflict(pi1,pi2))$$

holds. That is, if $pi1$'s and $pi2$'s noninterference conditions hold then they do not interfere and consequently can be executed together if both $pi1$'s and $pi2$'s executability conditions hold. If $pi1$ and $pi2$ do not interfere under any conditions, we set $NI(pi1,pi2)$ to $\{ \}$, the null set, meaning that $NoConflict(pi1,pi2)$ inevitably holds. If $pi1$ and $pi2$ interfere under all conditions, we set $NI(pi1,pi2)$ to $\{FALSE\}$, where FALSE is a statement that is logically false. We also restrict NI so that $NI(pi1,pi2)=NI(pi2,pi1)$, which is justified since

$$NoConflict(pi1,pi2) \equiv NoConflict(pi2,pi1).$$

When describing noninterference conditions, one can be conservative in the following sense. If one does not know whether or not two concurrent plan instances interfere, their noninterference conditions can be set to $\{FALSE\}$. The effect of this is that a plan will never be accepted containing both these plan instances since all noninterference conditions for plan instances in the plan must be achieved, and FALSE can never be achieved. Also, stating that the noninterference conditions for $pi1$ and $pi2$ is $\{FALSE\}$ does not mean that they necessarily interfere, it just says that if FALSE is true then $pi1$ and $pi2$ do not interfere, a statement that is vacuously true. We must note that failure means that a plan could not be found using the information currently available, not that a plan does not exist to achieve the goal.

3.6.2 The Algorithm

The planning algorithm is a backward chaining algorithm adapted from the algorithm described in chapter 1. A **goal stack** is maintained, which refers to a set of conditions to be achieved. Initially, the goal stack is set to the goal conditions G. During each cycle, a planning operation that is "applicable" is chosen to remove a condition from the goal stack, and new conditions may be added. The algorithm terminates in success if the goal stack becomes empty. In this case, the composition of all the plan instances that have been introduced into the plan form a solution, namely, a composite plan instance that can be successfully executed to achieve the goal conditions in a context given by the world description.

The state of the planning process is given by two state variables *INPLAN* and *GS* where

> **INPLAN** is a set of plan instances indicating the plan instances that have already been entered into the plan; and

> **GS** is a set of Interval Logic statements indicating the conditions in the goal stack.

Initially, *INPLAN* is set to the null set (indicating that initially there are no plan instances in the plan) and *GS* is set to the goal conditions. Any state where *GS* is empty is a solution state.

There are two planning operators, **REMOVE** and **INTRO**. REMOVE is used to remove a condition from the goal stack that holds in the world description. REMOVE(C) is applicable in any state where C is in the goal stack and C is derivable (in Interval Logic) from the set of sentences capturing the world description. Since any condition derivable from W holds under all circumstances no matter which actions the agent performs, C can simply be removed from the goal stack.

The planning operator INTRO introduces a new plan instance into the plan to remove a goal condition. INTRO(C,pi) is applicable in any state where C is in the goal stack and C is derivable from the set formed by adding pi's effects to W. That is, C is a condition that would be true if pi could be successfully executed in a context given by the world description. INTRO(C,pi) updates INPLAN to indicate that pi belongs to the plan, and modifies GS by removing C and adding pi's executability conditions along with noninterference conditions between pi and any overlapping plan instance already in the plan. Formally, the applicability conditions and effects of the planning operators are as follows, where $\vdash$ denotes provability in Interval Logic:

REMOVE(C) is applicable in state <INPLAN,GS> if $C \in$ GS and W ⊢ C.
The resulting state is <INPLAN,GS – {C}>

INTRO(C,pi) is applicable if $C \in$ GS and W $\cup$ EFF(pi) ⊢ C. The resulting
state is <INPLAN $\cup$ {pi}, (GS – {C}) $\cup$ EC(pi) $\cup$ {n | n $\in$ NI(pi,pix) and
pix∈ INPLAN}>.

3.6.3   Planning Examples

In this section, a number of simple planning problems are presented to
demonstrate the basic features of our planning algorithm. In particular, we
illustrate the treatment of both sequential and concurrent interactions. We also
show how our approach enables us to relax some of the restrictions that must be
imposed using other methods.

For the examples in this section, we make use of a simple date-line
structure that is indexed by the terms $I0, i1, I2, ...$, where $I0$ refers to the time of
planning, $I0$ meets $I1, I1$ meets $I2$, and so on. Thus, the set {$Meets(I0,I1)$,
$Meets(I1,I2), ...$} belongs to W in each of our planning examples.

The Two Planning Operators

To start, we present a simple planning example that illustrates the use of the
two planning operators REMOVE and INTRO. Consider a safe which is locked
at the time of planning $I0$. At this time also, the key that opens this safe rests
on a nearby table. The agent's goal is to have the safe opened by the end of
interval $I2$. We show that this goal can be solved by a plan instance composed of
the two simple plan instances "grasp the key during $I1$" and "open the safe with
the key during $I2$". We will use the term $GraspKey(I1)$ to refer to this first plan
instance and $OpenSafe(I2)$ to refer to the second.

The input specification capturing this planning problem is listed below.
Note that it does not need to include noninterference conditions because
$GraspKey(I1)$ and $OpenSafe(I2)$ do not overlap in time.

G: {∃ $i . SafeIsOpen(i) \land EndsBefEq(i,I2)$}

W: {$SafeIsLocked(I0), KeyOnTable(I0), Meets(I0,I1), Meets(I1,I2)$}

GraspKey(I1)
EC: {∃ $i . KeyOnTable(i) \land Meets(i, I1)$}
EFF: {∃ $i . HoldingKey(i) \land EndsEq(i,I1)$}

OpenSafe(I2)
EC: {∃ $i . HoldingKey(i) \land Meets(i,I2)$}
EFF: {∃ $i . SafeIsOpen(i) \land EndsEq(i,I2)$}.

The goal statement is true if the safe is open during an interval that ends before
or at the same time as $I2$, that is, by the end of $I2$. The world description set W
indicates that the safe is locked during planning time $I0$ and the key is on the

table during $I0$. Plan instance $GraspKey(I1)$'s executability conditions are true if the key is on the table during a time just prior to $GraspKey(I1)$'s execution. Its effect is that the key is being grasped during an interval that ends at the same time as $I1$. Finally, $OpenSafe(I2)$'s executability conditions are true if the key is grasped just prior to its execution, and its effect is true if the safe is open at its completion.

Before execution, $INPLAN$ is set to the null set and GS is set to G. Initially, the $INTRO$ operator applied to $OpenSafe(I2)$ is applicable, while $INTRO$ using $GraspKey(I1)$ and $REMOVE$ are not. $INTRO$ using $OpenSafe(I2)$ is applicable because the goal condition is derivable in Interval Logic from $\{\exists i . SafeIsOpen(i) \land EndsEq(i,I2)\}$, a subset of $W \cup EFF(OpenSafe(I2))$.

The result of introducing plan instance $OpenSafe(I2)$ is that the goal G is removed from GS and $OpenSafe$'s executability conditions and relevant noninterference conditions are added. Because $INPLAN$ is empty, there are no noninterference conditions to be added. Thus, GS at the end of the first cycle is set to

$$\{\exists \ i . HoldingKey(i) \land Meets(i,I2)\}$$

and INPLAN is set to $\{OpenSafe(I2)\}$.

At the second cycle, $INTRO$ using $GraspKey(I1)$ is applicable since the condition on the goal stack is derivable from $\{\exists i . HoldingKey(i) \land EndsEq(i,I1)), Meets(I1,I2)\}$, a subset of $W \cup EFF(GraspKey(I1))$.

The result of introducing $GraspKey(I1)$ is that $INPLAN$ is set to $\{OpenSafe(I2), GraspKey(I1)\}$, and GS is set to

$$\{\exists i . KeyOnTable(i) \land Meets(i,I1)\}.$$

As before, no noninterference conditions are added, this time because $OpenSafe(I2)$ does not overlap with $GraspKey(I1)$.

At cycle three, $REMOVE$ can be used to remove the condition making up the goal stack since this condition is derivable from $\{Meets(I0,I1), KeyOnTable(I0)\}$, a subset of W. Since GS is now empty, the algorithm terminates indicating that the plan instance $Comp(GraspKey(I1),OpenSafe(I2))$, which is the composition of the members of $INPLAN$, solves the goal G.

Sequential Interactions and Maintenance

We now consider a situation where an earlier plan instance may ruin a later one's executability conditions, this being the principal conflict detected in state-based systems. To illustrate this situation, we complicate our first example by adding a second condition that must hold in order for $OpenSafe(I2)$ to be executable: the agent must be within arm's reach of the safe just prior to execution. Thus, $OpenSafe(I2)$'s executability conditions are now taken to be

OpenSafe(I2)
EC: $\{\exists i . HoldingKey(i) \land Meets(i,I2)),$
$\quad \exists j . CloseToSafe(j) \land Meets(j,I2))\},$

where the term $CloseToSafe(j)$ means that the agent is close to the safe (within arm's length) during interval j. We also assume that this property holds at planning time, and thus modify W from the above example to include $CloseToSafe(I0)$.

Let us now examine the operation of the planning algorithm with these two modifications. We first iterate through three cycles of the planning algorithm as before. The only difference from our earlier example is that there are two conditions, not a single one, in the goal stack after $INTRO$ using $OpenSafe(I2)$ is applied. Consequently, there are two conditions after $GraspKey(I1)$ is introduced and one after $REMOVE$ is applied. In particular, after $INTRO$ using $OpenSafe(I2)$ is applied, GS is set to

$$\{\exists\, i \,.\, HoldingKey(i) \wedge Meets(i,I2),$$
$$\exists\, j \,.\, CloseToSafe(j) \wedge Meets(j,I2)\}.$$

After applying $INTRO$ using $GraspKey(I1)$ to remove the first condition above, GS is set to

$$\{\exists\, i \,.\, KeyOnTable(i) \wedge Meets(i,I1),$$
$$\exists\, j \,.\, CloseToSafe(j) \wedge Meets(j,I2)\}.$$

Finally, after applying $REMOVE$ to remove the first condition above, GS is set to

$$\{\exists\, j \,.\, CloseToSafe(j) \wedge Meets(j,I2)\}.$$

At this stage, the planner is at an impasse. The condition on the goal stack cannot be removed using $INTRO$ applied to any plan instance presented so far. Neither can $REMOVE$ be used; from the world description, one can infer only that the property $CloseToSafe$ holds during $I0$. This specification is noncommittal as to whether this property holds at any later times, such as a time just prior to $I2$. Unlike existing systems, which use a STRIPS or persistence assumption, we do not operate as if a property remains true unless it can be determined otherwise. Instead, a plan instance must be introduced to guarantee that a property remains true over an interval; that is, the property must be maintained. We now extend our example by introducing such a plan instance.

Recall that whether there exists a plan instance to maintain a property depends on whether the agent can affect that property. In this example, we assume that being within arm's length of the safe is solely within the agent's control, and we use the term $mtn(CloseToSafe,I1)$ as the plan instance that maintains this property over interval $I1$. The specification for this plan instance is given by:

mtn(CloseToSafe,I1)
EC: $\{\exists\, i \,.\, CloseToSafe(i) \wedge Meets(i,I1)\}$
EFF: $\{CloseToSafe(I1)\}.$

The above specification captures that $mtn(CloseToSafe,I1)$ is executable if the safe is within arm's length at a time just prior to execution, and its effect is that this property holds during execution. This specification implies that there are no external events that can prevent the agent from maintaining this property during $I1$. If it were possible for external events to interfere with this property, $mtn(CloseToSafe,I1)$'s executability conditions would have to mention that these events do not occur.

Since $GraspKey(I1)$ and $mtn(CloseToSafe,I1)$ overlap in time, their non-interference conditions must be specified. If the performance of $GraspKey(I1)$ does not involve a change in location, then $GraspKey(I1)$ and $mtn(CloseToSafe,I1)$ do not interfere under any conditions. In this case, we can set their noninterference conditions to { }. On the other hand, if grasping the key necessarily involves moving out of arm's reach from the safe, $GraspKey(I1)$ and $mtn(CloseToSafe,I1)$ would interfere under all conditions, and consequently we would set their noninterference conditions to {FALSE}. The third alternative is where the two plan instances interfere only under certain conditions. As an example, suppose that grasping the key involves moving out of arm's distance from the safe only if the key is not resting on the side of the table closest to the safe. In this case, we could set their noninterference conditions to $\exists i \, . \, KeyCloseBy(i) \wedge Meets(i,I1))$, namely, that the key is on the side of the table closest to the safe at the time just before the key should be grasped. Let us now investigate the operation of our planning algorithm for this last case, where there is conditional interference.

Remember that GS is set to $\{\exists i \, . \, CloseToSafe(i) \wedge Meets(i,I2)\}$ and $INPLAN$ is set to $\{OpenSafe(I2), GraspKey(I1)\}$. The result of introducing $mtn(CloseToSafe,I1)$ into the plan is that the goal condition above is removed and the action's executability conditions and the noninterference conditions (between $mtn(CloseToSafe,I1)$ and $GraspKey(I1)$) are added. Thus, the result of introducing $mtn(CloseToSafe,I1)$ would be the following goal stack:

$$\{(\exists i \, . \, CloseToSafe(i) \wedge Meets(i,I1)),$$
$$(\exists i \, . \, KeyCloseBy(i) \wedge Meets(i,I1))\}.$$

During the next cycle, the first condition could be removed by applying $REMOVE$ because it follows from $\{CloseToSafe(I0), Meets(I0,I1)\}$, a subset of W. To remove the second condition, we would need to show that this condition is derivable from the world description.[5] If this is the case, then we can use REMOVE and the problem is solved.

For the case where the two plan instances interfere under all conditions, and consequently their noninterference condition is set to FALSE, the result of adding $mtn(closeToSafe,I1)$ is that FALSE is added to GS. Thus, the problem will not be

---

5. Note that this second condition cannot be removed using $INTRO$ since this condition is not in the future of planning time and we can only introduce plan instances that occur after planning time.

solvable since FALSE is not derivable from any set. For efficiency reasons, we can simply consider any actions that would result in FALSE being added to GS as not being applicable.

Note that whether $GraspKey(I1)$ ruins $OpenSafe(I2)$'s executability conditions is detected through the concurrent interaction between $GraspKey(I1)$ and $mtn(CloseToSafe,I1)$, which is computed from their noninterference conditions. There are a number of advantages gained by detecting interactions in this fashion, as opposed to the standard approach where interactions are detected by looking at the relation between preconditions and effects and using phantom nodes. First, harmful sequential interactions and harmful concurrent interactions are treated in the same way. Second, our method is more expressive in the type of sequential interactions that can be treated. In other systems, either an earlier action ruins a later one's preconditions, or does not. We can also model the situation where an earlier plan instance conditionally ruins a later one's precondition as in the last example.

Third, we have more flexibility in how we describe plan instance (action) effects because they are used in our system only to determine if an action can achieve a condition, rather than to determine both achievement relations and action conflicts, as is done in the STRIPS assumption. For example, our algorithm does not require a complete and nondisjunctive specification of a plan instance's (action's) effects. This is in contrast to the standard methods, which must work under the assumption that each action's effect list is complete and must preclude the use of disjunctive effects.[6]

Finally, the use of maintenance plan instances allows us to make a distinction that cannot be captured using phantom nodes. In particular, we are able to distinguish between three cases: 1) the agent cannot affect property pr during time ix; in which case, there does not exist a plan instance that maintains pr any time during ix, 2) property pr is completely in the agent's control during interval ix; in which case, the only executability conditions for maintaining pr during ix is that pr holds just prior to ix, and 3) property pr is affected by both the agent and the external world during interval ix; in which case, the executability conditions for a plan instance that maintains pr during ix must mention the external events or conditions that could prevent this property from holding.

---

6. In our system, if we have a nondeterministic plan instance that brought about either property p at time ix or property q at time ix, we would set its effect list to this disjunction. We must also set to FALSE the noninterference conditions between pi and any plan instance that either maintains the negation of p during a time overlapping with ix and between pi and any plan instance that maintains the negation of q during a time overlapping with ix.

Concurrent Interactions

We now examine plan instance interactions that would be detected as concurrent interactions in other systems. We first present a simple example showing the conflict between two plan instances that share the same type of resource. We then complicate this example to take into account the possibility that an external event is also competing for this resource type.

Consider plan instances $RunHeater(I1)$, which refers to running a space heater during interval $I1$, and $RunSaw(I1)$, which refers to running a power saw at the same time. Whether these machines can be run together depends on the amount of power being supplied during $I1$. We assume that one unit of power is needed for each task; if there is just one unit of power being supplied, then one but not both can be executed, while if there are two or more units, they can be run together. We will use the formula $MinPowerSupplied(n,i)$ to denote that at least n units of power are being supplied during interval i. To focus on the interaction between $RunHeater(I1)$ and $RunSaw(I1)$, we set up the simple planning problem that follows:

G: $\{pr1(I1),pr2(I1)\}$

W: $\{((\forall\ i\ .\ MinPowerSupplied(2,i)\ \supset MinPowerSupplied(1,i)),$
          $(\forall\ i\ .\ MinPowerSupplied(3,i)\ \supset MinPowerSupplied(2,i)),$
          $Meets(I0,I1),\ Meets(I1,I2)\}$

$RunHeater(I1)$
EC: $\{MinPowerSupplied(1,I1)\}$
EFF: $\{pr1(I1)\}$

$RunSaw(I1)$
EC: $\{MinPowerSupplied(1,I1)\}$
EFF: $\{pr2(I1)\}$

$\{RunHeater(I1),RunSaw(I1)\}$
NI: $\{MinPowerSupplied(2,I1)\}.$

In the world description set W, we include two instances of a general law capturing that if at least n units of power is being supplied during any time i, then at least n-1 units of power is being supplied during i. The executability conditions for $RunHeater(I1)$ and $RunSaw(I1)$ capture that both plan instances can be executed individually as long as one unit is being supplied. The non-interference conditions capture that the two plan instances do not interfere if at least two units are being supplied. Implicit in the executability and non-interference specifications is that there are no external events or other plan instances that can compete for the power being supplied.

Using the algorithm, the interaction between $RunHeater(I1)$ and $RunSaw(I1)$ would first be considered when one of them is already in the plan and we are considering introducing the other. Such a state can be reached by first introducing either $RunHeater(I1)$ or $RunSaw(I1)$ into the plan, both of which are applicable at the first cycle when GS is set to G. Suppose we first introduce $RunHeater(I1)$ to remove the first condition in GS. The result of applying this operator is that G is set to

$$\{pr2(I1), MinPowerSupplied(1,I1)\}$$

and INPLAN is set to $\{RunHeater(I1)\}$.

At the second cycle, $RunHeater(I1)$ can be introduced to remove $pr2(I2)$ from the goal stack. The new goal stack produced by this operator is formed from the previous one by removing $pr2(I2)$ while adding $RunHeater(I1)$'s executability conditions and the noninterference conditions between $RunHeater(I1)$ and $RunSaw(I1)$ yielding

$$\{MinPowerSupplied(1,I1),\ MinPowerSupplied(2,I1)\}.$$

This new goal stack contains the conditions that must hold or be brought about in order for the composition of $RunHeater(I1)$ and $RunSaw(I1)$ to be executable. If statements in the world description capture that at least two units of power will be supplied during $I1$, the planning operator $REMOVE$ can be applied two times to remove the two conditions in the goal stack. For similar reasons, if there is a plan instance that can be executed with the effect that at least two units of power will be supplied during $I1$, then this plan instance can be introduced to remove the conditions.

Let us now complicate the above example by taking into account an external event that competes for the same type of resource used by $RunHeater(I1)$ and $RunSaw(I1)$. For simplicity, we will assume that only one external event— someone running a dishwasher during $I1$—is competing for the power being supplied. In this case, each plan instance is executable only if either there are at least two units being supplied during $I1$ (so that whether or not $DishwasherRunning$ occurs during $I1$ there will still be enough power to run one appliance), or $DishwasherRunning$ does not occur during $I1$ and there is at least one unit being supplied. We therefore modify the above example so that $RunHeater(I1)$'s and $RunSaw(I1)$'s executability conditions are both given by

$$\{MinPowerSupplied(2,I1)\ \vee$$
$$(MinPowerSupplied(1,I1)\ \wedge\ \sim\!DishwasherRunning(I1))\}.[7]$$

We must also modify the noninterference conditions between $RunHeater(I1)$ and $RunSaw(I1)$ to provide for the possibility where $DishwasherRunning$ occurs during $I1$; in which case they would interfere if at least three units were not supplied. Thus, we assume that their noninterference conditions are now given by

---

7. For simplicity, we are not distinguishing between $\sim\!DishwasherRunning(I1)$ and $\sim(\exists i2\ .\ \sim Disjoint(i2,I1)\ \wedge\ DishwasherRunning(i2))$, which we would want if the interval $I2$ were decomposable.

$\{MinPowerSupplied(3,I1) \lor$
$\quad (MinPowerSupplied(2,I1) \land \sim DishwasherRunning(I1))\}.$

A similar specification could be used if a third plan instance, rather than an external event, was competing for the resource.

Using these modifications, the goal stack produced by introducing both $RunHeater(I1)$ and $RunSaw(I1)$ is given by

$\{ (MinPowerSupplied(2,I1) \lor$
$\quad (MinPowerSupplied(1,I1) \land \sim DishwasherRunning(I1))),$
$\quad (MinPowerSupplied(3,I1) \lor$
$\quad\quad (MinPowerSupplied(2,I1) \land \sim DishwasherRunning(I1)))\}.$

If there are statements in the world description capturing that at least three units are being supplied during $I1$, then both conditions can be removed. That is, if $MinPowerSupplied(3,I1)$ is derivable from W, then we could remove both conditions from the goal stack using *REMOVE*. Similarly, if some plan instance could be introduced to remove $MinPowerSupplied(3,I1)$, then this plan instance could be introduced to remove the conditions.

We could also remove both conditions if the world description captures that *DishwasherRunning* will not occur during $I1$ and at least two units of power will be supplied during interval $I1$ (i.e., $\sim DishwasherRunning(I1)$ and $MinPowerSupplied(2,I1)$ are derivable from W). However, we could not introduce a plan instance to achieve the negation of *DishwasherRunning* since it is an external event that the agent cannot prevent, and thus we are assuming that no plan instance can affect it. Instead, only if $\sim DishwasherRunning(I1)$ is derivable from W, and plan instance *pi* achieves $MinPowerSupplied(2,I1)$, could we introduce *pi* to remove the conditions from the goal stack.

3.6.4 Limitations of the Planning Algorithm

The presentation of the simple planning algorithm above did not consider efficiency issues. In a number of places, the algorithm is abstract in the sense that there are many implementations, affording various degrees of efficiency, that meet the specification. Thus, we must fill in the details, trying to find an efficient implementation. In particular, we would need a mechanism that wisely chooses the appropriate operator from the set of applicable ones at each cycle, and a mechanism that detects when the goal stack is unsolvable and consequently backtracking should be performed. It should be noted that although operator applicability is defined in terms of Interval Logic provability, this does not necessitate an Interval Logic theorem prover implementation. Any procedure can be used as long as it can be interpreted as meeting our criteria for applicability.

Efficiency can also be improved by adapting techniques employed by some state-based planning systems, such as constraints [Stefik 1981], abstract actions [Sacerdoti 1974; Tenenberg 1986; see also chapter 4 of this book], and decomposable actions [Sacerdoti 1977]. To incorporate these capabilities it would be necessary to modify our algorithm rather than just plugging in the details.

One particularly restrictive aspect of our simple planning algorithm is that each plan instance must be completely specified when it is entered into the plan. By "completely specified" we mean that the plan instance is represented by a ground term. This is in contrast to current planning systems, such as MOLGEN [Stefik 1981], SIPE [Wilkins 1988], DEVISER [Vere 1981], and the ILP planner in chapter 1 that permit features of an action, such as the objects manipulated by the action or the action's time of occurrence, to be only partially specified when the action is first entered into the plan. As the planning process continues, additional constraints may be imposed on these values for such reasons as preventing the plan instances in the solution from conflicting with each other. The use of partially described plan instances permits more flexible control strategies than those that can be employed using our simple algorithm, since more choices are available at each decision point.

In order to modify our algorithm to allow partially described plan instances, a number of issues must be considered. For example, there are number of ways we can try to relate a planner that returns a partially described plan instance and the correctness criteria we identified in section 3.5.1. Possible interpretations of correctness include: i) the planner returns a partially described plan instance having the property that *all* of its completions *solve* the goal (as defined by our correctness criteria), ii) the planner returns a partially described plan instance having the property that *there exists* a completion that solves the goal, or iii) constraints on the partially described plan instance are ones that need to hold, otherwise the plan would provably fail.

Another issue that needs to be investigated is the interaction between constraints and the noninterference conditions. Recall that we enter non-interference conditions into the goal stack when we find two plan instances in the plan that overlap in time. Now, if the plan instances are only constrained, one currently may not be able to tell whether they overlap or not. The question then becomes: when do we consider noninterference conditions? Do we consider them only when we deduce that two plan instances overlap, or do we take them into account when it is possible that they overlap?

If two plan instances necessarily interfere, then one can add the constraint that they do not overlap in time when it is known that they are both in the plan. This is the approach taken by De Lacaze [1990], which describes a planning implementation that extends our simple algorithm so that plan instances with constrained, rather than grounded, execution times can be treated. However, this same approach cannot be taken if two plan instances just conditionally interfere: constraining these plan instances so they do not overlap in time is overly restrictive. One approach that can be taken is to immediately make a decision whether or not they should overlap and to backtrack from this decision if it is not appropriate. However, this approach is antithetical to the least commitment strategy. A more sophisticated approach would try to delay this decision until more information is gathered or not make this decision at all if achievement of the goal does not depend on it.

Another issue that needs to be addressed stems from the fact that action specifications are given for individual plan instances. Instead, what needs to be done is to employ descriptions that describe classes of actions, as is typically done. De Lacaze [1990] demonstrates that schematas can be easily employed to describe effects, executability conditions, and noninterference conditions for classes of plan instances. Other modifications to afford a more succinct description of the action specifications also need to be addressed. For example, we would like a more succinct way to describe the interaction between three or more actions and events to avoid the cumbersome encoding used in section 3.6.3.

One approach to achieve a more succinct description of actions is to employ descriptions that describe the *difference* between the situation where an action is executed and the situation where it is not, a technique we presented in section 3.5.3 for handling simultaneous effects. For example, to handle resource conflicts, we could capture that if a plan instance *pi* is attempted in a situation where it does not occur, and there are *n* other plan instances using the *n* available resources, then the resulting world-histories are ones where *pi* occurs (since there is at least one resource available), but not all of the other plan instances. If, on the other hand, *pi* is attempted in a situation where there are *n* resources available, but less than *n* plan instances using them, then *pi* does not interfere with any of these plan instances.

3.7   Discussion

In this chapter, we presented a formal basis for planning with concurrent actions and external events by first developing an appropriate model of action. We then defined the planning problem in terms of this model by formulating a notion of planner correctness and showing how the description of a planning problem can be expressed in the logic.

Our model of action was obtained by extending the Interval Logic model with a structure analogous to the "result function" found in the state-change model of action. This allowed us to exploit the complementary strengths of these two types of models: the ability of Interval Logic to represent concurrent actions and external events, and the ability of the state-change model to capture the conditions that an action affects and does not affect, and to provide a simple basis for (sequential) action composition.

In our models, world-histories and basic action instances take the place of states and actions. Basic action instances refer to primitive actions at specified times and are used to construct plan instances, our analog to plans, which can be thought of as collections of actions at specified times. A world-history serves as the context in which the execution of a basic action at a specified time (i.e., a basic action instance) is given. For each world-history *h* and basic action instance *bai,* the model specifies the world-histories that differ from *h* solely on the account of *bai*'s occurrence. This structure enables us to model the influence of conditions that may hold during the time that a plan instance is to be executed, and it provides a simple basis for modeling concurrent interactions and for composing basic action instances to form plan instances.

By developing an appropriate semantic model, we were able to cast planning with concurrent actions and external events deductively. This allowed us to avoid the problems caused when nonmonotonic inference is used in conjunction with partial or imprecise world descriptions. Specifically, we were able to avoid the use of a STRIPS assumption [Waldinger 1977] to handle the frame problem and the use of nonmonotonic inference to reason about concurrent interactions as is done in chapter 1 and in GEM [Lansky 1985]. Moreover, we showed how our model provided a different light on the frame problem: it is the problem of determining what events, properties, and other actions, each action (plan instance) does not affect. It is not simply the problem of determining what properties remain unchanged as an action is executed. An important feature of our model is that it provides a simple structure for capturing what an action does not affect. This allowed us to employ simple rules to reason about compositions, such as one that captures that if two actions can be done individually and they do not affect each other, then they can be done simultaneously.

Finally, we presented a simple planning algorithm that handles concurrent actions and external events and is applicable with partial world descriptions. This algorithm is novel in that all action interactions, both sequential and concurrent, derive from a conditional interference relation that is specified by the user and relates only concurrent plan instances. Another novel feature is that we employ plan instances that maintain properties, rather than resorting to the STRIPS assumption to infer that a property remains true.

3.7.1   Issues Outside the Scope of the Deductive Logic

In this section, we briefly look at some issues that are not fully addressed by developing a deductive logic to express planning problems. We first discuss the problem of deciding what possibilities to take into account when forming a plan. We then discuss planning with an incomplete description, where it may be necessary to plan to obtain relevant information. We then mention the problem of planning with incorrect descriptions where planned actions might fail or not produce desired results. Finally, we discuss the frame problem. These discussions will elicit the role that the deductive logic can play in these reasoning tasks, demonstrating that a deductive logic still plays an important function when considering these practical and more encompassing issues.

We formulated the deductive planning problem: given a description of the world S and a goal G, find a plan instance pi such that it deductively follows from S that under all possible circumstances pi is executable and if pi occurs then G holds. One might argue that this framework is inappropriate because real agents do not actually derive that a plan works under all possibilities. What is important to note, however, is that our framework derives airtight plans *with respect to a particular world description S*, not with respect to all conceivable possibilities. This world description may be a simplified view of the world that only takes into account the few possibilities that the agent is actively considering.

This is in line with a more encompassing view of what a reasonable plan is: the plan must at least be airtight with respect to the possibilities that are actively being considered. For example, if you tell me that my plan would not work if so and so happens, a typical response would be "Oh, I was not taking that into account", and I would either argue that it is not necessary to take it into account or would modify my plan to take it into account. Developing a deductive logic is essential for formalizing this more encompassing planning view because it provides the notion of "being airtight". However, the other problem, that of determining the possibilities to take into account, is not addressed by a deductive logic.

There has been some work relevant to this problem of producing a simplified world description. Of particular relevance is any framework for handling the qualification problem [McCarthy 1977]. The problem is that, typically, precondition specifications for actions and causal statements only take into account certain possibilities. For example, in the preconditions for starting a car, one might include such conditions as the key is in the ignition and there is gas in the tank. Typically, however, one would not mention the condition that there is no potato in the tail pipe, although this situation could conceivably arise and prevent the car from starting. This suggests how we may describe simplified scenarios in our framework; our specifications of executability conditions, noninterference conditions, and causal statements need only mention conditions being actively considered.

There have been a number of schemes addressing the qualification problem that employ nonmonotonic logics, such as Ginsberg and Smith [1987] and Shoham [1986]. In both these approaches, when describing a general domain theory that is to be used for a number of different problems, one explicitly mentions only the conditions that are considered normal, that is, conditions that are to be taken into account in all given problems. When solving a problem, these systems take into account these normal conditions plus any abnormal conditions explicitly given for this particular problem. However, these systems do not address the difficult problem of deciding which conditions to be considered as normal and which ones not to.

Work by Weber [1989] is relevant to the problem of determining the most appropriate conditions to consider as being normal. Weber uses conditional probability statements to describe a world model and addresses the problem of determining what is the relevant body of evidence to consider when assessing a belief about some statement. He exploits the idea that it is only necessary to include evidence whose addition can have significant impact on one's assessment of the hypothesis. To adopt this approach in our framework, we can take advantage of Haddawy's work [1990], which incorporates our modal logic in a probabilistic framework. An interesting aspect of Haddawy's approach is the way that probability statements and our modal operators are related: he equates the probability of *IFTRIED(pi,C)* with the conditional probability P(C | *attempt(pi)*), that is, the belief in *C* given evidence that *pi* is attempted. This connection between conditionals—which are what *IFTRIED* statements can be thought of—and subjunctive conditional probabilities has previously been explored in the philosophic literature [Harper, Stalnaker, and Pearce 1981].

3.7.2 Incomplete Descriptions and Obtaining Additional Information

Working with an incomplete world description means that the planning agent may be missing relevant information when planning is initiated. If it is recognized that relevant information is missing, then it is necessary to determine what type of information is needed and how this information can be obtained. Once the means for obtaining the needed information has been identified, one can either suspend planning until this information is gathered, or include conditional actions in the plan along with actions to gather information needed by the conditional actions. Thus, to plan with a partial world model requires that we address the following problems: i) recognizing that relevant information is missing, ii) determining what type of additional information is needed, iii) determining how to obtain needed information, and iv) using conditional actions.

Our deductive logic provides a starting point for addressing these issues. Relevant information pertains to whether a *useful* plan or action—one that the agent is considering for execution—can be executed and if so what its results would be. If *S* refers to an important question about a useful plan or step in a plan, but the truth of *S* is undetermined, then relevant information is missing. An approach described in Mark, Weber, and Mcguire [1990] addresses the problem of determining what relevant information needs to be obtained. In this approach, one first tries to find a deductive proof to answer the question under consideration. If relevant information is omitted then a proof will not be established, but the partial proof tree constructed in the process can be very useful: the leaves in this partial proof tree that could not be proved or disproved suggest relevant questions to ask.

In order to obtain needed information, it is necessary to reason about actions or procedures that gather knowledge. This in turn requires that statements about the agent's knowledge are represented so that we can describe the effects of these "knowledge-producing actions." Directly relevant to this endeavor is work presented by Moore [1977; 1985], Haas [1983] Morgenstern and Stein [1988], and Shoham [1989], which present logics that relate knowledge and action. In these logics, one can explicitly make statements about the agent's knowledge and the effect of knowledge-producing actions. We say "explicitly" to contrast with our logic; in our discussions we have been equating knowledge with provability, a metaconcept; thus, we cannot directly make statements in our logic about the agent's knowledge, or lack of knowledge, or the effect of knowledge-producing actions. Thus, future work must investigate explicitly incorporating a knowledge modality in our framework.

A promising approach to introducing a knowledge modality is the possible-worlds approach. This would allow us, as Moore [1977; 1985] and Shoham [1989] did, to closely relate knowledge and action by treating both as relations on the set of possible worlds (world-histories). Thus, our first step would be to introduce another accessibility relation on the world-histories to capture the planning agent's knowledge. Moreover, this may allow us, as Shoham suggests, to get rid of temporal possibility (which is captured by our *INEV* operator) and treat all possibility as stemming from a lack of knowledge.

Finally, consider the use of conditional actions. While we allow plan instances that are conditional actions, we have not provided any mechanism for *forming* conditional plan instances from more basic entities. For example, we may want to consider a composition function such as *IfElse(cnd,pi1,pi2)*, which refers to executing plan instance *pi1*, if the agent determines that condition *cnd* is true, otherwise to executing plan instance *pi2*. In order for *IfElse(cnd,pi1,pi2)* to be executable, the planning agent must be able to determine the truth-value of *cnd* (at a time prior to *pi1*'s and *pi2*'s execution times). Thus, incorporating such a construct in our logic would first require that we could explicitly reason about the agent's knowledge and knowledge-producing actions.

3.7.3   Planning With an Incorrect World Description

During planning time, one's view of the world may be incorrect—a fact that may be verified by later observations indicating such things as a planned action that could not be executed or an expected result that was not produced. Deductive logic can be used to provide a precise characterization of this conflict between one's view at planning time and later observations. Each of these conflicts can be formalized as an inconsistency between sentences describing one's view during planning time and sentences describing later observations.

Along with detecting that a conflict exists, one wants to isolate the cause of the conflict and use this information, if possible, to fix the plan. One can first use techniques such as TMS dependencies [Doyle 1979] to efficiently find the set of sentences that collectively led to the inconsistency. One can then use techniques in model-based diagnosis [Davis 1984; Genesereth 1984; deKleer and Williams 1986] to further prune this set.

Although a deductive logic can help to localize the source of a problem by looking for minimal inconsistent sets, it cannot completely solve the problem; it cannot be used to indicate exactly what part of the plan to modify to fix the problem. This is because, even with minimal inconsistent sets, there may be many candidates to potentially modify. The deductive logic says nothing about the choice that is the most appropriate. One needs to employ additional criteria such as a notion of minimal change or what is easiest to fix.

3.7.4   Addressing the Frame Problem

We take the frame problem to be the general problem of describing what an action does not affect, a problem that manifests in any model of action. In tackling the frame problem, there are two issues to be considered: i) defining what the frame problem is for the particular model of action under consideration, and ii) finding ways to describe what an actions does not affect in a succinct, natural way that promotes efficient reasoning. In the state-based model—the context where the frame problem originated—the first problem is trivial: it is clear that the frame problem is the problem of determining what properties remain true as an action is applied in a state. On the other hand, for a model of action that treats simultaneous events (actions), the first problem is nontrivial. In fact, there has been much confusion because this issue has not been adequately addressed, as evident by the amount of debate concerning the Yale shooting problem [Hanks and McDermott 1986]. When work moved away from the state-based representation to explicit temporal logics, such as McDermott's [1982] and Allen's [1984], nonmonotonicity was introduced immediately (to address the second problem) without first understanding how the frame problem could be expressed deductively.

Our contribution is a precise semantic characterization of the frame problem in a model of action that treats concurrent actions and external events. In particular, we have developed a semantic model that explicitly interprets "action (plan instance) *al does not affect* condition C." Its interpretation is that if C holds in a world-history h, then C would hold in a world-history that would result from attempting *al* in h. This conception of the frame problem is more general than previous approaches because not only does it refer to the properties that each action does not affect, but also to the external events and other simultaneous actions that are not affected. Thus, we have addressed the first problem. However, we have employed a limited approach to describe what an action does not affect, using statements that can be seen as analogs to frame axioms. We took this simple approach because it allowed us to initially stay within a deductive framework. Thus, additional work is needed to adequately address problem two.

There are two basic approaches that can both be used to develop an appropriate way for describing what an action does not affect. One of these approaches is to partition the world into parts that either do not interact or only interact in very limited ways through specific channels. This type of approach has been adopted by Hayes [1982] and Lansky [1985; 1988]. Hayes carves the world into local space/time regions, which only interact if they share a spatial or temporal border. Lansky, whose approach we described in section 3.2.2, allows the user to partition the set of events into a hierarchically-organized set of classes that either interact through specified channels or are causally independent. We can incorporate this work into our framework by introducing constructs in our language that carve up the world into these type of regions; we can then relate these constructs to our formalism by using axioms saying that a plan instance does not affect other plan instances or conditions in "disjoint regions". This would allow us to use these structures in conjunction with the statements we presented earlier that directly specify lack of interference.

The other approach that can be used to capture what actions do not affect is to incorporate an analog to the STRIPS assumption. To take this approach, we would describe plan instances by specifying only what they affect and assume that they do not affect any conditions not mentioned in the effects specifications (or derivable from the effects specifications and causal laws). The STRIPS assumption in our framework would refer to the relationship between two world-histories differing on the account of a plan instance; it could be implemented as a nondeductive schema, such as

> If a condition C holds in a world-history and one cannot deduce that C does not hold in a world-history $h2$ produced by attempting $pi2$ in h, we assume C holds in $h2$.

Because this assumption involves nonmonotonic inference, we would have to be careful about its use with partial world descriptions. For example, we would have to assume that the planning description contains all relevant causal laws and effects specifications that tell us what each plan instance affects. However, the world description could be incomplete in what it says about the external events that may occur.

3.8   Appendix A. The Semantic Model and Logical Language

3.8.1   The Semantic Model

A model consists of the following elements

H   is a nonempty set designating the world-histories
           (i.e., complete worlds over time).

I   is a nonempty set designating the temporal intervals
           (i.e., stretches of time in a dateline).

Meets   is a relation defined on $I \times I$ specifying the *meets* interval relation;
           Meets(i1,i2) means that interval i1 immediately precedes interval i2.

PROP   is a nonempty subset of $2^{I \times H}$ designating the propositions. A
           proposition is equated with the interval/world-history pairs over which
           it holds.

BA   is a nonempty subset of PROP referring to the set of basic actions
           (i.e., primitive actions having the planning agent as the actor).

PI   is a nonempty subset of $2^{PROP \times I} \times 2^{BA \times I}$ designating the plan instances. The first element of the ordered pair (i.e., the set of proposition/interval pairs) indicates the abstract steps associated with the plan instance. The second element of the order pair (i.e., the set of basic-action/interval pairs) indicates exactly how the plan instance is to be performed.

R   is a relation on $I \times H \times H$; $R(i,h1,h2)$ means that world-histories h1 and h2 share a common past through at least the end of interval i and they are possible alternatives with respect to their common past.

CL   is a function from $BA \times I \times H$ to 2^H; the members of CL(ba,i,h) constitute all the world-histories that are closest to h with respect to the execution of basic action ba during interval i.

O   is a nonempty set of objects distinct from the plan instances and intervals.

Constraints that relate to the temporal structure
(taken from Allen and Hayes [1989] and chapter 1 of this book)

MT1)   For every interval i1, there exist intervals i0 and i2 such that Meets(i0,i1) and Meets(i1,i2).

MT2)   For all intervals i1, i2, i3, and i4, if Meets(i1,i2) and Meets(i2,i3) and Meets(i3,i4), then there exists an interval (ic) such that Meets(i1,ic) and Meets(ic,i4).

MT3)   For all intervals i1, i2, i3, and i4, if Meets(i1,i2) and Meets(i1,i3) and Meets(i4,i2), then Meets(i4,i3).

MT4)   For all intervals i1, i2, i3 and i4, if Meets(i3,i1) and Meets(i3,i2) and Meets(i1,i4) and Meets(i2,i4), then i1=i2.

MT5)   For all intervals i1, i2, i3, and i4, if Meets(i1,i2) and Meets(i3,i4), then one of the following is true:
      1)   Meets(i1,i4), or
      2)   there exists an interval ix such that Meets(i1,ix) and Meets(ix,i4), or
      3)   there exists an interval iy such that Meets(i3,iy) and Meets(iy,i2).

Definitions of other temporal relations

Equal(i1,i2) $=_{def}$ i1=i2.

Starts(i1,i2) $=_{def}$ there exist intervals i0, i3, and i4 such that Meets(i0,i1) and Meets(i0,i2) and Meets(i1,i3) and Meets(i3,i4) and Meets(i2,i4).

Finishes(i1,i2) =$_{def}$ there exist intervals i0, i3, and i4 such that Meets(i1,i0) and Meets(i2,i0) and Meets(i3,i1) and Meets(i4,i3) and Meets(i4,i2).

During(i1,i2) =$_{def}$ there exist intervals ix, i0, i3, and i4 such that Meets(ix,i0) and Meets(i0,i1) and Meets(i1,i3) and Meets(i3,i4) and Meets(ix,i2) and Meets(i2,i4).

In(i1,i2) =$_{def}$ Equal(i1,i2) or Finishes(i1,i2) or Starts(i1,i2) or During(i1,i2).

EndsBeforeEqual(i1,i2) =$_{def}$ there exist intervals i3, i4, and i5 such that Meets(i1,i3) and Meets(i2,i3), or
Meets(i1,i4) and Meets(i4,i5) and Meets(i2,i5).

Ints(instS) =$_{def}$ {i I there exist a proposition p such that <p,i>∈ instS}.

Covers(i,S) =$_{def}$ (for every interval ix if ix∈ S then In(ix,i)) and (there exist intervals iy and iz such that iy∈ S and iz∈ S and (Starts(iy,i) or Equal(iy,i)) and (Finishes(iz,i) or Equal(iz,i))).

Constraints on the R relation, CL function, and plan instances

R0) For all world-histories h1 and h2 and intervals i1 and i2,
if EndsBeforeEqual(i1,i2) and R(i2,h1,h2), then R(i1,h1,h2).

R1) R is reflexive: For every world-history h and interval i, R(i,h,h).

R2) R is symmetric: For all world-histories h1 and h2 and every interval i,
if R(i,h1,h2), then R(i,h2,h1).

R3) R is transitive: For all world-histories h1, h2, and h3 and every interval i,
if R(i,h1,h2) and R(i,h2,h3), then R(i,h1,h3).

R4) For all world-histories h1 and h2, every proposition p, and all intervals i1 and i2,
if EndsBeforeEqual(i1,i2) and R(i2,h1,h2), then <i1,h1>∈ p iff <i1,h2>∈ p.

PI1) For all plan instances <priS,baiS>, there exist intervals ic1 and ic2 such that Covers(ic1,Ints(priS)), Covers(ic2,Ints(baiS)), and (Equal(ic2,ic1) or Starts(ic2,ic1)).

PI2) For all plan instances <priS1,baiS1> and <priS2,baiS2>,
<priS1∪priS2,baiS1∪baiS2> is a plan instance.

BA-R1) For all world-histories h1 and h2, every basic action ba, and all intervals i1 and i2, if h2∈ CL(ba,i2,h1) and Meets(i1,i2), then R(i1,h2,h1).

BA-R2) For all world-histories h1, h2, and hcl1, every basic action ba, and all intervals i and ix, if R(ix,h1,h2) and hcl1∈ CL(ba,i,h1), then there exists a hcl2∈ CL(ba,i,h2) such that R(ix,hcl1,hcl2).

BA1) For every basic action ba, interval i, and world-history h, if $<i,h> \in$ ba, then CL(ba,i,h) = {h}.

BA2) For every world-history h, basic action ba, and interval i,
   if CL(ba,i,h)$\neq$ {h} then CL(ba,i,h) $\subseteq$ {h2 | $<i,h2> \in$ ba}.

Constraints relating to composition

We make use of the following definitions:

$fx*fy(h) =_{def} \bigcup_{hx \in fx(h)} fy(hx)$.

CompF({$<ba,i>$}) $=_{def}$ { $\lambda h.CL(ba,i,h)$}.

CompF(baiS) $=_{def}$ {bai*cmp | bai $\in$ baiS and cmp $\in$ CompF(baiS − {bai})},
   where |baiS|>1.

AllOccur(h,cmp,baiS) $=_{def}$
   cmp$\in$ CompF(baiS) and cmp(h) $\subseteq$ {h2 | $<i,h2> \in$ ba for all
   $<ba,i> \in$ baiS}.

Constraints:

BA-CMP1) For every world-history h, every basic action instance set baiS, and
   all composition functions cmp1 and cmp2, if AllOccur(h,cmp1,baiS)
   and AllOccur(h,cmp2,baiS), then cmp1(h)=cmp2(h).

BA-CMP2) For every world-history h, all basic action instance sets baiS1 and
   baiS2 and all composition functions cmp1 and cmp2, if
   AllOccur(h,cmp2,baiS2) and AllOccur(h,cmp1*cmp2,baiS1$\cup$baiS2),
   then AllOccur(h,cmp2*cmp1, baiS1 $\cup$ baiS2).

Definition of the closeness function
(which is used for the interpretation of IFTRIED)

FCL-DEF) $F_{cl}(baiS,h) =_{def}$
   cmp(h), if there exists a composition function (cmp) of baiS
         such that AllOccur(h,cmp,baiS);
   {h} Otherwise.

3.8.2   The Syntax

The primitive symbols
   The set of individual variables VAR,
   The set of function symbols FN,
   The set of temporal predicate symbols PT,
   The set of eternal predicate symbols PE,
   The set of modal operators MO.

The arity function DEG
   DEG is a function from FN $\cup$ PT $\cup$ PE to the nonnegative integers,
   which indicates the arity of each function and predicate symbol.

Restriction: For every temporal predicate (p), $DEG(p) \geq 1$.

The set of sorts TYPES
>TYPES = {Object, Interval, PlanInstance}.

The TYPEOF function
>TYPEOF is a function from $FN \cup VAR$ to TYPES, which indicates the type associated with each function symbol and variable.

The domain function DOM
>DOM is a function from $\{x \mid x \in FN \cup PT \cup PE \text{ and } DEG(x) \geq 1\}$ to $TYPES^+$ (i.e., all finite tuples formed from TYPES), which indicates the type restrictions for the arguments of the function and predicate symbols.
>Restrictions:
>If $p \in FN \cup PE$ and $DEG(p)=n$ then $DOM(p) \in TYPES^n$.
>If $p \in PT$ and $DEG(p)=n$ then $DOM(p) \in TYPES^{n-1} \times \{Interval\}$.

The interpreted primitive symbols

The language always includes the following interpreted symbols:

TimeOf belongs to FN
>$DEG(TimeOf)=1$, $TYPEOF(TimeOf)=Interval$,
>$DOM(TimeOf)=<PlanInstance>$.

Comp belongs to FN
>$DEG(Comp)=2$, $TYPEOF(Comp)=PlanInstance$,
>$DOM(Comp)=<PlanInstance,PlanInstance>$.

Meets belongs to PE
>$DEG(Meets)=2$, $DOM(Meets)=<Interval,Interval>$.

Occ belongs to PE
>$DEG(Occ)=1$, $DOM(Occ)=<PlanInstance>$.

IFTRIED and *INEV* belong to MO.

Formation rules

The set of terms TERMS is defined as follows:
>all members of VAR belong to TERMS;
>if c belongs to FN and $DEG(c)=0$, then c belongs to TERMS;
>if f belongs to FN and $DEG(f)=n>0$, and
>>$<TYPEOF(t_1),TYPEOF(t_2),....,TYPEOF(t_n)>=DOM(f)$,
>>then $f(t_1,t_2, ...,t_n)$ belongs to TERMS.

The set of sentences in our language L is defined as follows:

if p belongs to PE and $DEG(p)=0$, then p belongs to L;

if p belongs to $PT \cup PE$ and $DEG(c)=n>0$ and
$\quad\quad <TYPEOF(t_1),TYPEOF(t_2),...,TYPEOF(t_n)>=DOM(p)$,
$\quad\quad\quad$ then $p(t_1,t_2, ...,t_n)$ belongs to L;

if i belongs to TERMS, TYPEOF(i)=Interval and s belongs to L,
$\quad\quad\quad$ then INEV(i,s) belongs to L;

if pi belongs to TERMS and TYPEOF(pi)=PlanInstance and s belongs to L,
$\quad\quad\quad$ then IFTRIED(pi,s) belongs to L;

for every variable v and all sentences s1 and s2 in L,
$\quad\quad\quad$ (s1), ~s1, s1∨s2, and $\forall$v.s1 belong to L;

if t1 and t2 belong to TERMS, then t1=t2 belongs to L.

Defined expressions

We make use of the following definitions:

$s1 \wedge s2 =_{def} \sim(\sim s1 \vee \sim s2).$

$\exists v . s =_{def} \sim(\forall v.\sim s).$

$\forall v_1,v_2, ...,v_n .s =_{def} \forall v_1.(\forall v_2, ..., v_n . s).$

$\exists v_1,v_2, ...,v_n .s =_{def} \exists v_1.(\exists v_2, ..., v_n . s)$

$s1 \equiv s2 =_{def} (s1 \supset s2) \wedge (s2 \supset s1).$

$s1 \otimes s2 =_{def} (s1 \wedge \sim s2) \vee (s2 \wedge \sim s1).$

$(\otimes\ s1\ s2\ s3) =_{def} (s1 \wedge \sim s2 \wedge \sim s3) \vee (s2 \wedge \sim s1 \wedge \sim s3) \vee (s3 \wedge \sim s1 \wedge \sim s2).$

$POS(i,s) =_{def} \sim INEV(i,\sim s).$

$Executable(pi) =_{def} IFTRIED(pi,Occ(pi)).$

$Comp(pi_1,pi_2, ...,pi_n) =_{def} Comp(pi_1,Comp(pi_2,...,pi_n)).$

$BeforeMeets(i1,i2) =_{def} (\exists\ ix . Meets(i1,ix) \wedge Meets(ix,i2)) \vee Meets(i1,i2).$

$EndsBeforeEqual(i1,i2) =_{def}$
$\quad\quad (\exists\ ix,iy . Meets(i1,ix) \wedge Meets(ix,iy) \wedge Meets(i2,iy)) \vee$
$\quad\quad\quad (\exists\ iz . Meets(i1,iz) \wedge Meets(i2,iz)).$

3.8.3   The Interpretation of the Language

We will use the function V to specify the interpretation of all our syntactic
entities.

For convenience, to relate types and their semantic counterparts we introduce the
TMAP function:
$\quad\quad$ TMAP(Interval) = I,
$\quad\quad$ TMAP(PlanInstance) = PI,

TMAP(Object) = O, and

if $<ty_1,ty_2, ...,ty_n> \in$ TYPES^n, then TMAP($<ty_1,ty_2, ...,ty_n>$) = $<$TMAP(ty$_1$),TMAP(ty$_2$),...,TMAP(ty$_n$)$>$.

The interpretation for the function, variable, and predicate symbols:

if $x \in$ VAR, then $V(x) \in$ TMAP(TYPEOF(x));

if $c \in$ FN and DEG(c)=0, then $V(c) \in$ TMAP(TYPEOF(c))

if $f \in$ FN and DEG(f)=n>0, then V(f) is a function from TMAP(DOM(f)) to TMAP(TYPEOF(f));

if $p \in$ PT, then V(p) is a function from OMITLAST(TMAP(DOM(p))) to PROP,

where OMITLAST($<x_1,x_2, ...,x_n,x_{n+1}>$) =$_{def}$ $<x_1,x_2, ...,x_n>$;

if p belongs to PE and DEG(p)=0, then V(p) is a subset of H; and

if p belongs to PE and DEG(p)=n>0, then V(p) is a subset of H×TMAP(DOM(p)).

The interpreted function symbols:

V(Comp)($<$priS1,baiS1$>$,$<$priS2,baiS2$>$)=$<$priS1∪prS2,baiS1∪baiS$>$.

V(TimeOf)($<$priS,baiS$>$) =

the interval in the singleton set {ix | Covers(ix,Ints(priS))}

The interpreted (eternal) predicate symbols:

V(Meets) = {$<$hx,i1,i2$>$ | hx∈ H and Meets(i1,i2)}

V(Occ) = {$<$h,$<$priS,baiS$>>$ | $<$priS,baiS$>$∈ PI and for every proposition p and interval i, if $<$p,i$>$∈ priS∪baiS then $<$i,h$>$∈ p}.

The interpretation of the sentences

The interpretation of the sentences is given as function from L×H to {T,F}.

If p is a temporal predicate,

V(p(t$_1$,t$_2$, ...,t$_n$,i),h) = T iff $<$V(i),h$>$∈ V(p)(V(t$_1$),V(t$_2$),...,V(t$_n$)).

If p is an eternal predicate and DEG(p)=0, V(p,h) = T iff h∈ V(p).

If p is an eternal predicate and DEG(p)=n>0,

V(p(t$_1$,t$_2$, ...,t$_n$),h) = T iff h∈ V(p)(V(t$_1$),V(t$_2$),...,V(t$_n$)).

V(P1∨P2,h)=T iff V(P1,h)=T or V(P2,h)=T.

V(~P,h)=T iff V(P,h)≠T.

V($\forall$u.P,h)=T iff for all objects x if x∈ TMAP(TYPEOF(u)), then V[u;x](P,h)=T where V[u;x] is identical to V with the exception that V[u;x](u)=x.

V(t1=t2,h)=T iff V(t1)=V(t2).

V(INEV(i,P),h)=T iff for every world-history h2, if R(V(i),h,h2) then V(P,h2).

V(IFTRIED(pi,P),h)=T iff for every world-history h2, if h2∈ F$_{cl}$(V(pi)|$_2$,h), then V(P,h2).

3.9   Appendix B.   Proof Theory

Below are a set of axioms and inference rules that form a sound proof theory. See Pelavin [1988] for a proof of soundness.

First-order axioms

AX-FO1)   ⊢ (P ∨ P) ⊃ P.

AX-FO2)   ⊢ Q ⊃ (P ∨ Q).

AX-FO3)   ⊢ (P ∨ Q) ⊃ (Q ∨ P).

AX-FO4)   ⊢ (Q ⊃ R) ⊃ ((P ∨ Q) ⊃ (P ∨ R)).

AX-FO5)   ⊢ ∀v . P1 ⊃ P2

where P2 differs from P1 in having all free occurrences of v in P1 replaced by some term t that has the same type as variable v, and if term t has any variables in it, they must not become bound by the substitution.

AX-FO6)   ⊢ t=t.

AX-FO7)   ⊢ t1=t2 ⊃ (P1 ⊃ P2)

where P2 differs from P1 in having one or more free occurrences of t1 in P1 replaced by t2, and if term t2 has any variables in it, they must not become bound by the substitution.

AX-FO8)   ⊢ ~(t1=t2)

where t1 and t2 have different types.

Interval relation axioms

AX-IR1)   ⊢ (Meets(i1,i3) ∧ Meets(i2,i3)) ⊃ (Meets(i1,i4) ≡ Meets(i2,i4)).

AX-IR2)   ⊢ (Meets(i1,i2) ∧ Meets(i1,i3)) ⊃ (Meets(i0,i2) ≡ Meets(i0,i3)).

AX-IR3)   ⊢ (Meets(i1,i2) ∧ Meets(i3,i4)) ⊃

(⊗   Meets(i1,i4)

(∃ix . Meets(i1,ix) ∧ Meets(ix,i4))

(∃iy . Meets(i3,iy) ∧ Meets(iy,i2))).

AX-IR4)   ⊢ ∃ i0,i2 . Meets(i0,i1) ∧ Meets(i1,i2).

AX-IR5)   ⊢ Meets(i1,i2) ⊃

∃ix,iy,iz . Meets(ix,i1) ∧ Meets(i2,iy) ∧

Meets(ix,iz) ∧ Meets(iz,iy).

Nonmodal axioms relating to the Comp function

AX-CMP1)   ⊢ Comp(pi,pi)=pi.

AX-CMP2)   ⊢ Comp(pi1,pi2)=Comp(pi2,pi1).

AX-CMP3)   ⊢ Comp(pi1,Comp(pi2,pi3))=Comp(Comp(pi1,pi2),pi3).

AX-CMP4)   ⊢ Occ(Comp(pi1,pi2)) ≡ (Occ(pi1) ∧ Occ(pi2)).

AX-CMP5)   ⊢ Spans(TimeOf(Comp(pi1,pi2)),TimeOf(pi1),TimeOf(pi2))

where Spans(is,i1,i2) =$_{def}$ (∃ i0 . Meets(i0,is) ∧

$$\qquad\qquad (Meets(i0,i1) \lor Meets(i0,i2))) \land$$

$$\qquad\qquad (\exists\ i3 . Meets(is,i3) \land (Meets(i1,i3) \lor Meets(i2,i3)))).$$

Axioms relating to the INEV modal operator

AX-INV1)   ⊢ INEV(i,P) ⊃ P.

AX-INV2)   ⊢ INEV(i,P ⊃Q) ⊃ (INEV(i,P) ⊃ INEV(i,Q)).

AX-INV3)   ⊢ INEV(i,P) ⊃ INEV(i,INEV(i,P)).

AX-INV4)   ⊢ POS(i,P) ⊃ INEV(i,POS(i,P)).

AX-INV5)   ⊢ EndsBeforeEqual(i1,i2) ⊃ (INEV(i1,P) ⊃ INEV(i2,P)).

AX-INV6)   ⊢ EndsBeforeEqual(i1,i2) ⊃

(POS(i2,p(t1,t2,...,i1)) ⊃ INEV(i2,p(t1,t2,...,i1)))

where p is a temporal predicate.

AX-INV7)   ⊢ EndsBeforeEqual(TimeOf(pi),i) ⊃

(POS(i,Occ(pi)) ⊃ INEV(i,Occ(pi))).

AX-INV8)   ⊢ POS(i,Meets(i1,i2)) ⊃ INEV(i,Meets(i1,i2)).

Axioms relating to the IFTRIED modal operator

AX-IFTR1)   ⊢ IFTRIED(pi,P) ⊃ ~IFTRIED(pi,~P).

AX-IFTR2)   ⊢ IFTRIED(pi,P ⊃Q) ⊃ (IFTRIED(pi,P) ⊃ IFTRIED(pi,Q)).

AX-IFTR3)   ⊢ Occ(pi) ⊃ (IFTRIED(pi,P) ≡ P).

AX-IFTR4)   ⊢ IFTRIED(pi,IFTRIED(pi,P)) ≡ IFTRIED(pi,P).

AX-IFTR5)   ⊢ BeforeMeets(i,TimeOf(pi)) ⊃ (INEV(i,P) ⊃ IFTRIED(pi,P)).

AX-IFTR6)   ⊢ IFTRIED(pi,INEV(i,P)) ⊃ INEV(i,IFTRIED(pi,P)).

AX-IFTR7)   ⊢ IFTRIED(pi1,IFTRIED(pi2,Occ(pi1) ∧ Occ(pi2))) ⊃

$$(\text{IFTRIED}(\text{Comp}(pi1,pi2),P) \equiv$$
$$\text{IFTRIED}(pi1,\text{IFTRIED}(pi2,P))).$$

AX-IFTR8) ⊢ BeforeMeets(TimeOf(pi1),TimeOf(pi2)) ⊃
$$(\text{Executable}(\text{Comp}(pi1,pi2)) \supset$$
$$(\text{Executable}(pi1) \wedge \text{IFTRIED}(pi1,\text{Executable}(pi2))))).$$

AX-IFTR9) ⊢ Executable(pi1) ⊃
$$(\text{IFTRIED}(pi2,\text{IFTRIED}(pi1,\text{Occ}(pi1) \wedge \text{Occ}(pi2))) \supset$$
$$\text{IFTRIED}(pi1,\text{IFTRIED}(pi2,\text{Occ}(pi1) \wedge \text{Occ}(pi2))))).$$

The derivability relation

We define a two-place derivability relation, which takes a set of sentences and a single sentence as arguments. We specify this relation using the form "S ⊢ P", meaning that sentence P is derivable from the set of sentences in S.

This relation meets the following properties:

DER1) S ⊢ P if P ∈ S

DER2) { } ⊢ P iff ⊢ P

Inference rules

Modus Ponens)
    From: S1 ⊢ P and S2 ⊢ P ⊃ Q
    To: S1 ∪ S2 ⊢ Q,
    where S1 and S2 are any set of sentences, and P and Q are any sentences.

AND Introduction)
    From: S1 ⊢ P and S2 ⊢ Q
    To: S1 ∪ S2 ⊢ P ∧ Q

Universal Introduction)
    From: S ⊢ P ⊃ Q
    To: S ⊢ P ⊃ ∀v . Q,
    where S is a set of sentences, P and Q are any sentences, v is a variable, and there does not exist any free occurrences of v in P or in any member of S.

RL-INV)
    From: ⊢ P
    To: ⊢ INEV(i,P).

RL-IFTR)
    From: ⊢ P
    To: ⊢ IFTRIED(pi,P).

Chapter 4
Abstraction in Planning

Josh D. Tenenberg

4.1   Introduction

The computational cost of automated problem solving so far has proven to be quite high. With simple state-based representations, complete search strategies will generally be exponential as a function of solution length. With more expressive representations, such as that of Pelavin in chapter 3, determining if solutions to arbitrary problems exist is an undecidable problem. Such disconcerting results have led several researchers [Chapman 1990; Firby 1987; Whitehead and Ballard 1990; Rosenschein 1989] to abandon the use of explicit or declarative problem representations. However, it appears that doing so requires that the goals of the agent be within a narrow range that are hard-coded into the problem representation. The approach that is pursued here is not to abandon the use of explicit representations, but to consider a formalization of heuristic methods as a means for directing search.

A general class of approaches that has been advocated for this purpose is the use of abstraction. Although abstraction has served to label a number of quite different research efforts [Anderson and Farley 1988; Nau 1987; Knoblock 1990a; Korf 1987; Alterman 1987; Fikes, Hart and Nilsson 1972], some commonalities exist. Typically, an abstraction is taken as a mapping between representations, from a *concrete* level to an *abstract* level (or to several abstract levels through repeated mappings). The abstract level typically does not contain certain concrete-level details which expand the state-space, but which are usually unnecessary to consider in order to obtain an approximate solution. The search strategy is to abstract the operators and initial state of a system, problem solve at the abstract level, and use the abstract solution to guide the search back at the original level. A view of this is provided in figure 1. I will refer to this as the Map, Plan, Inverse-Map (MPI) paradigm. Implicit in this approach are several assumptions, which serve both as justification and motivation for using abstraction methods:

Abstract Search: Abstract representations are simpler, and hence, faster to search for solutions than the detailed representations.

Abstract Plan Refinement: Abstract solutions constrain search at more detailed levels.

Positive Cost/Benefit Trade-off: Computational efficiencies gained with abstract search and refinement are sufficient to offset its cost, as compared to alternative heuristic methods used within the original problem space.

Plan Reuse: Abstract solutions may correspond to a set of concrete refinements, serving as a basis for plan saving and reuse, reducing the planner's need to solve each problem from first principles.

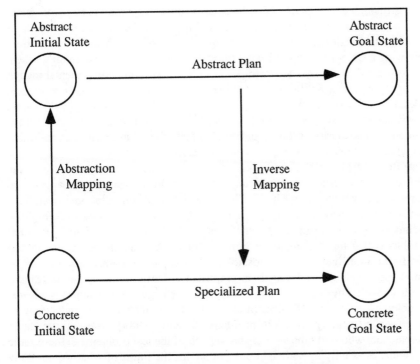

Figure 1: Relationship between discrete levels

Since these assumptions in past research have been largely implicit, there has been little recognition of them, let alone rigorous attempts to establish their verity. Crucial questions such as the following have not been examined:

- What is the relationship between the nature of the mapping and the search control strategy, so as to exploit the heuristic content embedded in the mapping?
- How do abstract- and concrete-level problem states correspond?
- How do abstract- and concrete-level plans correspond?

My intent in pursuing the research described in this chapter of the book is to formalize previously vague notions of abstraction, and to make the above assumptions and associated formal questions the focus of discussion. Because of the broad range of uses, both formal and informal, to which the term abstraction has been applied, I will make no attempt to provide a universal, encompassing definition. Rather, I will focus on definitions and extensions of two forms of abstraction that have appeared in the literature, **inheritance abstraction**, and **relaxed model** abstraction. Before discussing these different types of abstraction, a few words are in order about the use of state-based representations, as well as about the difficulties of measuring the effectiveness of heuristic methods.

Although earlier parts of this book have advocated a move away from state-based problem-solving representations and methods, they nonetheless serve as useful idealizations, especially regarding issues of search and computation. Viewing problem solving as search through a space of state descriptions, where actions are denoted by state changing operators, is a compelling mental model, bringing with it a wealth of descriptive terminology and past research efforts. Despite its obvious drawbacks, eloquently described in earlier parts of this book, I will adopt the state space model. For defining abstraction, I will rely on the simplicity and clarity of this model, hoping that others can extend this definition to representations not having the same expressive limitations.

Because abstraction as defined here is a heuristic method, there is the difficulty of ascertaining its efficacy. That is, problem spaces are mapped into new spaces which do not have a lower worst-case computational cost. This difficulty is inherent in *any* heuristic method, since worst-case asymptotic behavior has not been improved. This is, of course, one of the perennial problems that has accompanied virtually all work in automated planning and artificial intelligence. One possible approach to dealing with this is to implement systems and test them empirically. Unfortunately, this is fraught with considerable hazards, especially given that generating appropriate test problem instances for NP-hard problems is just beginning to be understood as itself an extremely difficult problem [Sanchis 1989]. Having the same researchers who build the systems provide all of the test problems to these same systems, especially in artificial domains, strains the limits of what we normally take to be scientific methods of theory testing and accountability. Even for those striving to be objective, it is difficult to ensure that the problem sample provided to the system does not fall within a lower-complexity subclass of problems for which a particular system has been optimized.

Another possible approach would be to improve analytical techniques used to evaluate planning systems or theories. An example of this would be crisper definitions of average-case behavior, and an understanding of how to apply such definitions to artificial domains. But what constitutes an average or random sampling of problems in a blocks-world domain, for instance, since no such domains exist within the real world from which we can obtain data? The approach taken here is a third alternative and follows the standard "logicist" methodology: to precisely state formal definitions and to prove theorems about the properties that follow from these definitions. The danger is that when going from actual domains (such as real blocks, or real kitchens), to idealized representations from which formal properties can be proven (such as a STRIPS encoding of the blocks world or the kitchen world), these nice properties may follow *only* as a result of the idealization process. In such a case, we obtain few insights that extend beyond these idealized models. However, with these risks in mind I nonetheless see this as one of the few viable alternatives. Such formal work *does* provide a clear basis on which people can agree or disagree. All of the cards are on the table, all of the assumptions clearly stated, all of the premises explicit. Thus, no systems have been built, and no claims are made about their performance. Rather, the issues and properties explored here will hopefully provide a terminology and desiderata with which future work can be evaluated. Some promising work, which I will briefly discuss in section 4.3.10, is already emerging.

4.1.1   Inheritance Abstraction

Inheritance abstraction extends the notion of inheritance from object types to actions, much as is described by Kautz in chapter 2. However, its use in plan *generation*, as opposed to plan recognition, necessitates a significantly different treatment (the reasons are discussed in section 4.2.11). Consider a kitchen domain, similar to that described by Kautz. This domain consists of many different objects, such as carving knives, fry pans, microwaves, mushrooms, refrigerators. Some of these objects can naturally be classed together, since, within this domain, they function similarly with respect to the common kitchen operations: knives (cleaver, chef, carving), food (ham, zucchini, mushroom), food store (pantry, refrigerator). That is, objects can be structured into an inheritance type hierarchy to inherit common attributes from a superclass (e.g., all knives have a cutting edge and handle), typical of ISA-hierarchies. Additionally, meaningful object superclasses will allow inheritance of *operations* on those objects (e.g., all knife operations involve separating a food into pieces). Using planning terminology, all operators belonging to the same superclass will have similar preconditions and effects, relative to the ISA-hierarchy on objects.

The central idea I pursue here is how an inheritance hierarchy of objects and actions can be defined *so as to permit planning using the high-level operations*, in concord with the Map, Plan, Inverse-Map paradigm. For instance, low-level operations might include slicing zucchini with a chef knife or chopping an onion with a cleaver, each being an instance of the abstract operation of cutting food in pieces with a knife. When faced with a planning problem, the planner would first solve an abstract version of the problem using the abstract operators and then specialize each plan step. For example, an abstract plan to cook a ham might be the sequence *<putInVessel, putInCooker, cook>*, while its specialization might be *<putInBakeDish, putInOven, bake>*.

Based upon this description of inheritance abstraction, one would prefer a guarantee that each abstract solution to a problem be refinable through an operator-by-operator specialization into a concrete-level solution (the **downward solution property**). In the formalism that I present, this property is shown to hold, but it requires somewhat strong constraints on the mapping function in order to do so.

The main difficulty in defining this formalism is in dealing with the frame problem at the abstract levels [McCarthy and Hayes 1969] . The frame problem is concerned with specifying in some economical fashion those aspects of the domain which do not change as a result of an action. In virtually all logic-based planning formalisms, operators, or action denoting terms, are taken as *completely* characterizing all change associated with the action (chapter 3 of this book being a notable exception). This is the case whether the representation language is a state-based STRIPS-like language, as it is here, or languages having explicit temporal terms, as those of Allen (chapter 1), Lifschitz [1987], and McCarthy and Hayes [1969], to name a few. These approaches all encode, in one fashion or another, that the truth of each proposition remains unchanged in the future unless an operator that changes the truth-value is explicitly known to occur. But this inference embeds an assumption that the planning agent knows about all effects of its acts. Unfortunately, such an assumption with regard to abstract operators is of dubious validity, since abstract operators by definition are underspecified. The complete effects of an abstract operator are not determined until a concrete specialization is chosen. For example, in Kautz's cooking domain, if *MeatInFridge* is true initially, what will its truth-value be after *PrepareMeal* ? This will depend upon whether a pasta dish or a meat dish is chosen as the specialization. In Tenenberg [1991], I discuss the frame problem in greater detail and the reliance that standard solutions place on inappropriate completeness assumptions.

The approach I use to overcome this problem is to abstract not only object types and operators, but to abstract every predicate in the domain through a **predicate mapping function**, and to use this mapping function to induce an abstraction mapping on state descriptions (sets of first-order sentences). Abstract operators thus completely characterize state change, *relative to the abstract state descriptions*. For example, suppose the operator *cook* is an abstraction of the concrete operators *bake*, *steam*, and *boil*. Further, suppose a precondition of each concrete operator is that the food be uncooked. However, the effects of cooking the food will be different (i.e., baked, steamed, boiled), depending upon which operator is chosen to specialize *cook*. Given a state to which the cook operator is applied at the abstract level, one cannot specify what the resulting food state will be at the concrete level. However, regardless of which specialization is chosen, the food will be cooked in any case! Thus, in the resulting abstract state, asserting that the food is cooked, and not specifying in any greater detail in what manner, is the. appropriate level of description.

Applied generally, this means that concrete operators abstracted to be the same abstract operator must have precisely analogous preconditions and effects. In this way, *all* effects of an abstract operator are sufficient to completely characterize abstract state change. Much of the technical content describing this approach is concerned with defining the abstraction mapping on predicates and state descriptions so that

1)   the mapping preserves the logical consistency of the abstract levels, that is, guarantees that no inconsistent states can be reached, assuming a consistent concrete level, and

2)   the mapping enforces an inheritance semantics between corresponding state descriptions at the abstract and concrete levels.

An inheritance semantics is one in which for each model of the concrete state description, there exists an abstract model for which its interpretation of each abstract predicate is exactly the union of the interpretations of all concrete predicates that it abstracts. For example, the set of all knives is the union of chef knives, paring knives, cleavers, carving knives, and so on. One of the objectives of this research is simply to explore this natural extension of inheritance hierarchies to the planning domain in an attempt to uncover its properties and uses. Potential advantages of its use include:

1) The abstract-level state descriptions and state space are smaller, and hence, weak search methods employed on them will generally be able to plunge deeper into the search space than in the original search space.

2) Certain choices about which objects to use to fill certain roles in a plan (e.g., type of knife) can be deferred, either until later in the planning process when new constraints have emerged or until execution time.

3) Plans having an operator that fails (e.g., chef knife unavailable at execution time) might be easily fixed by choosing an analogous operator (e.g., use available cleaver instead).

4) Abstract plans encode a set of specializations, and thus, will be more useful to store and reuse in plan libraries than any of the specializations.

Not all of these advantages are pursued or exploited here, and determining whether their potential can be realized for a net gain requires further research. A short discussion on research that has attempted to do this is included in section 4.2.12. There are, of course, disadvantages associated with this approach to abstraction, including:

1) The information lost in going from the concrete to the abstract levels might be crucial to solving a given problem. That is, the solution might depend, not on the features of an object *common* to those in its class, but rather on its *distinguishing* features. Unfortunately, determining if a problem does or does not have this characteristic will generally not be determinable *a priori*.

2) Choosing which objects to group into the same abstract class is a very difficult problem, and the formalism to be described provides only weak constraints on doing this.

3) The constraints required on the domain formalization in order to ensure well-behaved relations between abstract- and concrete-level solutions may be too strong to be of use. This point is discussed further after the formalization is presented.

By precisely defining the abstraction formalism, I hope to present a sound basis upon which other researchers can evaluate and weigh the advantages against the disadvantages.

4.1.2   Relaxed Model Abstraction

The precondition of an operator in state-based planning is a set of sufficient conditions for applying the operator to a state. Although this requirement of sufficiency is the subject of considerable controversy, giving rise to the well-known qualification problem [McCarthy 1977], I assume sufficiency throughout, considering this one of the possible pitfalls of the idealized model-building approach discussed earlier. Thus, one can view preconditions as constraints on world states, each precondition specifying a constraint that a state must satisfy prior to operator application. The representation makes no commitment as to the effects of an operator when it is applied in a state *not* satisfying all of the preconditions.

In an attempt to focus the search of a planning agent, Sacerdoti developed the following idea in his ABSTRIPS system [Sacerdoti 1974], one which is both clever and simple: 1) for each operator in a given representation of a domain, distinguish between preconditions which are typically easy to establish from those which are difficult to establish, 2) construct an abstract planning level identical to the original (concrete) representation, except that the easy preconditions are eliminated at the abstract level. Thus, eliminating the easily established preconditions is equivalent to assuming that they are satisfied in every state of the abstract level. Pearl [1984] refers to this type of abstraction as **relaxed model** problem solving.

Extending this description from 2 to n levels is trivial. simply order the preconditions on a discrete spectrum of ease of achievability by assigning to each a nonnegative integer, a **criticality**. The original domain description is then level 0, and the level i description is identical to level 0, except all preconditions having criticality less than i are eliminated. For simplicity of presentation, much of the subsequent discussion will be in terms of a simple two-level system. However, all results, without exception, extend to an arbitrary but bounded level system by simple induction. The proofs are in terms of such k-level systems. An example ABSTRIPS system from Sacerdoti [1974] is a STRIPS encoding of a domain in which a robot pushes boxes between rooms. Whether the robot is next to the box it is to push is a low-criticality precondition, the status of doors to rooms (open or closed) is a medium-criticality precondition, and whether an object is pushable is a high-criticality precondition.

The search strategy that relaxed model abstraction naturally gives rise to, a refinement of the MPI paradigm termed *length first search* by Sacerdoti [1974], is

1) search for a solution at the abstract level,

2) refine this solution at the concrete level by reintroducing eliminated preconditions of each abstract plan step, and use these preconditions as a set of ordered subgoals to achieve.

That is, search in the less constrained space first, and then refine this by inserting small subplans between abstract plan steps to establish the reintroduced preconditions.

For example, an abstract plan to get a box from one room to an adjacent one might be *<pushThruDr >*. Refining this at the next lowest level, where doors must be opened prior to going through doorways, might yield, *<open, pushThruDr >*. And refining at the lowest level, where robots must be near the boxes they push, might yield *<gotoB, pushB, open, pushThruDr >*. As the plan is refined, notice that the relative ordering of the abstract operators is preserved, and that operators are added only to satisfy preconditions that are introduced at the lower levels.

Despite the simplicity and appeal of Sacerdoti's approach, there are several problems which must be addressed.

1) Defining a metric for measuring the ease and hardness of establishing a precondition appears difficult (both conceptually and computationally), as well as problem dependent.

2) Assuming the truth of preconditions at abstract levels is unsound and may lead to contradictions.

3) Although the proposed search strategy is intuitively appealing, as yet it has no formal basis, that is, no justification for believing that it will lead to search efficiencies.

Point 1 is concerned with choosing a good abstraction, while points 2 and 3 deal with clearly defining the hierarchy and uncovering its formal properties. Although my intent in pursuing this research has been to explore all of these, the latter definitional issues are prerequisites to uncovering criteria for performance improvements. The surprising difficulties I encountered with these issues of consistency and search left little time to explore the former issue of performance. However, Knoblock [1990a; 1990b], Yang [1990] and myself (singly and jointly), have pursued the fundamental issue of building good abstractions, the results of which are briefly reported on in section 4.3.10.

The existence of inconsistent states is readily apparent at the abstract level in systems that have what I term **static axioms**, that is, axioms that are true in every state. In a block-stacking domain, a static axiom might be that the agent can only hold a single block at a time. Suppose that the *HandEmpty* precondition of a *pickup* action is assigned a low criticality. At the abstract level, then, the *pickup* action might be applied when the agent is already holding a block. The resulting state is thus inconsistent, since the agent will be holding the original block and the block it has just picked up, violating the static axiom pertaining to holding only a single block. Note that this inconsistency is a result of the abstraction process, since the concrete precondition that the agent's hand be empty before a *pickup* prevents the agent from violating the static axiom at the concrete level.

As will be discussed later, the existence of inconsistencies presents both computational and semantic problems, and it would be preferable to define relaxed model abstraction so as to ensure that such inconsistencies did not arise. A natural approach would be to assign criticalities to effects, and eliminate effects along with preconditions. But it is not obvious which effects to eliminate with which preconditions. For instance, the problematic effect from the above example (*Holding*) involves a different predicate than the precondition that gets eliminated. Computing all effects which will result in inconsistencies as a result of eliminating particular preconditions appears to be a computationally intractable problem.

The approach that I have pursued involves finding a quickly computable determination of which effects to eliminate with which preconditions such that the abstract levels are guaranteed to be consistent. In exchange for ease of computability, the constraints will be overly cautious in that they might eliminate some effects which would *not* cause inconsistencies, but for which determining this fact would generally be too expensive. Precondition and effect literals are grouped together whenever they can *possibly* occur together in the proof of any precondition, as determined by the transitive closure of their implicational relationship in the given domain axioms.

Taking the domain axioms to all be Horn clauses (a disjunction of literals with, at most, one unnegated), two literals are connected if and only if they occur together in a clause, and are grouped together if and only if they are related by the transitive closure of connected. For example, given the clauses:

$$Holding(x) \land y \neq x \supset \sim Holding(y) \tag{1}$$
$$HandEmpty \supset \sim Holding(x) \tag{2}$$
$$\sim On(x, x) \tag{3}$$
$$On(x, y) \supset \sim Clear(y) \tag{4}$$
$$On(x, y) \supset \sim On(y, x) \tag{5}$$
$$On(x, y) \supset Above(x, y) \tag{6}$$
$$Above(x, y) \land Above(y, z) \supset Above(x, z) \tag{7}$$

Holding and *HandEmpty* are grouped together by virtue of axiom 1, and *On*, *Clear*, and *Above* are grouped together by virtue of axioms 4 and 6.

This grouping forms a partition on literals, and criticalities are assigned identically to all preconditions and effects within the same partition. Further, domain axioms are assigned the criticality of their constituent literals which by definition is unique. The level i representation is obtained from the concrete level by eliminating not only preconditions having criticality less than i, but effects and axioms having criticality less than i as well. Because of this syntactic, implication-based method for assigning criticalities, it is straightforward to show that inconsistencies can never arise as the result of abstraction. That is, abstract levels preserve the consistency of the concrete level.

Despite the crispness of this result, it suffers from a potentially debilitating drawback: in some domains, all literals will be implicationally related, hence grouped together and assigned the same criticality. The severity of this problem may depend upon the actual domains represented. Regardless, it would be more reassuring to develop alternative analytic constraints that do not suffer from this problem.

Summarizing the discussion thus far:

1) Assigning criticalities arbitrarily to preconditions can result in inconsistencies.

2) Assigning criticalities to both preconditions and effects, and eliminating both, holds promise, but requires determining which effects are eliminated with which preconditions.

3) In the worst case, a precise determination of precondition-effect groupings appears undecidable, thus leading us to seek sufficient but perhaps overly strong constraints for grouping preconditions and effects.

4) Grouping based on the transitive closure of existence in the same Horn clause is one such constraint sufficient, but possibly it is too strong.

My approach toward finding better constraints on literal groupings is to weaken the grouping constraint such that literals satisfying certain properties with respect to the domain representation are never considered in the connected relation or its transitive closure. These literals, such as those involving the equality or sort predicates (predicates such as *Door* or *Box* indicating the sort of an object), often serve as the only implicational link in two otherwise disjoint subparts of the axiomatization. Making these literals opaque with respect to the transitivity relation preserves the disjointness in many domains, hence allowing several levels of abstraction. This abstract description hopefully will become clearer to the reader when the formalism is presented.

An equally important, but orthogonal, issue to consistency is determining the relationship between the concrete- and abstract-level solutions, so as to provide constraints on search. In fact, without such relationships, it is difficult to justify the use of abstraction. As described above, search is first attempted at the abstract level. If a solution is found, it is refined at the concrete level by inserting new operators between the abstract plan steps in order to satisfy the reintroduced concrete-level preconditions (those that are eliminated at the abstract level).

In the formalization of relaxed model abstraction in section 4.3, I prove the following properties:

1) Whenever a low-level plan ω to a problem exists, there exists an abstract-level plan ω' that solves the problem at the abstract level. This is called the **upward solution property**. Further ω' refines to ω by inserting operators between the abstract plan steps, as just described.

2) By the converse, if no abstract-level solution exists to a problem, no concrete-level solution exists.

3) In refining the abstract-level plan, one can protect all establishment literals without loss of completeness.

If in the abstract plan, the literal p is an effect of operator o_1 and a precondition of o_2, and o_2 is required in order to solve the goal, then p is an establishment literal, and is protected by prohibiting the insertion of an operator between o_1 and o_2 that negates p. In essence, the last property above states that one never needs to consider refinements of the abstract plan in which inserted operators negate the establishment relations of the abstract level.

This last property has heuristic merit, but its strength should not be overstated. If a problem has a solution, then it has an abstract solution that is refinable through protected insertion. This abstract solution is termed **monotonically refinable**. Unfortunately, there is no way of determining *prior* to refinement if a *given* abstract solution is one of the solutions that refines in this manner. Nonetheless, property 3 provides a useful criterion for backtracking in the refinement process by stating that if we are attempting to insert a new operator that violates a protected establishment, then this plan is clearly *not* the one which is monotonically refinable, and we should backtrack until we find the abstract plan which is. If we are pursuing a complete search strategy, property 1 guarantees that we will eventually find the monotonically-refinable solution.

The proofs of properties 1 through 3 are straightforward. Let ρ be a concrete-level problem solved by concrete plan ω. Consider ω at the abstract level. That is, only abstract level preconditions need be satisfied in any abstract solution of ρ. Thus, several plan steps in ω may no longer be necessary, since they existed solely to satisfy the eliminated preconditions. By removing these operators (if any), the new plan is no longer, and possibly shorter, than ω, and monotonically expands to ω. The difficult part of the proof is in ensuring that once plan steps are removed at the abstract level, every abstract precondition of the remaining operators is still satisfied in the state in which it is applied.

For example, suppose the problem is one of getting a box from one room to an adjacent room, which as we saw earlier, is solved at the concrete level by the plan $<gotoB, pushB, open, pushThruDr>$. At the next higher level of abstraction, preconditions for getting the robot to the box before pushing it are eliminated. Thus, the plan step $gotoB$ is unnecessary. And at the highest level of abstraction, where door status preconditions are eliminated, the *open* plan step is unnecessary, yielding the abstract plan $< pushB, pushThruDr >$.

4.1.3 Macro Expansion

Although I do not claim to be presenting a complete coverage of abstraction, one type that is not being covered deserves mention. This type of abstraction involves naming sequences of operators, called **macro operators**, or **macros**, and using these named sequences in plans in precisely the same fashion as primitives. In this sense, using macros is analogous to the use of subprocedures in programming. Once a subprocedure (or macro) has been defined in terms of well-defined primitives, it can be used to stand for the corresponding sequence of instructions (or operators). In addition, it can be used itself by other subprocedures or macros.

In planning, the canonical example system that uses macros is MACROPS [Fikes, Hart, and Nilsson 1972], although there are excellent examples as well in Korf [1985] and Minton [1985]. The preconditions of a macro operator are the union of the preconditions of each step, less each precondition which is established by preceding operators in the sequence. Likewise, the effects are the union of the individual operator effects less those which are negated by subsequent operators. For instance, let $MAC1(A, B, C)$ stand for the sequence $<stack(A, B),stack(B, C)>$, which stacks a tower of size 3 in a blocks-world domain. The preconditions for $MAC1$ are that A, B and C are clear, and the effects are that A is on B and B is on C.

Typically, macros are used in planning in the identical way that primitive operators are used: in the backward direction, the effects of each macro are checked for a match with the current goal, and if a match exists, the preconditions of the macro are used as the new subgoals. Of course, macros can also be used in the forward direction, where the current state is matched against the preconditions of the macro, with the subsequent state having the effects.

Allowing names to stand for aggregates of other objects is indeed compelling and powerful, and is certainly an important component of human problem solving. However, in the context of state space planning, it presents formidable technical challenges. Primary among these are the following:

1) As the number of named sequences grows, the cost of referencing the appropriate sequence for a given problem can exceed the cost of searching in the primitive operator space.

2) The number of states that satisfy the preconditions of a named sequence *decreases* as the length of the sequence increases.

The first point suggests that naming every sequence is an ill-advised strategy. One must clearly use some criteria to choose sequences for which the benefit of their use exceeds the cost of reference. This cost might be deceptively high, since adding a new macro generally will increase the average cost of search for each problem, while providing benefit only for the subset of problems to which it applies. Thus, one would prefer to name only those sequences that can be frequently applied to solve problems, or whose benefit is sufficiently high to offset its infrequent use. Finding such a set of sequences is quite a difficult problem, especially in the absence of information about the distribution of problems that the agent will encounter.

As macros increase in length, so do their preconditions. The greater the number of preconditions, the fewer states there are that satisfy these preconditions. Thus, it is an irony that those macros that are the most powerful, in that they plunge deepest into the search space, are also the ones that can be applied to the fewest number of states. The designers of MACROPS were acutely aware of this problem [Fikes, Hart, and Nilsson 1972, p. 27]:

The source of this difficulty is that the level of detail in a MACROPS description does not match the level of planning at which the MACROPS is used. . . . It may be necessary to consider more sophisticated abstraction schemes involving alteration of predicate meanings or creation of new predicates.

Macro operators might eventually prove to be a more useful form of abstraction than those explored here; however, it appears that a means for generalizing or eliminating preconditions, similar to inheritance and relaxed model abstraction, respectively, may be a prerequisite to effective macro-operator use. In fact, it was with this motivation that I began exploring the two forms of abstraction which are formally defined in the following pages.

4.1.4   Outline

The order in which the technical material will be presented is as follows. First, the STRIPS formalism that I employ will be presented. Inheritance abstraction is then presented. Included are several theorems regarding the preservation of consistency, the inheritance semantics that is enforced between concrete- and abstract-level world states, and the downward solution property. A brief comparison with the similar use of inheritance abstraction by Kautz in chapter 2 is also made. Following this, relaxed model abstraction is defined. Two different sets of constraints which ensure that consistency is preserved at the abstract levels are presented. The first set is overly strong, but it provides the basic intuitions and proofs that make the second set of constraints more accessible. It is shown that abstract plans can be refined by inserting operators between the abstract plan steps, none of which violate the establishment protections, in order to satisfy the reintroduced preconditions. In addition, it is shown that using this constraint provides a criterion for backtracking that preserves the completeness of the search strategy. Finally, results of recent and related work are briefly described. All theorems and lemmas are stated without proof in the body of the text, with the proofs appearing at the end in section 4.5.

4.1.5   STRIPS

STRIPS-like representations have been used extensively in planning systems [Chapman 1987; Sacerdoti 1977; Waldinger 1977; Wilkins 1988]. Despite many shortcomings of STRIPS, especially those outlined in earlier chapters of this book, it serves as a simple, well-understood representation for exploring abstraction. One of the few attempts at a rigorous formalization is provided by Lifschitz [1986], from which much of the formalization to be presented has been adapted. Although most planning researchers are familiar with STRIPS, I provide a detailed description, since there are several variants described in the literature with some nontrivial differences between them, and because a crisp formalization allows for a precise statement of the main definitions and theorems. In the original system [Fikes and Nilsson 1971], STRIPS is both a planning language and a stack-based control structure for searching the plan space. In the following discussion, all references to STRIPS refer only to the language component.

In STRIPS, the world is viewed as being in a particular state at each moment, and only through the actions of a single agent can the world change state. The state of the world is represented by a set of sentences in a first-order language, called a **situation**, and the actions of the agent are represented by **operators**. Associated with each operator is a set of preconditions specifying the conditions that must be satisfied by a situation in order for the operator to apply. The effects of each operator are represented by the deletion and addition of sentences to the situations in which they apply. In addition, there is a rule base of **static axioms** representing those constraints that are true of each situation, such as that an object can only be in one room at a time, or that only one object can ever be held at a time. Thus, a situation is determined by a set of facts which might change as a result of actions and the static axioms.

STRIPS can thus be viewed as a knowledge base (KB) manager, where the effects of an action are realized as operations on the KB. In particular, suppose one has situation S' and action o, with the associated sentences A_O to be added, and D_O to be deleted. The new situation resulting from applying o to S' is $(S' \setminus D_O) \cup A_O$, that is, the old situation minus the deleted sentences, plus the added sentences. By virtue of this syntactic operation, those sentences not deleted continue to hold in the new situation (the so-called *STRIPS assumption* Waldinger [1977]) without the necessity of a separate axiom and inference step for each such sentence, as is typically required in situation calculus approaches [McCarthy and Hayes 1969]. The STRIPS assumption, then, provides a simple approach to handling the *frame problem* [McCarthy and Hayes 1969] in domains having only a single active agent with complete knowledge.

Some propositions about the world might inferentially depend upon others; hence, this affects the form in which the world state is encoded so as to facilitate updates in the knowledge base as a result of applying an operator. For instance, suppose that in a typical blocks-world scene, there is a stack of blocks. If the top block is removed from the stack, then the fact that it is no longer above the remaining blocks in the stack must be reflected in the axioms used to represent the world. If *Above* is encoded explicitly in the knowledge base, then the operator associated with removing a block must specify the deletion of all of the appropriate *Above* relationships from the KB. Alternatively, one could store only the *On* relationships in the KB, along with axioms stating that *On* implies *Above*, and *Above* is transitive. In this way, only the single *On* relation between the top block and the one just below it need be changed as a result of the remove action.

This approach will be generalized to all of the object relationships encoded in the system and will be reflected in the description of the syntax of STRIPS systems. A predicate will be either **essential** (referred to as *primary* in Fikes and Nilsson [1971] and Janlert [1987]), meaning that it is not dependent upon or derivable from any others, or **inessential** (*secondary*, in Fikes and Nilsson

L: *Constants: C1, C2,...*
   Variables: w, x, y, z
   Predicates: On, Clear, Above, ≠
E: *On, Clear*
K: *~Above(TABLE, x)*
   ~Above(x, x)
   $On(x, y) \supset \neg Clear(y)$
   $On(x, y) \land y \neq z \supset \neg On(x, z)$
   $On(x, y) \land y \neq TABLE \land x \neq z \supset \neg On(z, y)$
   $\{C_i \neq C_j \mid i, j \in N \text{ and } i \neq j\}$
   $On(x, y) \supset Above(x, y)$
   $Above(x, y) \land Above(y, z) \supset Above(x, z)$
O: *stack(x, y)*
           P: $On(x, TABLE), Clear(y), Clear(x), x \neq y$
           D: $On(x, TABLE), Clear(y)$
           A: $On(x, y)$
    unstack(x, y)
           P: $On(x, y), Clear(x)$
           D: $On(x, y)$
           A: $On(x, TABLE), Clear(y)$
σ: $\{T \mid K \cup T \text{ is consistent and } T \subseteq E_\phi\}$

Figure 2: A simple STRIPS system

[1971] and Janlert [1987]), meaning that it is derivable from the essential relations.

Formally, a STRIPS system Σ is a quintuple (L, E, O, K, σ), where L is a first-order language, E is a subset of the predicates of L, (E being the essential predicates), O is a set of operator schemata, K is a nonempty set of clauses in language L (the static axioms), and σ is a set whose elements are sets of ground atoms (the problem space). There are additional constraints on K and σ discussed below. In the balance of this chapter, *Preds(L)* will stand for the set of predicate symbols in L. An example STRIPS system for the standard blocks world is given in figure 2. Unbound variables are taken as universally quantified throughout this chapter.

The set K is taken to be Horn in the balance of this chapter. A clause C is **Horn** if and only if there is at most one unnegated literal in C, and a clause set is Horn if all of its elements are Horn. Theorem 3 relies upon K being Horn; however, none of the theorems for relaxed model abstraction have such a requirement. K includes those axioms true in every situation. In figure 2, this includes things like "The table is never *above* anything", and "Each object can only be *on* one thing". Every essential predicate that appears in K is required to occur only in negated literals, that is, as the antecedent of a Horn clause. This ensures that essential atoms are never derivable from other clauses in any situation, the only derivable atoms are those having inessential predicates. This requirement simply makes explicit common usages regarding primary and secondary predicates

The set E_ϕ is defined as the set of ground atoms formed from predicates in E:

$E_\phi = \{P(x_1,....,x_n) \mid P \in E,$ and $x_1,....,x_n$ are ground terms$\}$.

Each element of σ is composed from atoms in E_ϕ. So, for example, $On(A, B)$ and $Clear(C)$ are both elements of E_ϕ.

An operator consists of a name and a description, an example of which is the operator *stack*. An **operator schema name** is an expression which has the form

$op(arg_1, arg_2,....,arg_n)$,

where *op* is a symbol not in L, and the arg_i are all variables of L, an example being *stack(x, y)*. Associated with each operator schema name o is an operator schema **description** (P_O, D_O, A_O), referred to as the preconditions, deletes, and adds, which are sets of atoms. The atoms in D_O and A_O must be atoms using predicates from E, which insures that only atomic expressions formed from essential predicates are explicitly managed by the KB operations. The only variables occurring in (P_O, D_O, A_O) are the arg_i of the associated operator schema. An operator schema name together with its description will be called an **operator schema.**

If τ is a substitution of terms for variables, and o is an operator schema, then $o\tau$ is understood in the standard way as the substitution of each variable in o by its pairing under τ. We take the set O_ϕ to be the set of operator schemata in O under all *ground* substitutions:

$O_\phi = \{o\tau \mid o \in O$ and τ is a ground substitution$\}$.

Operator schemata will never occur in expressions partially instantiated. An **operator** is an operator schema fully instantiated by ground terms—likewise for operator description and operator name. When the context is clear, the term *operator* will often informally be used to refer to just the operator schema name under a particular substitution.

The state of the world is represented by sets of sentences, called **situations**. Situations are composed of two parts, one containing the essential statements, such as $On(A, B)$, which might be deleted or subsequently added by operator application, and the other part containing the static axioms, such as

$\forall\, x, y \,.\, On(x, y) \supset Above(x, y)$.

The part containing the essential statements is called the **dynamic situation**, and is a subset of E_ϕ. A situation is a dynamic situation unioned with K, the static axioms.

A **problem** is a pair $\rho = (T_0, G)$, where T_0 is the initial dynamic situation and G, the goal, is a set of atoms.

A **plan** is a finite sequence of operator names (fully instantiated), with the **length** of the plan being the number of operator names in the sequence. The length n plan $\omega = <o_1,.....,o_n>$ defines a sequence of dynamic situations T_0, $T_1,.....,T_n$, where T_0 is the initial dynamic situation, and

$$T_i = (T_{i-1} \setminus D_{o_i}) \cup A_{o_i}, 1 \leq i \leq n.$$

That is, T_i is the dynamic situation T_{i-1} without the deletes of action o_i but including the adds of action o_i. This in turn defines a sequence of situations S_0 $S_1,.....,S_n$ composed of the dynamic situations unioned with the static axioms:

$$S_i = T_i \cup K, 0 \leq i \leq n.$$

An operator o is **applicable** in situation S if $S \vdash P_o$. The plan ω is **accepted** in Σ with respect to S_0, under the condition that

$$S_i \vdash P_{a_{i+1}}, 1 \leq i < n:$$

where S_i is defined as above. That is, a plan is accepted if each operator is applicable in the situation in which it is applied. S_n, the final situation achieved by executing plan ω from initial situation S_0, is called the **result** and is denoted $Result(\omega, S_0)$. The null plan, denoted $<>$, will be considered a plan of length zero accepted in Σ with respect to every situation, where $Result(<>, S_0) = S_0$. A situation S_i is accessible from S_0 if and only if there exists a plan ω that is accepted in Σ with respect to S_0 and $Result(\omega, S_0) = S_i$. The initial situation is accessible to itself by the existence of the null plan. Plan ω solves problem $\rho = (T_0, G)$ if

$$Result(\omega, T_0 \cup K) \vdash G:$$

A problem is solvable if there exists a plan that solves it.

The dynamic situations are considered changing parameters of the system. There are only some dynamic situations that we will want to consider as possible values for the changing parameters. These are characterized by the set σ of the quintuple defining Σ. We take σ_K to be the set of elements of σ, each unioned with K:

$$\sigma_K = \{T \cup K \mid T \in \sigma\}$$

Under this definition, σ_K defines the problem space. A situation that is an element of σ_K, is called a **legal situation**. By definition, we place the following constraint on STRIPS systems: σ_K is closed under operator application. That is, for all $S \in \sigma_K$ and all $o \in O_\phi$ applicable in S, $Result(<o>, S) \in \sigma_K$. For the balance of this chapter, the Σ associated with the concrete level of a STRIPS system will be taken as the set of all sets of essential sentences that are consistent with the static axioms:

$$\sigma = \{T \mid T \subseteq E_\phi \text{ and } T \cup K \text{ is consistent}\}.$$

Given these definitions, the notion of a consistent system can now be precisely stated.

Definition 1

A STRIPS system $\Sigma = (L, E, O, K, \sigma)$ *is* consistent *if and only if for every situation* $S \in \sigma_K$, *every situation accessible from S is (logically) consistent.*

4.2   Inheritance Abstraction

4.2.1   Generalizing Inheritance

The intent of using inheritance abstraction is to formalize the notion that analogous action types can be structured together into an action class at the abstract level characterized by the common features of all elements of this class. So, for instance, a *MakeFettucini* and a *MakeLinguini* act can be considered as instances of a more general *MakePasta* act. Planning a meal can then take place at the abstract (*MakePasta*) level, deferring the choice of specialization until the overall shape of the plan has first been determined. Note, however, that *MakeFettucini* and *MakeLinguini* are analogous only when *Fettucini* and *Linguini* are viewed as analogous, just as *MakeMarinara* and *MakePesto* are analogous only when *Marinara* and *Pesto* are viewed as analogous. The clustering of actions is thus driven by the way in which objects are clustered.

When objects are structured in what has commonly been referred to as an *inheritance hierarchy* (or *ISA-hierarchy*) [Brachman 1979; Hendrix 1979; Tenenberg 1985; Wasserman 1985], each class is characterized by the features common to all of its members as described by the domain theory. Details are considered to be those features that distinguish the elements of the class. For example, *Bottles* and *Cups* can be considered abstractly as *Containers*. Common features include the ability to hold liquid and to be poured from. Distinguishing features include that *Bottles* have narrow necks and *Cups* do not.

The semantics of inheritance is that of the subset relationship. For instance, in using inheritance hierarchies, the intent is that the set of objects that the predicate *Bottle* (or the node in the ISA-hierarchy labeled *Bottle*) denotes is a subset of the objects that the predicate (or node) *Container* denotes. *Bottles* thus inherit all of the features of *Containers*, since any property true of each *Container* must be true of each *Bottle*.

This clustering of object types into classes in the system to be subsequently described is specified by a mapping function on predicate symbols. This function takes predicate names from a concrete language, and maps them into abstract predicate names. This then induces a mapping on theories written in these languages. The inheritance semantics is enforced by restricting those concrete axioms which are mapped to be those which do not distinguish between the analogous concrete predicates.

This mapping function is defined in section 4.2.2, followed by the definition of theory mappings (since each state of a STRIPS system can be viewed as a first-order theory), and finally, by the mapping of operators and STRIPS systems.

4.2.2   Predicate Mappings

Formally, predicate mappings are functions that map predicate symbols from one first-order language to another. Given two sets of predicate symbols R and R', $f:R \rightarrow_{onto} R'$ is a predicate mapping, where f is not necessarily one-to-one. This is extended to a mapping between two first-order languages, $f: L \rightarrow_{onto} L'$, where the predicates are the only symbols that possibly distinguish L and L', and all nonpredicate symbols map to themselves under f. Two or more concrete predicates mapping to the same abstract predicate will be called **analogues**. The expression $f^{-1}(\psi')$ is to be interpreted in the obvious way as the set of concrete symbols, each of which maps to ψ' under f.

4.2.3   Model Abstraction

Under what conditions might we consider a model M' of L' to be an abstraction of model M of L? In other words, if f is taken as a syntactic abstraction mapping between languages, how do we wish to define the abstraction mapping between models of these languages? A reasonable definition is that we want to do this when the respective models all exhibit the previously mentioned inheritance semantics between mapped symbols. That is, a model M' of L' is taken as an abstraction of model M of L if and only if both models have the same objects in their universes, the interpretations assigned to the nonpredicate symbols are identical, and all tuples of the interpretation of an abstract predicate P' in M' are exactly those tuples of the interpretation of all predicates P in M that map to P' under f. This is stated formally in definition 2 below. Recall that $Pred_L$ is the set of predicates of language L. In addition, the notation $M[\psi]$ denotes the interpretation of ψ under model M .

Definition   2
   *Let M and M' be models of languages L and L' respectively, and $f : L \rightarrow L'$ be a predicate mapping function. M' is the **abstract model of M through f** (that is, M' is $AM_f(M)$) if and only if*

   1. $Domain(M')=Domain(M)$,

   2. $M'[\psi'] = M[\psi']$, for all nonpredicate symbols $\psi' \in L'$, and

   3. $M'[R'] = \bigcup_{R \in f^{-1}(R')} M[R]$, for all symbols $R \in Pred_{L'}$.

Note that neither exceptions nor inductions are captured by the abstraction-specialization relationship between models as defined above. If Cup maps through f to $Container$, then it is required without exception that *every Cup* be a *Container* in the corresponding models. In addition, each object taken to be a *Container* must be an element of the extension of a predicate that maps to

$S:$	$Bottle(x) \supset Graspable(x)$
	$Cup(x) \supset Graspable(x)$
	$Bottle(x) \supset MadeOfGlass(x)$
	$Cup(x) \supset MadeOfCeramic(x)$
	$MadeOfGlass(x) \supset \sim MadeOfCeramic(x)$
	$Graspable(x) \wedge MadeOfGlass(x) \supset GraspWithCare(x)$
	$Graspable(x) \wedge MadeOfCeramic(x) \supset GraspWithCare(x)$
	$Bottle(A) \vee Cup(A)$
	$\sim Bottle(B)$
	$\sim Cup(B)$
	$Bottle(C)$
$f:$	$f(Bottle) = f(Cup) = Container$
	$f(Graspable) = Graspable$
	$f(GraspWithCare) = GraspWithCare$
	$f(MadeOfGlass) = Breakable$
	$f(MadeOfCeramic) = Breakable$
$f(S):$	$Container(x) \supset Graspable(x)$
	$Container(x) \supset Breakable(x)$
	$Breakable(x) \supset \sim Breakable(x)$
	$Graspable(x) \wedge Breakable(x) \supset GraspWithCare(x)$
	$Container(A)$
	$\sim Container(B)$
	$Container(C)$

Figure 3: Predicate mapping of clause set

Container (in the corresponding models). No induction is made that allows an object to be a *Container* that is not one of the specializations of *Container* .

4.2.4   Theory Abstraction

Sentences will be taken to be in clause form, where clauses are taken to be disjunctions of *distinct* literals, that is, no literal appears more than once in any clause. Therefore, each clause can be represented as a set of literals. The predicate mapping on languages is extended to a mapping on sets of sentences in these languages in the obvious way. Intuitively, this amounts to rewriting the original expression and replacing all predicate symbols by their image under f. By definition, we take $f(\varnothing) = \varnothing$ for every abstraction mapping f. If ψ' is an abstract expression, then $f^{-1}(\psi')$ is the set of concrete expressions mapping to ψ' under f. An example of a clause set rewritten under a predicate mapping function is provided in figure 3. Note that $Pred_L$ and $Pred_{L'}$ need not be disjoint. Also, these clauses are written as implications rather than as disjunctions for clarity. I will use these equivalent syntactic variations interchangeably.

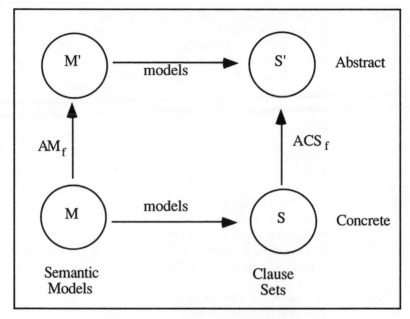

Figure 4: Relationship of ACS$_f$ to AM$_f$

The abstraction relationship between languages and models has been defined. Simply applying the predicate mapping function f to an axiomatization S is insufficient to guarantee that $f(S)$ is an abstract clause set of S, for every such f. One can see this in figure 3, where the concrete axiom

MadeOfGlass ⊃ ~MadeOfCeramic(x)

is abstracted to

Breakable(x) ⊃ ~Breakable(x)

which sanctions the inference at the abstract level of both *Breakable(A)* and its negation. The concrete level is consistent, however, which means that the concrete-level theory has a model, but the abstract theory does not. Thus, the desired abstraction relationship between theories S and S' is when, for each model M of the concrete theory S, the abstract model of M satisfies S'.

Definition 3

*Let S and S' be sets of clauses in L and L', respectively, and let f: L→ L' be a predicate mapping function. S' is an **abstract clause set of S** **through f** (that is, S' is ACS$_f$ of S) if and only if for every model M that satisfies S, AM$_f$(M) satisfies S'.*

A view of this is provided in figure 4.

By the definition of ACS$_f$, if some clause set S' is ACS$_f$ of S, then it will also be the case that any subset of S' is also ACS$_f$ of S, since if some model satisfies every clause of S', then surely it satisfies every clause of each subset of S'. One can, therefore, define clause sets which are maximal abstract clause sets.

Definition 4

*Let S and S' be sets of clauses in L and L', respectively, and let $f : L \rightarrow L'$ be a predicate mapping function. S' is a **maximal abstract clause set** of S **through** f (that is, S' is MACSf of S) if and only if*

1) S' is ACSf of S, and

2) for every S'' which is ACSf of S, $DC(S'') \subseteq DC(S')$, where DC stands for deductive closure.

For a given abstraction mapping f and clause set S, one might reasonably inquire if there exists an S' which is an abstract clause set (or a maximal abstract clause set) of S through f. That is, do there exist abstractions of arbitrary theories whose models satisfy the abstract model definition? These questions are answered affirmatively in the following section, where a constructive definition is provided.

4.2.5   Theory Mappings

Suppose we have an axiomatization in the concrete language that encodes our knowledge about the objects and relations in the world. In addition, we also have a predicate mapping function that indicates the categories of objects and relations that we consider analogous. We would like to construct a weaker axiomatization in the abstract language such that

1) it is faithful to the original axiomatization in that no statements true in the abstract theory will be falsified at the concrete level;

2) it contains no contradictions, assuming that the concrete axiomatization does not;

3) it includes abstract assertions that hold of all specializations; and

4) it preserves the abstract model property between the abstract and concrete theories with respect to the predicate mapping.

As indicated earlier, simply applying f is insufficient to satisfy all of these constraints, since consistency is not preserved. The problem with simply using f is that axioms in the original clause set might distinguish between the analogous predicates, as with the axiom that an object cannot be both ceramic and glass. What is needed is some constraint prohibiting concrete-level clauses which distinguish between analogous predicates to be abstracted.

The following definition of a clause set mapping defines one such set of constraints, and satisfies the above criteria. In this definition, for any clause C, $|C|$ denotes the number of literals in C; $neg(C)$ denotes the disjunction of the negative literals of C, or $\varnothing$ if there are none; and $pos(C)$ denotes the disjunction of the positive literals of C, or $\varnothing$ if there are none.

Definition 5 (Abs Clause Mapping)

$Abs_f(S) = \{C' \mid for\ every\ N \in f^{-1}(neg(C'))\ having\ |neg(C')|\ distinct\ literals,$
$there\ exists\ P \in f^{-1}(pos(C'))\ such\ that\ S \vdash N \vee P \}$

Informally, this says that an abstract clause is such that for every specialization of the negated literals, there exists some specialization of the unnegated literals such that the disjunction of these specializations is derivable from the concrete clause set. For example, let S and f be as in figure 3. Then $Abs_f(S)$ must include

$\sim Container(x) \vee Graspable(x),$

since for every specialization of *Container* having a single literal—in this case, $\sim Bottle$ and $\sim Cup$—there exists a specialization of *Breakable* such that the disjunction of the respective specializations, namely,

$\sim Bottle(x) \vee MadeOfGlass(x)$
$\sim Cup(x) \vee MadeOfCeramic(x)$

are derivable from the concrete clause set.

In the degenerate case where C' has no negative literals, the membership condition for C' is not trivially satisfied. Rather, $neg(C')$ is defined as $\emptyset$, and by definition $f^{-1}(\emptyset) = \emptyset$. Therefore, if C' has no negative literals, then there exists a unique $N \in f^{-1}(\emptyset)$ having no literals, namely, $\emptyset$ itself, and it is required that there exist a $P \in f^{-1}(C')$ such that $S \vdash \emptyset \vee P$. Put simply, if C' has no negative literals, there must exist a $P \in f^{-1}(C')$ such that $S \vdash P$. For example, if $Bottle(A) \vee Cup(A)$ is an element of S, then $Container(A)$ is an element of $Abs_f(S)$.

The case where there are no positive literals in C' is similar. For every $N \in f^{-1}(neg(C'))$ having $|neg(C')|$ literals, it must be that $S \vdash N$. For example, if $\sim Bottle(B)$ and $\sim Cup(B)$ are elements of S, then $\sim Container(B)$ is an element of $Abs_f(S)$. Similarly, in the above example, the clause

$Breakable(x) \supset \sim Breakable(x)$

is not an element of $Abs_f(S)$, since neither of

$\sim MadeOfGlass(x)$
$\sim MadeOfCeramic(x)$

are derivable from the initial clause set. If C' has neither negative nor positive literals, that is, $C' = \emptyset$, then $S \vdash \emptyset$. Therefore, if S is inconsistent, so is $Abs_f(S)$. Taking S from figure 3, $Abs_f(S)$ is the deductive closure of the set $f(S)$ minus clause $Breakable(x) \supset \sim Breakable(x)$.

Given these definitions, it can be shown that $Abs_f(S)$ is the strongest axiom set that abstracts S.

Theorem 1

S' is ACS_f of S *if and only if* $S' \subseteq Abs_f(S)$.

Due to this strength, however, Abs_f is not practical to use, since it contains its own deductive closure. Thus, for all but the empty clause set, it is infinite in size. However, since each subset of Abs_f is also ACS_f of S, one can consider subsets of Abs_f that are not of infinite size but that satisfy the criteria for theory mappings stated earlier. We demonstrate one such subset below, which additionally has a useful proof-theoretic property.

Definition 6 (MembAbs Clause Mapping)

$MembAbs_f(S) = \{ C' \mid$ *for every* $N \in f^{-1}(neg(C'))$ *having* $|neg(C')|$ *distinct literals, there exists* $P \in f^{-1}(pos(C'))$ *such that* $N \vee P \in S$.

The only difference between $MembAbs_f$ and Abs_f is that specialized clauses must be elements of the original clause set in $MembAbs_f$, instead of derivable from the original clause set, as they are in Abs_f. This results in the following lemma:

Lemma 1

If S *is a set of atoms, then* $MembAbs_f(S) = f(S)$.

$MembAbs_f$ is computable in the worst case in time quadratic in the size of S, and by the above lemma, linear in the best case. The clause set $f(S)$ minus clause $Breakable(x) \supset {\sim}Breakable(x)$ from figure 3 is $MembAbs_f(S)$.

Since $MembAbs_f$ depends upon membership and not derivability, it is sensitive to the way in which the axiom writers choose to encode their domain theories. I do not argue that it is the optimal or best subset of Abs_f to choose, simply that it is a natural one with useful computational and proof-theoretic properties.

4.2.6   Proof-Theoretic Relationship Between Levels

In addition to the model-theoretic properties associated with $MembAbs_f$ stated above, there is an important proof-theoretic property. Informally, for every abstract proof of a clause from a Horn clause set, there is an isomorphic proof of the specializations at the concrete level. The case for non-Horn sets is similar, and is given in Tenenberg [1988]. For our purposes in this chapter, the Horn case is all that is required.

Before this theorem can be formally stated, a nonstandard definition of proof is first given. Typically, proofs are formalized as either sequences of clauses, where parents of inference steps must appear earlier in the sequence, or as graphs, where input clauses are the leaves of the graph, and arcs point from parents to children. The reason why these definitions are inadequate is that if there is an abstract clause that is used more than once in a proof, it might be specialized differently for each inference in which it is used. Thus, a definition of proof is required that identifies each separate use of each clause in a proof, this being the only motivation for introducing this definition.

Definition 7 (Proof)

A proof from S is taken to be a directed acyclic graph F = (V, E) such that

1. *F is a forest of binary trees (see Aho, Hopcroft, and Ullman [1983]),*

2. *there exists a labeling function l_F labeling each node of V with a theorem of S,*

3. *all leaf nodes are leaf-labeled (per definition 8), and*

4. *if $<v, w> \in E$, then $l_F(v)$ is the child of a full-resolution inference [Robinson 1965] with $l_F(w)$ as one of the parents.*

Definition 8 (Leaf-label)

All clauses of S are leaf-labels. All clauses labeling nodes on a path to a leaf-labeled node are leaf-labels. No other clauses are leaf-labels.

A **proof from** S **of clause** C is a proof F from S where C labels the root of some tree of F. A **refutation proof from S of formula C** is a proof of the null clause from S unioned with the negation of C in clause form. The length of a proof is the number of nodes in the forest. The following recursive definition identifies all of the nodes that are ancestors of a clause in a proof.

Definition 9 (Out-forest)

The out-forest of a node v is

1. *All nodes in the tree rooted at v are in out-forest(v).*

2. *All nodes in a tree rooted by a node with an identical label to an element of out-forest(v) are in out-forest(v).*

3. *No other nodes are in out-forest(v).*

It will often be more convenient to talk about nodes as if they were clauses, rather than labeled by clauses. Recall, however, that the same clause can label more than one node.

Given the clause set S from figure 3, an example proof from $MembAbs_f(S)$ is given in figure 5. Note that the clause $Container(C)$ labels two separate nodes in the proof, since it is used in two separate inferences. Every node in the proof is an element of the out-forest of the node labeled by $GraspWithCare(C)$. The out-forest of $Graspable(C)$ contains only the top two nodes in the graph. The leaves are all labeled by elements of $MembAbs_f(S)$.

The following theorem states that every abstract proof can be specialized by replacing each node label by one of its specializations.

Theorem 2

Let S be a Horn clause set, f be a predicate mapping, and $F' = (V, E)$ be a proof of clause C' from $MembAbs_f(S)$ under labeling function $l_{F'}$. For each $N \in f^{-1}(neg\ (C'))$ having $|neg\ (C')|$ literals, there exists $P \in f^{-1}(pos(C'))$ and proof F such that

1. *$F = (V, E)$,*

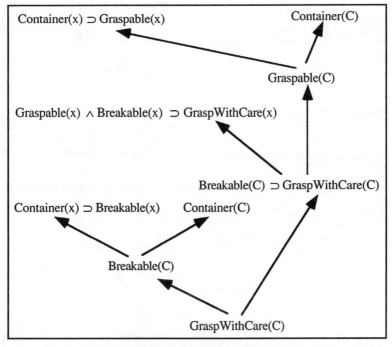

Figure 5: Example of proof

2. *there exists a labeling function l_F such that F proves $N \lor P$ from S, and*

3. $f(l_F(v)) = l_{F'}(v), \text{ for each } v \in V$.

This theorem demonstrates that finding an abstract solution (proof) provides a strong constraint on finding a solution to the original problem, since the only concrete-level proofs that need to be pursued are those that exhibit the isomorphism. That is, given an abstract proof, the concrete-level search space has been reduced from the set of all proofs to the set of isomorphisms of this abstract proof.

Figure 6 demonstrates this theorem with a specialized proof of the abstract proof of figure 5. The proof structures are identical, and each label of the abstract proof is the abstraction through f, the predicate mapping, of the corresponding label of the concrete proof.

Rather than searching in the original problem space, then, a problem can be abstracted, search can be pursued in the abstract space, and an abstract solution, if found, can be specialized under the constraints of the above correspondence. Note that there might exist problems having a solution at the concrete level for which no abstract solution exists. In particular, these will be problems that rely upon distinguishing features of analogous concrete-level classes.

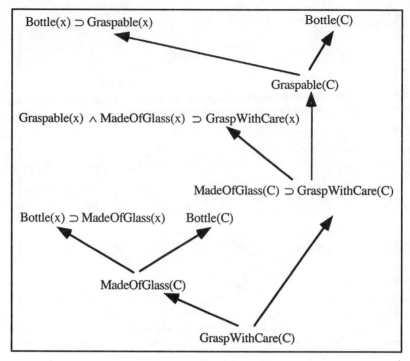

Figure 6: Specialized proof

4.2.7   Abstract STRIPS Systems

The intent of abstracting STRIPS systems is similar to that of abstracting first-order theories—to enable the agent to perform search within a smaller space. This requires abstracting all elements of the quintuple that define the STRIPS system.

The intuition associated with abstracting the operators is that actions performed on analogous objects for analogous purposes can be considered the same at the abstract level. These actions will be determined to be analogous based upon a mapping and comparison of the preconditions, deletes, and adds of the operators under the given predicate mapping function.

The STRIPS system resulting from abstracting all operators will have the downward solution property. That is, for every abstract plan ω' solving abstract goal G', there exists some specialization ω of ω', and G of G' such that ω solves G.

Let $\Sigma = (L, E, O, K, \sigma)$ be a STRIPS system and $f : L \to L'$ be a predicate mapping function. The abstract system $\Sigma' = (L', E', O', K', \sigma')$ associated with Σ is itself a STRIPS system. First, f is restricted so that if P_1 is an essential predicate and P_2 is an inessential predicate, then $f(P_1) \neq f(P_2)$. The other tuples are defined as

Concrete	Abstract
sliceShroomWSlicer(x, y, z)	*makeInPieces(x, y, z)*
P: *On (x, z), Slicer(y);*	**P:** *On(x, z), Knife(y),*
Mushroom(x), Whole(x)	*Food(x), Whole(x)*
D: *Whole(x)*	**D:** *Whole(x)*
A: *Sliced(x)*	**A:** *InPieces(x)*

Figure 7: Mapping operators

$L' = f(L),$
$E' = \{f(P) \mid P \in E\},$
$\sigma' = \{f(T) \mid T \in \sigma\},$
$K' = MembAbs_f(K).$

What remains is to define the abstract operator set O'. The predicate mapping function f can be extended to a mapping on operator schemata by assigning an abstract name to each schema name, and mapping each atom of the description to its image under f. For example, in figure 7, the concrete operator *sliceShroomWSlicer* maps to the abstract operator *makeInPieces*, where f maps the predicates in the corresponding positions on the precondition, add, and delete lists.

Given operator schema $o = opname:(P, D, A)$, define

$f(o) = f(opname) : (f(P), f(D), f(A)):$

Do likewise for instantiated operator schemata. In addition, define

$f(O) = \{f(o) \mid o \in O\}$

This mapping is extended to plans, so that if $\omega = <o_1,....,o_n>$ then $f(\omega) = <f(o_1),....,f(o_n)>$.

Only a subset of $f(O)$ will be used in the abstract-level system—in particular, those abstract operators that do not distinguish between the analogous predicates. This is similar to the mapping on axiomatizations, where given first-order theory S, only the subset $MembAbs_f(S)$ of $f(S)$ was used for performing abstract-level inference. For instance, in order to map *PourFromBottle* to *PourFromContainer* it is required that *PourFromCup* also exist at the concrete level, assuming that cups and bottles are the only predicates that map to container. Abstracting an operator o from Σ to Σ' requires that there exists in Σ a complete set of analogues of o with respect to the objects over which o is applied. The set of abstract-level operator schemata $O' \in \Sigma'$ are defined below. It is assumed that all corresponding variables in analogous operator schemata in O have been named identically.

Definition 10 (Operator Abstraction)

$O' = \{o' \mid o' \in f(O)$ *and there exists* $Q \subseteq O$ *such that*

1   for each $o \in Q$, $f(o) = o'$

2.   for each set $P \in f^{-1}(P_{o'})$ *such that each element of* P *is atomic, there*
   exists $o \in Q$ *such that* $P = P_o$,

3.   for each $o \in Q$, *ground substitution* ϕ, $d_i \in D_o\phi$, *and atomic*
   $d_j \in f^{-1}(f(d_i))$, *either* $d_j \in D_o\phi$ *or* $K \cup P_o\phi \vdash \sim d_j\}$.

Informally, for each $o' \in O'$, there exists a subset Q of the concrete operator schemata, all of which are analogous and map to o' (under the uniform variable assignments). In addition, each specialization of the precondition list of o' is the precondition list for some element of Q. That is, Q is a *complete* set of analogues. Also for each element of Q, for every deleted atom, every analogous atom either co-occurs on the delete list, or its negation is derivable whenever the preconditions of this operator hold. This last requirement is imposed in order to insure a correspondence between the abstract and concrete levels, since otherwise, if two analogous propositions hold in some situation at the concrete level and only one is deleted by an operator o, then in the corresponding abstract situation, the abstraction of both propositions will be deleted by the abstraction of o.

A concrete-level problem is abstracted as $\rho' = (T', G') = (f(T), f(G))$. Since the abstraction of a STRIPS system is itself a STRIPS system, definitions of legal situation, plan, and consistency hold for the abstract level. Figure 8 illustrates how several operators in a concrete-level kitchen domain can map to the same operator at the abstract level. The predicate mapping function maps all predicate symbols to themselves, except

$f(Slicer) = f(ChefKnife) = f(Cleaver) = Knife,$
$f(Mushroom) = f(Ham) = Food,$
$f(Sliced) = f(Diced) = InPieces.$

Thus, several different predicates have been abstracted in this example: the cutting tool, the type of food, and the type of cutting.

4.2.8   Downward Solution Property

Given the abstract STRIPS system defined above, the abstract level will correspond to the concrete level in a precise way. Each abstract plan is specializable by an isomorphic concrete plan such that each intermediate abstract situation is *MembAbs f* of the corresponding concrete situation. In addition, each abstract-level precondition proof is specializable by an isomorphic concrete-level precondition proof for the corresponding operator. Thus, for every abstract-level inference, there exists a set of isomorphic images that defines the space of specializations.

Concrete	Abstract
$sliceShroomWSlicer(x, y, z)$	$makeInPieces(x, y, z)$
P: $On(x, z), Slicer(y),$	**P:** $On(x, z), Knife(y),$
$Mushroom(x), Whole(x)$	$Food(x), Whole(x)$
D: $Whole(x)$	**D:** $Whole(x)$
A: $Sliced(x)$	**A:** $InPieces(x)$
$sliceShroomWChefKnife(x, y, z)$	
P: $On(x,z), ChefKnife(y),$	
$Mushroom(x), Whole(x)$	
D: $Whole(x)$	
A: $Sliced(x)$	
$\vdots$	
$diceHamWCleaver(x, y, z)$	
P: $On(x, z), Cleaver(y),$	
$Ham(x), Whole(x)$	
D: $Whole(x)$	
A: $Diced(x)$	

Figure 8: Operator abstraction

Theorem 3 (Downward Solution Property)

Let $\Sigma' = (L', E', O', K', \sigma')$ be an abstraction through f of the consistent STRIPS system $\Sigma = (L, E, O, K, \sigma)$, and let $\omega' = <o'_1,....,o'_n>$ solve $\sigma' = (T'_0, G')$ for some $T'_0 \in \sigma'$. For every $T_0 \in \sigma$ such that $f(T_0) = T'_0$, there exists a plan $\omega = <o_1,....,o_n>$ accepted at the concrete level such that

1. $f(\omega) = \omega'$,

2. $MembAbs_f(Result(<o_1,....,o_m>, T_0 \cup K)) = Result(<o'_1,....,o'_m>, T'_0 \cup K'), 1 \leq m \leq n,$

3. *there exists $G \in f^{-1}(G')$ such that $Result(\omega, T_0 \cup K) \vdash G$,*

4. *for each proof F' of preconditions $P_{o'_{m+1}}$ from $Result(<o'_1,....,o'_m>, T'_0 \cup K')$, there exists proof F of preconditions $P_{o_{m+1}}$ from $Result(<o_1,....,o_m>, T_0 \cup K)$ such that F and F' are isomorphic as specified in Theorem 2, $0 \leq m < n$.*

Although the stated theorems are between only two levels, the results extend to additional levels, since the abstract level is itself a STRIPS systems that can be abstracted in precisely the same fashion. Therefore, rather than searching in the original problem space, a problem can be abstracted, search can be pursued in the abstract space, and an abstract solution, if found, can be specialized under the constraints of the above correspondence.

Concrete	Abstract	Concrete	Abstract
Slicer(x)	*Knife(x)*	*MicroWave(x)*	*Cooker(x)*
ChefKnife(x)	*Knife(x)*	*Oven(x)*	*Cooker(x)*
Cleaver(x)	*Knife(x)*	*StoveTop(x)*	*Cooker(x)*
Sliced(x)	*InPieces(x)*	*Sauteed(x)*	*Cooked(x)*
Diced(x)	*InPieces(x)*	*MicroWaved(x)*	*Cooked(x)*
Whole(x)	*Whole(x)*	*Baked(x)*	*Cooked(x)*
Mushroom(x)	*Food(x)*	*HandEmpty*	*HandEmpty*
Ham(x)	*Food(x)*	*Held(x)*	*Held(x)*
Broccoli(x)	*Food(x)*	*Raw(x)*	*Raw(x)*
Onion(x)	*Food(x)*	*Empty(x)*	*Empty(x)*
Off(x)	*Off(x)*	*On(x)*	*On(x)*
In(x, y)	*In(x, y)*		

Figure 9: Predicate mapping

4.2.9   Example

An example of a simplified kitchen domain is given in figures 9 through 11. For simplicity, no static axioms are given for this domain, although we can imagine axioms stating that different sorts are disjoint, that an object cannot be both raw and baked, and so on. In addition, all of the constants are assumed to denote objects of the correct sort. Note that each step of the abstract plan is refined by a single specialization.

The downward solution theorem provides a formal constraint on the concrete-level solution given the existence of an abstract solution, but it is weaker than we might hope. First, since the converse of the theorem does not hold, there might exist problems at the concrete level which do not have abstract solutions. The abstract level encodes a simplified domain with a smaller search space, but at the cost of incompleteness. In addition, even in cases where an abstract solution to a problem exists, there is no guarantee that there exists a concrete solution to *every* specialization, rather, it is guaranteed only that *some* concrete solution exists—not necessarily the desired one. This would be the case in the cooking example above if the goal were to microwave the food, and the microwave was not initially empty. If, however, the goal is originally stated as a disjunction of predicates that exactly characterize an abstract predicate, for example,

   Baked(H) ∨ *Sauteed(H)* ∨ *MicroWaved(H)*,

then the theorem states that, given an abstract solution, *some* concrete solution can be found that satisfies the problem.

Concrete	Abstract
putIn(x, y)	*putIn(x, y)*
P : *Held(x), Empty(y)*	**P :** *Held(x), Empty(y)*
D : *Held(x), Empty(y)*	**D :** *Held(x), Empty(y)*
A : *HandEmpty , In(x, y)*	**A :** *HandEmpty , In(x, y)*
get(x, y)	*get(x, y)*
P : *HandEmpty , On(x, y)*	**P :** *HandEmpty ,On(x, y)*
D : *HandEmpty , On(x, y)*	**D :** *HandEmpty ,On(x, y)*
A : *Held(x)*	**A :** *Held(x)*
zap(x, y, z)	*cook(x, y, z)*
P : *In(x, y), In(y, z), MicroWave(z),*	**P :** *In(x, y), In(y, z),*
Raw(x)	*Cooker(z), Raw(z)*
D : *Raw(z)*	**D :** *Raw(z)*
A : *MicroWaved(z)*	**A :** *Cooked(z)*
bake(x, y, z)	
P : *In(x, y), In(y, z), Oven(z), Raw(x)*	
D : *Raw(z)*	
A : *Baked(z)*	
sautee(x, y, z)	
P : *In(x, y), In(y, z), StoveTop(z), Raw(x)*	
D : *Raw(z)*	
A : *Sauteed(z)*	

Figure 10: Example operators

Concrete	Abstract
Initial State:	
HandEmpty	*HandEmpty*
On(H, C)	*On(H, C)*
On(P, C)	*On(P, C)*
Raw(H)	*Raw(H)*
Empty(O)	*Empty(O)*
Empty(P)	*Empty(P)*
Whole(H)	*Whole(H)*
Goal:	
Baked(H)	*Cooked(H)*
Sliced(H)	*InPieces(H)*
Plan:	
sliceHamWSlicer(H, S, C)	*makeInPieces(H, S, C)*
get(H, C)	*get(H, C)*
putIn(H, P)	*putIn(P, C)*
get(P, C)	*get(P, C)*
putIn(P, O)	*putIn(P, O)*
bake(H, P, O)	*cook(H, P, O)*

Figure 11: Plan abstraction

4.2.10   The Frame Problem

The constraints specified above for ensuring both consistency and the downward solution property are quite strong. In particular, requiring that a concrete action, such as *PourFromBottle*, be abstracted only under the condition that all other *Containers* have isomorphic pour actions is not often met. Suppose that three out of four types of *Containers* are pourable, and one is not. Then, the abstract pour action would not be permitted.

One might additionally prefer that two or more concrete operators can be mapped to the same abstract operator if they are *similar*, but not necessarily isomorphic (under the predicate mapping). The preconditions might then be those that are common to all of the concrete operators. For instance, suppose that there is an additional precondition of microwaving, such as that the electronic timer and heat setting be encoded.

The problem with relaxing these strong constraints is that one runs into the frame problem. Abstract operators are underspecified, since, at the abstract level, one is uncommitted as to which specialization will eventually be used. In fact, this is the primary motivation for using abstraction! However, in order to plan further steps, one needs some means for maintaining the belief in all of the unaffected assertions that denote the world state. The typical way in which this has been done—and STRIPS is exemplary—is to assume that the operator descriptions are complete in that they characterize *all* of the changes that the operator brings about. The inferential strength of this assumption has been crucial in constructing a plan for a problem, since it allows for the persistence of truth-values of all the propositions unaffected by an initial sequence of operators but required at some subsequent point in a plan. Thus, the detailed knowledge encapsulated in the initial state description is not lost after the application of an action, but instead is persisted.

However, with abstract operators, it is clearly *not* the case that the operator descriptions are complete relative to the original problem description. The primary accomplishment in the above formalization is to express the state description at a suitable level so that the abstract operators completely describe the world *at the abstract level*. Thus, if you *cook* some food, although it is unclear whether the food will be microwaved, baked, or sauteed, one can certainly guarantee that the food will indeed be cooked. However, the cost of having this abstract-level completeness of operator descriptions is a rigid set of syntactic constraints, which may be difficult to enforce. Hopefully, future research will provide a more flexible means for using inheritance-style abstractions that also addresses the frame problem.

4.2.11   Comparison With Kautz

Kautz's use of inheritance abstraction in plan recognition(chapter 2) is quite different than the use defined here for plan generation. In plan recognition, one ascends an action hierarchy in order to determine an agent's highest-level plan.

One might consider reversing this process in plan construction. That is, one would *descend* the plan hierarchy to determine the low-level actions that an agent can perform to achieve its goals. For instance, suppose that an agent had an encoding of Kautz's cooking hierarchy, and the goal of having a cooked meal. Starting from the top of the hierarchy, one could look for a specialization of *AnyEvent* that satisfies this goal, an instance being the *PrepareMeal* node. One could then expand by descending the hierarchy, choosing one of each *or*-node, and all of the *and*-nodes, until one reached the bottom of the hierarchy. So, for instance, one such completed plan to cook a meal would be *Boil, MakeSpaghetti, MakePesto* .

Although this approach looks promising, there are many obstacles to its development as a general strategy for planning. In particular:

1) One cannot assume that plan libraries are complete. For instance, what if one instead wished to make linguine with clam sauce? Kautz's library has no such plan. One might consider adding this plan to the library, but one could not do so for every possible plan, since this would result in a library of infinite size.

2) Kautz's stored plans are insufficient for planning from arbitrary initial states. That is, *Boil, MakeSpaghetti, MakePesto* is only a successful plan when the preconditions for these subactions are satisfied at their time of application. But what if this is not the case? For instance, we might presume that a *Boil* action has as preconditions that water is in a pot, the pot is on a stove, the agent is in the kitchen, and so on. So, this plan is insufficient from an initial state in which the agent is not in the kitchen, all of the pots are dirty, all of the stove's burners are already occupied, or any of a host of other states that do not satisfy the preconditions of the subactions. In fact, using only an abstraction-decomposition hierarchy, the plans obtained from descending the hierarchy as discussed earlier will almost never result in a plan that can be applied from some initial state chosen randomly. This is clearly inadequate for plan generation.

3) The correctness of plans used in Kautz's recognition hierarchy is never verified. Therefore, one may not be able to deductively prove that a given goal is satisfied in the state following the application of a plan. This is because Kautz never specifies an approach to the frame problem. So, for instance, although it might be provable that the water is boiling immediately after a *Boil* act (because of, say, an explicit axiom to this effect), there is no means for inferring whether the water is still boiling after the *MakeSpaghetti* or *MakePesto* acts. This is not a drawback to Kautz's approach for plan recognition, since it in fact never arises, the recognizer never needs to chain through the steps of a plan to infer what goals are satisfied, the recognizer can simply assume that this mental effort was expended at the time the plan was stored. But an approach to

the frame problem must be specified with the plan formation task. And, as we have just seen, this is a nontrivial problem.

4.2.12   Related Research in Plan Generation

There have been several recent suggestions focused upon abstracting actions, such as that of Nau [1987], Anderson and Farley [1988], and Alterman [1987]. All of these researchers propose operators that inherit preconditions and effects, and yet none considers abstract operators to actually be operations on an abstract representation of the domain. Therefore, none of their proposals enables the composition of operators, and hence the completion of an entire plan, at the abstract level. Without the ability to compose abstract operators, the meaning of such abstract operators is called into question, as well as the nature of their contribution to the eventual construction of a concrete-level plan.

Abstraction appears useful for plan adaptation or repair. That is, if one has a particular plan that is being executed, errors or unforeseen events might occur at runtime—for instance, the chef's knife is not available or the microwave oven is not functioning. In this case, then, the hierarchical structure of the plan provides a basis for quickly repairing the problem online. This type of computation can be found in Alterman [1987] who uses a script-based problem representation [Schank and Abelson 1977]. When a plan step fails due to its inability to satisfy the precondition of an operator, an analogous operator is attempted that has the same abstract effect but a different specialized precondition. This would amount to using a cleaver as a substitute for the missing chef knife.

Because recovering from unexpected failures exacts a computational cost, it would be best to develop strategies to avoid them. One such strategy is to defer the choice of resources as late as possible. For instance, in the above example, if the agent were to defer the choice of knife until execution time, then the above problem might be avoidable since the availability of many resources changes rapidly over time. Using abstraction, one can construct plans using a generic knife (as well as generic objects for many other tasks) without specifying the particular knife, a generalization of Stefik's least-commitment strategy Stefik [1981]. Not only can one generalize by replacing specific object constants by variables, but by using an encoded object taxonomy, one can specify the most general class of object for the given task (a serrated-edge knife as opposed to a straight-edge knife, for instance). The intuition behind why least commitment is beneficial in the above example is that the larger a set of knives that one considers for cutting, the greater the likelihood that the plan will eventually succeed, since it only requires that some knife within the candidate set be available, rather than a particular knife. The larger the class of objects one considers, the greater the chance that some element from this class will be available at execution time.

4.2.13   Summary

The inheritance abstraction described in this chapter formalizes the notion that different actions can be viewed analogously, based upon a hierarchical structuring of the objects and relations in the world. Bottles are similar to cups, and hence, pouring from a bottle is analogous to pouring from a cup. Likewise, slicing and dicing food are analogous, although at the detailed level, the knives used might differ and the effects will differ.

A mapping on first-order languages is defined by means of a renaming function on predicates. This is extended to a mapping on theories and STRIPS systems. The resulting system exhibits the downward solution property, in that the existence of an abstract-level plan for a problem implies the existence of some specialization of this plan that solves a specialization of the problem. Search for a concrete plan is thus constrained to be in the space of specializations, these being the set of isomorphic plans under the inverse of the predicate mapping function. In addition, for each model of each world state in the concrete-level plan, there is a model of the corresponding abstract world state that preserves the inheritance (subset) relationship between renamed predicates.

4.3   Abstraction Using Relaxed Models

4.3.1   ABSTRIPS

In this section, I formalize Sacerdoti's original ABSTRIPS system by extending the definitions for STRIPS systems. Recall that relaxed model abstraction involves removing precondition constraints as one ascends the abstraction hierarchy. Once a problem is solved at an abstract level, the solution is refined at the next level by taking the reintroduced preconditions of the abstract plan operators as new subgoals.

A k-level ABSTRIPS system $\aleph$ is a sextuple $\aleph = (L, E, O, K, \sigma, crit)$, where (L, E, O, K, σ) are defined as in a STRIPS system, and $crit$ is a function that assigns to each precondition one of the first k nonnegative integers:

$$crit: \bigcup_{o \in O} P_o \rightarrow \{0, 1,...,k-1\}$$

If P_o is the set of preconditions of operator class o, then we denote the set of preconditions of o having criticality i or greater as P^i_o. That is,

$$P^i_o = \{P \mid P \in P_o \text{ and } crit(P) \geq i\}.$$

The description for each operator class o is defined at level i by the triple (P^i_o, D_o, A_o), and the set of operator descriptions at level i is denoted O^i. This in turn implicitly defines a STRIPS system for each criticality level:

$$\aleph^i = (L, E, O^i, K, \sigma).$$

L: *Constants: A, B, C*
   Variables: x, y, z
   Predicates: On, Clear, HandEmpty, Holding, ≠
E: *On, Clear, HandEmpty, Holding*
K: *Holding(x) ∧ y ≠ x ⊃ ~Holding(y)*
   HandEmpty ⊃ ~Holding(x)
   ~On(x, x)
   On(x, y) ⊃ ~Clear(y)
   On(x, y) ⊃ ~On(y, x)
   A ≠ B, B ≠ C, C ≠ A
O: *stack(x, y)*
         P: *Clear(y), Holding(x)*
         D: *Clear(y), Holding(x)*
         A: *On(x, y), Clear(x), HandEmpty*
   unstack(x, y)
         P: *On(x, y), Clear(x), HandEmpty*
         D: *On(x, y), Clear(x), HandEmpty*
         A: *Clear(y), Holding(x)*
σ: {T | K ∪ T is consistent and T ⊆ E$_\phi$ }
crit:
   {<On, 1>, <Clear, 1>, <Holding, 0>, <HandEmpty, 0>}

Figure 12: Example of an ABSTRIPS system

Note that the original STRIPS system, that is, the system with the full set of preconditions, is simply $\aleph^0$.

A k-AB $\aleph$ is consistent under the condition that every $\aleph^i$ is consistent. Given this definition, it is simple to demonstrate how an inconsistency can result in an ABSTRIPS system, even when the original system is consistent. That is, the inconsistency is introduced unintentionally by the abstraction mapping. The two-level ABSTRIPS system in figure 12 is an example showing how the inconsistency can arise for a simple block-stacking problem. For simplicity, the criticalities are assigned to predicates, indicating that the same criticality is assigned to each literal that uses the same predicate. In this and all subsequent examples, level 0 will be called the primitive level, and level 1 will be called the abstract level.

$\aleph^0$ is consistent, which can easily be verified, however, $\aleph^1$ is not. The counterexample is the initial dynamic situation

T_0 = {On(A, B), Clear(A), Holding(C)}.

The operator unstack(A, B) is applicable since the preconditions with criticality 1 are satisfied in $S_0 = K \cup T_0$, yielding

{Holding(A), Clear(B), Holding(C)}.

The inconsistency is derivable from the axiom stating that two blocks cannot be held at the same time. Intuitively, this is reasonable, since if one ignores the *HandEmpty* precondition, and the agent attempts this action in a situation in which the agent is already *Holding* an object, then two objects will be held in the resulting situation.

4.3.2 Planning With Inconsistent Systems

Sacerdoti [1974, p. 119] did not seem to notice that inconsistencies could arise from applying precondition elimination indiscriminately:

> The world model can remain unchanged; there is no need to delete unimportant details from it because they can simply be ignored.

As has been seen above, these unimportant details might be logically related to important details, and hence cannot simply be ignored.

One might argue that it is necessary to give up consistency at the abstract levels in order to gain an improvement in performance. As Nilsson [1980, p. 352] states " ... a contradictory state description may result, but this causes no problems." However, since all preconditions of every operator are satisfied in an inconsistent situation, once such a situation is reached, there are no constraints on the future choice of actions. In some systems [Rich 1983], especially those that do backtracking search, the detection of inconsistencies indicates that a wrong choice has been made, at which point the system must backtrack through some previous choice.

It is perhaps an even greater problem if the inconsistency is never detected. This might be the case where a refutation theorem prover is used (as described in the original STRIPS paper [Fikes and Nilsson 1971]) which might be misled from inconsistent situations into inferring that a desired theorem is provable. Suppose that a planner solves a problem at an abstract planning level, where the solution passes into some inconsistent situation. Under the assumption that plans at the next-lowest level will be required to bear some relationship to the abstract solution, a considerable amount of resource might be wasted in attempting to specialize this errant plan.

There are also semantic problems associated with a system that allows inconsistencies if we wish to associate some truth-functional semantics with each of the states, as in Lifschitz [1986]. For example, how does one interpret a system with an axiom stating that no more than one object can be held at a time, but which has additional axioms stating that both objects *A* and *B* are being held? Whatever correspondence that held between our formal system and the domain we wished to represent, however tenuous, certainly seems to be invalidated at the abstract levels of these inconsistent systems. In total, inconsistent systems present computational, proof-theoretic, and semantic problems.

Of course, one could avoid this consistency problem by trivializing the representation. Such is the case with TWEAK, which is similar to STRIPS, but which has no static axioms. In such a representation, a state is consistent if and only if it does not contain contradictory propositions. Thus, determining state consistency can be done in time $O(n^2)$ in the number of propositions in the state description. Determining the consistency of a TWEAK system is likewise trivial, requiring only that the initial states be consistent, and that proposition ~P be deleted by an operator whenever P is added by that operator.

Most of this discussion has concerned the preservation of consistency while ascending the hierarchy. This is because, in general, it will be impossible to decide if a STRIPS system is consistent. But if a STRIPS system *is* consistent, it seems highly desirable that the abstraction process itself should not introduce an inconsistency. Thus, a set of domain-independent constraints will be provided in the next section which guarantee the preservation of consistency.

4.3.3   Restricted ABSTRIPS

We can consider preconditions to constrain the set of states in which an operator can be applied. For instance, in figure 12, the *HandEmpty* precondition of *unstack* ensures that *unstack* cannot be applied in any state in which *HandEmpty* is false. When *HandEmpty* is eliminated as a precondition, then this constraint no longer applies and it is then possible to apply the operator in unintended states. For instance, when the agent is already *Holding* an object, in the resulting state two objects are being held thus violating one of the static axioms.

There is an irony in this, since it seems that one of the objects of using relaxed models is for the express reason of violating domain axioms. That is, the intent is for planning to first occur in worlds with far fewer constraints, for instance, without regard to whether the robot's hand is empty or not. But eliminating *HandEmpty* is equivalent to assuming that it is always true at the abstract levels, which can lead to inconsistency.

As discussed earlier, one obvious approach to solving this problem would be not only to eliminate preconditions as one ascends the abstraction hierarchy, but also effects. In particular, one would like to eliminate precisely those effects which would result in inconsistencies if they were to remain. However, determining this grouping of preconditions and effects is quite difficult, and may not be unique.

The approach to be described constrains the assignment of criticalities, so that, in general, predicates that are implicationally related within clauses of the static theory are considered to be in the same equivalence class, and are assigned the same criticality. The different levels of abstraction are then made distinct by eliminating not only preconditions, but adds, deletes, and static axioms as well. Each abstraction has its own coherence, based upon those sentences and relaxed operators remaining within its subtheory. Dividing the levels in this fashion preserves consistency from the lowest levels to the highest.

Two different formalizations of restrictions on an ABSTRIPS system will be provided. The latter system is the most general. However, the motivation for many of its constraints, and its proof of consistency are best understood by looking first at a simpler system. The former system, then, is primarily for illustrative purposes, detailing the general approach and proof structures.

4.3.4   Simple Restrictions

A restricted k-level ABSTRIPS system (referred to as k_{R1}-AB) is a sextuple $\aleph_{R1} = (L, E, O, K, \sigma, crit_{R1})$, where (L, E, O, K, σ) is as in a STRIPS system. The definition of $crit_{R1}$ is as follows. If Q is a predicate and C is a clause, we write $Q \in C$ if Q occurs in some literal of C. Given predicates Q_1 and Q_2, Q_1 *Connects* Q_2 if and only if by definition, there exists a clause in the static axioms in which both Q_1 and Q_2 occur. That is, *Connects* is a binary relation on predicates:

Connects $=_{def} \{<Q_1, Q_2> \mid Q_1, Q_2 \in Preds(L)$ and there exists $C \in K$ s.t. $Q_1, Q_2 \in C\}$.

Connects is therefore reflexive and symmetric. Let *Connects** be the transitive closure of *Connects*. *Connects** is thus an equivalence relation and partitions those predicates that appear in K into equivalence classes. The function $crit_{R1}$ is a mapping from each predicate to one of the first k nonnegative integers, subject to the constraint that any two predicates related by *Connects** must have the same criticality. That is,

$crit_{R1}$: $Preds(L) \rightarrow \{0, 1, ..., k - 1\}$, and
   if $<Q_1, Q_2> \in Connects^*$, then $crit_{R1}(Q_1) = crit_{R1}(Q_2)$.

Note that there are no constraints upon the assignment of a criticality level to predicates not appearing in K.

Predicates, then, are grouped into the same class based upon their connections to one another in the static axioms. If two predicates are not related by *Connects**, then these predicates are independent, in that they cannot appear together in any proof. This is formalized in lemma 16 in section 4.5.2.

Criticality assignments are extended to the remaining parts of the planning system The criticality of a literal is the criticality of the predicate that occurs in the literal. Clauses in K are assigned the same criticalities as their constituent literals, which all must have the same criticality by the definition of *Connects** . If some clause $C \in L$ contains literals with different criticalities, then $crit_{R1}(C)$ is undefined. In addition, $crit_{R1}(\emptyset)$ is undefined. Using a superscript i to the right of a set name will be used to denote those elements in the set that have criticality i or greater. For instance, K^i is

$K^i = \{C \mid C \in K$ and $crit(C) \geq i\}$.

If we take the elements of O, the set of operator classes, to all have the form $opName(P, D, A)$, then

$O^i = \{opName(P^i, D^i, A^i) \mid opName(P, D, A) \in O\}$.

Note that add and delete literals are eliminated at the different abstraction levels along with the elimination of preconditions.

If T is an element of σ, then T^i contains all sentences of T having no literals of criticality less than i. If σ is the set of legal dynamic situations, then the set of legal dynamic situations at level i consists of each set of σ containing only those sentences at level i or higher:

$$\sigma^i = \{T^i \mid T \in \sigma\}$$

S^i is similarly defined, for each element of σ_K.

A k_{R1}-AB $\aleph_{R1} = (L, E, O, K, \sigma, crit_{R1})$ therefore implicitly defines an abstraction hierarchy of k separate STRIPS systems, one for each level of abstraction

$$\aleph^i_{R1} = (L^i, E^i, O^i, K^i, \sigma^i), 0 \le i < k,$$

where L^i contains all nonpredicate symbols of L and only those predicates of L having at least criticality i.

I will sometimes want to refer to those elements of a set that are assigned a particular criticality without referring to the other elements that have a higher criticality. Therefore, if S is a set and i is a criticality,

$$S^{=i} = \{s \mid s \in S \text{ and } crit_{R1}\text{as}) = i\}.$$

For example, by this definition,

$$K^i = K^{i+1} \cup K^{=i}.$$

That is, the static axioms at level i or greater is the union of the static axioms at level i and the static axioms greater than level i.

Given a k_{R1}-AB, situations will be legal *relative to a particular level of the* k_{R1}-AB. A k_{R1}-AB is consistent under the condition that each level is consistent.

An additional condition that will be useful in later discussion concerns whether, for each operator, legal situations exist from which its preconditions are derivable. More formally, if O is the set of operator classes of Σ, Σ satisfies the **usability condition** if and only if, for every $o \in O$, for every ground substitution ϕ, there exists $S \in \sigma_K$ such that $S \vdash P_o \phi$. I initially require that systems satisfy this constraint in order to ensure consistency at the abstract levels, but subsequently relax this requirement. Note, however, that determining if an arbitrary planning system satisfies this condition is undecidable. However, for particular systems we are able to easily determine that they do or do not satisfy the usability condition.

As an example of a k_{R1}-AB, take the ABSTRIPS system of figure 12, and, given the same (L, E, O, K, σ), take $crit_{R1}$ to be

$$crit_{R1} = \{<On, 1>, <Clear, 1>, <HandEmpty, 0>, <Holding, 0>, <\ne, 0>\}.$$

L^1: *Constants: A, B, C*
       Variables: x, y, z
       Predicates: On, Clear, ≠
E^1: *On, Clear*
K^1: *~On(x, x)*
       On(x, y) ⊃ ~Clear(y)
       On(x, y) ⊃ ~On(y, x)
       A ≠ B, B ≠ C, C ≠ A
O^1: *stack(x, y)*
          P: *Clear(y)*
          D: *Clear(y)*
          A: *On(x, y), Clear(x)*
       unstack(x, y)
          P: *On(x, y), Clear(x)*
          D: *On(x, y), Clear(x)*
       A: *Clear(y)*

Figure 13: Example of a restricted ABSTRIPS system

The system $\aleph^0{}_{R1}=(L, E, O, K, \sigma)$, and $\aleph^1{}_{R1}$ is shown in figure 13. Note that each level satisfies the usability condition.

Situations are partitioned by the criticality function, and each partition is independent with respect to deriving preconditions, deleting clauses, and adding clauses. This is due to the constraint on the assignment of criticalities. Since the partitions are independent, there are no ordering constraints on the assignment of criticalities between the different partitions. Any partition can be taken as a detail or as an abstraction.

Lemma 2

Let $\aleph_{R1}$ be a consistent k_{R1}-AB having k levels for which the usability condition holds of $\aleph^0{}_{R1}$. $\aleph^i{}_{R1}$ is consistent, $0 \leq i < k$.

4.3.5   Relaxing the Simple Restrictions

One of the main problems with the restricted system described above is that the partitioning constraint might result in only a single partition. For instance, including the axioms

$On(x, y) \wedge y \neq z \supset ~On(x, z)$
$On(x, y) \wedge y \neq TABLE \wedge x \neq z \supset ~On(z, y)$

in figure 13 results in a collapsing of the equivalence classes to a singleton.

More generally, given a particular domain language, if we continue to add axioms to our domain theory, at what point are all of the predicates likely to be in the same equivalence class? In other words, what size axiomatizations are likely to have predicates that are all implicationally related as above? As pointed out by Michael Swain (personal communication), this problem is isomorphic to the connectivity problem for random graphs, for which a well-defined answer exists. To see the isomorphism, let each predicate in the axiomatization be a node in a graph, and let there be an edge in the graph between any two predicates that appear in the same clause. A random graph is one in which edges are added randomly. We can ask of this graph, at what point is it fully connected? As described in Bollobás [1985], the probability that a random element G from the set of graphs having n nodes approaches 1 as n approaches infinity, if the number of edges in G is greater than $1/2n \log n$.

If we take each new domain axiom as relating random predicates in the language, then the above theorem is rather disconcerting. One might make the argument that domain axioms for common-sense rule bases do not typically relate random predicates. In fact, if we take them to represent structure in the real world, we might insist that there is sufficient regularity to invalidate the randomness assumption. Although such a question might only be answerable empirically, it is difficult to do so with only artificial domains. Regardless, another approach is to weaken the partitioning constraints so that full connectivity occurs less often. I pursue this approach below.

The motivation for the partitioning constraint is to relate predicates based upon their implicational relationships to one another in the static axioms. It would be desirable to relax the partitioning constraint to accommodate the presence of predicates (such as inequality) that may occur in different parts of the theory, but which should not be used in determining the equivalence classes. This is done by defining a set of what are termed the *fixed* predicates of a planning system, all of which are inessential predicates and not derivable (in atomic form) in any situation, enabling them to be ignored when assigning predicate partitions without affect to the consistency of the abstract level.

Additionally, theorem 2 relies upon the truth of the usability condition. Unfortunately, this condition may not hold. An example of this would be an operator schema that only applies to a subset of the domain. For instance, one might consider a domain having bottles and blocks, where a *pour* operator only applies to bottles. Syntactically, this is achieved by having the atom $Bottle(x)$ appear as a precondition to *pour*. But this operator will never apply to non-bottles, violating the usability condition. To remedy this, the **sort-usability condition** is defined, which requires for each operator, only that a subset of the instantiations of an operator be usable.

Let $\Sigma = (L, E, O, K, \sigma)$ be a STRIPS system. The **fixed predicates** of L (*fixed(L)*) are those predicates of L that are

1) inessential, and

2) negated whenever they appear in nonatomic clauses of K.

These are the predicates of the language that, in some senses, are primitive in that no atoms composed of these predicates can be inferred from the domain theory, and none are ever added by any operator application. The only fixed predicate of figure 13 is $\neq$ (taking $\neq$ as atomic and $=$ as its negation). A **fixed literal** is a literal containing a fixed predicate, and a **fixed clause** is a clause containing only fixed literals. Let the **sort predicates of L** (*sort(L)*) be that subset of the fixed predicates which are monadic.

One could take the fixed predicates as a special *subset* of those defined here, and designate this subset by an additional element of the $\aleph_{R1}$ tuple. For simplicity, this approach is not taken. This is likewise the case for the sort predicates, which could be explicitly distinguished by the axiom writer. Criticalities can now be redefined, so that the fixed predicates are disregarded with respect to determining the predicate partitions. Given the syntactic constraints on these predicates, having them appear in axioms from different partitions will never result in inferences being made between the partitions.

Let $\aleph_{R2}$ be a sextuple $(L, E, O, K, \sigma, crit_{R2})$, where each element of the tuple is identical to $\aleph_{R1}$, except that the criticality function is redefined to ignore the fixed predicates as follows. *Connects* is first redefined as

$Connects = \{<Q_1, Q_2> \mid Q_1, Q_2 \in Preds(L)$ *and there exists* $C \in K$ *s.t.* Q_1, $Q_2 \in C$ *and* $Q_1 \notin fixed(L)$, $Q_2 \notin fixed(L)\}$.

As before, *Connects** is the transitive closure of *Connects*. The criticality function is

$crit_{R2}: Preds(L) \rightarrow \{0, 1,...,.k - 1\}$

subject to the constraint that

1) if $<Q_1, Q_2> \in$ *Connects** then $crit_{R2}(Q_1) = crit_{R2}(Q_2)$,

2) if $Q_1 \notin fixed(L)$ occurs in some clause with $Q_2 \in fixed(L)$, then $crit_{R2}(Q_1) \leq crit_{R2}(Q_2)$, and

3) $crit_{R2}(P) = k - 1$, for every sort literal P.

That is, nonfixed predicates must have the same criticality if they are related by *Connects**, a nonfixed predicate P must have a lower criticality than all fixed predicates that occur with P in any clause, and all sort predicates must be assigned the maximum criticality.

Note that there are no constraints on the criticalities of fixed predicates that appear in the same clause. Since clauses may now be composed of literals having different criticalities, the criticality of a clause will be taken to be the minimum criticality of the literals of the clause. As before, $crit_{R2}(\varnothing)$ is undefined.

Definition 11

If O is the set of operator classes of the STRIPS system Σ, Σ satisfies the **sort-usability condition** *if and only if, for every operator name* $o(x_1,...,x_n)$, *there exists* $Q_1 \in sort(L),....,Q_n \in sort(L)$ *such that*

1. $Q_i(x_i) \in P_o$, $1 \leq i \leq n$,

2. for every substitution ϕ of ground terms for the variables $x_1,...,x_n$, if $K \vdash (Q_1(x_1) \wedge...\wedge.Q_n(x_n))\phi$, then there exists $S \in \sigma_K$ such that $S \vdash P_o\phi$.

Intuitively, a system is sort usable if for each operator, there exists a legal situation that derives its preconditions whenever its arguments are of the correct sorts.

Consistency Under the Relaxed Restrictions

It can be shown that systems abstracted under these new constraints are consistent under the sort-usability condition. The reason for this is similar to that for the previous restriction. A level i precondition is proven only by clauses with the same or greater criticality. Thus, when one moves to a higher abstraction level, all of the preconditions remaining that were provable at the lower level are still provable.

Lemma 3

> Let $\aleph_{R2}$ be a consistent k_{R2}-AB having k levels for which the sort-usability condition holds of $\aleph^0_{R2}$. $\aleph^i_{R2}$ is consistent, $0 \leq i < k$.

It should be noted that consistency under these systems is a somewhat delicate condition to preserve. The proof of the above lemma relies on all of the following conditions:

1) The system is sort usable.

2) The fixed predicates have maximum criticality.

3) No essentials appear unnegated on the right-hand side of implications in static axioms.

4) Preconditions, deletes, and adds are all atomic, and deletes and adds are essential.

This set of constraints is sufficient for consistency, but it is not clear if a weaker set will also provide consistency. Certainly, it would be desirable to find a weaker set, as the above are difficult to guarantee and the sort-usability condition is undecidable to determine.

4.3.6   Example

An illustrative example is provided in figures 14 through 16, adapted from the domain of Sacerdoti [1974] and Nilsson [1984]. In Nilsson's example, containing over thirty predicates and over 170 axioms, all axioms are atomic and hence there are *no* constraints on criticality assignments to any of the predicates. Such simple systems are thus trivially k_{R2}-AB systems, regardless of the assignment of criticalities. Sacerdoti's system is likewise similarly unconstrained. However, more complex examples will include additional axioms, particularly "integrity constraints" [Reiter 1978], since, as seen in Nilsson's system, nothing axiomatically prohibits any object from being at more than one place at a time, or the same door connecting an arbitrary number of rooms, or rooms being in rooms. In addition, since no explicit sorting has been placed on

Constants: $\{ROB, B_i, D_i, R_i, L_i\}$
Variables: $\{x, y, z, rob_i, bx_i, dr_i, rm_i, loc_i\}$
Sort Predicates: $\{Box, Door, Location, Room, Robot\}$
Other Predicates:

$Open(Door)$	$InRoom(\{Location, Robot, Box\}, Room)$
$Closed(Door)$	$At(\{Bx, Robot\}, Location)$
$HandEmpty()$	$Connects(Door, Room, Room)$

Essentials:

$Holding(Box)$	$NextTo(Location, Door, Room)$
$DoorOf(Door,Room)$	$\neq(anysort, anysort)$
$\{At, Open, Closed, ClearLoc, Holding, HandEmpty, NextTo\}$	

Predicate Partitions:

$P_0 = \{Open, Closed\}$
$P_1 = \{HandEmpty, Holding\}$
$P_2 = $ all other predicates

$crit(P_i) = i$
$\sigma = \{T \mid$ every element of T is essential, and $T \cup K$ is consistent$\}$.

Figure 14: Predicates and partitions of example system

$Connects(dr, rm1, rm2) \supset Connects(dr, rm2, rm1)$
$Connects(dr, rm1, rm2) \wedge rm1 \neq rm3 \wedge rm2 \neq rm4 \supset$
$\qquad \sim Connects(dr, rm3, rm4)$
$\sim Connects(dr, rm, rm)$
$Connects(dr, rm1, rm2) \supset DoorOf(dr, rm1)$
$Connects(dr, rm1, rm2) \supset DoorOf(dr, rm2)$
$DoorOf(dr, rm1) \wedge DoorOf(dr, rm2) \wedge rm1 \neq rm2 \supset Connects(dr, rm1, rm2)$
$Open(dr) \supset \sim Closed(dr)$
$InRoom(x, rm1) \wedge rm1 \neq rm2 \supset \sim InRoom(x, rm2)$
$InRoom(loc, rm) \wedge At(x, loc) \supset InRoom(x, rm)$
$At(bx1, loc) \wedge bx1 \neq bx2 \supset \sim At(bx2, loc)$
$At(bx, loc) \supset \sim ClearLoc(loc)$
$Holding(bx1) \wedge bx1 \neq bx2 \supset \sim Holding(bx2)$
$Holding(bx) \supset \sim HandEmpty$
$\{\alpha \neq \beta \mid \alpha, \beta$ different constants$\}$
$Robot(ROB)$
$\{Box(B_i) \mid i \in N\}$
$\{Door(D_i) \mid i \in N\}$
$\{Location(L_i) \mid i \in N\}$
$\{Room(R_i) \mid i \in N\}$
Axioms stating that sorts are disjoint, of the form
$\qquad Box(x) \sim Door(x)$
for all sorts.

Figure 15: Static axioms

```
goto(loc₁, loc₂, rm)
                    P: At(ROB, loc₁), InRoom(loc₁, rm), InRoom(loc₂, rm)
                    D: At(ROB), loc₁)
                    A: At(ROB), loc₂)
goThru(loc₁, loc₂, dr, rm₁, rm₂)
                    P: At(ROB, loc₁), Connects(dr, rm₁, rm₂),
                            NextTo(loc₂, dr, rm₂), NextTo(loc₁, dr, rm₁)
                            Open(dr), InRoom(loc₁, rm₁}, InRoom(loc₂, rm₂)
                    D: At(ROB, loc₁)
                    A: At(ROB, loc₂)
open(dr, loc, rm)
                    P: At(ROB, loc), NextTo(loc, dr, rm), HandEmpty, Closed(dr)
                    D: Closed(dr)
                    A: Open(dr)
close(dr, loc, rm)
                    P: At(ROB, loc), NextTo(loc, dr, rm), HandEmpty, Open(dr)
                    D: Open(dr)
                    A: Closed(dr)
get(bx, loc)
                    P: At(box, loc), At(ROB, loc), HandEmpty
                    D: At(box, loc), HandEmpty
                    A: ClearLoc(loc), Holding(bx)
put(bx, loc)
                    P: At(box, loc), At(ROB, loc), Holding(bx)
                    D: ClearLoc(loc), Holding(bx)
                    A: At(box, loc), HandEmpty
```

Figure 16: Operators

the operator class parameters, any ground term can be replaced in any class. Therefore, the robot can, strangely enough, push coordinate locations to other locations, open and close boxes, and even push itself to boxes. Hence, a more realistic representation will require the addition of these axioms. However, these additional axioms make the problem considerably more difficult. A many-sorted notation is used, where the sorts of the arguments to each nonsort predicate are given. For instance,

$$InRoom(\{Location, Robot, Box\}, Room)$$

is used to denote that the first argument must be either a *Location*, *Robot*, or *Box*, and the second argument must be a *Room*. This will be used as shorthand for restricting the quantification of the variables in the axioms in which the nonsort predicates appear. So, for instance, the axiom

$$InRoom(x, rm1) \wedge rm1 \neq rm2 \supset \sim InRoom(x, rm2)$$

is to be understood as

$\forall x, rm1, rm2 . Room(rm_1) \wedge Room(rm_2) \wedge$
$(Location(x) \vee Robot(x) \vee Box(x)) \supset$
$InRoom(x, rm_1) \wedge rm_1 \neq rm_2 \supset \sim InRoom(x, rm_2).$

If there are no restrictions on the quantification, then the variable denotes an object of any sort.

In addition, each of the precondition lists of each operator is implicitly augmented by atoms indicating the sorts of the arguments. So, for example, one can think of $goto(loc_1, loc_2, rm)$ as having the additional preconditions $Location(loc_1)$, $Location(loc_2)$, $Room(rm)$. These preconditions were not written only for reasons of notational simplicity.

Intuitively, one can think of the different predicate partitions as being inferentially disjoint. For instance, the truth-values of any instance of *InRoom* will bear no relation to whether some door is *Open* or not. Likewise, the location of the robot will have no effect on whether it is holding anything. However, some object being at a location might affect whether or not it is in some particular room. The first level of abstraction (the level above the primitive level) is one in which doors need not be opened or closed. This is also true of the second level, but in addition, the status of the robot's hand is of no concern. Thus, at the highest level, a path will be found between different locations, where the agent can carry any number of boxes, and doors need not be opened or closed; at the next level, the robot will be required to insert actions that empty its hand at the appropriate times so that it never carries more than a single object; and in the most detailed level, doors will have to be opened in order for the robot to pass from one room into another.

A difference between this axiomatization and that of the original [Sacerdoti 1974] is that in this one, a greater reliance is placed on the static axioms to infer indirect effects of actions. For instance, one does not need a separate operator for pushing a box to a new location as opposed to moving the robot to a new location, since the latter will suffice. If the robot happens to be holding some object while moving, then by the static axioms, the object will go to the new location. This is likewise true for pushing through doors. Thus, eight operators of the original system (*gotoB, goto, gotoL, pushB, pushD, pushL, goThruDr, pushThruDr*) are replaced by two within the restricted system (*goto, goThru*).

Note that there are schemata for asserting the uniqueness of different terms, that different terms are of different sorts, and that the sorts are disjoint. A sample problem using this system is presented in section 4.3.7.

4.3.7   Upward Solution Property

Of equal importance to preserving consistency is to ensure that there exists a structural relationship between solutions obtained at the different levels, so that abstract-level search constrains search at lower levels. Showing that ABSTRIPS systems (restricted and unrestricted) have the upward solution property is in fact quite simple. Recall that this property states that whenever there exists a lowest-

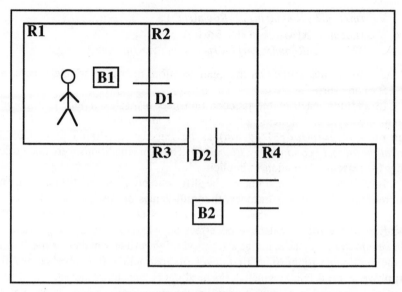

Figure 17: Moving box problem

level solution to a problem, there exists a solution at all higher levels. The central observation is that solutions that satisfy the more stringent constraints of the concrete level will also satisfy the relaxed constraints of successive levels. Thus, trivially, the upward solution property is satisfied.

Theorem 4

> *Let $\aleph_{R2}$ be a k_{R2}-AB having k levels, and let ω be a plan accepted by $\aleph^0{}_{R2}$ with respect to some legal situation S^0. ω is accepted by $\aleph^i{}_{R2}$ with respect to S^i, $0 \leq i < k$.*

As an example of this property, consider the problem illustrated in figure 17, relative to the system of section 4.3.6. The formulas in figure 18 indicate the initial dynamic situation; the goal, as given, is to get box B_1 (the one near the robot) to room R_2. A solution at the lowest level is given in figure 19.

At the first level of abstraction, the preconditions for doors being open or closed are disregarded. However, this has no effect on the applicability of the plan—the remaining preconditions of all operators are satisfied in the situations in which they are applied, and the goal is satisfied in the final situation. This is likewise the case at the next abstraction level, where the preconditions for holding boxes (or the hand being empty) are disregarded. Conversely, we have the following corollary:

Corollary 4

> *Let $\aleph_{R2}$ be a k_{R2}-AB . If $\rho = (T_0, G)$ is not solvable at the highest level of abstraction, then it is not solvable at any lower level of abstraction.*

$Connects(D_1, R_1, R_2)$	$InRoom(L_7, R_1)$	$ClearLoc(L_7, R_1)$
$Connects(D_2, R_2, R_3)$	$InRoom(L_8, R_1)$	$ClearLoc(L_{10}, R_2)$
$Connects(D_1, R_1, R_2)$	$InRoom(L_9, R_1)$	
$Closed(D_1)$	$InRoom(L_{10}, R_2)$	
$Open(D_2)$	$InRoom(L_{11}, R_2)$	$ClearLoc(L_{11}, R_2)$
$Closed(D_3)$	$InRoom(L_{12}, R_2)$	$ClearLoc(L_{12}, R_2)$
$HandEmpty$	$InRoom(L_{13}, R_3)$	$ClearLoc(L_{13}, R_3)$
$NextTo(L_1, D_1, R_1)$	$InRoom(L_{14}, R_3)$	$ClearLoc(L_{14}, R_3)$
$NextTo(L_2, D_1, R_2)$	$InRoom(L_{15}, R_3)$	$ClearLoc(L_{15}, R_3)$
$NextTo(L_3, D_2, R_2)$	$InRoom(L_{16}, R_4)$	$ClearLoc(L_{16}, R_4)$
$NextTo(L_4, D_2, R_3)$	$InRoom(L_{17}, R_4)$	$ClearLoc(L_{17}, R_4)$
$NextTo(L_5, D_3, R_3)$	$InRoom(L_{18}, R_4)$	$ClearLoc(L_{18}, R_4)$
$NextTo(L_6, D_3, R_4)$		
$At(ROB, L_8)$	$At(B_1, L_9)$	$At(B_2, L_{15})$
GOAL: $InRoom(B_1, R_2)$		

Figure 18: Moving box problem

$< goto(L_8, L_9, R_1),\ get(B_1, L_9),\ goto(L_9, L_1, R_1),\ put(B_1, L_1),$
$open(D_1, L_1, R_1),\ get(B_1, L_1),$
$goThru(L_1, L_2, D_1, R_1, R_2),\ put(B_1, L_2) >$

Figure 19: Concrete-level plan

That is, from the upward solution property, it follows that if there is no abstract-level solution, then there is no solution at any lower level. However, the utility of this corollary in search is limited since one is rarely able to exhaust the abstract-level state space.

4.3.8   The Monotonicity Property

In addition to the upward solution property, there is a stronger result obtainable: it would be advantageous if the abstract levels permitted shorter plans than the concrete level, where the lower levels would expand upon the abstract plans by inserting operators between the abstract plan steps to achieve the reintroduced preconditions. Knoblock [1990a] defines such a property, the *monotonicity* property, which roughly states that for each problem solvable at the lowest level, there exists a solution ω' at the highest level such that ω' can be expanded at each lower level solely by inserting plan steps, none of which violate the *precondition-establishment* structure of the abstract level. For instance, if in ω, operator o_1 establishes a precondition P of some subsequent operator o_2, then there exists a solution at the lower level in which no step inserted between o_1 and o_2 deletes P. This section extends Knoblock's definitions from ABSTRIPS systems with no static axioms, to k_{R2}-AB systems.

Formalizing this strong solution property between levels requires defining the establishment relationship between steps in a plan. I first define a simple temporal relationship, and then the precondition-establishment relationship between plan steps.

Let $\omega = <o_1,....,.o_n>$ be a plan. Let $<_\omega$ denote the *sometime before* relation between plan steps. That is, $o_i <_\omega o_j$ if and only if $i < j$. The plan subscript to $<$ is dropped if the context clearly identifies the referenced plan. The relations $>_\omega$, $\leq_\omega$, $\geq_\omega$ are defined in the obvious way.

The causal relationships to be defined state when the effect of one plan step establishes the precondition of a subsequent step. All steps in a plan should ultimately be shown to have a role in the satisfaction of the goal; any plan step that does not can be removed from the plan without any adverse effect. Given a concrete-level plan, as one abstracts this plan, preconditions of operators are removed and hence the plan steps that were present solely to bring about the removed preconditions can themselves be removed.

In the following definitions, let $\omega = <o_1,....,.o_n>$ be a plan accepted by STRIPS system Σ with respect to legal situation S_0. $S_i = (T_i \cup K_i)$ is the ith situation generated by ω from S_0. $<$ is extended to situations, where $S_i < S_j$ if and only if $i < j$.

The first definition specifies that a literal from one state is required to prove the truth of a literal from a subsequent state.

Definition 12
> B *in* S_i *yields* C *in* S_j *($Yields(B, S_i, C, S_j)$) if and only if*
> 1. $B \in T_i$,
> 2. $S_i \leq S_j$,
> 3. *for every* o_k *such that* $o_1 < o_k \leq o_j$, $B \notin D_{o_k}$ *and* $B \notin A_{o_k}$, *and*
> 4. B *labels a node in the out-forest of the null clause in a refutation proof of* C *from* S_j.
>
> B *is called the establishing literal.*

The **establishment** relation is now defined in one of three ways. One operator establishes another when an added literal from the former is used to prove a precondition of the latter. The initial state establishes an operator when one of its literals proves a precondition of the operator. An operator establishes a goal when one of its added literals is used in the final state to prove the goal.

Definition 13
> o_i *establishes* o_j *($Establishes(o_i, o_j)$) if and only if there exists* $B \in A_{o_i}$ *and* $C \in P_{o_j}$ *such that* $Yields(B, S_i, C, S_{j-1})$.

Definition 14
> S_0 *establishes* o_j *($Establishes(S_0, o_j)$) if and only if there exists* $B \in S_0$ *and* $C \in P_{o_j}$ *such that* $Yields(B, S_i, C, S_{j-1})$.

Definition 15

*o_i **establishes** G (Establishes(o_i, G)) if and only if there exists B ∈ A_{o_i} and C ∈ G such that Yields(B, S_i, C, S_n).*

For example, in the plan in figure 19, $goto(L_8, L_9, R_1)$ establishes $get(B_1, L_9)$, with $At(ROB, L_9)$ the establishing literal, S_0 establishes $get(B_1, L_9)$, with $At(B_1, L_9)$ the establishing literal, and $put(B_1, L_2)$ establishes the goal $InRoom(B_1, R_2)$ with $At(B_1, L_2)$ the establishing literal. An operator is justified in a plan if it is used, directly or indirectly, to prove one of the goals.

Definition 16

*o_i is **justified** in ω with respect to goal G if and only if*
   1.   Establishes(o_i, G), or
   2.   there exists a justified operator o_j such that Establishes(o_i, o_j).

A plan is justified under the condition that each of its operators is justified. At the lowest level of abstraction, the plan in figure 19 is justified, which can be verified by working backward from the goal: the last operator is justified since it establishes the goal, the two previous operators establish the last operator, and so on.

One can justify a plan by removing all unjustified operators:

Definition 17

***justified**(ω, S, G) is the plan resulting from removing from ω all operators that are not justified.*

A simple way of viewing a justified plan is as a graph, where there is a node for each operator, the initial situation S_0, and the goal set G. There is an edge <o_i, o_j> if Establishes(o_i, o_j), an edge <o_i, G> if Establishes(o_i, G), and an edge <S_0, o_i> if Establishes(S_0, o_i), there being no other edges. Each edge is labeled by the establishing literal. An example plan graph for the plan in figure 19 is given in figure 20. For readability, the node for the initial situation and all of its outbound establishment edges are not displayed. It is trivial to show that a justified plan will be a directed acyclic graph where every node is visited on a depth-first traversal backward from the goal node. Thus, an unjustified plan can be justified by removing all nodes not visited on such a traversal.

If a plan is justified, it does not mean that it is optimal, or even efficient. For instance, the plan <$stack(A,B)$, $unstack(A,B)$, $stack(A,B)$> is a justified plan for getting A on B, since the last operator establishes the goal, and each previous operator establishes its successor. Justification simply eliminates those actions which do not causally contribute to the plan of which they are a part.

The following lemma states that if a plan solves a problem, then the plan after justification also solves the problem.

Lemma 5

Let Σ be a STRIPS system, and ω = <o_1,....,o_n> be a plan that solves ρ = (T_0, G). Then justified(ω, (K ∪ T_0), G) solves ρ.

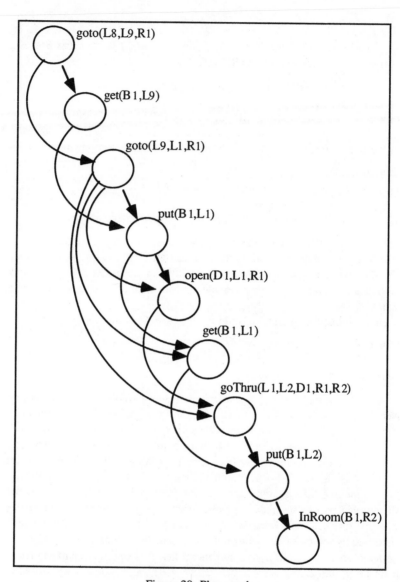

Figure 20: Plan graph

As one ascends the abstraction hierarchy, a plan that solves the problem at the lowest level will solve the problem at each successive level when stated in the language at that level. Therefore, this initial plan when justified at the abstract levels will also solve the abstract-level problem statement. Plan steps are thus possibly eliminated, since it is no longer necessary to achieve preconditions that are removed at the abstract level. The plan from figure 20 is given at level 1 in figure 21, where the *open* node and all associated arcs are

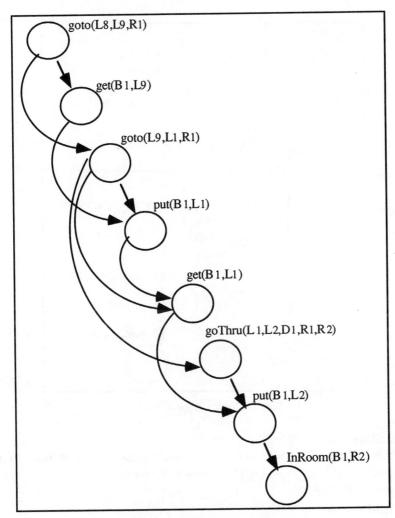

Figure 21: Plan graph at level 1

removed, and at level 2 in figure 22, where the nodes and arcs relating to whether the robot is holding anything are also removed. An eight-step plan at the concrete level becomes a four-step abstract plan.

Theorem 5

Let $\aleph_{R2}$ be a consistent kR_2-AB having k levels, and let ω be a plan accepted by $\aleph^0_{R2}$ that solves $\rho^0 = (T^0, G^0)$. For $0 \le i < k$, justified(ω, ($K^i \cup T^i$), G) solves ρ^i with respect to level i.

The monotonicity property can now be stated as follows:

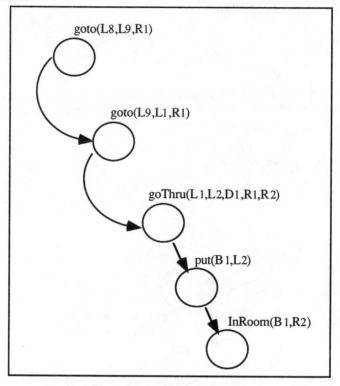

Figure 22: Plan graph at level 2

Definition 18

Let ω' solve ae at level i. ω is a monotonic refinement *of ω' at level i - j if and only if ω solves ρ at level i - j, and ω' is equal to the level i justification of ω.*

Definition 19

A k level abstraction space is monotonic if and only if for every problem ρ = (S₀, G) solvable at the concrete (0th) level, there exists a sequence of plans ωₖ₋₁,....,ω₀ such that ωₖ₋₁ is a justified plan for solving ρ at level k-1, and for 0 < i < k, ωᵢ₋₁ is a monotonic refinement of ωᵢ.

From these definitions and theorem 5, the next theorem trivially follows:

Theorem 6

Every k_{R2}-AB *is a monotonic abstraction space.*

4.3.9   Search

The discussion of search in this section is adapted from work done jointly with Qiang Yang of the University of Waterloo, Waterloo, Ontario [Yang and Tenenberg 1990]. Although this work with Yang has been in extending the definitions and theorems proven earlier to nonlinear, least commitment planners, such as TWEAK [Chapman 1985], much of that discussion on search relates to the linear planner described here.

Suppose that a problem has a concrete-level solution. Then there exists a monotonically-refinable abstract-level solution. Search, however, proceeds in a length-first fashion from the highest level to the lowest. Since the downward solution property does not hold, one cannot be sure if an abstract plan initially obtained is a plan having a monotonic refinement. But one can use the monotonic property to prune the search space by *protecting* all abstract-level establishments during refinement at lower levels; protection violations thus provide a criterion for backtracking. And using this search constraint does not sacrifice completeness. This is made more precise below.

Definition   20

*A search strategy is **globally complete** if it is guaranteed to find a highest-level solution and a monotonic refinement of this solution at each lower level, whenever a lowest-level solution exists.*

A search strategy can be viewed as a generate and test algorithm, which for each level, proposes new operators, and checks if the current plan with the inclusion of these new operators solves the problem. A planning algorithm is locally complete at a given level if it is guaranteed to find a solution at that level, if such a solution exists. For any level, it is known that A^*, Breadth-First Search (BFS), Depth-First Iterative Deepening (DFID), and so on are all locally complete and *admissible* (they find the shortest-length solution when a solution exists). However, one cannot simply apply one of these algorithms at each level in succession to arrive at a globally complete algorithm. For instance, suppose that BFS is employed at the highest level of abstraction, on a problem for which a lowest-level solution exists. The algorithm is guaranteed to find an optimal solution at the highest level, if such exists. Unfortunately, this abstract solution might not be monotonically refinable, in which case the system will be required to backtrack and try another abstract solution.

However, by redefining the state space to include not only the search operations of a single-level system (i.e., generating and testing new plan operators), but additionally to include plan refinement (i.e., generating and testing new plan operators at the level below) whenever an abstract plan is found that solves the abstract goal, any of the locally complete strategies can be used for global completeness. There thus exist globally complete, although semi–decidable, algorithms for searching abstraction spaces.

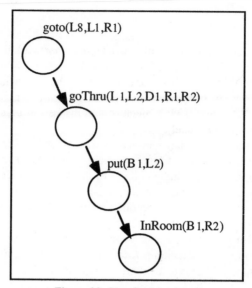

Figure 23: Unrefinable plan 1

The monotonic property provides a criterion for backtracking guaranteed to preserve global completeness. All establishing literals of an abstract plan can be protected [Waldinger 1977] during refinement at the next lowest level.

There are two cases when this backtracking can occur. First, when a new operator is generated which deletes an establishing literal of the abstract plan, and second, when a new operator is proposed which adds an establishing literal which would appear in the abstract plan. Suppose that plan $\omega' = <o'_1,...,o'_n>$ solves problem $\rho = (T_0, G)$ at level i. Recall that an establishing literal of ω' is a literal added by an operator that satisfies a precondition of a subsequent operator. Let P be a literal added by o_i which is an establishing literal of o_j. If, in the level i-1 refinement of ω', an operator is generated that occurs between o_i and o_j which deletes P, then this refined plan cannot be justified to yield ω'.

For instance, suppose that the plan from figure 23 has been found to solve the abstract-level goal $(InRoom(B_1, R_2))$, and is being refined at the concrete level. The abstract-level plan does not include going to the location of the box (L_9)before going to the door, and hence, this must be corrected at the concrete level. However, if in the concrete refinement, the robot goes to the box location (or any other location) immediately from the initial state, then this violates $At(L_8)$, the protected establishing literal of the operator $goto(L_8, L_1, R_1)$ from the abstract plan. Thus, this current refinement with the new $goto$ is not abstractable to the plan in figure 23, and all of its refinements can be abandoned.

Corollary 6

If S is a globally complete search strategy, then S can abandon proposed plans at level i that violate any of the protected establishing literals from levels greater than i, without loss of completeness.

The other case is when a new operator is proposed which adds a literal that becomes an establishing literal for an operator that is justified in the abstract plan. For instance, in refining the plan of figure 23, suppose that the operators

$$<goto(L_2, L_{10}, R_2), put(B_1, L_{10})>$$

were proposed to be appended to the end of the abstract plan. As a result, this new *put* operator is justified, since it establishes the goal, and hence, if this new plan were justified at the abstract level, it would not be identical to the original abstract-level plan.

Corollary 7

If S is a globally complete search strategy, then S can abandon plans at level i that propose operators which add establishing literals for operators that are justified at any higher level.

Another way to view this, is that these new operators are replacing operators earlier in the plan which originally established the preconditions now established by the new operators.

4.3.10   Related Research

Because abstract plans can be considerably shorter than their concrete refinements, relaxed model abstraction offers promise in reducing the cost of planning. One of the issues of primary concern that is not addressed in this chapter, is that of choosing good criticality assignments. Knoblock [1990b] addresses this issue by proposing an additional set of restrictions on the criticality assignment guaranteeing that literals established at lower levels will never add or delete literals with higher criticalities. A spectrum of restrictions and solution properties is further explored in [Knoblock, Tenenberg, and Yang 1990] for a simple representation language that does not include any static axioms, and for which issues of correctness are trivialized.

An additional direction that has been explored [Yang and Tenenberg 1990] is in extending the monotonicity results detailed here to nonlinear least-commitment planners, such as that of Chapman [1985]. By formalizing justification rigorously for partial plans (those in which there are only partial constraints on temporal order and operator instantiation), the beneficial properties of both least-commitment and abstraction are preserved. In addition, Yang is seeking to demonstrate empirically that abstraction results in search efficiencies. This work suggests that the number of establishment protection violations is inversely related to the efficiency of the criticality assignments—the fewer the violations, the better the assignment.

4.3.11   Summary

ABSTRIPS provides an elegant means for producing relaxed models, by associating a criticality value with each precondition, and abstracting at level i

by considering only preconditions having criticality i or greater. The drawback is that this approach is too simplistic for systems having static axioms that represent the inferential relationships between the predicates. In these more expressive systems, abstracting by eliminating preconditions can lead to inconsistencies.

In addition to problems with inconsistency, there has been little previous understanding of the precise relationship between solutions obtainable at different levels. Hence, it has been difficult to specify search procedures that exploit the represented abstractions.

A set of restrictions on ABSTRIPS is presented which guarantees that consistency is preserved in ascending the abstraction hierarchy. These restrictions assign criticalities not just to preconditions, but to all parts of the system, including adds, deletes, and static axioms, based upon the inferential relationship of the predicates as expressed in the static axioms.

The upward solution property holds of all of the ABSTRIPS-style systems. Further, such systems are shown to be monotonic, in that the presence of a concrete solution implies the presence of an abstract solution refinable at lower levels by adding operators that never violate any higher-level establishment relations. Search is therefore constrained, in that refinements to an abstract plan violating the establishment structure need never be considered, without loss of completeness.

4.4   Conclusion

4.4.1   Discrete Levels

This chapter has presented two different views on abstraction in plan construction. The focus has been on unearthing the relationships between the different levels of the systems. Inherent in this entire approach is the use of discrete levels of representation, where the abstract states and operators are partitioned from the concrete level. This is as opposed to having a single level, such as Kautz's hierarchy, where assertions about abstract and concrete objects and relations are together within the same representation, and thus can directly interact. The multilevel approach dates to Amarel [1968], if not earlier, but has been used many times subsequently [Knoblock 1990a; Tenenberg 1988; Sacerdoti 1974; Giunchiglia and Walsh 1989; Plaisted 1981; Korf 1987]. Its advantages are that one can more easily define precisely what an abstraction *is*, and explore the formal relationship between levels, as has been done in this chapter.

However, the rigidity of the discrete-level approach gives cause for concern. It does not allow the kind of flexibility that people appear to have, by allowing them to plan some subtasks to a considerable amount of detail, while leaving others very loosely sketched. Our natural language reflects this flexibility, since, for some tasks, we can talk of knives in general when the distinctions between the kinds of knife are irrelevant, while for others, we can speak of 10" chef knives, since a related task demands this precision.

But if we forego the discrete-level approach, then we are faced with some considerable technical problems. Among these are defining precisely what abstract operators or assertions are. Kautz is able to address this issue by defining abstract operators using implication. However, for plan construction, one has the additional complexity of developing an approach for inheriting frame axioms, as discussed earlier. Further, without discrete levels, it is not clear what guides search. How does a plan that might contain abstract operators relate to its eventual concrete refinement?

4.4.2   Solution Properties

The two different types of abstraction exhibit different solution properties. This suggests that combining both reduced model and inheritance abstraction into a single system will not be straightforward. In particular, does one lose both the upward and downward solution properties? How, then, is such an abstract plan specialized? That is, how does the existence of an abstract plan constrain the search for a low-level plan? With reduced model abstraction, having an abstract plan does not guarantee that one of its refinements will solve the concrete-level problem, while with inheritance abstraction, there is no guarantee that there even exists an abstract plan. The construction of a search strategy that exploits the abstraction is a nontrivial task, especially if one wishes to preserve completeness.

As an alternative, perhaps one could define inheritance abstraction in such a way that it exhibits the upward, rather than the downward solution property, thus making its combination with reduced model abstraction easier. Although this might be possible, intuition leads me to believe it is not a fruitful way to proceed. This is not to say that the presence of the downward solution property was a fortuitous consequence of the syntactic constraints that I enforced. Rather, the constraints were designed so as to ensure this property. But this was only after it became clear that the "essential nature" of inheritance operators was for plans to also inherit: plans that solve the abstract-level problem will specialize to solve specializations of this problem.

Might we want to prefer one type of abstraction to another? Giunchiglia and Walsh [1989] point out that with downward solution abstractions, there exist problems solvable at the concrete level that are not solvable at the abstract level. "This means that completeness is lost .... We consider this the one property you do not want to lose." For the general case, this appears to be a difficult position to defend. Although one sacrifices completeness at the abstract level with downward solution abstractions, obtaining an abstract solution guarantees a finite, constrained search for its concrete realization. This may well offset the loss of completeness. Further, having completeness with an upward solution abstraction might be of little use, if the abstractions are poorly chosen and the abstract solutions typically lie in distant parts of the search space. The use of abstraction for problem solving is too little understood yet to be doctrinaire about which types of abstraction, in general, will be best.

Perhaps then, we might want to forego the guarantees associated with having these solution properties. Abstract plans would not guarantee the existence of refinements, or vice versa. What, then, justifies the use of abstraction? What defines an abstract operator, an abstract plan, and what principles are used to guide search and abstract plan refinement? The use of probabilities in planning might provide some insights [Dean and Kanazawa 1988b; Weber 1989; Tenenberg 1991], where rather than having solution guarantees, abstract solutions will simply be *evidence* for the existence of low-level solutions, or vice versa. However, it is as yet unclear whether such methods will provide further understanding into the nature of problem solving and abstraction. Hopefully, providing a formal investigation of abstraction within the constrained systems examined in this chapter begins to establish a context—a coherent set of issues and problems—in which deeper insights might be obtained.

4.5   Proofs

4.5.1   Proofs for Inheritance Abstraction

Model-Theoretic Proofs

In the following proofs, the interpretation of symbol ψ in model M under value assignment v is notated as $M_v[\psi]$. If C is a clause, then $M[C]$ is true if and only if $M_v[C]$ is true for every value assignment v of variables to domain elements. Before proving theorem 1, several lemmas and corollaries will be established. In addition, the main definitions are rewritten here for easier reference.

Definition 2

*Let M and M' be models of languages L and L' respectively, and $f : L{\rightarrow}L'$ be a predicate mapping function. M' is the **abstract model of M** through f (that is, M' is $AM_f(M)$) if and only if*

1. Domain(M')=Domain(M),

2. $M'[\psi] = M[\psi]$, for all nonpredicate symbols $\psi \in L'$, and

3. $M'[R'] = \bigcup_{R\in f^{-1}(R')} M[R]$, for all symbols $R \in Pred_{L'}$.

Definition 3

Let S and S' be sets of clauses in L and L', respectively, and let $f:L{\rightarrow}L'$ be a predicate mapping function. S' is an abstract clause set of S through f (that is, S' is ACS_f of S) if and only if for every model M that satisfies S, $AM_f(M)$ satisfies S'.

Definition 4

Let S and S' be sets of clauses in L and L', respectively, and let f : L→L'
*be a predicate mapping function. S' is a **maximal abstract clause set***
of S through f (that is, S' is MACSf of S) if and only if

1. *S' is ACSf of S, and*
2. *for every S" which is ACSf of S, DC(S") ⊆ DC(S'), where DC*
   stands for deductive closure.

Definition 5

$Abs_f(S) = \{C' \mid$ for every $N \in f^{-1}(neg (C'))$ having $|neg(C')|$ distinct
literals, there exists $P \in f^{-1}(pos(C'))$ such that $S \vdash N \vee P$ }

Lemma 8

$Abs_f(S)$ is ACSf of S.

Proof: Let M be a model of S, let $M' = AM_f(M)$, and $S' = Abs_f(S)$. It must be
shown that M' is a model of S'. Suppose by way of contradiction, that M' is not
a model of S'. Then there is a clause $C' \in S'$ such that $M'[C']$ is false. There are
four cases to consider: C' has all positive literals, C' has all negative literals, C'
has both positive and negative literals, and C' has no literals.

C' has only positive literals: By the definition of Abs_f, there exists
$P \in f^{-1}(C')$ such that $S \vdash P$, and therefore this $M[P]$ is true. C' is, by
definition, of the form $C'_1 \vee ... \vee C'_k$, where each C'_i is an atom. Since
$M'[C']$ is false, there exists a value assignment v such that $M'_v[C']$ is false.
Then $M_v[C'_i]$ must be false, for each C'_i. Let $R'(x_1,....,x_n)$ be one such C'_i.
Then

$$<M'_v[x_1],....,M'_v[x_n]> \notin M'_v[R_0].$$

But by the definition of AM_f, then it must be that, for every $R \in f^{-1}(R_0)$

$$<M_v[x_1],....,M_v[x_n]> \notin M_v[R].$$

since otherwise the tuple would be an element of the interpretation in M' of
R'. This must also be the case of every C'_i. Therefore, for every $P \in f^{-1}(C')$,
$M_v[P]$ is false, since each such P is a disjunction of the specializations of
each C'_i, and $M[P]$ is false, a contradiction.

C' has only negative literals: By the definition of Abs_f, for every N
$\in f^{-1}(C')$ having $| C' |$ literals, $S \vdash N$, and therefore each $M[N]$ is true. C' is
of the form $\sim C'_1 \vee ... \vee \sim C'_k$, where each C'_i is an atom. Since $M'[C']$ is false,
there exists an assignment v of individuals to variables such that $M'_v[C']$ is
false. Then $M'_v[\sim C'_i]$ is false for each C'_i, and hence $M'_v[C'_i]$ is true. Let
$R'(x_1,....,x_n)$ be one such C'_i. Then

$$<M'_v[x_1],....,M'_v[x_n]> \in M'_v[R'].$$

By the definition of AM_f, there must exist an $R \in f^{-1}(R')$ such that

$$<M_v[x_1],....,M_v[x_n]> \in M_v[R],$$

and hence $M_v[\sim R(x_1,\dots,x_n)]$ is false. This must also be the case of every C'_i. But then there exists a specialization of C' having $|C'|$ literals which is false under v, and hence false in M, since one can take this specialization as the disjunction of each of the specializations with truth-value false of the C'_i. But this contradicts the assumption that M satisfies S.

C' has both negative and positive literals: By definition, for every $N \in f^{-1}(neg(C'))$ having $|neg(C')|$ literals, there exists $P \in f^{-1}(pos(C'))$ such that $S \vdash N \vee P$, and therefore $M[N \vee P]$ is true. Since $M'[C']$ is false, there exists a value assignment v such that $M'_v[C']$ is false. By the arguments of the previous case, there exists $N \in f^{-1}(neg(C'))$ having $|neg(C')|$ literals such that $M_v[N]$ is false. And by the arguments of the first case, for every $P \in f^{-1}(pos(C'))$, $M_v[P]$ is false. But then, for this particular $N \in f^{-1}(neg(C'))$ having $|neg(C')|$ literals, there does not exist $P \in f^{-1}(pos(C'))$ such that $S \vdash N \vee P$, a contradiction.

C' has no literals: This case is trivial, since if $\varnothing \in S'$ then $S \vdash \varnothing$, by the definition of Abs_f, and therefore there do not exist any models for S, a contradiction.

Corollary 9
If $S' \subseteq Abs_f(S)$ then S' is inconsistent only if S is inconsistent.

Proof: If S is consistent, then by definition there must exist some model M satisfying S. Then $AM_f(M)$ must satisfy $Abs_f(S)$, and must additionally satisfy any subset of $Abs_f(S)$. Therefore, if S is consistent, then any subset of $Abs_f(S)$ is also consistent. The contrapositive establishes the corollary.

Corollary 10
If S is inconsistent then $Abs_f(S)$ is inconsistent.

Proof: Trivially, since $\varnothing$ is its own abstraction.

Lemma 11
If S' is ACS_f of S and $S' \vdash C'$, then $C' \in Abs_f(S)$.

Proof: It is established that for each theorem C' of S', a set of specializations of C' are theorems of S, where this set is precisely those theorems required for inclusion of C' in $Abs_f(S)$. Let S' be some abstract clause set of S, and C' be a theorem of S'. The same four cases are considered as in the previous lemma.

C' has only positive literals: C' is of the form $C'_1 \vee \dots \vee C'_k$, where each C'_i is an atom. Define clause P to be the clause of $f^{-1}(C')$ having the maximum number of distinct literals. That is,

$$P = \bigvee\nolimits_{C'_i \in C'} disj(f^{-1}(C'_i)),$$

where $disj(f^{-1}(C'_i))$ denotes the disjunction of all atomic specializations of C'_i.

It can be shown that $S \vdash P$. To prove this, suppose by way of contradiction that $S \nvdash P$. Then there must exist a model M of S and value assignment v

such that $M_v[P]$ is false, since otherwise, P would be true in all models of S, and hence derivable from S. Therefore, for every literal P_i of P, $M_v[P_i]$ is false. Since every specialization of each C'_i of C' is a literal of P, and each is false in M under v, then $AMf(M)_v[C']$ is false, by the definition of $ACSf$. Therefore, $AMf(M)[C']$ is false. But by the definition of an abstract clause set, $AMf(M)$ must satisfy S', which contradicts the assumption that $S' \vdash C'$. This, then, establishes that $S \vdash P$. But by the definition of $Absf$, $C' \in Absf(S)$, since there exists $Q \in f^{-1}(C')$, namely P, such that $S \vdash Q$.

C' has only negative literals: C' is of the form $\sim C'_1 \vee ... \vee \sim C'_k$, where each C'_i is an atom. It can be shown that for each $N \in f^{-1}(C')$ having k distinct literals, $S \vdash N$. To prove this, suppose by way of contradiction that there exists $N \in f^{-1}(C')$ having k distinct literals such that $S \nvdash N$. N is of the form $\sim N'_1 \vee ... \vee \sim N'_k$, where $N_i \in f^{-1}(C_i)$, $1 \leq i \leq k$. Then there exists a model M of S such that $M[N]$ is false, and thus a value assignment v such that $M_v[N]$ is false. Therefore, for every disjunct $\sim N_i$ of N, $M_v[\sim N_i]$ is false, and thus $M_v[N_i]$ is true. Then by the definition of AMf, for every C'_i, $AMf(M)_v[C'_i]$ is true, since some specialization is true in M, and hence $AMf(M)_v[\sim C'_i]$ is false, $AMf(M)_v[C']$ is false, and hence $AMf(M)[C']$ is false. But by the definition of an abstract clause set, $AMf(M)$ must satisfy S', and hence, C' cannot be derivable from S', which contradicts the assumption that $S' \vdash C'$. This, then, establishes that, for every $N \in f^{-1}(C')$ having k distinct literals, $S \vdash N$. Then by the definition of $Absf$, $C' \in Absf(S)$.

C' has positive and negative literals: Define P as the element of $f^{-1}(pos(C'))$ having the maximum number of literals. It can be shown that for every $N \in f^{-1}(neg(C'))$ having $|neg(C')|$ literals, $S \vdash N \vee P$.

Suppose by way of contradiction that there exists $N \in f^{-1}(neg(C'))$ having $|neg(C')|$ literals such that $S \nvdash N \vee P$. Then there exists a model M of S and a value assignment v such that $M_v[N \vee P]$ is false. Therefore $M_v[N]$ is false, and $M_v[P]$ is false. But by the first case, $AMf(M)_v[f(N)]$ is false, and by the second case, $AMf(M)_v[f(P)]$ is false, and hence $AMf(M)[C']$ is false. But by the definition of an abstract clause set, $AMf(M)$ must satisfy S', and hence, C' cannot be derivable from S', which contradicts the assumption $C' \in S'$. This, then, establishes that, for every $N \in f^{-1}(neg(C'))$ having $|neg(C')|$ distinct literals, there exists $P \in f^{-1}(pos(C'))$ such that $S \vdash N \vee P$. Then by the definition of $Absf$, $C' \in Absf(S)$.

C' has no literals: This case is trivial, since if $\varnothing \in S'$ then $S \vdash \varnothing$, since otherwise, there would exist a model M of S for which $AMf(M)$ is not a model of S'. And by definition, then, $\varnothing \in Absf(S)$.

Corollary 12

$Absf(S)$ is $MACSf$ of S.

Proof: Trivially from lemma 11 and the definition of $MACSf$.

Corollary 13

$DC(Abs_f(S)) = Abs_f(S)$, where DC denotes deductive closure.

Proof: Trivially from lemma 11, by taking S' to be the deductive closure of $Abs_f(S)$.

Theorem 1

S' is ACS_f of S if and only if $S' \subseteq Abs_f(S)$:

Proof: The only if direction trivially follows from lemma 11. Suppose that S' $\subseteq Abs_f(S)$. By definition, for any model M satisfying S, $AM_f(M)$ satisfies $Abs_f(S)$, and hence, $AM_f(M)$ must satisfy any subset of $Abs_f(S)$.

Corollary 14

$Abs_f(S)$ is finite if and only if S is the empty clause set.

Proof: Trivially, by corollary 13.

Corollary 15

There is no effective procedure for constructing $Abs_f(S)$, for arbitrary S and f.

Proof: Trivially, by corollary 13.

Proof-Theoretic Proofs

Definition 7

A **proof** from S is taken to be a directed acyclic graph $F = (V, E)$ such that

1. F is a forest of binary trees [Aho, Hopcroft, and Ullman 1983],

2. there exists a labeling function l_F labeling each node of V with a theorem of S,

3. all leaf nodes are leaf-labeled (per definition 8), and

4. if $<v, w> \in E$ then $l_F(v)$ is the child of a full resolution inference [Robinson 1965] with $l_F(w)$ as one of the parents.

Definition 8

All clauses of S are **leaf-labels**. All clauses labeling nodes on a path to a leaf-labeled node are leaf-labels. No other clauses are leaf-labels.

A **proof from S of clause** C is a proof G from S where C labels the root of some tree of G. A refutation proof from S of formula C is a proof of the null clause from S unioned with the negation of C in clause form. The length of a proof is the number of nodes in the forest.

Definition 9

The **out-forest** of a node v is:

1. All nodes in the tree rooted at v are in out-forest(v).

2. All nodes in a tree rooted by a node with an identical label to an element of out-forest(v) are in out-forest(v).

   3. No other nodes are in out-forest(v).

Theorem 2

Let S be a Horn clause set, f be a predicate mapping, and $F' = (V, E)$ be a proof of clause C' from $MembAbs f(S)$ under labeling function $l_{F'}$. For each $N \in f^{-1}(neg(C'))$ having $|neg(C')|$ literals, there exists $P \in f^{-1}(pos(C'))$ and proof F such that

   1. $F = (V, E)$
   2. there exists a labeling function l_F such that F proves $N \vee P$ from S,
   3. $f(l_F(v)) = l_{F'}(v)$, for each $v \in V$.

Proof: This is proven inductively on the size of a proof. The base case where V is a singleton is trivially satisfied by the definition of *MembAbs f* . Assume the theorem holds for all proof forests of size $n\text{-}1$. Take F' as a proof of size n, and let v be the node labeled by C' that roots some tree in F'. Let *edges(v)* be the set of outgoing edges from v. By the induction hypothesis, the theorem holds for the root of each tree in $F'_{-v} = (V - \{v\}, E - \{edges(v)\})$. If $l_{F'}(v)$ is a clause from S, then v is a leaf node, and this reduces to the base case. If v is has no outgoing edges but is not an input node, then there exists some other node w in F' identically labeled, and by the induction hypothesis, the theorem holds.

If v has outgoing edges to u, w, then $l_{F'}(u)$, $l_{F'}(w)$ are labeled by the parents of a resolution inference of C'. Without loss of generality, u is labeled by a clause of the form $Q' \vee M'$, and w by a clause of the form $P' \vee W' \vee U'$, where Q', P' are atoms, and M', W', U' are disjunctions of negated atoms, P', M', W' possibly being null. Further, these clauses resolve under some substitution ϕ on Q', W', yielding $C' = (P' \vee M' \vee U')\phi$. Since no node in a proof has more than one incoming edge, u and w root trees in F'_{-v}, and these trees by definition have no nodes in common. Let F^1_{-v} be some proof that specializes F'_{-v}, by the induction hypothesis. u is labeled by a specialization of its labeling in F'_{-v}. That is, it is of the form $Q \vee M$, where $f(Q) = Q'$ and $f(M) = M'$. There must also exist a proof F^2_{-v}, where w is labeled by a clause $P \vee W \vee U$, where $f(P) = P'$, $f(W) = W'$, $f(U) = U$, and W resolves with Q under ϕ yielding $C = (P \vee M \vee U)\phi$. Note that the proofs F^1_{-v} and F^2_{-v} are identical graphs, but having possibly different labeling functions. Then there must exist proof $F = (V, E)$ whose labelings are identical to that of F^1_{-v}, except the nodes of the tree rooted at w are labeled as in F^2_{-v}, and v is labeled by C. This graph satisfies the three conditions of the theorem, by construction, for one particular specialization of C'. And by the induction hypothesis, such a proof will exist for every other specialization C' required by the theorem, by a similar argument, since the appropriate specializations exist for the parents.

4.5.2   Proofs for Relaxed Model Abstraction

Consistency Proofs

Lemma 16

> Let $\aleph_{R1}$ be a k_{R1}-AB, S^i be a legal situation at level i, and F be a proof
> forest from $S^i \cup \{\sim C\}$, for some atom C. For every node v in F not labeled
> by the null clause, there exists criticality j such that every literal in the label
> of v has criticality j, and the label of every element of out-forest(v) has
> criticality j.

Proof: The following is proven inductively on the size of F. As the base case,
let F contain only a singleton node set. Then v must be labeled by a static
axiom, and by the definition of $crit_{R1}$, every literal in $l_F(v)$ must have the same
criticality, and $out\text{-}forest(v) = \phi$. Assume the lemma holds of all forests of size
$n\text{-}1$. Let F be a proof forest of size n. Let v be a node that roots a tree in F. If v
is a leaf node and labeled by a static axiom, then this reduces to the base case. If
v is a leaf node and not labeled by a static axiom, then there must exist another
node w labeled identically, and by the induction hypothesis, the lemma is
satisfied for w in a proof forest of size $n\text{-}1$, and hence must be satisfied for v in F

Suppose that v is not a leaf and not labeled by the null clause. Then from v
there exist edges to nodes w_1 and w_2 labeled by parents of a resolution step of
the label of v. By the induction hypothesis, there exists a proof of size $n\text{-}1$ in
which each w_1 and w_2 satisfy the lemma. Since $l_F(w_1)$ and $l_F(w_2)$ resolve on
some literal, then they must have the same criticality (call it j), and thus every
literal in $l_F(v)$ will have criticality j, and every element of $out\text{-}forest(v)$ has
criticality j.

Lemma 17

> Let F be a refutation proof of a precondition atom P from S^i. For every
> node v in the out-forest of the null clause, $crit_{R1}(l_F(v)) = crit_{R1}(P)$.

Proof: By the definition of a legal situation, S^i is consistent, and $\sim P$ must
therefore label some leaf node in $out\text{-}forest(\varnothing)$. But by lemma 16, all nodes in
$out\text{-}forest(\varnothing)$ must have the same criticality.

Lemma 18

> Let $\aleph_{R1}$ be a k_{R1}-AB having k levels. If the usability condition holds over
> $\aleph^0_{R1}$, then the usability condition holds over $\aleph^j_{R1}, 0 \leq j < k$.

Proof: This is proven by induction on the level of criticality. The base case of
the 0th level is given. Suppose that the usability assumption holds over $\aleph^j_{R1}$,
$0 \leq j < i$, for some $i < k\text{-}1$. Then there exists a legal situation S at level i that
derives P^i_o. By lemma 17, the proof of each precondition of P^{i+1}_o requires no
clauses at level i or lower. But then there exists a legal situation at level $i+1$ that

derives $P^{i+1}{}_o$, since $P^{i+1}{}_o \subset P^i{}_o$ and those clauses of S at level $i+1$ or higher form a legal situation at level $i+1$.

Lemma 2

Let $\aleph_{R1}$ be a consistent k_{R1}-AB having k levels for which the usability condition holds of $\aleph^0{}_{R1}$. $\aleph^i{}_{R1}$ is consistent, $0 \leq i < k$.

Proof: This is proven by induction on the level of criticality, with the base case given. Assume the theorem holds for $\aleph^n{}_{R1}, 0 \leq n < j$, where $j < k\text{-}1$. Let o be an arbitrary operator. By lemma 18, there exists a legal situation S at level j such that $S \vdash P^j{}_o$, and for which $Result(<o>, S)$ is consistent. But then, S^{j+1} (the clauses of S having at least criticality $j+1$) must be legal and consistent, and $S^{j+1} \vdash P^{j+1}{}_o$, by lemma 17. Further,

$$Result(<o>, S^{j+1}) \subseteq Result(<o>, S^j),$$

by the definition of $Result$, and since $Result(<o>, S^j)$ is consistent, so must its subset $Result(<o>, S^{j+1})$, and hence the theorem holds of level $j+1$.

Lemma 19

Let $\aleph_{R2}$ be a k_{R2}-AB, S^i be a legal situation at level i, and F be a proof forest from $S^i \cup \sim\!C$, for some atom C. For every node v in F not labeled by the null clause, there exists criticality j such that every nonfixed literal in the label of v has criticality j, the nonfixed literals in the label of every element of out-forest(v) has criticality j, and the fixed literals in v and out-forest(v) have criticality greater or equal to j.

Proof: The following is proven inductively on the size of F . The base case where F contains a single node is trivially satisfied by the definition of criticality. Assume the lemma holds of all forests of size $n\text{-}1$. Let F be a proof forest of size n. Let v be a node that roots a tree in F . If v is a leaf node then the lemma is again trivially satisfied, by arguments analogous to lemma 16.

Suppose that v is not a leaf and not labeled by the null clause. Then from v there exist edges to nodes w_1 and w_2 labeled by parents of a resolution step of the label of v. By the induction hypothesis, there exists a proof of size $n\text{-}1$ in which each w_1 and w_2 satisfy the lemma. Let C_1 and C_2 be the labels of w_1 and w_2. There are two cases depending upon whether C_1 and C_2 resolve on a fixed predicate or not.

Fixed Predicate: Let P be the predicate resolved on. Without loss of generality, assume P is negated in C_1 and unnegated in C_2. Then C_2 must be an atomic element of the static axioms since P can never appear unnegated in any but unit clauses, by the definition of fixed predicates. But by the induction hypothesis, all of the nonfixed literals of $l_F(v)$ must have the same criticality, since these literals all come from C_1. Likewise, since $out\text{-}forest(w_2)$ is empty, then all nonfixed literals of labels of $out\text{-}forest(v)$ have the same criticality, since this was true of w_1. Similarly, the fixed literals of v and $out\text{-}forest(v)$ must have criticality at least j.

Nonfixed Predicate: The lemma trivially holds in this case, since it holds for the labels of the parents, and the parents have a nonfixed predicate in common.

Lemma 20

Let F be a refutation proof of a precondition atom P from S^i. For every node v in the out-forest of the null clause, $crit_{R1}(l_F(v)) \geq crit_{R1}(P)$.

Proof: Since S^i is consistent, $\sim P$ must label a leaf node in the out-forest of the null clause. Further, there exists j such that the criticality of each nonfixed literal in each label of the out-forest of the null clause is j, and the fixed literals of these clauses all have criticality at least j. If P is not a fixed literal, then $j \geq crit_{R2}(P)$, by lemma 19. If P is a fixed literal, then by the definition of fixed predicates, P can appear unnegated only in atomic clauses, and hence the proof consists only of the single inference, $\sim P$ and P yielding the null clause, which satisfies the lemma.

Lemma 21

Let $\aleph_{R2}$ be a k_{R2}-AB having k levels. If the sort-usability condition holds over $\aleph^0_{R2}$, then the sort-usability condition holds over $\aleph^j_{R2}$, $0 \leq j < k$.

Proof: This is proven by induction, with the base case given. Assume that this lemma holds for all levels up to and including $\aleph^n_{R2}$, $n < k\text{-}1$. Let o be an arbitrary operator under some fully ground substitution, and assume the static axioms satisfy the preconditions of o involving sorted predicates. There exists a legal situation S^n at level n such that $S^n \vdash P^n_o$, by the induction hypothesis. But then, there exists a legal situation at level $n+1$ that derives P^{n+1}_o, namely S^{n+1} (i.e., all clauses of S^n having criticality $n+1$ or higher), since all level $n+1$ preconditions are provable from only clauses at level $n+1$ or greater, by lemma 20.

Lemma 3

Let $\aleph_{R2}$ be a consistent k_{R2}-AB having k levels for which the sort-usability condition holds of $\aleph^0_{R2}$. $\aleph^j_{R2}$ is consistent, $0 \leq i < k$.

Proof: This is proven by induction, with the base case given. Assume that the theorem holds for all levels up to and including $\aleph^n_{R2}$, $n < k\text{-}1$. Let o be an arbitrary operator (under a fully ground substitution) such that the static axioms derive the sort preconditions of o. By lemma 21, there exists a legal situation S^n at level n such that $S^n \vdash P^n_o$, and for which $Result(<o>, S^n)$ is consistent. But then, S^{n+1} (the clauses of S^n having criticality at least $n+1$) must be legal and consistent, and $S^{n+1} \vdash P^{n+1}_o$, by lemma 20. Further,

$$Result(<o>, S^{n+1}) \ Result(<o>, S^n),$$

by the definition of Result, and hence, the theorem holds of level $n+1$. Finally, note that if the static axioms do not derive the sort preconditions of o, then there exists no legal situation at any level that derives the sort preconditions. This is because the sort preconditions are by definition inessential predicates, only appear negated in nonunit static axioms, and can never appear as an element of any dynamic situation.

Upward Solution Proofs

Theorem 4

Let $\aleph_{R2}$ be a k_{R2}-AB having k levels, and let ω be a plan accepted by $\aleph^0_{R2}$ with respect to some legal situation S^0. ω is accepted by $\aleph^i_{R2}$ with respect to S^i, $0 \leq i < k$.

Proof: This is proven trivially by an induction on the level of abstraction, since each precondition of every operator in ω are proven by clauses having $crit_{R2}(P)$ or greater, and the resulting situations at the abstract levels are always a subset of the corresponding situation at the concrete level.

Corollary 4

Let $\aleph_{R2}$ be a k_{R2}-AB . If $\rho = (T_0, G)$ is not solvable at the highest level of abstraction, then it is not solvable at any lower level of abstraction.

Proof: Trivially by taking the contrapositive of theorem 4.

Lemma 5

Let Σ be a STRIPS system, and ω be a plan that solves $\rho = (T_0, G)$. justified(ω, $K \cup T_0$, G) solves ρ.

Proof: This is proven by an induction on the length of ω, with the base case of a null plan trivially satisfied. Assume the lemma holds for all plans of length n-1, and suppose $\omega = <o_1,....,o_n>$ solves ρ. By the induction hypothesis,

$$\beta = justified(<o_2,....,o_n>, Result(<o_1>, K \cup T_0), G)$$

solves G with respect to $Result(<o_1>, K \cup T_0)$. That is, the original plan without the first operator satisfies the goal when applied from the second world state. If $<o_1>$ establishes G or enables an operator in β, then $justified(\omega, K \cup T_0, G)$ is equal to $<o1>$ appended to the front of β, in which case it solves ρ. Otherwise, $justified(\omega, K \cup T_0, G) = \beta$, in which case it also solves ρ.

Theorem 5

Let $\aleph_{R2}$ be a consistent k_{R2}-AB having k levels, and let ω be a plan accepted by $\aleph^0_{R2}$ that solves $\rho^0 = (T^0, G^0)$. For $0 \leq i < k$, justified(ω, $(K^i \cup T^i)$, G) solves ρ^i with respect to level i.

Proof: Trivially by lemma 5, by justifying ω as one ascends the abstraction hierarchy.

References

Aho, A., J. Hopcroft, and J. Ullman. *Data Structures and Algorithms*. Reading, Mass.: Addison-Wesley, 1983.

Allen, J.F. "Maintaining knowledge about temporal intervals", *Comm. ACM* 26 (11): 832-843, 1983a.

Allen, J.F. "Recognizing intentions from natural language utterances", in *Computational Models of Discourse*, M. Brady and R. Berwick (eds.). Cambridge: MIT Press, 1983b.

Allen, J.F. "Towards a general theory of action and time", *Artificial Intelligence* 23 (2): 123-154, 1984.

Allen, J.F. and P.J. Hayes. "A common-sense theory of time", *Proc. Int'l. Joint Conference on Artificial Intelligence*, 1985.

Allen, J.F. and P.J. Hayes. "Moments and points in an interval-based temporal logic", *Computational Intelligence 5* (4):225-238, 1989.

Allen, J.F. and J.A. Koomen. "Planning using a temporal world model", *Int'l. Joint Conference on Artificial Intelligence*, 1983.

Alterman, R. "Issues in adaptive planning", TR 304, Dept. of Computer Science, U. California at Berkeley, 1987.

Amarel, S. "On representations of problems of reasoning about actions", in *Machine Intelligence 3*, D. Michie (ed.), 131-171. Edinburgh: Edinburgh Univ. Press, 1968.

Anderson, J. and A. Farley. "Plan abstraction based on operator generalization", *Proc. National Conf. on Artificial Intelligence*, 1988.

Bollobas, B. *Random Graphs*. London: Academic Press, 1985.

Bacchus, F., J. Tenenberg, and J.A. Koomen. "A non-reified temporal logic", *Proc. of the First Int'l Conf. on Principles of Knowledge Representation and Reasoning,* Morgan Kaufmann, 1989.

Brachman, R. "On the epistemological status of semantic networks", in *Associative Networks*, N. Findler (ed.), New York: Academic Press, 1979.

Bratman, M. *Intention, Plans and Practical Reason*. Cambridge: Harvard Univ. Press, 1987.

Bruce, B.C. "Plans and social action", in *Theoretical Issues in Reading Comprehension*, R. Spiro, B. Bruce, and W. Brewer (eds.), Hillsdale, N.J.: Lawrence Erlbaum, 1981.

Carberry, S. "Tracking goals in an information seeking environment", *Proc. National Conf. on Artificial Intelligence*, 1983.

Chapman, D. "Planning for conjunctive goals", *Artificial Intelligence 32* (3): 333-377, 1987.

Chapman, D. "Vision, instruction, and action", A.I. TR 1204, MIT, Cambridge, 1990.

Charniak, E. Unpublished talk presented at the Univ. of Rochester, New York, 1983.

Charniak, E. and R. Goldman. "A semantics for probabilistic quantifier-free first-order languages, with particular application to story understanding", *Proc. Int'l. Joint Conference on Artificial Intelligence*, 1074-1079, 1989.

Charniak, E. and D. McDermott. *Introduction to Artificial Intelligence*. Reading, Mass.: Addison-Wesley, 1985.

Clark, K. "Negations as failure", in *Logic and Data Bases*, H. Gallaire and J. Minker (eds.), 293-322, New York: Plenum, 1978.

Cohen, P. "Referring as requesting", *Proc. COLING*, 207-211, Stanford Univ., Stanford, California, 1984.

Cohen, P.R., J. Morgan, and M. Pollack. *Intentions in Communication*, Cambridge, Mass.: MIT Press, 1990

Cohen, P., R. Perrault, and J. Allen. "Beyond question-answering", Report No. 4644, BBN Inc., Cambridge, Mass., 1981.

Davidson, D. "The logical form of action sentences", in *The Logic of Decision and Action*, N. Rescher (ed.). Pittsburgh, Pa.: Univ. Pittsburgh Press, 1967.

Davis, M. "The mathematics of non-monotonic reasoning", *Artificial Intelligence 13*: 73-80, 1980.

Davis, R. "Diagnostic reasoning based on structure and behavior", *Artificial Intelligence 24*, 347-410, 1984.

Dean, T. "An approach to reasoning about time for planning and problem solving", TR 433, Computer Science Dept., Yale Univ., New Haven, Conn., 1985.

Dean, T. and K. Kanazawa. "Probabilistic causal reasoning", *Proc. CS/CSI*, 125-132, 1988a.

Dean, T. and K. Kanazawa. "Probabilistic temporal reasoning", *Proc. National Conf. on Artificial Intelligence*, 524-528, 1988b.

Dean, T. and D. McDermott. "Temporal database management", *Artificial Intelligence 32* (1):1-56, 1987.

Dean, T., J. Firby, and D. Miller. "Hierarchical planning involving deadlines, travel time and resources", *Computational Intelligence, 6* (1) 1990.

deKleer, J. "An assumption-based TMS", *Artificial Intelligence 28*:127-162, 1986.

deKleer, J. and B. Williams, "Reasoning about multiple faults", *Proc. National Conf. on Artificial Intelligence*, 132-139, 1984.

De Lacaze, R. "Planning with concurrent actions and external events", Masters thesis, Computer Science Dept., New York Univ., New York, 1991.

Doyle, A. C. *The Sign of Four*, Chapter 6, 1890, Reprint. New York: Ballantine, 1987.

Doyle, J. "A truth maintenance system", *Artificial Intelligence 12* (3):231-272, 1979.

Etherington, D. "Reasoning with incomplete information: Investigations of non-monotonic reasoning", TR 86-14, Dept. of Computer Science, Univ. British Columbia, Vancouver, 1986.

Fikes, R.E. and N.J. Nilsson. "STRIPS: A new approach to the application of theorem proving to problem solving", *Artificial Intelligence 2* (3/4):189-208, 1971.

Fikes, R.E., P. Hart, and N.J. Nilsson. "Learning and executing generalized robot plans", *Artificial Intelligence 3*: 251-288, 1972.

Firby, R.J. "An investigation into reactive planning in complex domains", *Proc. National Conf. on Artificial Intelligence*, 1987.

Genesereth, M. "The role of plans in automated consulting", *Proc. Int'l Joint Conference on Artificial Intelligence*, 119, 1979.

Genesereth, M. "The use of design descriptions in automated diagnosis", *Artificial Intelligence 24*: 411-436, 1984.

Georgeff, M. "The representation of events in multiagent domains", *Proc. National Conf. on Artificial Intelligence*, 70-75, August 1986.

Ginsberg, M.L. "Counterfactuals", *Artificial Intelligence 30*: 35-80, 1986.

Ginsberg, M.L. and D.E. Smith. "Possible worlds and the qualification problem", *Proc. National Conf. on Artificial Intelligence*, 212-217, 1987.

Giunchiglia, F. and T. Walsh. "Abstract theorem proving", *Proc. Int'l Joint Conference on Artificial Intelligence*, 1989.

Goldman, A.I. *A Theory of Human Action*. Englewood Cliffs, N.J.: Prentice-Hall, 1970.

Goodman, B. and D. Litman. "Plan recognition for intelligent interfaces", *Proc. IEEE Conference on Artificial Intelligence Applications*, Santa Barbara, Calif., 1990.

Haas, A.R. "Planning Mental Actions", Ph.D. diss. and TR 106, Computer Science Dept., Univ. of Rochester, New York, 1982.

Haas, A.R. "Possible events, actual events, and robots", *Computational Intelligence 1* (2):59-70, 1985.

Haas, A. R. "The case for domain-specific frame axioms", in *The Frame Problem in Artificial Intelligence, Proc. 1987 Workshop*, F. M. Brown (ed.).Los Altos, Calif.: Morgan Kaufmann, 1987.

Haddawy, P. "Time, chance and action", *Proc. Sixth Conference on Uncertainty in Artificial Intelligence*, 147-154, 1990.

Hanks, S. and D. McDermott. "Default reasoning, nonmonotonic logics, and the frame problem", *Proc. National Conf. on Artificial Intelligence*, 1986.

Harper, W.L., R. Stalnaker, and G. Pearce (eds.). *Ifs*. Holland: D. Reidel, 1981.

Harel, D. "Dynamic logic", in *Handbook of Philosophical Logic, Vol. II*. New York: Reidel, 1984.

Hayes, P.J. "The logic of frames", in *Readings in Knowledge Representation*, R.J. Brachman and H.J. Levesque (eds.). Los Altos, Calif.: Morgan Kaufmann, 1985.

Hendrix, G. "Encoding knowledge in partitioned networks", in *Associative Networks*, N. Findler (ed.), New York: Academic Press, 1979.

Hobbs, J.R., M E. Stickel, P. Martin, and D. Edwards. "Interpretation as abduction", *Proc. Annual Meeting of the Association for Computational Linguistics*, 32-37, Buffalo, N.Y., 1988.

Huff, K. and V. Lesser. "Knowledge-based command understanding: An example for the software development environment", TR 82-6, Computer and Information Sciences, Univ. Massachusetts at Amherst, 1982.

Hughes, G.E. and M.J. Cresswell. *An Introduction to Modal Logic*, London: Methuen and Co. Ltd., 1968.

Janlert, L.E. "Modeling change-the frame problem", in *The Robot's Dilemma: The Frame Problem in Artificial Intelligence*, Z. Pylyshyn (ed.), 65-76. Norwood, N.J.: Ablex Publishing Co., 1987.

Kautz, H. "The logic of persistence", *Proc. National Conf. on Artificial Intelligence*, 401-405, Philadelphia, Pa., August 1986.

Koomen, J.A. "Localizing temporal constraint propagation", *Proc. First Int'l Conf. on Principles of Knowledge Representation and Reasoning*, Los Altos, Calif.: Morgan Kaufmann, 1989.

Knoblock, C. "A theory of abstraction for hierarchical planning", in *Change of Representation and Inductive Bias*, P. Benjamin (ed.), 81-104. Norwell, Mass.: Kluwer Academic, 1990a.

Knoblock, C. "Learning effective abstraction hierarchies", *Proc. National Conf. on Artificial Intelligence*, 1990b.

Knoblock, C., J. Tenenberg, and Q. Yang. "A spectrum of abstraction hierarchies", *AAAI Workshop on Automatic Generation of Approximations and Abstractions*, 1990.

Korf, R. "Macro-operators: A weak method for learning", *Artificial Intelligence* 26: 35-77, 1985.

Korf, R. "Planning as search: A quantitative approach", *Artificial Intelligence* 33: 68-88, 1987.

Kowalski, R. *Logic for Problem Solving*. New York: North Holland, 1979.

Ladkin, P. and R. Maddux. "Representation and reasoning with convex time intervals", TR KES.U.88.2, Kestrel Institution, Palo Alto, Calif., 1988.

Lansky, A.L. "Behavioral specifications and planning for multiagent domains", TR 360, SRI International, Menlo Park, Calif., 1985.

Lansky, A.L. "A representation of parallel activity based on events, structure, and causality", in *Reasoning about Actions and Plans: Proc. of the 1986 Workshop*, M. Georgeff and A.L. Lansky (eds.), 123-159. San Mateo, Calif., Morgan Kaufmann, 1987.

Lansky, A.L. "Localized event-based reasoning for multi-agent domains", TN 423, SRI International, Menlo Park, Calif., 1988.

Lewis, D.K. *Counterfactuals*. Cambridge, Mass.: Harvard Univ. Press, 1973.

Lifschitz, V. "Pointwise Circumscription: Preliminary report", *Proc. National Conf. on Artificial Intelligence*, 1986.

Lifschitz, V. "On the semantics of strips", in *Reasoning about Actions and Plans: Proc. of the 1986 Workshop*, M. Georgeff and A.L. Lansky (eds.), 1-9. San Mateo, Calif., Morgan Kaufmann, 1987.

Litman, D. and J. Allen. "A plan recognition model for subdialogues in conversation", *Cognitive Science 11*: 163-200, 1987.

Mark, B., J. Weber, and J. Mcguire. "Incremental validation as a design tool", Tech. Report, Lockheed AI Center, 1990.

McCarthy, J. "Epistemological problems of artificial intelligence", *Int'l. Joint Conference on Artificial Intelligence*, 1038-1044, 1977.

McCarthy, J. "Circumscription: A form of non-monotonic reasoning", *Artificial Intelligence 13*: 27-39, 1980.

McCarthy, J. and P.J. Hayes. "Some philosophical problems from the standpoint of artificial intelligence", in *Machine Intelligence 4*, B.M.D. Michie (ed.), 463-502. Edinburgh: Edinburgh Univ. Press, 1969.

McDermott, D. "A temporal logic for reasoning about processes and plans", *Cognitive Science 6* (2): 101-155, 1982.

McDermott, D. "Reasoning about plans", in *Formal Theories of the Commonsense World*, J.R. Hobbs and R.C. Moore (eds.), 269-317. Norwood, N.J.: Ablex, 1986.

Minsky, M. "A framework for representing knowledge", in *The Psychology of Computer Vision*. New York: McGraw-Hill, 1975.

Minton, S. "Selectively generalizing plans for problem solving", *Proc. Int'l. Joint Conference on Artificial Intelligence*, 595-599, 1985.

Moore, R. "Reasoning about knowledge and action", *Proc. Int'l. Joint Conference on Artificial Intelligence*, 1977.

Moore, R. "A formal theory of knowledge and action", in *Formal Theories of the Commonsense World*, J.R. Hobbs and R.C. Moore (eds.), Norwood, N.J.: Ablex, 1986.

Morgenstern, L. and L.A. Stein. "Why things go wrong: A formal theory of causal reasoning", *Proc. National Conf. on Artificial Intelligence*, 518-523, 1988.

Mourelatos, A. "Events, processes, and states", *Linguistics & Philosophy 2*: 415-434, 1978.

Nau, D. "Hierarchical abstraction for process planning", *Proc. Int'l Conference in Applications of Artificial Intelligence in Engineering*, 1987.

Nilsson, N. "Shakey the robot", TR 323, SRI International, Menlo Park, Calif., 1984.

Pearl, J. *Heuristics*. Reading, Mass.: Addison-Wesley, 1984.

Pednault, E.P.D. "Synthesizing plans that contain actions with context-dependent effects", *Computational Intelligence 4* (4): 356-372, 1988.

Pelavin, R. "A formal approach to planning with concurrent actions and external events", TR 254, Computer Science Dept., Univ. Rochester, New York, 1988.

Plaisted, D. "Theorem proving with abstraction", *Artificial Intelligence 16*: 47-108, 1981.

Pollack, M. "A model of plan inference that distinguishes between the beliefs of actors and observers", *Proc. Annual Meeting of the Association for Computational Linguistics*, 1986.

Pople, H. "Heuristic methods for imposing structure on ill-structured problems: The structuring of medical diagnostics", in *Artificial Intelligence in Medicine, AAAS Select Symposium 51*, P. Szolovits (ed.), Boulder, Colo.: Westview Press, 1982.

Reggia, J., D.S. Nau, and P.Y. Wang. "Diagnostic expert systems based on a set covering model", *Int'l Journal of Man-Machine Studies 19:* 437-460, 1983.

Reiter, R. "On closed world databases", in *Logic and Data Bases*, H. Gallaire and J. Minker (eds.), New York: Plenum, 1978.

Reiter, R. "A theory of diagnosis from first principles", *Artificial Intelligence 32* (1): 57-96, 1987.

Rich, E. *Artificial Intelligence*, New York: McGraw-Hill, 1983.

Robinson, J. "A machine-oriented logic based on the resolution principle", *Journal of the ACM 12* (1): 23-41, 1965.

Rosenschein, S.J. "Plan synthesis: A logical perspective", *Proc. Int'l Joint Conference on Artificial Intelligence,* 331-337, 1981.

Rosenschein, S.J. "Synthesizing information-tracking automata from environment descriptions", *Proc. First Int'l Conference on Principles of Knowledge Representation and Reasoning*, San Mateo, Calif.: Morgan Kaufmann, 1989.

Sacerdoti, E.D. "Planning in a hierarchy of abstraction spaces", *Artificial Intelligence 5* (2): 115-135, 1974.

Sacerdoti, E.D. *A Structure for Plans and Behavior*. New York: American Elsevier, 1977.

Sanchis, L. "Language instance generation and test case construction for NP-hard problems", Ph.D. diss. and TR 296, Computer Science Dept., Univ. Rochester, New York, 1989.

Schank, R. *Conceptual Information Processing*. New York: American Elsevier, 1975.

Schank, R. and R. Abelson. *Scripts, Plans, Goals, and Understanding*. Hillsdale, N.J.: Lawrence Erlbaum, 1977.

Schmidt, C.F., N.S. Sridharan, and J.L. Goodson. "The plan recognition problem: An intersection of psychology and artificial intelligence", *Artificial Intelligence 11*: 45-83, 1978.

Schoppers, M. "Representation and automatic synthesis of reaction plans", Ph.D. diss., Computer Science Dept., Univ. of Illinois and Urbana-Champaign, 1989.

Schubert, L.K. "Monotonic solution of the frame problem in the situation calculus: An efficient method for worlds with fully specified actions", in *Knowledge Representation and Defeasible Reasoning,* H. Kyburg, R. Loui, and G. Carlson (eds.). Norwell,N.J.:Kluwer Academic, 1989.

Shoham, Y. "Chronological ignorance: Time, nonmonotonicity, necessity and causal theories", *Proc. National Conf. on Artificial Intelligence,* 389-393, Philadelphia, Pa., 1986.

Shoham, Y. "Temporal logics in AI: Semantical and ontological considerations", *Artificial Intelligence 33* (1): 89-104, 1987.

Shoham, Y. "Time for action: On the relation between time, knowledge and action", *Proc. Int'l Joint Conference on Artificial Intelligence,* 954-959, 1989.

Stalnaker, R. "A theory of conditionals", in *Studies in Logical Theory,* N. Rescher (ed.), 98-112. Oxford: Basil Blackwell, 1968.

Stefik, M. "Planning with constraints (MOLGEN: Part 1)", *Artificial Intelligence 16* (2): 111-140, 1981.

Stickel, M.E. "Automated deduction by theory resolution", *Proc. Int'l Joint Conference on Artificial Intelligence,* 1181-1186, 1985.

Tate, A. "Generating project networks", *Proc. Int'l. Joint Conference on Artificial Intelligence,* 888-893, 1977.

Tenenberg, J. "Reasoning with exclusion", *Proc. Int'l Journal Conference on Artificial Intelligence,* 1985.

Tenenberg, J.D. "Planning with abstraction", *Proc. National Conf. on Artificial Intelligence,* 76-80, 1986.

Tenenberg, J. D. "Abstraction in planning", Ph.D. diss. and TR 250, Computer Science Dept., Univ. Rochester, New York, 1988.

Tenenberg, J. "Abandoning the completeness assumptions: A statistical approach to the frame problem", in *Advances in Human Cognition, Vol.1, The Frame Problem in Artificial Intelligence.* K. Ford and P. Hayes (eds.). Greenwich, Conn.:JAI Press, 1991.

Vendler, Z. *Linguistics in Philosophy.* Ithaca, N.Y.: Cornell Univ. Press, 1967.

Vere, S. "Planning in time: Windows and durations for activities and goals", *IEEE Trans. Pattern Analysis Mach. Intell. 5* (3): 246-267, 1983.

Vilain, M., H. Kautz, and P. vanBeek. "Constraint propagation algorithms for temporal reasoning: A revised report", in *Readings in Qualitative Reasoning About Physical Systems,* D. Wild and J. deKleer (eds.), 373-381. San Mateo, Calif.: Morgan Kaufmann, 1990.

Waldinger, R. "Achieving several goals simultaneously", in *Machine Intelligence 8*: 94-136, 1977.

Warren, D. "Generating conditional plans and programs", *Proc. Artificial Intelligence and Simulation of Behavior*, Edinburgh, 1976.

Wasserman, K. "Unifying representation and generalization: Understanding hierarchically structured objects", Ph.D. diss., Columbia Univ., New York, 1985.

Weber, J. "A parallel algorithm for statistical belief refinement and its use in causal reasoning", *Proc. Int'l Joint Conference on Artificial Intelligence*, 900-906, 1989a.

Weber, J. "Principles and algorithms for causal reasoning with uncertain knowledge", Ph.D. diss. and TR 287, Computer Science Dept., Univ. Rochester, New York, 1989b.

Whitehead, S. and D. Ballard. "Active perception and reinforcement learning", TR 331, Computer Science Dept., Univ. Rochester, New York, 1990.

Wilensky, R. *Planning and Understanding*. Reading, Mass.: Addison-Wesley, 1983.

Wilkins, D. *Practical Planning*, San Mateo, Calif.: Morgan Kaufmann, 1988.

Yang, Q. and J. Tenenberg. "Abtweak: A hierarchical, least-commitment planner", in *Proc. National Conference on Artificial Intelligence*, 1990.

Index

AFJ4724 -1

DATE DUE

MAY 26 1995			

DEMCO 38-297